CONTROVERSIAL ISSUES IN MENTAL HEALTH

CONTROVERSIAL ISSUES IN MENTAL HEALTH

Edited by

Stuart A. Kirk

Columbia University

Susan D. Einbinder

University of Southern California

Series Editors

Eileen Gambrill
Robert Pruger

University of California, Berkeley

ALLYN AND BACON

Boston London Toronto Sydney Tokyo Singapore

To

Allison Kirk and Brandon Kirk

Lynn and Jason Einbinder

Editor-in-Chief, Social Sciences: Susan Badger
Senior Editor: Karen Hanson
Editorial Assistant: Sarah Dunbar
Production Administrator: Susan McIntyre
Editorial-Production Service: Ruttle, Shaw & Wetherill, Inc.
Cover Administrator: Suzanne Harbison
Composition Buyer: Linda Cox
Manufacturing Buyer: Louise Richardson

A Division of Simon & Schuster, Inc.
160 Gould Street
Needham Heights, MA 02194

Library of Congress Cataloging-in-Publication Data

Controversial issues in mental health/edited by Stuart A. Kirk,
Susan D. Einbinder.
p. cm.
Includes bibliographical references.
ISBN 0–205–14675–9
1. Mental health policy. I. Kirk, Stuart A.
II. Einbinder, Susan D.
RA790.5.C653 1994
362.2--dc20 93–15442
CIP

Printed in the United States of America

10 9 8 7 6 5 4 3 2 98 97 96 95

Contents

II. Debates about Understanding Mental Disorders

III. Debates about Treating Mental Disorders

IV. Debates about Interprofessional Issues

Foreword

Controversial Issues in Mental Health is one of a series published by Allyn and Bacon that presents opposing sides of controversial issues to inform readers about topics of concern. This book presents different controversial topics on mental health.

We are all affected in one way or another by the mental health topics addressed: Has deinstitutionalization failed? Is managed care good for psychiatric patients? Should committing people involuntarily be easier? Different views about the nature of ''mental illness'' and what can be done to prevent and alter behaviors considered to reflect mental illness touch all of our lives. Such topics are the focus of casual conversations as well as the concern of impassioned consumer advocacy groups. How could it be otherwise? Mental illness involves behavior that is labeled as deviant by someone. If not troubling to the person said to have it, it is troubling to those who are affected by it. The integral relationship between mental illness and deviance explains the changing view of unusual, disliked, or disruptive behavior from sinful, to criminal, to reflective of mental illness. Thus, the topics discussed in this book are of concern not only to those who work in the field of mental health but to others as well.

The remedies proposed for mental illness are as varied as the kinds of behavior viewed as signs of mental illness. The history of mental health intervention depicts a panorama of suggested treatments, many of which harmed rather than aided those unfortunate enough to experience them. Some of the contributors to this book argue that harm is still being done. For example, some argue that electroconvulsive shock therapy does more harm than good. Harmful side effects of neuroleptic medication may not be disclosed to patients or their families ''for the good of the patient.'' Given the influence of cultural values on what is considered to be mental illness (the extent of this influence is itself controversial, as can be seen in one of the debates in this book), the possibility of undue intrusion is high.

I wish I had had access to a book like this when I was in graduate or, better yet, undergraduate school. The advantages of including differing views on a topic is well illustrated in *Controversial Issues in Mental Health.* I learned new facts in areas in which I thought I was informed, such as issues related to deinstitutionalization of patients. The format ensures that different perspectives on a topic are presented. A unique feature of the format in this series on controversial issues is the inclusion of replies to each statement. This offers the reader another ''insider view'' of opposing positions. The happy result is that the reader benefits by being better informed.

This book offers a welcome antidote to sources that provide only one side of controversial issues related to mental health. Professionals, clients, and indeed all people have a right to be well informed about important issues that affect their lives or the lives of others they care about. It is not as easy to hide embarrassing facts that relate to a position when people holding different perspectives openly debate a topic. The statements in this book are often argued with a passionate concern for the consumers of services. They illustrate that passion does not rule out a well-reasoned and well-supported argument. The essays in this book are a testament that passion and rationality (critical thinking) are not incompatible.

The topics included are notable for their timeliness. The editors have done a fine job of selecting authors from a wide variety of professions, perspectives, and positions, including academics, practitioners, and consumer advocates. This book will be valuable to those who work in the field of mental health as well as to policymakers and legislators who struggle to address such problems as homelessness and to ensure the rights of patients. This book could be used as a text in courses on mental health to highlight points that should be considered when discussing or thinking about important issues, or it could be used to supplement a main text.

The statement with reply format, which is unique to this series and to the flagship book *Controversial Issues in Social Work,* should encourage critical thinking. It demonstrates that differences of opinion, far from being undesirable, are valuable in arriving at informed beliefs. This book will help readers to think more critically about the difficult problems that confront the mental health field. Given scarce resources and the possibility of harming rather than helping people, it is important that we understand the nature of problems in this field so that resources can be effectively used and consumers protected from bogus and harmful practices. This book will advance this understanding. What I appreciate most about this book is the engaging writing style. The debates are enjoyable to read as well as informative. I was sorry when I came to the end of the manuscript. All too often, becoming better informed is arduous. Not so here.

Eileen Gambrill

Preface

Controversies are provocative. As William Hazlitt (1778–1830) said "When a thing ceases to be a subject of controversy, it ceases to be a subject of interest." By polarizing an issue into two opposing views, controversies force those involved to take one side, justify that choice, define and defend assumptions, and clarify beliefs. Through this process, controversies can challenge, hone, and change deeply held opinions. Our interest in controversy is more substantial than simply encouraging the spectacle of a free-for-all. Conflict that is ad hominem, malicious, vengeful, or vindictive rarely sheds light on anything other than personal animosities. There is plenty of that in the world and we do not need to encourage it. By contrast, conflict that is structured and focused creates an environment where participants must clearly articulate their points to convince others to agree with them. Each side has the opportunity to shake unexamined assumptions, question unfounded conclusions, spot leaps of logic in an opponent's stance, and address every facet of the complicated and often value-laden issue. This kind of conflict can inform, enliven, and contribute to our collective knowledge. It was this latter potential that stimulated the design of this book.

Avoiding Voices in the Dark

The word *controversy* derives from the Latin *contra* (against) and the verb *vertere* (to turn). According to Webster's Dictionary, controversy is a discussion of a question in which opposing positions clash. *Controversial Issues in Mental Health* identifies important questions, showcases impressive advocates for each side, and structures a clash of viewpoints that juxtapose opposing positions and elucidate underlying factors of the issue at hand. Here, controversy uses conflict to clarify the issue and make it coherent.

Often, controversies are neither structured nor reasoned, generating—as the cliche goes—more heat than light. At times, controversies are no more than animosities rooted deeply in ideology, personal experience, or prejudice—voices in the dark shouting epithets. Usually little is learned from such clashes, other than to illustrate people's propensity to act uncivilly, speak without thinking, and hear without listening.

Even when we are exposed to reasoned controversies, the forum is often inadequate. For example, we frequently hear both sides of a controversy from only one side. In this arrangement we listen to or read about what has been written by an ardent proponent who believes in one half of the controversy. The proponent selectively summarizes the "other side" as a way of highlighting his or her favored and more fully developed position. Thus, we learn about the "other" side from someone who has no stake in making in persuasive, logical, or desirable. While the proponent gives the impression that he or she is offering an unbiased account of the other side, the opposing view is presented in a weakened, flawed, or inept form. The "other" position is drawn unattractively, sketched without conviction or passion. Instead of a balanced portrayal of the opposing position, we are offered a straw man, a deliberately drawn clumsy foe, quick to stumble and fall at the first jab—which the presenting proponent eagerly provides.

Another inadequate forum is provided by an "objective" third party seeking to "find the truth," who serves not only as judge and jury but also as both defense and prosecuting attorney, all the while maintaining no personal stake in the outcome. These arrangements can be found in a classroom when a professor presents all sides of the issue or in a textbook where an author summarizes and sifts through different views of a controversial issue to distinguish the chaff from the wheat. To be sure, a more accurate rendering of a controversial issue is likely in this setting because the issue is described by a supposedly objective reporter. But everyone has an opinion, although the stated emphasis is on fairness and balance. Implicitly or explicitly, that comes through in such a forum. Worse still, an "objective" presenter lacks conviction and passion about the issue. Precisely because the discussant is a third party, the topic is presented without acute sensitivity to the nuances of opposing positions. The discourse often lacks a personal commitment to making the argument persuasive and opts for neutrality instead of using the rhetorical power of language to aid and abet one side. Under these circumstances, an important emotional tone to a controversy may be lost, not necessarily weakening its logic but certainly dampening its motivating spirit. In the hands of a third party, a controversial issue becomes boring, denuded of interest or zest.

Sometimes opponents strive to speak to each other, but the dialogue fails because they lack a structured forum. Harsh words may fly between two people exchanging arguments without recognizing that they are speaking about slightly different, but related questions; arguing, as it were, around the target. You say tomato, and I say tomato, without vocalization to illuminate different pronunciations. Such misfires help to identify issues, if not common answers. Other times, the issue may be clear, but dissenting contributions are offered at different times and places so that no common audience sees or hears both sides. For example, an argument is made forcefully in one issue of a professional journal about a controversial issue. Months later, someone writes a letter to the editor offering a critique of the initial argument and laying out evidence for an opposing position. The next year, in a different journal, a third author extends the original argument. A fourth author, incensed, pens another critical letter to the editor. Two years later, in a chapter of a book, someone else lays out what they think is a stronger argument or counterargument. And so it goes. The participating authors rarely confront one another directly or have an opportunity to respond to one another. Only a reader with a serious interest in the controversy is likely to track down the pieces of this fragmented, fractious, ongoing debate. The emotional tone may be strong, but the immediacy and interest of people concerned about the issue is depleted. Without consideration of time and place, even where opposing arguments are closely drawn and compelling, the controversy is lost.

This book attempts to remedy the structural problems of forums for controversies by asking informed opponents to address the same question, at the same time and place, and to speak back to each other. We'll say more about this format in a moment.

Controversies in Mental Health

The field of mental health is a fertile area for controversy. This is understandable; the mind is a terrible thing to misconstrue. Throughout modern history, the study of the mad, the insane, and the mentally ill has served as a barometer of our growing understanding or misunderstanding of human behavior and a sensitive indicator of the humanity of our social institutions. How we understand and treat the mentally disordered has been a reflection of how we, as a society, choose to care for those of misfortune. Understandably, treatment of the mentally ill is affected by the outcome of debates about the role of the states vis-a-vis the federal government, about the proper balance of protecting citizens' civil liberties when they clash with their health and welfare, and about the extent to which social intervention can produce desired outcomes. These larger political, legal, and social issues find their way into mental health debates.

The sensitivity of the mental health field to cultural and social cross-currents stems, in part, from its focus on very human characteristics: cognition, emotion, and behavior. Understanding mental disorder requires assumptions about normal development and natural functioning, topics rife with disagreement. As normality involves complex assumptions about biological facts and social values, so too do approaches to mental disorder. Thus, making judgments about who is mentally ill and how or if they should be treated can quickly turn into a quagmire of arguments about what is normal and what is just.

On these questions, the level of uncertainty of the mental health field's knowledge base provides opportunities for disagreements. For example, the causes of most mental disorders have not been identified, although there is a profusion of rival theories. And on specific treatment for specific disorders, considerable room exists for disagreement about what works and why, how it should be financed and at what level, and who should do it and with what monitoring or oversight mechanisms.

The mental health field is composed of a diverse array of professions and disciplines. The field is inhabited by psychiatrists, psychoanalysts, clinical psychologists, social workers, nurses, and counselors of various kinds. Each profession has its own history, perspectives, proclivities, and interests. The mental health field also enjoys the attention of social and behavioral scientists, humanists, and biomedical researchers. This potpourri of talent brings great intellectual variety to this field. But the diversity reaches beyond disciplinary perspectives, because within most professions and disciplines are sharp differences of belief and approach. These internal disputes are also reflected in each discipline's approaches to mental health. For example, among psychiatrists there are sharply differing views of the role of psychiatric medications, involuntary treatment, and managed care. Psychologists disagree about the relative effectiveness of types of psychotherapy. Social workers argue about the amount of emphasis that should be placed on environmental intervention as opposed to psychological means. These many disputes are not idle talk among scholars; the outcomes have real consequences for how money is allocated for research and services, who receives help and how, and how influence is distributed among professions, each of which wants to claim some territory for itself in the vast and shifting terrain covered by mental health. Money, power, and influence shape the struggle for truth in mental health as elsewhere, but one sometimes must read between the lines to detect it.

The Process and Format

This book intends to capture the spirit of some of these important contemporary disputes in the field of mental health. Moreover, we wanted to structure disagreements so that the authors inform as they attempt to persuade. We also wanted to avoid some of the structural arrangements of time and place and question that so often allow willing opponents to speak past each other or speak to different audiences. We tried to accomplish this in three ways.

First, we identify significant controversies in mental health. Since positions become controversial only if there are at least two sides (*contra vertere*), we reviewed recent issues of mental health journals and looked for topics on which there were finely drawn opposing positions published as articles, rebuttals to articles, or letters to the editors. We surveyed colleagues with a list of potential topics, and asked them to indicate which topics they thought were important controversies as well as to suggest others. From this process, we identified nearly forty controversial issues. We then winnowed and refined the list. Some of the topics were too similar, some did not excite any of our preliminary respondents, and some we realized had been worded so poorly that the debate would be skewed or impossibly clumsy. Finally, we wanted an array of topics to cover different levels of conflict within mental health. The result is the nineteen topics in this book.

Second, we needed not just topics, but articulate advocates—people who care about the issue, who are ready to address or had already articulated a position, and who have little fear of speaking out. Most of the contributors to this book had already written forcefully about the controversial issue. Some of them had repeatedly staked out a position, taken on opponents, and remained confident in their arguments; others were new to the published controversy, but eager to express a point of view; and a few were uneasy converts to the format, agreeing to argue a point of view before they had completely worked out their own position on it. This latter group adopted their views to the structure of our book to illuminate the controversial elements and elucidate the issue.

Many of our debate topics were shaped by discussions with prospective authors. In some cases, we discovered that our initial wording of a debate question was biased or did not focus the issue appropriately. These active participants in published controversies were acutely tuned to nuance, and they helped us tighten the focus. Sometimes, however, a tightened focus comforted one author, but made it more difficult to find an opponent. Not surprisingly, authors were great sources of leads about possible worthy opponents. At other times, we were easily able to find an advocate to argue one side, but were repeatedly unable to find someone to argue the other side. For example, one of our preliminary topics was "Are psychiatric diagnoses race biased?" We quickly found an author to argue YES, but failed to find anyone who would publicly argue NO. Ultimately, this topic was dropped. We also abandoned questions about whether mothers are still being blamed for their children's disorders, whether diagnostic labels are themselves harmful, and questions about codependency, schizophrenia, alcoholism, and other topics.

Third, in addition to specifying the question to be addressed by both sides, we allow rejoinders. After each pair of authors had submitted their papers (in almost all cases without knowing the identity of their opponent), we exchanged their essays (in all cases with identifying information about the authors) and asked them to write a brief rebuttal. Knowing that you will have a certain, immediate critique of your argument is a prod to logical reasoning and careful wording. Our purpose was to encourage reasoned statements and to allow reasoned rejoinders, and in so doing to allow both sides to articulate opposing positions and to speak back. We think the authors have succeeded.

To accomplish all this in the confines of a small book is not easy. We insisted on brevity. Many of our worthy contributors have argued their points at great length in other scholarly arenas. They knew, more than most, about the complexity of their case, the scattered evidence that should be brought to bear, and what the full convincing argument should look like. Who better, we thought, to distill the essence of the argument, to get quickly to the bone, than those who are most informed and most knowledgeable. We asked them to provide not complete comprehensive reviews of their position, but the outlines of the full argument—its essence—as they saw it. And without being asked for it, they gave us their passion for the topic.

The Outline of the Book

This book is organized into five sections, each of which encompasses a general area of mental health controversy. We make no claim to cover these general areas exhaustively or even to having selected the most important contemporary controversies. Because this book is intended for an audience relatively new to the field of mental health, we wanted to introduce a sample of fascinating subjects. The sections are ordered to raise issues about how we define and identify mental disorder, how we understand the causes of mental disorders, how we treat persons who have mental disorders, how mental health and other professions may differ, and how social policies affect the field of mental health. Although it is possible to read the book from start to finish, readers may want to read selectively in a particular area of interest, starting in one section and returning to an earlier one at a later date. In fact, other latent structures to these debates might suggest a different organization, for example, along a medical/nonmedical axis or between defenders and critics of conventional wisdom. An instructor who uses this book for a mental health course may well find that grouping these debates differently has pedagogical value.

The first section of the book, Debates about Identifying Mental Disorders, addresses controversies among mental health professionals about how we define and identify mental disorders. The influence of cultural factors is the issue of the first debate, which explores whether the concept of mental disorder itself is culturally relative. The second debate asks whether personality disorders, as described in the *DSM-III-R,* are gender biased. Whether a "personality" itself can be disordered is the topic of the third debate. This section concludes with a debate about whether computers can replace human diagnosticians in making diagnoses. These four debates highlight fundamental questions about our conceptualizations and approaches to mental disorder.

The second section of the book, Debates about Understanding Mental Disorders, contains controversies about the causes and consequences of mental illness. These issues—and mental health professionals' opinions about them—

greatly influence how we allocate scarce resources. The first debate discusses whether prevention through social structural changes should have primacy over clinical treatment. The next debate exchanges views about whether mental illness should be considered a cause of homelessness. Finally, this section concludes with a debate about whether the emphasis on genetics distorts approaches to mental disorders. These debates each reflect differences of opinions about the importance of social structural factors in the generation and consequences of mental illness.

The third section of the book, Debates about Treating Mental Disorders, identifies controversies about three specific treatment approaches. The first topic focuses on the relevance and empirical foundations of psychoanalytic therapy for public mental health programs. The second debate addresses the continued use of electroshock treatment. The final issue explores the use of neuroleptics, a class of drugs frequently used to treat people with severe mental disorders. These debates challenge the reader to explore the consequences of each treatment for consumers of mental health services.

The fourth section, Debates about Interprofessional Issues, addresses some of the controversies that arise because the field of mental health is comprised of a variety of professions and has involvements in other social arenas. This section asks questions about whether the remedicalization of psychiatry is good for the mental health field, whether non-physicians should be allowed to prescribe medicine, and whether mental health experts should be allowed to testify in court. Finally, this section concludes with an exchange debating whether different professions offer the same service to clients. The debates in this section highlight conflicts within and between professionals in mental health.

The final section, Debates about Policy Issues, discusses many broad social policy developments and how they have and continue to affect clients' access to mental health services. The first topic discusses whether deinstitutionalization has failed. The next debate asks whether the National Alliance for the Mentally Ill (NAMI), an influential advocacy group formed by families of the mentally ill, represents the needs of all families with members who are psychiatric patients. The third topic addresses the emergence of managed care and its likely influence on service provision and on clients. This debate is followed by an exchange about whether it should be easier to involuntarily commit persons for treatment. Finally, this section poses the question of whether mental health professionals have abandoned the chronically mentally ill.

The Participants

The participants in these debates took their tasks seriously, very much in keeping with their opinions about their respective topics. Their cooperation is appreciated as much as their commitment. Compiling a book of original contributions from forty-four authors is no small task. For nine months, we kept telephone lines and fax machines busy; letters, notes, and essays were exchanged through the mail; and word processors hummed across the country and over time zones. The authors graciously accepted our invitation to contribute, diligently answered our many calls and letters, and paid attention to the details and deadlines of our requests. We thank them all, and their secretaries and assistants, for their cooperation and good spirits in this endeavor.

We knew many of the contributors to this book only through their written work or through their colleagues' positive recommendations to us. But in working with them (some of them may describe it as pestering, and for that we apologize!), they have become a group to us, an extended family of sorts, with a shared dedication to improving the lives of those with mental disorders and with sharp but respectful differences of opinion and style. We have learned from them, not only through their written contribution, but also from the different ways in which they approached their tasks and in the many ways they have been helpful to us.

We sought and have achieved diversity among our authors. Represented are psychiatrists, psychologists, social workers, psychotherapists, sociologists, philosophers, government officials, and poets. There are essays written by quantitative researchers and theoreticians, by policymakers and policy advocates, by clinicians and former patients, by defenders of the status quo and their vociferous critics, by well-known eminent figures in mental health and by relatively new voices, in short, from people who often have very different backgrounds, commitments, and perspectives. This, of course, was our intention.

Seeking such diversity has its drawbacks. Even though we attempted to structure the debates and provide a single focus for each one, these topics are sufficiently complex and multilayered to allow our debaters to partially miss one another, to address slightly different aspects of the general issue, or to highlight different bodies of evidence. It is our challenge to the reader to identify such disjunctions, to spot arguments that are flawed, and to scrutinize the uses of facts and values and the logical chains from premises to conclusions. In this regard, the essays in this book are a wonderful introduction to the dilemmas, diversity, and divisiveness of the mental health field today.

In preparing this book, we incurred debts beyond those to our very able authors. We also sought and received advice, and at times solace, from many others. Eileen Gambrill and Karen Hanson were the first to invite us to undertake this task and supported us from the very beginning. Among our professional colleagues who were kind enough to offer us helpful advice and other assistance, but who are not included among the contributors to this book, are Ronald Feldman, Lynn Videka-Sherman, Uri Aviram, Wally Gingerich, Ed Mullen, Linda Freeman, and Joanne Turnbull. The constant support of Carol Ann Koz cannot be adequately acknowledged. Additional thanks go to Madelin Einbinder Foti and John Foti and Morgan Einbinder for their love and friendship. The book is dedicated to our respective progeny and parents: Allison and Brandon Kirk and Lynn and Jason Einbinder.

Finally, a note on co-editing. Developing a book with forty-four authors, thirty-eight essays, and thirty-eight rebuttals is not a task for the disorganized. It required a jointly coordinated volley of phone calls, missives, and mailings and demanded a level of communication and flexibility that challenged even the most obsessively organized. It called for attention to minute detail, tight time schedules, and a level of coordination that is almost foreign to academic life and temperaments. Working closely with a colleague, particularly one who thinks that they are the better organized, has the potential of becoming a controversy in itself. To our mutual delight, we found that assembling this book was not only intellectually stimulating, but fun. We hope that our readers ''catch'' our enthusiasm about these controversies and this book.

Stuart A. Kirk
Susan D. Einbinder

DEBATE 1

Is the Concept of Mental Disorder Culturally Relative?

Presenting the YES argument is Laurence J. Kirmayer, M.D., FRCPC, who is Associate Professor of Psychiatry and Director, Division of Social and Transcultural Psychiatry, McGill University, Montreal. He is Editor-in-Chief of *Transcultural Psychiatric Research Review.* He is also a staff psychiatrist and research associate, Institute of Community and Family Psychiatry, Sir Mortimer B. Davis–Jewish General Hospital, Montreal, and psychiatric consultant, Inuulitsivik Health Centre, Povungnituk, Quebec. His research interests include somatization, cultural idioms of distress, and comparative studies of psychotherapy and symbolic healing.

Taking the opposing position, NO, is Jerome C. Wakefield, who is an Associate Professor in the School of Social Work and a Core Member of the Institute for Health, Health Care Policy, and Aging Research at Rutgers University. Dr. Wakefield has also taught at the University of California at Berkeley, the University of Chicago, and Columbia University. He holds a doctorate in Social Welfare and a master's degree in Mathematics with a concentration in Logic and Methodology of Science and has completed all course work for a doctorate in Philosophy, all from Berkeley. His main area of research is the conceptual foundations of the mental health professions, and he has published on such topics as the concept of mental disorder, the validity of DSM-III-R diagnostic criteria, conceptual foundations of psychoanalytic theory, hermeneutic approaches to psychology, and the history of sexuality.

YES

LAURENCE J. KIRMAYER

While people in most cultures recognize bizarre behavior as a special type of problem, they do not always understand it as an illness, nor do they classify such "crazy" behavior with the other forms of deviance or distress that we include in the category of mental disorder. It is not only the boundaries of disorder that differ across cultures, however, the concept of "mental disorder" itself is a creation of Western cultural history for which no exact parallel can be found in many other traditions.

Cultural concepts of mental disorder can be distinguished from cultural variations in the actual manifestations of distress. Cultures may differ in the recognition, classification, and explanation of deviant behavior even though people suffer from similar afflictions all over the world. In fact, cultural concepts influence psychological processes so that there is also great cultural variation in the nature of emotional and behavioral problems (Kirmayer, 1989). In this essay, though, I will focus on the issue of cultural concepts rather than the actual manifestations of mental disorders.

A culture includes the shared belief system of a people. However, much cultural knowledge is not accessible as explicit beliefs but resides in the private, public, and institutional practices that constitute a people's way of life. Cultural beliefs and practices are not freely picked up and dropped—over time and through development, they construct both individuals' sense of self and their social identity.

This view of culture has an important implication for our discussion of cultural concepts. We usually expect that people can describe their concepts or that cultural concepts are directly represented in their lexicon. If culture consists of practices, however, cultural knowledge is encoded not only as mental representations in phototypical images, narratives, or more abstract models, but also as skills, procedures, habits, and stances that may not be easy for people to describe. We can get at these embodied aspects of culture only by observing how people actually live their lives.

Consider, then, this vignette from the Arctic of Québec where I do clinical work and ethnographic research:

> Markoosie is a 32-year-old Inuit man living in a remote village. He has auditory and somatic hallucinations and a persistent delusion that three men from the south, whom he has never met, are planning to come north to kill him. One day he mistakes three coworkers driving the water truck for his southern assassins and shoots at them with his rifle. He flees home in fear and is brought to the nursing station by police who ask that he be taken south to be hospitalized. When he returns from the southern psychiatric

> hospital, where he receives a diagnosis of paranoid schizophrenia, he is put back to work as a dog catcher, shooting strays with his rifle. Although he continues to have hallucinations and delusions even on neuroleptic medication, he keeps these experiences to himself and is viewed by most community members as recovered.

While Markoosie's illness is long-standing and the trained interviewer can find evidence of thought disorder and hallucinations that never entirely remit, he is not identified as having a problem by most people in the community until his behavior becomes dangerous to others. Some people in the community have heard that he has a kind of sickness, and they assume it is an illness like any other. Others have noticed him walking around the settlement talking to himself and view him as worried or preoccupied. Still others find him strange and believe he is possessed by demons and recommend exorcism.

Among these disparate views, the notion that he has a mental illness is the minority opinion held by a few Inuit health workers knowledgeable about psychiatry. The two most common interpretations of his behavior are both culturally distinctive concepts of disorder. The first is that he is worried, preoccupied, or thinking too much. This concept (the term in Inuktitut is *isumaluktuq*) blurs the distinction between ordinary worry, which is clearly not an illness, and excessive worry, which can make one withdrawn and disabled. The concept of *isumaluktuq* then puts Markoosie's affliction on a continuum with quite ordinary states of worry and preoccupation. It normalizes his odd behavior. Along with the Inuit tendency to label behavioral states and conditions rather than personality traits in describing people and problems, the concept of *isumaluktuq* protects Markoosie from some of the stigmatization that accompanies our own labels of schizophrenia and other mental disorders. Our own labels carry more pejorative weight because they are sharply distinguished from ordinary states (they are "disorders") and because of a more general tendency in Western societies to label people with characterological traits, and so to attach illness labels as reflections of a permanent change in a person's status (one can be a schizophrenic in remission, but the label sticks).

The second common interpretation for Markoosie's violent and peculiar behavior offered by some Inuit is that he is possessed by a demon. This concept is derived from the recently established Pentecostal church, but it is likely that it owes part of its popularity to a continuity with traditional Inuit shamanic ideas and practices. For those who see Markoosie as possessed, his problem is neither mental nor an illness—it is his soul that is afflicted. He has been bodily invaded by spectral or satanic forces that can speak through him, control his actions, and make life hell for himself and others. The appropriate treatment is spiritual—prayer, laying on of hands, and exorcism. If these treatments fail, this indicates either that the demons are too strong or that Markoosie himself is lacking in moral strength or religious conviction. This conceptualization has the virtue of offering him reintegration into the community if he is healed but poses the danger of ostracism if the healing fails.

Certainly, the Inuit have terms for ''losing one's mind,'' ''being crazy,'' and so on, but these apply to overt extremes of bizarre behavior and, in fact, function more as descriptions of behavior than as theories of the locus and nature of the problem (Vallee, 1966). Inuit are reluctant to use these terms even for individuals with schizophrenia, bipolar disorder, or other major psychiatric disorders. Instead, they tend to use the word *isumaluktuq* and, when pressed for a general term for mental disorder, this is also the word they offer. In Inuit thinking, then, mental disorders are largely assimilated to worry or problems in living.

From this brief example, it is clear not only that cultural concepts of deviant behavior and mental disorder vary but also that they have important consequences for the course of psychiatric disorders. Another cogent example of this has been provided by Janis Jenkins in her work with Mexican-American families with a schizophrenic member. Jenkins (1988) has found that many of these families make a sharp distinction between *locura* (craziness) and *nervios* (nervousness). *Locura* is evidenced by violent and unpredictable behavior and may indicate a mental illness. In contrast, *nervios* is not a mental illness but a reaction to difficult life events or social stress, expressed through a multitude of emotional and somatic symptoms, which may include many of the symptoms of schizophrenia. The person with *nervios* is very sensitive to interpersonal conflict and so the appropriate response is to avoid conflict or confrontation with them. In this case, a specific cultural belief about the nature of mental disorder leads to a reduction in negative expressed emotion within the family—exactly the sort of behavioral change that has been shown to improve the prognosis of schizophrenia.[1]

If such cultural variations occur in the way of conceptualizing major—and probably universal—psychiatric disorders like schizophrenia, differences in cultural conceptions are all the more profound for milder disorders which, if one accepts cognitive theory, can themselves be created by specific beliefs.

For example, Obeyesekere (1985) discusses how, from a Buddhist perspective, many of the cardinal symptoms of depression are not indicative of pathology but of accurate understanding of the inevitability of suffering and loss. He suggests that some individuals who would be labeled depressed by psychiatric criteria are, in Sri Lanka, viewed as having acquired important religious insights. From the Buddhist perspective, the ''disorder,'' if it can be called that, resides not in morbid thoughts but in the struggle to hold on to transient experiences. The goal of spiritual development is not a strong ego but the dissolution of the self of which western psychology is so enamored!

Of course, culture is not something exotic ''out there''—every product of knowledge is, in some measure, a cultural construction. So our own psychiatric nosology and scientific theories of psychopathology must also be understood as a product of a cultural history (Gaines, 1992). One way to see this is to consider the meaning of the term *mental disorder;* each word is a metaphor carrying a freight of cultural meaning. What we have in the term *mental disorder* is a culture-specific way of classifying and explaining human problems.

Mental is a term that evokes the Cartesian dualism central to Western culture. It denotes a special category of experience, one distinct from and valued over the merely physical or bodily (Kirmayer, 1988). The everyday use of *mental* involves a localization of experience to a private interior. The mental then is a disembodied essence that resides in our brains (or behind our foreheads) and involves inner dispositions, thoughts, desires, and plans that constitute who we really are. In academic psychology, *mental* stands for cognitive and emotional processes that give rise to the observable organization of behavior. The effort to explain the mental in terms of information processing or physiological mechanisms is a distinctive feature of contemporary psychology. Other cultures do not split off the mental from the physical and do not situate the process of thinking and feeling entirely within the person.

In fact, three of the great medical traditions of the world, Islamic, Ayurvedic, and Chinese, treat the person as a psychophysical unity and so make no fundamental distinction between mental and physical illness. For example, in traditional Chinese medicine bizarre behavior was recognized as a medical problem and presumed to be due to some derangement of the bodily humors. However, because these humors or energetic principles that govern health have both physical and emotional correlates, there is no need for a special category of mental illness. Nor is the derangement simply a disorder situated within the body since the body is open to the environment. Illness may be a manifestation of social-moral problems or of cosmological forces. As well, milder somatic disturbances all have emotional concomitants and any strong emotion points toward an organic imbalance. In this system, there is no distinct category of mental disorder. This traditional view survives in contemporary Chinese medical practice both in the popularity of the diagnosis of neurasthenia (nervous weakness) for a host of social, emotional, and physical complaints (Kleinman, 1986) and in the theoretical basis and prescription of herbal medicines (Ots, 1990).

An example not tied to an elaborate textual tradition is supplied by the traditional Amhara of rural Ethiopia (Young, 1975). The Amhara do not refer their thoughts, feelings and desires to a disembodied, internal mental state. Instead, they understand themselves as physically and socially embodied beings. Asked how they feel they may gesture to the body and describe a somatic sensation. Asked whether they have cried much in the last week, they may reply that there have not been any funerals recently (Kortmann, 1987). Crying is understood not so much as a manifestation of an inner mental state of sadness but as a bodily response or gesture appropriate to a specific social situation. This makes even the simplest self-report of symptoms of psychiatric ''disorder'' problematic.

But are mental processes really internal mechanisms? Have other cultures simply got it wrong? Perhaps not. Many philosophers and social psychologists have argued that mind is a social creation. We learn to think, feel, and acquire an identity through interaction with others. Much of our thinking and feeling continues to be done in interaction with others or with collective representations or social institutions. The most profound expressions of mind are cooperative creations that are not held in one individual's mind but circulate among individuals.[2] The tendency to locate mind within the individual is itself a feature of our folk psychology that ignores the social distribution of mental processes.

Our concept of the mental then is a specific cultural category. While it can be redefined in sufficiently abstract terms to allow us to apply it cross-culturally, the cognate terms in other cultures do not have quite the same connotations. Similarly, *disorder* is a technical term for problematic patterns of behavior made popular by DSM-III. Its utility is directly related to its ambiguity. It sits somewhere between two concepts used in physical medicine: that of *syndromes*—that is, correlated patterns of co-occurring symptoms—and *disease*—entities identified by distinctive anatomical or pathophysiological processes.

There is an underlying assumption that psychiatric disorders will ultimately be mapped onto diseases but, at present, they reflect groupings of symptoms and syndromes that are related because they are held to involve some similar disturbance in function or response to treatment. Yet, the functions we use to identify disorders reflect our theoretical models of psychology and physiology. Cultural beliefs and values may make one or another function more prominent in our thinking and so lead us to reorganize our nosology.

For example, a distinctive form of social phobia, *taijin kyofusho* (TKS), is an extremely common psychiatric diagnosis in Japan (Kirmayer, 1991). While social phobia in North America centers on fear of potential public embarrassment, the chief symptom of TKS is the fear of injuring others with one's gaze or inappropriate social behavior. This is an exaggeration of culturally normative concerns about harmonious social relations. Many Japanese psychiatrists believe that social phobia reflects a fundamental impairment in self-concept and social-relatedness that is more central than, and hence overrides, other psychological disturbances. Consequently, they view patients with delusions, anxiety, and avoidant behavior as having closely related problems, which they label as a single disorder, *taijin kyofusho.* These same patients would be viewed by American psychiatrists as having distinctly different sorts of problems. The central importance given to the status hierarchy and the social presentation of self leads Japanese psychiatrists to organize the whole domain of anxiety differently and to view as similar many types of problems that would be sharply distinguished by American psychiatrists (Tseng et al., 1992).

Clearly, the notion of mental disorder arises from a specific scientific tradition of nosology. Although it can be framed in an abstract manner that allows us to apply it with profit to the categorization and explanation of people's problems elsewhere in the world, it is not used by most of these people themselves in understanding their own problems. Instead, to explain deviant or problematic behavior, people appeal to other processes that are central to their cultural belief systems. Interpretations of deviance may invoke religious, magical, environmental, or moral explanations. Each form of understanding gives rise to a different categorization and social response to deviance.

Finally, many problems in other cultures (and perhaps in our own) that current nosology attempts to construct as discrete disorders are not deviant or disorders at all. They are culturally constituted and sanctioned *idioms of distress*—vocabularies and styles for explaining and expressing a wide range of personal and social problems. These idioms of distress cannot simply be added to our lists of discrete entities. Instead, they must be understood as rhetorical devices for making sense of human predicaments.

I have tried to present a few examples of the divergent cultural concepts of deviant behavior that may be applied to people with identifiable psychiatric disorders. There are many more examples of social problems and predicaments that do not neatly correspond to any Western psychiatric category. Similarly, there are many well-established examples of cultural interpretations of psychiatric distress that invoke neither the concept of the mental nor of disorder. Understanding these differences is an obvious prerequisite to applying psychiatric theory and practice across cultures. Just as important, it can help us to rethink and refine current psychiatric theory to transcend some of the limiting assumptions we inherit from our own cultural system.

Endnotes

1. Guarnaccia and colleagues (1992) describe a similar cultural pattern among Puerto Ricans and Cuban-Americans.
2. See, for example, Dennett's (1991) discussion of ''memes.''

References

Dennett, D. C. (1991). *Consciousness explained.* Boston: Little, Brown & Company.

Fabrega, H., Jr. (1992). The role of culture in a theory of psychiatric illness. *Social Science and Medicine, 35*(1), 91–103.

Gaines, A. D. (1992). From DSM-I to III-R: Voices of self, mastery and the other: A cultural constructivist reading of U.S. psychiatric classification. *Social Science and Medicine, 35*(1), 3–24.

Guarnaccia, P. J., Parra, P., Deschamps, A., Milstein, G., & Argiles, N. (1992). Si Dios quiere: Hispanic families' experiences of caring for a seriously mentally ill family member. *Culture, Medicine and Psychiatry, 16*(2), 187–216.

Jenkins, J. H. (1988). Ethnopsychiatric interpretations of schizophrenic illness: The problem of nervios in Mexican-American families. *Culture, Medicine and Psychiatry, 12,* 303–331.

Kirmayer, L. J. (1988). Mind and body as metaphors: Hidden values in biomedicine. In M. Lock & D. Gordon (Eds.), *Biomedicine examined* (pp. 57–92). Dordrecht: Kluwer.

Kirmayer, L. J. (1989). Cultural variations in the response to psychiatric disorders and emotional distress. *Social Science and Medicine, 29*(3), 327–339.

Kirmayer, L. J. (1991). The place of culture in psychiatric nosology: Taijin kyofusho and DSM-III-R. *Journal of Nervous and Mental Disease, 179*(1), 19–28.

Kleinman, A. (1986). *Social origins of distress and disease.* New Haven: Yale University Press.

Kortmann, F. (1987). Problems in communication in transcultural psychiatry: The self reporting questionnaire in Ethiopia. *Acta Psychiatrica Scandinavia, 75,* 563–570.

Obeyesekere, G. (1985). Depression, Buddhism, and the work of culture in Sri Lanka. In A. M. Kleinman & B. Good (Eds.), *Culture and depression* (pp. 134–152). Berkeley, CA: University of California Press.

Ots, T. (1990). The angry liver, the anxious heart and the melancholy spleen: The phenomenology of perception in Chinese culture. *Culture, Medicine and Psychiatry, 14*(1), 21–58.

Tseng, W.-S., Asai, M., Kitanishi, K., McLaughlin, D. G., & Kyomen, H. (1992). Diagnostic patterns of social phobia: Comparison in Tokyo and Hawaii. *Journal of Nervous and Mental Disease, 180*(6), 380–385.

Vallee, F. G. (1966). Eskimo theories of mental illness in the Hudson Bay region. *Anthropologica, 8,* 53–83.

Young, A. (1975). Why Amhara get *kureynya:* Sickness and possession in an Ethiopian zar cult. *American Ethnologist, 2,* 567.

Annotated Bibliography

Kleinman, A. (1988). *Rethinking psychiatry.* New York: Free Press.

Thoughtful critique of the cultural assumptions of contemporary psychiatric theory and practice.

Kleinman, A. & Good, B. (Eds.). (1985), *Culture and depression,* Berkeley, CA: University of California Press.

Fascinating collection of essays on the diversity of interpretations of depression as affect and disorder.

Littlewood, R. (1990). From categories to contexts: A decade of the 'new cross-cultural psychiatry.' *British Journal of Psychiatry, 156,* 308–327.

Provocative review of recent studies emphasizing a relativistic perspective.

Marsella, A. J., & White, G. M. (Eds.). (1982) *Cultural conceptions of mental health and therapy.* Dordrecht, Netherlands: D. Reidel.

Essays on the diversity of concepts of mental health, illness, and psychotherapy.

Shweder, R. A., & LeVine, R. A. (Eds.). (1984). *Culture theory: Essays on mind, self, and emotion.* Cambridge, England: Cambridge University Press.

Explorations of different "ethnopsychologies."

Rejoinder to Professor Kirmayer

JEROME C. WAKEFIELD

Kirmayer and I are to some degree talking past each other. I understood the question, "Is the concept of mental disorder culturally relative?" to be asking, literally, whether different cultures have different concepts that qualify specifically as concepts of mental disorder. I argued that the notion of different concepts of mental disorder makes no sense; the concept of mental disorder is the concept of a harmful mental dysfunction, where a dysfunction is a deviation from the way the organism is designed to function. All cultures are concerned about such conditions, although they may differ in how they explain their existence and in exactly which conditions they recognize as falling under the concept. But either a concept is this concept of mental disorder or else it is some other concept entirely; there is no in-between of "different concepts of mental disorder."

Kirmayer interpreted the question much more broadly, as asking whether different cultures "differ in the recognition, classification, and explanation of deviant behavior." This interpretation trivializes the question. Differences in explanation and recognition of disorder are so widespread that, if this were the meaning of the question, one would have to conclude that, not only cultures, but also virtually every individual and certainly every theoretician in the mental health field has his or her own concept of mental disorder. According to Kirmayer's construal, when two physicians disagree on a diagnosis—which is in effect a disagreement over the explanation of symptoms—they must have different concepts of disorder. But this confuses theories and explanations with concepts and undermines the value of the concept as a shared theory-neutral "glue" that holds together the disparate members of the mental health field and connects them to the general population. It is precisely because the concept is more abstract and widely shared than specific theories and explanations that it has some value as a framework for inquiry.

Each of Kirmayer's examples shows one or another of the confusions I pointed out in my article. Because of space limits, I can consider only Kirmayer's main example, the case of Markoosie, an Innuit Eskimo suffering from delusions and hallucinations. Kirmayer claims that this example displays cross-cultural differences in both recognition and explanation of deviant behavior, and thus proves the existence of "culturally distinctive concepts of disorder." First, as to recognition, although Markoosie is diagnosable by DSM-III-R standards and likely would be recognized within our community as disordered, many people in his community do not recognize him as having a disorder until he becomes a threat. This might be due partly to reticence about labeling in a small community, but it is also due to a difference in the degree of harm from Markoosie's condition. In our community, Markoosie's symptoms would likely cause substantial harm, perhaps including lack of employment and income as well as social friction, long before he became a threat. That, in conjunction with evidence that the harm is caused by a dysfunction, would justify an attribution of disorder. In less industrialized and less dense societies like the Inuits', there need not be as much harm from variations in mental functioning, and Markoosie's overall successful social adaptation, including continued employment at a simple task largely pursued in isolation, is testimony to that fact. Until he became violent, he was neither a problem for others nor, apparently, in subjective pain over his symptoms, so it is arguable that there was no significant harm. But, harm is a necessary requirement for the existence of disorder. If modern industrial societies did not require the degree of mental focus and impulse control that they do, we too would probably have a higher threshold for judgments of harm bearing on disorder, more like Markoosie's community. So, the difference between the Inuit and us in recognition of Markoosie's condition as disordered is explained not by a difference in the concept of disorder but rather by differences in judgments of whether Markoosie's condition meets the harm criterion for that concept.

Second, as to differences in explanation, Kirmayer notes that some Inuit explain Markoosie's behavior by demonic supernatural forces and others by excessive worry, and he claims that these explanations display different concepts of disorder. Comparable supernatural explanations are common in our own society and are compatible with our concept of disorder. When I was a child, I was told by Mrs. Siegel, a religious woman who took care of me when my parents were out of town, that illnesses are God's punishment for sins one has committed. Mrs. Siegel nonetheless understood the standard concept of disorder; indeed, it is only by using that concept that she was able to recognize the conditions that were candidates for being God's punishment. Today, some people misguidedly think that AIDS is a punishment by God for sinful activity, but that supernatural attribution does not mean that they do not think that AIDS is a disorder, it just means they have a different explanation than most of us for why the disorder occurs. Although the full story is more complex than I have space to go into here, the point is that supernatural attributions are often partial explanations of conditions that are already recognized as disorders by their harmful and dysfunctional features. It is the fact that we shared the concept of disorder that allowed Mrs. Siegel and me to have different theories about the cause of disorder.

A second Inuit explanation is that Markoosie is worrying too much. This is genuinely ambiguous. Is Markoosie worrying so much that he is disabled and thus disordered, or is he just at the extreme on a normal continuum? I suspect that the Inuit have trouble answering such questions, as do we, because the concept of mental disorder does not offer any easy answer to such complex dilemmas. We ourselves question whether problems are due to a normal reaction to stress or to a more serious breakdown in the individual's ability to function. The ambiguities of the Inuit category of *isumaluktuq* resonate with our own concept of disorder and are no counterexample to it.

Kirmayer falls prey to a common confusion when he tries to connect the question of the existence of mental disorder to the mind/body problem. The concept of a mental disorder is just the concept that something has gone wrong with the way the organism's mind is designed to function. In suggesting that such disorders exist, there need be no deep metaphysical assumptions about the nature of the mind, any more than there need be deep metaphysical assumptions about the nature of kidneys in saying that kidney disorders exist. Whatever the mind is made of, as long as the mind encompasses an identifiable realm of phenomena (e.g., perception, thought, feeling), then disorders within that realm are mental disorders. Similarly, Kirmayer's comments on social and physical views of the mind confuse specific theories of mind with the concepts of mind and disorder.

The study of cross-cultural differences is so fascinating, and the need to respect differences is so urgent, that one may easily become mesmerized by the differences and go beyond the data to make sweeping relativistic claims that deny the very commonalities that allow us to understand other cultures in the first place. Kirmayer's engaging presentation suffers from this problem. Instead of proving that the concept of mental disorder is culturally relative, his examples actually confirm my diagnosis of the errors leading to relativism.

NO

Jerome C. Wakefield

There are many ways that mental disorders vary across cultures. But does the *concept* of mental disorder itself vary across cultures? I will argue that the common assertion that "different cultures have different concepts of mental disorder'' is not only false but incoherent. I first present some preliminary points about concepts, then explain why the reasons usually given for the relativity of ''mental disorder'' are not good ones, and finally argue that the whole notion of the relativity of concepts makes no sense to begin with.

Relativisms of all kinds are popular these days, partly because they are seen as an antidote to the arrogance with which Western thinkers have traditionally approached non-Western cultures. If truth, values, and concepts are relative to culture, then no culture can justifiably impose its own standards on another. However, even the pursuit of an admirable goal such as humility can sometimes lead to intellectual error, and that is what has happened, I claim, with the acceptance of the doctrine of concept relativism. Note that my argument here is only about concept relativism; I make no claims about other, more common forms of relativism.

To understand concept relativism and why it is incoherent, one first has to understand what a concept is and how concepts differ from beliefs about what falls under the concept. Concepts are the ultimate criteria for classification of things under categories, and we use concepts to think and to formulate beliefs. For example, to believe that ''bachelors are sloppy,'' one first has to possess the concepts ''bachelor'' and ''sloppy.'' The concept ''bachelor'' just consists of the definition of the term *bachelor,* which is roughly ''unmarried adult male.'' The structure of a concept—that is, the criterion that determines what things fall under the concept—manifests itself largely through classificatory judgments, that is, beliefs about which things belong in which categories. For example, the fact that ''unmarried adult male'' is the conceptual criterion for ''bachelor'' emerges in beliefs about who is and who is not a bachelor.

However, it would be a mistake to think that, just because concepts are the ultimate criteria for classification, differences in classification always imply different concepts. Classificatory judgments depend not just on the conceptual criteria for the category, but also on a complex set of beliefs and theories on the basis of which one judges whether a specific thing actually meets the conditions set by the conceptual criteria. Differences in classification can reflect differences in those other beliefs and theories, rather than differences over the concept itself. For example, even though ''bachelor'' has fairly clear criteria that are shared among members of our culture, two people who attend a party may disagree afterwards about which men were bachelors. The disagreements might stem from different beliefs about the evidence (for example, your friend but not you might have noticed that a given individual was wearing a wedding ring, and you but not your friend might have heard one person say that he is not married) or from differences in beliefs about the meaning of the evidence (for example, you may think that wearing a wedding ring is conclusive proof of being married, while your friend may believe that a large number of bachelors wear wedding rings to fend off unwanted suitors; you may believe that a man's saying he is unmarried is good evidence of his marital status, while your friend may believe that many men lie about marital status to keep their courtship options open). It actually requires a complex inference from the available data (e.g., observations of wedding rings, listening to what people say) to the conclusion that someone does or does not meet the conceptual criteria for "bachelor." So, even though you and your friend share the concept "bachelor," you can disagree in your beliefs about whether particular people should be classified under that concept. I will argue below that, similarly, cross-cultural differences in classification of conditions as mental disorders are due to different circumstances and beliefs, and not to different concepts.

Now, before we can tell whether other cultures' concepts of mental disorder are the same as or different from ours, we have to identify our own culture's definition of *mental disorder*. [The following brief comments are developed in more detail in Wakefield, 1992a, b.] Two criteria are central to our judgment that a condition is a disorder. First, the condition must be harmful according to social values, because by definition a disorder must be a negative condition that warrants concern and social intervention in the form of treatment. However, not all undesirable mental conditions are mental disorders; for example, ignorance, criminal behavior, bad manners, and moral weakness are all clearly negative but are not considered disorders, because nothing has gone wrong with the person's internal functioning. Second, then, to be a disorder, a condition must be due to a mental dysfunction, meaning that one of the person's mental systems or mechanisms, such as cognitive, perceptual, linguistic, emotional, or motivational mechanisms, must be failing to perform the natural function for which it was designed. For example, people are evolutionarily designed to be able to think somewhat rationally, so the inability to do so is a disorder; people are designed to be able to communicate through language, so people who cannot speak are disordered; fear is a mechanism designed to enable us to avoid danger, so when fear becomes so excessive that it is no longer related to danger, a disorder exists; and so on. Note that this definition of mental disorder is exactly parallel to the definition of physical disorder; for example, the eye is clearly designed to enable us to see, and that is why blindness is a disorder; the muscles are designed to allow us to move, and that is why paralysis is a disorder; and so on. Each disorder, mental or physical, is a breakdown in the way that some internal mechanism was designed to function. In sum, a mental disorder is a harmful mental dysfunction, that is, a harmful breakdown in the ability of a mental system to perform a function it was naturally designed to perform.

There are two basic pieces of evidence that lead people to claim that the concept of mental disorder is different in different cultures. First, there is cultural diversity in the conditions that actually occur; some conditions that occur in other cultures do not occur in our culture, and some conditions that occur in our culture do not occur in other cultures. For example, in a society without snakes (as in New Zealand), there are no snake phobias; in a society with low levels of stress, there may be no stress disorders or anxiety conditions; and anorexia nervosa is extremely rare in cultures where the aesthetic ideal of thinness does not exist. Conversely, distinctive forms of intense shame reactions occur in cultures that are more shame-oriented than ours, and specific expressions of madness appear to be shaped by culture.

Does this diversity of conditions show that the concept of mental disorder is relative to culture? Clearly not, because all the described conditions would likely be categorized as disorders in any culture in which they occurred. If people did starve themselves to death in a non-Western culture, or if someone had a severe and debilitating chronic shame response in Western culture, the respective conditions would likely be classified as disorders. These examples do not show that the ultimate classificatory criteria are different in different cultures, but only that the specific disorders that occur in a given culture depend in complex ways on that culture's circumstances and nature. The same point can be made about physical disorders; we do not get hookworm, and many non-Western cultures do not experience heart disease, but that does not mean that the conceptual criteria that define ''physical illness'' are different in Western and non-Western cultures. So, the diversity of the conditions that actually occur in different cultures is not a good reason for embracing conceptual relativism.

The second reason for embracing relativism is diversity in the judgments members of different cultures make about the very same condition. For example, unlike us, some cultures do not classify certain symptoms of agoraphobia, schizophrenia, or (to take a physical example) malaria as disorders. If two cultures are familiar with the same condition, and one believes it to be a disorder and the other does not, then, the relativist claims, the two cultures must be using different conceptual criteria for classification.

However, as the earlier discussion of ''bachelor'' showed, differences in classificatory beliefs do not imply differences in concepts. People might categorize conditions in different ways because they have different beliefs about whether the conditions satisfy a shared conceptual criterion. Given the earlier analysis of ''mental disorder'' as ''harmful mental dysfunction,'' such a difference in beliefs would have to be a difference over whether the mental condition is harmful, or a difference over whether the condition is a dysfunction.

Before turning to cross-cultural examples, it is useful to consider a disagreement between two different eras within our own culture. In Victorian times, many physicians judged a woman who has orgasms during intercourse to be disordered, whereas in our own time many physicians consider women who do not have orgasms during intercourse to be disordered. One way to understand this disagreement is to say it is due to different concepts of mental disorder. However, the relativist view implies that in Victorian times it really was a disorder for a woman to have an orgasm during intercourse (because it really did fit their concept of disorder) and leaves no room for criticism of Victorian diagnostic practices. But, in fact, the Victorians were wrong (this does not imply that we are right; the question of when lack of orgasm is a disorder is a complex one that will not be considered here). A more fruitful and illuminating approach is to assume that we and the Victorians share the same concept of mental disorder as harmful dysfunction, and that the Victorian physicians in question simply had different views than we do about female orgasms with respect to harm and dysfunction. This indeed seems to be the case. The Victorians possessed different values than we do about sexual pleasure, and they saw orgasm as potentially harmful, especially in the case of women whose role was to restrain male lust. And, the Victorian physicians had a theory about God's design of women which implied that, like children, women are not designed to experience intense sexual pleasure and can only be brought to such pleasures through excessive stimulation by overly lustful males, in which case female orgasm constitutes a breakdown in the way the female's sexuality was designed to function. So, the difference between us and the Victorians on sexual dysfunction can be explained in terms of differing beliefs about harm and dysfunction (indeed, if we shared their beliefs and values, we would no doubt make the same classificatory judgment they did), and the differences are entirely consistent with our sharing the same concept of mental disorder as harmful dysfunction.

The examples cited by relativists of cross-cultural differences in disorder judgments can equally be explained as differences in classificatory beliefs rather than concepts. For example, agoraphobia is relatively rare in many non-Western societies, but when it does occur (generally in a woman) it is often not considered a disorder because a woman's place is perceived to be in the home and there is not the level of tension between the desire to stay home and the culture's expectations that there is in Western society, so the condition is not seen as harmful. Because different cultures have different values that determine judgments of what is harmful, judgments of disorder will also vary. For example, in some cultures, where color of skin is highly important, albinism is considered a serious disorder, whereas in other cultures it is not. The conditions that are harmful vary with cultural values, and the set of disorders varies correspondingly, but the concept of disorder itself does not vary; it is at a more abstract level and always refers to harmful dysfunctions.

Theories about dysfunction also cause variations in disorder judgments. Some cultures believe that certain schizophrenic symptoms are communications from the gods rather than manifestations of disorder, but that is a matter of a theory about the cause of the symptoms rather than a disagreement about the conceptual criteria for disorder; if we believed that someone was a conduit for the words of God, we too would not classify the person as disordered. Sometimes, a condition like malaria or hookworm is so endemic in an isolated culture that it is considered to be normal human functioning, that is, the way human beings were designed to be, rather than a dysfunction. (Usually, what is statistically normal is also functionally normal, but not always, as is shown by our own examples of almost universal periodontal disease, dental caries, atherosclerosis, and mild lung irritation.) But such judgments have their source in a mistaken belief, not in a different concept of disorder. This is shown by the fact that, as soon as such societies are exposed to Western medicine and find out that the condition is due to a specific pathogenic process and is not part of how human beings are designed to function, they too come to consider the condition a disorder and recognize their earlier judgment as an error. Because classifying a condition as a disorder involves the factual claim that it is a dysfunction, it is possible to be mistaken in this way. Such mistakes could occur in our culture, as well. For example, imagine what would happen if we discovered some isolated human group that aged much more slowly than we do, and we subsequently found out that our own aging rate is caused by a virus that had become almost universally endemic. We would no doubt reclassify our aging, which we now consider to be normal, as a disorder. The change would not be a change in the concept of disorder, but a correction of an incorrect judgment about dysfunction that led to a misclassification.

So far, I have argued that the evidence fails to prove that different cultures have different concepts of mental disorder. I conclude by briefly explaining why I think that the entire notion of conceptual relativism is confused. It is, of course, conceivable that another culture might use different concepts than we do to organize their reality and that they might not use the concept of disorder at all but rather use other concepts such as "deviance" or "undesirability." (In fact, however, the evidence suggests that virtually all societies possess the concept of mental disorder.) But those other concepts are not different versions of the concept of mental disorder, any more than our own concepts of deviance or undesirability are concepts of mental disorder. They are just different concepts, period. This points to the following problem: if another culture's concepts are different from our concept of mental disorder, then why would we say that they have a different concept of mental disorder, rather than that they do not use the concept of mental disorder at all? That is, what would make a different concept specifically a concept of mental disorder, rather than just some other concept? The relativist has no good answer to this question, for the simple reason that a concept is identified by the conceptual criteria of which it is composed (in the case of mental disorder, these are "harmful mental dysfunctions"), so any concept that is not exactly the same with respect to these criteria is no longer a concept of mental disorder. There is no other standard for identifying an instance of the concept of mental disorder in another culture, other than that it matches our own concept. For this methodological reason, it is incoherent to suggest that other cultures possess different concepts of mental disorder. There is nothing culturally imperialistic about this; it is a feature of the nature of translation of all concepts, not just "mental disorder."

This paradox of relativism may become clearer with an example. Suppose for example, that you find a culture that classifies criminal behavior and schizophrenia together under the same label. Does that mean that the culture has a different concept of mental disorder than we do? Not at all. Their label could mean "deviance" or "socially undesirable behavior" rather than "mental disorder." (And, why would one suggest that they have a different concept of mental disorder, rather than a different concept of crime?) Even if the term does mean "disorder," the other culture might have a theory (as do some of our own social scientists) that criminal behavior is caused by an underlying disorder, and they could be using that theory in classifying criminals as disordered. In neither case does their concept of disorder differ from ours; rather, either their judgment of who falls under the concept differs, or they are using a different concept altogether. In translating their language into ours, we must make sense of their assertions, and we cannot make sense of them if we translate a concept of theirs as "mental disorder" for which the criteria are not "harmful dysfunctions." Ironically, then, the doctrine of concept relativism fails because it is conceptually confused and fails to take into account the nature of concepts.

References

Wakefield, J. C. (1992). "The concept of mental disorder: On the boundary between social values and biological facts." *American Psychologist, 47,* 3, 373–388.

Wakefield, J. C. (1992). "Disorder as harmful dysfunction: A conceptual critique of DSM-III-R's definition of mental disorder." *Psychological Review, 99,* 2, 232–247.

Rejoinder to Professor Wakefield

Laurence J. Kirmayer

Wakefield makes two arguments: (1) the *concept* of mental disorder can be sharply distinguished from *beliefs* about etiology, symptoms, and so on and that, formulated in suitably abstract terms, the concept of mental disorder is universal; and (2) the claim that the concept of mental disorder is not universal is logically incoherent since no comparison at all can be made across cultures where similar categories do not exist. Unfortunately, both of these arguments rest on a definition of *concept* that lacks psychological reality.

For Wakefield, concepts are essentially propositions that define category or set membership. Concepts then are *monothetic* classifications—something either is or is not an instance of a concept; connotations and associations are irrelevant to its core meaning. This ignores much recent research in cognitive science and anthropology that suggests that the concepts people actually use are often based on *polythetic* classifications. The most common of these is probably classification (or conceptualization) by prototypes or exemplars: people have in mind a specific instance or an ideal case and then judge how closely other cases relate to this along many possible dimensions (Rosch, 1978). The mental representation of a prototype may not be in the form of a finite set of propositions but in an image-schema, metaphor, mode of practice, skill, or disposition to act (Lakoff, 1987). Specific instances may be related to an exemplar in different ways; thus, a concept groups together disparate events related by family resemblance rather than any single ''essence'' or basic characteristic that could be defined by a few propositions (Sperber, 1982). As a result of this polythetic structure, concepts are better understood as models or metaphors with rich connotative meanings that are inseparable from their denotation (Kirmayer, 1992).

Having divorced the notion of *concept* from its psychological reality, Wakefield can proceed with arguments based on his own formal definition of *mental disorder*. Of course, it is perfectly possible to construct a sufficiently abstract definition of *mental disorder* that we can find something that fits the concept in every culture. At this point, however, we are no longer discussing the actual concepts that people use but a philosophical abstraction that is, itself, the product of a particular cultural perspective. Indeed, while Wakefield's attempt to clarify the meaning of disorder by relating it to ''harmful dysfunction'' is interesting, it is certainly not culture-free. To see this, we must look more closely at how Wakefield's (1992) appeal to evolutionary theory serves to naturalize culturally based assumptions about deviance and distress.

Wakefield freely admits that the judgment of harm depends on cultural values. He suggests, however, that ''dysfunction'' can be judged against evolutionary criteria of the function for which certain biobehavioral systems evolved. Dysfunction refers to the inability or impairment of an organ or system to perform the natural function for which it was ''designed'' by evolution. The ability to identify ''natural functions'' assumes that there can be a consensus (both within and across cultures) on what our bodily systems and psychological functions are *for*. This may be true for the lungs which are designed to exchange oxygen and carbon dioxide (although even here it is difficult to identify *the* natural function because the lungs also serve endocrine and hemodynamic functions). But for what specific functions was the brain designed? We can offer only global notions like ''adaptation'' or an open-ended list that simply reflects our folk psychology: sensing, perceiving, feeling, imagining. Nor is the problem solved if we partition the brain into discrete subsystems—one designed to get food and regulate blood sugar, another to regulate water and electrolytes, yet another for sexual desire and reproduction—since these systems are related and intertwined in ways that depend on cultural values and practices. One has only to think of the eating disorders or of Wakefield's own example of female orgasm to appreciate how culturally and historically relative the definition of *natural function* remains.

Even if we grant that a specific ''natural'' function can sometimes be identified by evolutionary theory, the threshold of dysfunction is undetermined by evolutionary theory because the ecological niche or adaptive context is constantly changing. Consider, for example, psychological systems designed to seek out novelty. When are they functioning well and when poorly—that is, what is enough novelty? What about systems designed to form attachments with others? When are these too strong, too weak, or inappropriately directed? Clearly, the normal functioning of these more complex systems cannot be defined without reference to a specific social environment with its attendant cultural values. If this is so for admittedly universal motivations like novelty-seeking, attachment, and aggression, how much more so for socially and culturally acquired systems like the search for prestige, esthetic pleasure, or religious experience. Yet, these more elaborate motivational systems or functions are central to peoples' lives and are the first to be affected by "mental disorder."

There are many ways of framing or interpreting the "natural" functions of our bodies, and the ones we find most convincing reflect our own cultural values. For example, we tend to think of adaptation in terms of individuals rather than groups because of the individualistic bias of Euro-American societies, and so we are less likely to recognize or give central place to functions whose main purpose may be intragroup harmony rather than individual fitness. Labeling certain features of human behavior as "natural" is one way to ignore their cultural shaping. In fact, there is little consensus on what our psychological systems are for—they are so malleable that they can be for almost anything—and many evolutionary psychologists argue that we have evolved to be able to adapt to situations rather than to have fixed or specific functions. Any change in culture will change the fitness of specific psychological traits, give new meaning and purpose to psychological functions, and change their boundaries and interdependence. Beyond a few relatively simple physiological functions, it is impossible to identify what psychological systems or functions are *for* in any universal sense.

Wakefield's attempt to show that the notion of "concept relativity" is "incoherent" is similarly flawed by his reliance on a notion of concepts as monothetic categories. There are points of contact between our conceptual systems, no matter how profoundly different. This is so because most concepts are not defined by a single proposition—they have many ramifications, so that two cultures can make contact at specific points of conceptual similarity and diverge in others. The aim of cross-cultural comparison is to start from points of contact and explore these divergences. In the case of mental disorder, these points of contact have to do with forms of suffering and deviant behavior, which are of mutual interest to the psychiatrist and to sufferers, healers or helpers, and social control agencies within cultural communities. Profound differences between cultural worlds yield the sort of incommensurability that Wakefield warns of only when concepts are divorced from their experiential ground and practical use. The task of cross-cultural translation demands the sensibilities of the poet more than the logician, to capture something of the connotations of words and their music along with their denotation. These connotations can be appreciated only when we reconstruct the social context in which concepts are used. In the end, Wakefield's argument seems to miss the point because, like much of psychological and psychiatric theory, it ignores the social world in favor of an individualistic and abstract definition of *concept, mental,* and *dysfunction.* This approach explains away culture, rather than addressing its central importance in the construction of concepts and categories.

References

Kirmayer, L. J. (1992). The body's insistence on meaning: Metaphor as presentation and representation in illness experience. *Medical Anthropology Quarterly, 6*(4), 323–346.

Lakoff, G. (1987). *Women, fire, and dangerous things.* Chicago: University of Chicago Press.

Reznek, L. (1987). *The Nature of Disease.* London: Routledge & Kegan Paul.

Rosch, E. (1978). Principles of categorization. In E. Rosch & B. Lloyd (Eds.), *Cognition and categorization* (pp. 27–48). Hillsdale, NJ: Erlbaum.

Sperber, D. (1982). *On anthropological knowledge.* Cambridge: Cambridge University Press.

Wakefield, J. C. (1992). The concept of mental disorder: On the boundary between biological facts and social values. *American Psychologist, 47*(3), 373–388.

Debate 2

Are Personality Disorders Gender Biased?

Lenore E. A. Walker, Ed.D., argues YES. Dr. Walker is a licensed psychologist in independent practice with Walker & Associates in Denver, Colorado, and Executive Director of the Domestic Violence Institute. She earned a diplomate in clinical psychology from the American Board of Professional Psychology, which has pioneered the introduction of expert witness testimony on the "battered woman self-defense" in the United States' courtrooms. Her research on the psychological effects of battered women and dynamics of the battering relationship began in 1970 with research funded by the National Institute of Mental Health. She lectures internationally on women's mental health and on stopping all forms of violence against women and children. She is the author of nine books and many articles, including *The Battered Woman* (1979), *Women and Mental Health Policy* (1984), *The Battered Woman Syndrome* (1984), and *Terrifying Love: Why Battered Women Kill and How Society Responds* (1989).

Thomas A. Widiger, Ph.D., Elizabeth Corbitt, M.A., and Miriam Funtowicz, B.A., argue NO. Dr. Widiger is a Professor of Psychology at the University of Kentucky. He has published extensively in the area of personality disorders, diagnosis, and sex bias. He is a consulting editor to six journals, including *Journal of Abnormal Psychology, Psychological Assessment, Journal of Personality Assessment,* and *Clinical Psychology Review.* He is currently the Research Coordinator for the American Psychiatric Association's fourth edition of the *Diagnostic and Statistical Manual of Mental Disorders.*

Elizabeth Corbitt and Miriam Funtowicz are graduate students in clinical psychology at the University of Kentucky.

YES

LENORE E. A. WALKER

Accusations of inherent gender bias in the very structure of personality disorders, as defined by the *Diagnostic and Statistical Manual of Mental Disorders (DSM)* (APA; 1980; 1987), have existed since its publication, when the old classification of character disorder was changed and expanded using specific criteria that were created to fit separate personality disorder categories. In this essay, I argue that these new categories are gender biased. First, I contend that the criteria for the most commonly used personality disorder diagnostic categories are gender biased and, second, that the construct of personality can be better understood using experience by gender as a critical variable.

Many clinicians and researchers have criticized the lack of scientific rigor in the formation of what the *DSM* currently defines as the personality disorders (Braude, 1986; Brown, 1992; Caplan, 1987, 1991; Kaplan, 1983; Kirk & Kutchins, 1992; Kutchins & Kirk, 1986; Rosewater, 1987; Walker, 1987). In fact, the criticisms of gender bias throughout the entire diagnostic system go beyond the personality disorder categories to cover most mental illness. Chesler (1972) made one of the earliest arguments that women's higher rate of diagnosed mental illness in general is due to male therapists' (and society's in general) lack of acceptance of the normality of women's sex-role socialization patterns and that the frequency of such diagnoses does not represent inherent individual or even gender weaknesses. The now classic Broverman et al. (1970) study as well as other American Psychological Association research (APA, 1978) document the differences in the standard of mental health for males and females. Despite almost twenty years of criticism, the most recent APA study of women and depression (McGrath, Keita, Strickland, & Russo, 1990), for example, documents the gender bias that still permeates the understanding of both the causes and interventions for treatment of depression in women.

The effects of inadequate research that results in gender bias were illustrated in the 1985–1986 politically based debates about the inclusion of several newly proposed personality disorder categories for the *DSM-III-R* and particularly around the inclusion of *Masochistic Personality Disorder* (ultimately changed to *Self-Defeating Personality Disorder*) (cf. debates in the 1987 issue of the *Journal of Personality Disorder* and the 1991 issue of *Canadian Psychology* for further information).

After feminist psychiatrists, psychologists, and other mental health professionals criticized this particular proposal, largely because the criteria assumed women's sex-role socialized responses to be pathological, the APA committee agreed to further study the proposed criteria that were originally tested on their mostly male psychiatry students (Kass, 1987). These psychiatric residents had not gathered information concerning abuse in their patients' lives, so criticisms that the criteria would be more likely to misdiagnose battered women and those who experienced physical and sexual abuse as a child with the disorder could not be scientifically evaluated in that field sample. After the criticisms of their unscientific methods, the *DSM* task force decided to further test the criteria reliability by field testing with another biased sample of psychiatrists who already indicated agreement with the new construct, again without evaluating the validity of the feminine socialized responses or those of abused women (Kass, MacKinnon, & Spitzer, 1986). Although there are still inadequate data to support this new diagnosis, the *DSM-IV* task force has not yet decided to remove the category from its special section.

What Is Personality and Its Disorders?

The concept of personality and its subsequent disorders is not an atheoretical concept as the *DSM-III-R* claims but, rather, has definite theoretical underpinnings. Psychodynamic theory suggests that a fundamental core of an individual exists that is developed and set in early childhood from a combination of biological and environmental forces. Once this core is internalized, it continues to guide the individual's life responses. Humanistic, behavioral, and cognitive theories also posit a construct akin to a core personality that guides the individual in his or her subsequent cognitive, emotional, and behavioral interactions, although these theories accept the continued development of personality throughout life (Millon, 1983; Young, 1990).

Disorders of personality represent ways in which a person's basic core has been altered in relation to adaptation to these adverse conditions. It is generally thought that personality disorders differ from symptom-generated disorders in pervasiveness and endurance—that is, they feel so ego-syntonic (or ''right'') to the individual that there is little motivation to modify the maladaptive behavior patterns even when they ultimately cause the individual pain and fail to satisfy his or her needs (Millon, 1983). Thus, those diagnosed with a personality disorder can be expected to be highly resistant to change through psychotherapy. This definition, of course, gives little credence to the adaptive qualities of personality in situational conditions that for many women (and some men) make it impossible to meet their needs fully in any other way. It has been suggested that many of the criteria for personality disorders are really appropriate coping strategies given certain situational experiences and, thus, should not be considered pathological (cf. Walker, 1991a). Thus, the resistance to changing personality traits when the situation that gave rise to them is unchanged should not be considered pathology.

Gender Bias and *DSM-III* Personality Disorders

Although all of the personality disorders are considered to be gender biased, several others prior to *Self-Defeating Personality Disorder* have been singled out as the most biased against women, particularly *Borderline, Dependent,* and

Histrionic Personality Disorders (see Caplan, 1987, 1991; Kaplan, 1983). Careful analysis of the text descriptions of these disorders as well as the criteria used to make the diagnosis indicates that their very definitions perpetuate the gender bias against women's socialized roles. These stereotypes already have been criticized by feminist psychologists in other contexts (cf. Brown & Ballou, 1992).

Kaplan (1983) was one of the first psychologists to demonstrate that *Dependent* and *Histrionic Personality* criteria overlap and reflect a labeling of women who "overconform" to sex-role stereotypes as pathological. Individuals with dependent personality disorder traits are defined as passive and submissive; those who are labeled histrionic are given to exaggerated expression of emotions as well as being dependent and vain. The double-bind for women is that those who are assertive and do not demonstrate dependent behavior often are subjected to unpleasant consequences including being disliked. Herman (1992) applied a similar analysis for *Borderline Personality Disorders* and found that a high percentage of those women who demonstrate what are labeled "borderline" traits, such as being unpredictably angry, having difficulty with interpersonal relationships, being dependent on others, and having problems in setting effective limits between themselves and others, are merely behaving in an assertive or even aggressive, although admittedly not feminine, manner. In fact, as Herman demonstrates, most of these women are predictable once the abuse etiology is known. Without understanding the survival purpose of the so-called personality traits, abused women are frequently misdiagnosed and receive inadequate treatment as is described later.

The second most common personality disorder category to misdiagnose abused women, after *Borderline Personality Disorder,* is *Masochistic* or *Self-Defeating Personality Disorder* even though the protests about lack of empirical data have kept this category in the *DSM-III-R* provisional section. Women who are labeled "masochistic" are defined as dependent and self-defeating. They are seen as overnurturing—putting others' needs before their own even when it causes great trouble and pain for themselves (Caplan, 1987). Here, too, there is no acknowledgment of the adaptive nature of these behaviors to their environments or of the confusion with other diagnoses such as *Borderline.* In fact, the diagnosed behaviors may actually prevent battered women and those who have been sexually abused from being further harmed and in that sense are not "self-defeating" (Walker & Browne, 1985). Thus, what are really adaptive coping strategies are instead labeled maladaptive behavior, meeting the current *DSM* criteria for personality disorders (Rosewater, 1987; Walker, 1987). Only after the developers of the *DSM* were presented with the empirical data did they add a caveat not to use the category with *currently* battered women. This does not, however, prevent misdiagnosis of those who have been previously battered (Walker, 1984; 1989a) or who are adult survivors of child sexual abuse (Herman, 1992; Brown, 1992; Root, 1992).

As Kaplan (1983) has pointed out, the concept of *dependency* appears repeatedly in the criteria for most of the personality disorders. Yet, the definition of disorders of dependency used includes the ways in which women express dependency on men and not the reverse. For example, men who rely on others to maintain their homes and take care of their children are not considered to be expressing personality-disordered dependency behaviors. In response to Kaplan's arguments, Williams and Spitzer (1983) inadvertently support the gender-bias argument by calling attention to how features of *Antisocial* and *Schizoid Personality Disorders* can be considered caricatures of masculinity. They point out how those criteria of lying, stealing, fighting, truancy, resisting authority, unusually early or aggressive sexual behavior, excessive drinking, use of illicit drugs, and impaired ability to sustain lasting, close, warm, and responsible behavior are more likely to be diagnostic of males who display the behavior measured by *Antisocial* or *Schizoid Personality Disorder.* It is not clear why the *DSM* creators (Kass, Spitzer, & Williams [1983]) do not believe it is also gender bias if men's difficulties with interpersonal relationships gains them different diagnostic categories than do the same difficulties of women. Perhaps the most salient message is that there is an unspoken context within which male and female behaviors are judged. I believe that context is what we now label *sex-role stereotypes.* To further support the uncovering of gender-based bias, it is important to recognize that the criteria in those disorders that more frequently are assigned to males are more behaviorally based, whereas those for women include more distortions of affect and cognition. Some of the earliest feminist critiques of gender bias pointed out how various materials given to boys were more active and behaviorally oriented, and those given to girls were more passive and feeling oriented (Chesler, 1972).

To help underscore the danger of not recognizing the gender bias inherent in currently used personality disorder criteria, Caplan (1991) set out to deliberately create a category that would pathologize male stereotyped behavior patterns (Pantony & Caplan, 1991). *Delusional Dominating Personality Disorder* was "field tested" by asking for comments from a nonrepresentative sample of feminist psychologists. These criteria met the minimum "tests of scientific rigor" that were claimed for the other personality disorder categories. Caplan (1991) presented the new category to the *DSM-IV* Task Force for possible inclusion in the next revision of the diagnostic manual. She describes their reaction as one of disbelief that anyone would actually design a category using known male sex-role stereotyped thoughts, feelings, and behavior that would then cause them to be described as male pathology. Nevertheless, the *DSM* Task Force has admitted in the past that they were well aware of the gender biases reflected in the current personality disorder categories and have not made a satisfactory attempt to reformulate them for the forthcoming *DSM-IV.* Caplan (1991), Pantony and Caplan (1991), Walker (1991b), and others insist that without including researchers and clinicians who specialize in gender issues on the *DSM* Task Force (we have been systematically excluded as unreliable "trouble-makers"), the diagnostic system will continue to reflect the personal biases (conscious and otherwise) of the committee members.

A Different Approach

What would a gender-sensitive view add to the theoretical construct of personality and its disorders? First, it would emphasize that the length of time for development of personality goes beyond the childhood years and lasts throughout a person's life. It would also incorporate the impact of situational factors such as trauma on human beings, recognizing that some traumas such as repeated family abuse profoundly change the way people think about the world and their place in it. I do not argue that with the experience of abuse such constructs as maladaptive personality styles or schemata cannot exist. Rather, I contend that we have not yet learned how to accurately classify or measure the impact of trauma on personality. A more comprehensive understanding of the entire range of traumatic reactions and disorders, including brief reactions, is a necessary preliminary step, without which we would make premature speculation about the most serious effects.

Second, a gender-sensitive view of personality would more carefully define observable behaviors, motivating factors, and pervasive and enduring patterns of thinking, feeling, and acting, differentiating them from adaptive responses of men and women in a changing and sometimes hostile world. It is important to understand the many different purposes of the same symptoms and traits given the new knowledge we have about contexts in which they occur.

Third, a gender-sensitive view of personality would better reflect the diversity of culture and its impact on definitions of what is normal and not normal. Norms for appropriate interpersonal relationships are different for males and females within different cultures. For example, Native American and Asian cultures have a different view of dependency than do European and American cultures. Such differences make it impossible to define pathological interpersonal relationships without using gender and culture as the context for comparisons.

Fourth, gender and culture would be used to help determine the validity of the criteria that are used to make a personality disorder diagnosis. This means using scientific methods of validating criteria that also use feminist and culturally sensitive methods, such as a combination of objective and subjective methods which also permit those being studied to comment on the categories relevant to them. Brown and Root (1990) and Walker (1989b) among others have suggested new feminist gender and culturally sensitive scientific methodologies.

Psychologists have demonstrated that stripping context from the diagnostic system results in misdiagnosis. Some have suggested ways of improving reliability and validity within a relatively intact *DSM* system (Herman, 1992). Brown (1992) suggests that a complete overhaul of the way we think diagnostically would necessarily mandate new criteria and categories for the system. Others suggest that the present system is too flawed to even patch up and use with African-Americans and other non-white women. Walker (in press) insists that the concept of personality and its disorders needs to be rethought in radically different ways, especially given the frequency with which abuse victims are erroneously labeled by clinicians untrained in working with them.

Herman (1992) suggests that research on the impact of trauma on the personality of victims, particularly those who were sexually abused as children, demonstrates a different kind of interference with personality development that is not a typical personality disorder but, rather, is a more severe form of *Post-Traumatic Stress Disorder.* I have proposed a continuum of traumatic reactions and disorders ranging from very mild with spontaneous recovery, often occurring with good initial support, through the traditional *Post-Traumatic Stress Disorder* subcategories of *Battered Woman Syndrome, Battered Child Syndrome, Child Abuse Accommodation Syndrome,* and *Rape Trauma Syndrome.* In addition, I suggest adding another dimension to assess a pervasive and enduring coping style that is closely associated with a high arousal and depressed cognitive style, Seligman's (1990) learned optimism and learned helplessness (1975) and Young's (1990) schema-focused approaches. This more severe end of the continuum of damage is not a different kind of personality disorder as is currently conceptualized by Herman (1992); rather, its assessment traces the development of different cognitive styles and coping strategies that are based on the realities of surviving oppression from gender, culture, and violence, which fundamentally change a person's total view of the world and their place in it. Like the current construct of personality disorder, such a pattern may be pervasive and enduring and difficult to treat. However, as the person is able to construct a safer place in the world, some of these strategies are not necessary and spontaneously are no longer used. For others, the movement from victim to survivor may require skilled professional intervention; perhaps therapies to help develop a different cognitive style and set of coping strategies. There is no question that for many women and men, gender bias in society in general matches the gender bias they face in assessment, diagnosis, and treatment from mental health professionals. This will be changed only when those responsible for the development of diagnostic systems on which effective therapies are based recognize the profound impact of gender and culture on people's behavior.

References

American Psychiatric Association. (1980). *Diagnostic and statistical manual of mental disorders (3rd ed.).* Washington, DC: Author.

American Psychiatric Association. (1987). *Diagnostic and statistical manual of mental disorders, third edition-revised (DSM-III-R).* Washington, DC: Author.

American Psychological Association. (1978). Task force on sex bias and sex role stereotyping in psychotherapeutic practice. *American Psychologist, 33,* 1122–1123.

Braude, M. (1986). Letter to the editor. *American Journal of Psychiatry, 2.*

Broverman, I. K., Broverman, D. M., Clarkson, F. E., Rosencrantz, P., & Vogel, S. R. (1970). Sex-role stereotypes and clinical judgments of mental health. *Journal of Consulting Psychology, 34,* 1–7.

Brown, L. (1992). A feminist critique of personality disorders. In L. Brown & M. Ballou (Eds.), *Personality and psychopathology.* New York: Guilford.

Brown, L. B., & Root, M. P. P. (Eds.). (1990). *Diversity and complexity in feminist therapy.* New York: Haworth.

Brown, L. S., & Ballou (Eds.). (1992). *Personality and psychopathology.* New York: Guilford.

Caplan, P. J. (1987). The Psychiatric Association's failure to meet its own standards: The dangers of self-defeating personality disorder as a category. *Journal of Personality Disorders, 1,* 178–182.

Caplan, P. J. (1991). How *do* they decide what is normal? The bizarre, but true, tale of the *DSM* process. *Canadian Psychologist, 32*(2), 162–170.

Chesler, P. (1972). *Women and madness.* New York: Avon.

Herman, J. L. (1992). *Trauma and recovery.* New York: Basic Books.

Kaplan, M. (1983). A woman's view of the *DSM-III. American Psychologist, 28,* 786–792.

Kass, F. (1987). Self-defeating personality disorder: An empirical study. *Journal of Personality Disorders, 1,* 168–173.

Kass, F., MacKinnon, R., & Spitzer, R. L. (1986). Masochistic personality: An empirical study. *American Journal of Psychiatry, 143,* 216–218.

Kass, F., Spitzer, R. L., & Williams, J. B. W. (1983). An empirical study of sex bias in the diagnostic criteria of *DSM-III* Axis II personality disorders. *American Psychologist, 28,* 799–801.

Kirk, S. A., & Kutchins, H. (1992). *The selling of* DSM: *The rhetoric of science in psychiatry.* Hawthorne, NY: Aldine de Gruyter.

Kutchins, H., & Kirk, S. A. (1986). The reliability of *DSM-III:* A critical review. *Social Work Research and Abstracts, 22,* 4, 3–12.

McGrath, E., Keita, G. P., Strickland, B., & Russo, N. F. (Eds.). (1990). *Women and depression: Risk factors and treatment issues. Final report of the APA National Task Force on Women and Depression.* Washington, DC: Author.

Millon, T. (1983). *Theories of personality and psychopathology.* New York: Holt, Rinehart, & Winston.

Pantony, K. L. & Caplan, P. J. (1991). Delusional dominating personality disorder: A modest proposal for identifying some consequences of rigid masculine socialization. *Canadian Psychology, 32,* 120–133.

Root, M. P. P. (1992). Reconstructing the impact of trauma on personality. In L. Brown & M. Ballou (Eds.) *Personality and psychopathology: Feminist reappraisals.* New York: Guilford.

Rosewater, L. B. (1987). A critical analysis of the proposed self-defeating personality disorder. *Journal of Personality Disorders, 1,* 190–195.

Seligman, M. L. (1990). *Learned optimism.* New York: Wiley.

Seligman, M. L. (1975). *Helplessness.* San Francisco: Wiley.

Walker, L. E. A. (in press). *The abused woman and survivor therapy: Assessment and treatment.* Washington, DC: American Psychological Association.

Walker, L. E. A. (1991a). Post-traumatic stress disorder in women: Diagnosis and treatment of battered woman syndrome. *Psychotherapy, 28*(1), 21–29.

Walker, L. E. A. (1991b). Discussion DDPD: Consequences for the profession of psychology. *Canadian Psychology, 32,* 136–138.

Walker, L. E. A. (1989a). *Terrifying love: Why battered women kill and how society responds.* New York: Harper & Row.

Walker, L. E. A. (1989b). Psychology and violence against women. *American Psychologist, 44,* 695–702.

Walker, L. E. A. (1987). Inadequacies of the masochistic personality disorder diagnosis for women. *Journal of Personality Disorders 1,* 183–189.

Walker, L. E. (1984). *The battered woman syndrome.* New York: Springer.

Walker, L. E. A., & Browne, A. (1985). Gender and victimization by intimates. *Journal of Personality, 53,* 179–195.

Williams, J. B. W., & Spitzer, R. L. (1983). The issue of sex bias in DSM-III: A critique of ''A women's view of DSM-III'' by Marcie Kaplan. *American Psychologist, 38,* 793–798.

Young, J. E. (1990). *Cognitive therapy for personality disorders: A schema-focused approach.* Sarasota, FL: Professional Resource Exchange.

Annotated Bibliography

American Psychological Association. (1978). Task force on sex bias and sex role stereotyping in psychotherapeutic practice. *American Psychologist, 33,* 1122–1123.

This is one of the original studies by the APA that demonstrated gender bias in clinician's assessment and intervention decisions.

Brown, L. (1992). A feminist critique of personality disorders. In L. Brown & M. Ballou (Eds.), *Personality and psychopathology.* New York: Guilford.

Brown has been one of the leading theorists to insist on integrating gender, culture, and diversity in the diagnostic process. This chapter as well as the one by Root in the same book are both important in understanding the shortcomings of the present models of personality disorders.

Caplan, P. J. (1991). How *do* they decide what is normal? The bizarre, but true, tale of the *DSM* process. *Canadian Psychologist, 32*(2), 162–170.

Caplan has been one of the most critical scholars into the process by which the diagnostic manual has been prepared. This special edition of *Canadian Psychology* presents numerous articles debating the issue.

Herman, J. L. (1992). *Trauma and recovery.* New York: Basic Books.

Herman's work on trauma victims and their misdiagnosis using the current diagnostic system is presented in this book along with her conceptualization of appropriate understanding and intervention techniques.

Kaplan, M. (1983). A woman's view of the *DSM-III. American Psychologist, 28,* 786–792.

This is the first article to appear following the publication of the *DSM-III* where the new concept of personality disorders was first included. Interestingly, although the authors of the personality disorder section of the manual have been aware of the debate for almost ten years following publication of this article, no attempts have been made to address the real concerns raised by Kaplan.

Rosewater, L. B. (1987). A critical analysis of the proposed self-defeating personality disorder. *Journal of Personality Disorders, 1,* 190–195.

Rosewater's critique of the newly proposed category addresses the issues raised by gender bias in the criteria proposed for all the other categories, too. This journal issue presents both sides of the argument.

Walker, L. E. A. (1989). Psychology and violence against women. *American Psychologist, 44,* 695–702.

This article describes the gender bias that is reflected in the assumption that science can be stripped of context and still be neutral and objective. It discusses the newer scientific methodology that avoids such bias.

Rejoinder to Dr. Walker

THOMAS A. WIDIGER, ELIZABETH CORBITT, AND MIRIAM FUNTOWICZ

Dr. Walker believes that calling attention to how features of the antisocial and compulsive personality disorders involve maladaptive variants of traits that are seen more often in males supports the gender-bias argument. She states that she does not understand why the authors of *DSM* "do not believe it is also gender bias if men's difficulties with interpersonal relationships gains them different diagnostic categories than do the same difficulties of women.'' This disagreement is at the essence of the dispute. Dr. Walker objects to the occurrence of different prevalence rates for personality disorders in men and women that reflect differences in the personality traits of men and women.

We can understand why one would not want this to occur. It would be desirable in a democratic and just world for there to be no differences in personality, for all persons to be the same, and for the rates of all disorders to be the same across all genders, cultures, and ethnic groups. But, contrary to Dr. Walker's assumption, men and women do not in fact have the same difficulties in interpersonal relationships. Differences between men and women exist with respect to a variety of personality traits (Deaux, 1985). Therefore, one would expect to find different prevalence rates between men and women with respect to the maladaptive variants of these traits. On average, men do tend to be more assertive than women (Deaux, 1985; Eagly & Steffen, 1986). As a result, there are different prevalence rates for maladaptive variants of this trait. More men than women are domineering (a symptom of the compulsive personality disorder) and more women than men are submissive (a symptom of the dependent personality disorder).

It is likely that Dr. Walker is correct that many of these traits were due in part to sexist social, cultural pressures (e.g., a parental and/or societal encouragement of males to be domineering or women to be submissive), but this would not negate their ultimate maladaptivity. Dr. Walker confuses the etiology for these traits (e.g., they may have been adaptive within the pathogenic environment in which they were created) with their pathology (they do constrain the person's ability to adapt flexibly to various situations). Dependent and submissive behavior will be adaptive within some situations (and clinicians are instructed in the *DSM* not to confuse a personality disorder with a situation-specific behavior), but adaptivity within a limited and pathogenic context (e.g., abusive family environment) does not suggest that the behavior is then generally desirable and adaptive. It is clearly preferable for a woman not to be dependent or submissive.

Dr. Walker is unfair to the authors of the *DSM* in her suggestion that they fail to appreciate the profound impact of gender and culture on behavior. The diagnosis of a dependent (and a compulsive) personality disorder facilitates the recognition of how our society impels women (and men) to develop behavior patterns that are ultimately maladaptive. Sexism does indeed occur in our society, and when it does occur it is extremely harmful and unjust, as in an encouragement of women to be submissive or men to be domineering, but a diagnosis of the effects of this sexism is not itself sexist. A taxonomy that took the politically correct position of ensuring that as many men as women would receive a diagnosis of dependency (e.g., by including such criteria as the reliance on someone else to care for one's home and children, as suggested by Dr. Walker) would and should be criticized for trying to hide the impact of social-cultural factors. Dr. Walker might then have accused such authors of trying to disguise how society encourages a maladaptive submissiveness in women by gerrymandering the criteria set to ensure that just as many men would receive the diagnosis.

The sex-bias issue has indeed been controversial. Regrettably, however, the literature has often provided more heat than light. As we indicated earlier, the empirical studies have indicated that sex-biased diagnoses have resulted from a failure to adhere to the *DSM* rather than from the manual itself. Even the ''now classic Broverman et al. (1970) study'' has been shown to be grossly misleading, fallacious, and simply wrong (Stricker, 1977; Widiger & Settle, 1987), yet it continues to be favorably cited with no recognition or even acknowledgment of the subsequent refutations. We urge the readers of this debate to question their own biases and presumptions, to review all of the data and arguments, and to look beyond the ad hominem acrimony to determine what the reality is, rather than what we want or presume it to be.

References

Deaux, K. (1985). Sex and gender. *Annual Review of Psychology, 36,* 49–81.

Eagly, A. H., & Steffen, V. J. (1986). Gender and aggressive behavior: A meta-analytic review of the social psychological literature. *Psychological Bulletin, 100,* 309–330.

Stricker, G. (1977). Implications of research for psychotherapeutic treatment of women. *American Psychologist, 32,* 14–22.

Widiger, T. A., & Settle, S. A. (1987). Broverman et al. revisited: An artifactual sex bias. *Journal of Personality and Social Psychology, 53,* 463–469.

NO

Thomas A. Widiger, Elizabeth M. Corbitt, and Miriam N. Funtowicz

A controversy concerning the American Psychiatric Association's (APA) *Diagnostic and Statistical Manual of Mental Disorders* (*DSM;* APA, 1987) is whether the personality disorder diagnoses are sex biased. The most explicit and thorough presentation of this argument was by Kaplan (1983). ''Masculine-biased assumptions about what behaviors are healthy and what behaviors are crazy are codified in diagnostic criteria'' (Kaplan, 1983, p. 786). She focused in particular on the histrionic and dependent personality disorders (HPD and DPD, respectively), suggesting that ''via assumptions about sex roles . . . a healthy woman automatically earns the diagnosis of Histrionic Personality Disorder'' (p. 789).

A variety of studies have documented the occurrence of sex bias in the diagnosis of personality disorders (e.g., Ford & Widiger, 1989; Hamilton, Rothbart, & Dawes, 1986; Warner, 1978). However, it is an error to infer from these studies that the diagnostic manual is itself sex biased. In fact, a consistent finding across all of these studies was that the participating clinicians failed to adhere to the diagnostic manual. It has been this failure to follow the *DSM-II, DSM-III,* or *DSM-III-R* diagnostic criteria that has been the major culprit for sex-biased diagnoses, not the *DSM* itself. Consider, for example, Hamilton et al. (1986), who obtained antisocial (APD) and HPD diagnoses from clinical psychologists for cases that varied with respect to the sex of the patient and the relative number of *DSM-III* APD and HPD criteria. When the patient was female, the clinicians were more likely to give histrionic than antisocial diagnoses, irrespective of the actual symptomatology. In other words, the clinicians were using the sex of the patient to make their diagnoses rather than the *DSM-III* diagnostic criteria. Even when a female patient had more APD than HPD symptoms and, therefore, should have received an APD rather than an HPD diagnosis if the clinician adhered to the diagnostic manual, she was still likely to be given an HPD diagnosis. Sex bias was evidenced in Hamilton et al., but the bias was in the clinicians and not in the manual.

The failure of clinicians to follow the *DSM-III* and, as a result, to then impose a sex bias was clearly demonstrated in a study by Ford and Widiger (1989). Ford and Widiger found that clinicians diagnosed females with HPD even when they did not meet the *DSM-III* criteria for HPD and met instead the *DSM-III* criteria for APD. Equally important, the sex of the patient had no effect on the assessments when the clinicians were asked to assess individually each of the *DSM-III* histrionic and antisocial criteria. The authors concluded that the bias that had been found in prior studies was due to clinicians failing to adhere closely to the *DSM-III* HPD diagnostic criteria. "It thus appears that sex biases may best be diminished by an increased emphasis in training programs and clinical settings on the systematic use and adherence to the criteria and diagnostic rules presented in the *DSM-III*" (p. 304).

There has not yet been any study to suggest that a normal woman would meet the *DSM-III-R* criteria for HPD, DPD, or any other personality disorder. It is true that HPD and DPD are diagnosed more often in women than in men, and it is also true that HPD and DPD involve, in part, exaggerated and maladaptive variants of stereotypic feminine traits. But the *DSM-III* and *DSM-III-R* criteria for these personality disorders do not involve normal feminine traits. It is not normal to express emotions with an *inappropriate* exaggeration, to be *overly* concerned with physical attractiveness, and to be *constantly* seeking or demanding reassurance, approval, or praise (APA, 1987). These are not normal or stereotypic feminine traits, and a *DSM-III-R* diagnosis of HPD requires not one, but four of these maladaptive behaviors. It is then difficult to imagine how a normal, healthy woman "automatically earns the diagnosis of Histrionic Personality Disorder" (Kaplan, 1983, p. 789).

To the extent that personality disorders represent extreme, maladaptive variants of normal personality traits, one would expect to find more women than men with the personality disorders that involve maladaptive variants of those personality traits that occur more often in women, just as one would also expect to find more men than women with the personality disorders that involve maladaptive variants of personality traits that are seen more often in men. A personality disorder (e.g., HPD) that involves variants of personality traits (e.g., emotionality) that are seen more often in women will naturally occur more often in women, and a personality disorder (e.g., compulsive) that involves variants of personality traits (e.g., control of emotionality) that are seen more often in men will naturally occur more often in men. It would be consistent with a (political) democratic ideal for men and women to obtain an equal prevalence rate for each personality disorder, but this would be more problematic to the construct validity of the respective personality disorders than to obtaining of a differential sex prevalence. Should the same number of men and women receive the diagnoses of antisocial personality disorder and compulsive personality disorder (CPD)? Most persons would question the validity of HPD, APD, DPD, and CDP if researchers and clinicians found no differential sex prevalence.

Just as many personality disorders occur more often in men as there are personality disorders that occur more often in women, and a man is just as likely to receive a personality disorder diagnosis as a woman (Kass, Spitzer, & Williams, 1983). Across all of the personality disorders there is no differential sex prevalence, and at least two of the *DSM-III-R* personality disorders involve maladaptive variants of stereotypic masculine traits (i.e., CPD and APD). An equal prevalence of personality disorder diagnoses across men and women does not refute the sex-bias argument because it could be the case that more men than women (or more women than men) have personality disorders (Widiger & Spitzer, 1991). It would again be a confusion of a social ideal with a scientific objectivity to assume that all of the personality disorders taken together should occur with equal frequency across the sexes. Nevertheless, the prevalence rates that have been obtained are inconsistent with the argument that women receive more personality disorder diagnoses than men.

A systematic review of the normal personality traits that may underlie each of the *DSM-III-R* personality disorders does suggest that the differential sex prevalence rates that have been obtained are consistent with theoretical expectations. For example, a compelling model of normal personality is the Five-Factor model, consisting of the dimensions of neuroticism, introversion versus extraversion, openness to experience, agreeableness versus antagonism, and conscientiousness (Digman, 1990). From the perspective of the Five-Factor model, borderline personality disorder consists essentially of extreme neuroticism (Costa & McCrae, 1990; Wiggins & Pincus, 1989), and a variety of studies have consistently indicated that females obtain higher scores on neuroticism than males (Costa & McCrae, 1988). One would then expect more women than men to be diagnosed with borderline personality disorder (APA, 1987). From the perspective of the Five-Factor model, HPD involves in part neuroticism, the extraversion facets of warmth and positive emotions, and openness to feelings (Costa & McCrae, 1992). These are again traits that occur more often in women (Costa & McCrae, 1988) and, as expected, HPD is diagnosed more often in women (APA, 1987). From the perspective of the Five-Factor model, DPD involves in part excessive neuroticism, low assertiveness (a facet of extraversion), and excessive modesty, compliance, and altruism (facets of agreeableness) (Costa & McCrae, 1992). These traits are seen more often in women (Costa & McCrae, 1988; Eagly & Crowley, 1986), and DPD is diagnosed more often in women (APA, 1987). From the perspective of the Five-Factor model, APD involves in part excessive excitement-seeking (a facet of extraversion) and excessively low straightforwardness, low altruism, low compliance, and low tendermindedness (facets of agreeableness) (Costa & McCrae, 1992). These traits occur more often in males (Costa & McCrae, 1988; Eagly & Steffen, 1986), and APD is diagnosed more often in males (APA, 1987). All of the differential sex prevalence rates that have been obtained for the personality disorders that occur more often in women are consistent with the sex differences that have been obtained for the personality traits that would underlie these personality disorders (Corbitt, 1992).

It is, however, understandable how a clinician might misdiagnose a normal woman with HPD. The *DSM-III-R* criteria indicate behaviors that are beyond the range of normal activity, but the criteria are so broad that clinicians have substantial leeway in their application. For example, the *DSM-III-R* indicates that there must be an *overconcern* with physical attractiveness (APA, 1987), but clinicians will disagree as to what constitutes overconcern. It is not clear when concern becomes overconcern, and clinicians with a biased attitude may consider a normal woman's attentiveness, care, and pride regarding her physical appearance to represent a vain overconcern. The same misdiagnoses could occur for personality disorders that involve maladaptive variants of normal masculine traits (e.g., APD and CPD), but research has indicated that clinical biases have been greater for the disorders that occur more often in women (Ford & Widiger, 1989; Hamilton et al., 1986). The *DSM-III-R* could have and should have done more to discourage this misapplication of the diagnostic criteria. The text of the *DSM* should warn clinicians that sex-biased misdiagnoses have occurred, and the diagnostic criteria should have been more specific and exact. For example, rather than simply indicate that there is an overconcern with physical attractiveness, the manual should specify clearly how this overconcern can be assessed reliably so that a misdiagnosis is much less likely to occur.

The concern that there may be sex bias in the *DSM-III* and *DSM-III-R* personality disorder diagnostic criteria themselves is also understandable. It is reasonable to expect that males will have a lower threshold for attributing maladaptivity to stereotypic feminine traits (Kaplan, 1983). Males might have a lower threshold for when they would consider emotionality to be "inappropriate" or when time spent on improving one's physical attractiveness represents an "overconcern." Males might likewise have a higher threshold than females for when they consider the expression of affection to be "restricted" or when devotion to work is considered to be "excessive" (i.e., CPD criteria; APA, 1987). Given that males have been the principal authors of the *DSM-III* and the *DSM-III-R* personality disorder diagnostic criteria, it is not unreasonable to be concerned that a masculine bias has had some impact on the development of these diagnostic criteria. The male authors of the *DSM-III* and the *DSM-III-R* could have imposed a masculine bias in the construction of the individual criteria and in the setting of the threshold at which a diagnosis would occur. However, the empirical research and an inspection of the set of personality disorder diagnoses and their criteria do not suggest that any such bias has in fact occurred. A normal woman would not meet the *DSM-III-R* criteria for a personality disorder; the differential sex prevalence rates that have been obtained when the assessments adhered to the diagnostic manual have been inconsistent with the sex-bias hypotheses and have instead been consistent with the theoretical expectations for the respective disorders; and the sex biases that have been observed empirically have been due to clinicians failing to follow the *DSM-III* and the *DSM-III-R* diagnostic criteria. Sex bias would be diminished not by eliminating or ignoring the *DSM-III-R* diagnostic criteria for HPD and DPD, but rather by adhering more closely to these criteria sets. Future revisions of the *DSM* could facilitate this adherence by providing more specific and explicit guidelines for the application and assessment of the diagnostic criteria.

References

American Psychiatric Association. (1987). *Diagnostic and statistical manual of mental disorders* (3rd ed.). Washington, DC: American Psychiatric Association.

Corbitt, E. M. (1992). *Sex bias and the personality disorders: A reinterpretation from the Five-Factor model.* Unpublished manuscript. Lexington, KY: University of Kentucky.

Costa, P. T., & McCrae, R. R. (1988). Personality in adulthood: A six-year longitudinal study of self-reports and spouse ratings on the NEO Personality Inventory. *Journal of Personality and Social Psychology, 54,* 853–863.

Costa, P. T., & McCrae, R. R. (1990). Personality disorders and the Five-Factor model of personality. *Journal of Personality Disorders, 4,* 362–371.

Costa, P. T., & McCrae, R. R. (1992). *Revised NEO Personality Inventory (NEO PI-R) and NEO Five-Factor Inventory. Professional manual.* Odessa, FL: Psychological Assessment Resources.

Digman, J. (1990). Personality structure: Emergence of the five factor model. *Annual Review of Psychology, 41,* 417–440.

Eagly, A. H., & Crowley, M. (1986). Gender and helping behavior: A meta-analytic review of the social psychology literature. *Psychological Bulletin, 100,* 283–308.

Eagly, A. H., & Steffen, V. J. (1986). Gender and aggressive behavior: A meta-analytic review of the social psychological literature. *Psychological Bulletin, 100,* 309–330.

Ford, M., & Widiger, T. (1989). Sex bias in the diagnosis of histrionic and antisocial personality disorders. *Journal of Consulting and Clinical Psychology, 57,* 301–305.

Hamilton, S., Rothbart, M., & Dawes, R. M. (1986). Sex bias, diagnosis, and DSM-III. *Sex Roles, 15,* 269–274.

Kaplan, M. (1983). A woman's view of DSM-III. *American Psychologist, 38,* 786–792.

Kass, F., Spitzer, R. L., & Williams, J. B. W. (1983). An empirical study of the issue of sex bias in the diagnostic criteria of DSM-III Axis II personality disorders. *American Psychologist, 38,* 799–801.

Warner, R. (1978). The diagnosis of antisocial and hysterical personality disorders. *Journal of Nervous and Mental Disease, 166,* 839–845.

Widiger, T. A., & Spitzer, R. L. (1991). Sex bias in the diagnosis of personality disorders: Conceptual and methodological issues. *Clinical Psychology Review, 11,* 1–22.

Wiggins, J. S., & Pincus, A. L. (1989). Conceptions of personality disorders and dimensions of personality. *Psychological Assessment: A Journal of Consulting and Clinical Psychology, 1,* 305–316.

Annotated Bibliography

Kaplan, H. (1983). A woman's view of DSM-III. *American Psychologist, 38,* 786–792.

This paper provides the most thorough and compelling argument that the *DSM* provides sex-biased diagnoses.

Widiger, T., & Settle, S. (1987). Broverman et al. revisited: An artifactual sex bias. *Journal of Personality and Social Psychology, 53,* 463–469.

This paper provides a good illustration of how sex-bias research is often misinterpreted.

Widiger, T., & Spitzer, R. (1991). Sex bias in the diagnosis of personality disorders: Conceptual and methodological issues. *Clinical Psychology Review, 11,* 1–22.

This paper provides a comprehensive overview of the conceptual and empirical issues with respect to the question of whether the *DSM* provides sex-biased personality disorder diagnoses.

Williams, J. B. W., & Spitzer, R. L. (1983). The issue of sex bias in DSM-III. A critique of ''A woman's view of DSM-III'' by Marcie Kaplan. *American Psychologist, 38,* 793–798.

This paper provides an official rejoinder to Kaplan (1983) by the two principal authors of *DSM-III.*

Rejoinder to Professor Widiger

LENORE E. A. WALKER

Widiger, Corbitt, and Funtowicz put forward the argument that the *DSM-III-R* diagnostic criteria for various personality disorders merely reflect the reality of the social context within which clinicians function, and therefore, that any bias acknowledged by the research data is normal and expected for several reasons and therefore is not bias. First, if gender bias exists, and the authors cite studies supporting such bias, it is because clinicians cannot properly interpret the meaning of the criteria. Second, such gender bias is due to application of criteria that reflect the normal social norms and, thus, this does not mean the personality disorder categories are biased themselves. Third, even if some personality disorder categories reflect more male or female diagnoses, the overall number of those diagnosed with a personality disorder is equally distributed between the sexes. These arguments do not adequately defend the inclusion of the various personality disorders with their admittedly biased criteria in a diagnostic manual that is supposed to guide clinicians in their mental health work.

The first argument, that human error and not the criteria, themselves, is to blame for any misdiagnosis reflective of gender bias is merely a defense of the conceptualizations that are stripped of their context. Of course, clinicians reflect the general stereotyped attitudes of the general population. This is not a pejorative view of clinicians' inability to get it right, but rather a reflection of the inability of the diagnostic manual to take human nature into account. Not only are issues of gender bias and mental health not systematically taught in all training programs, but neither is a nonsexist attitude required as an ethical value in most professional licensing examinations. Gender sensitivity is not respected by the developers of the theories encompassed in the *DSM,* so expecting clinicians who use the manual to hold such sensitive values has no factual basis. It is not so simple to overcome years of socialization by training when it is not initiated at the very beginning of the professional process nor displayed or valued by mentors.

Second, the argument that the criteria reflect social norms is precisely the argument that I make to demonstrate the detrimental effects of gender bias in reifying the status quo. It is folly to believe that scientific objectivity is not driven by social realities. Feminist psychology has provided numerous research studies to demonstrate the ways sexism impacts on what was thought to be science. Stripping diagnostic criteria from the social context within which they occur creates symptoms that have no validity in measuring disorders as separate from coping strategies. Third, the argument that equal numbers of both males and females are diagnosed with any personality disorder and, therefore, the higher prevalency rates for women in some and men in others is not important simply misses the importance of the potential usefulness of accurate diagnostic thinking in informing treatment goals. If male and female viewpoints on what constitute disorders of dependency, for example, are different, then gender-biased interventions will continue. It is incumbent on the diagnostic manual to present criteria that reflect the impact of gender and culture, rather than standing behind the outdated notion of scientific neutrality so that seekers of mental health services receive the very best analysis and treatment of their problems from all clinicians.

DEBATE 3

Can Personalities Be Disordered?

Arguing YES are Roger D. Davis and Theodore Millon. Roger Davis is a University Fellow at the University of Miami. His recent publications include "The Five-Factor Model for Personality Disorders: Apt or Misguided" in *Psychological Inquiry* and "Objective Assessment of Anxiety," a chapter in B. Wolman's *Handbook of Anxiety.*

Theodore Millon is a Professor of Psychology at the University of Miami and Professor of Psychiatry at Harvard Medical School/McLean Hospital. His most recent book is *Toward a New Personology: An Evolutionary Model* (John Wiley, 1990).

Arguing NO is Mark A. Mattaini, who is an Assistant Professor at the Columbia University School of Social Work. He was previously director of a community mental health center. His recent publications have been in the areas of clinical assessment, family practice, and behavior analysis of significant social problems. He is completing a book about the use of graphic visualization in clinical practice.

YES

ROGER D. DAVIS AND THEODORE MILLON

The science of psychopathology has long been dominated by schizophrenia, depression, anxiety, and other "classical" disorders. Although many of these Axis I disorders were first formalized by early nosologists such as Kraepelin and

Bleuler, some were recognized by ancient civilizations. The study of personality has a similarly long, and similarly disconnected history, extending back at least to the humoral theory of Hippocrates and to the more mystical Hebrew *Kabala* and Chinese *I Ching*. The notion of personality pathology, however, which synthesizes the construct of personality, borrowed from "normal" personality psychology, and the idea of abnormality, borrowed from classical psychopathology, has only recently achieved widespread acceptance in the multiaxial model adopted by *DSM-III* (American Psychiatric Association, 1987).

Before beginning, however, a few words should be said about language. Language predisposes us to think in certain ways, shaping how scientific problems are conceptualized and the character with which their "solutions" are formed. The words *disorder* and *pathology* have an affinity to the medical model of mental illness, leading one to conceptualize personality disorders in much the same way as medical diseases, that is, as external agents that somehow infiltrate the person and subvert healthy functioning (Millon, 1969). The notion that all forms of illness are the product of external intruders has its roots in the prescientific ideas of demonology and witchcraft. Modern medicine has recaptured this idea in the form of infectious agents, genetic abnormalities, constitutional frailties, and the like, so that all psychopathologies seem to be inflicted from "outside" on an individual who would otherwise be productive and healthy. This is not the way to think about the question that forms the title of this essay, and so, in a strict sense, the answer is, "No, personality cannot be disordered."

Rather than talk about personality disorders, we can talk about personality *patterns*. This nomenclature recognizes the existence of a kind of psychopathology that derives from the entire developmental matrix of the individual (Millon, 1969). Such patterns are not just a loose collection of attitudes, expectancies, needs, and instrumental behaviors. Instead, they are tightly organized and interactive, so much so that they merit the term *personality*. This essay examines persons and personality from an integrative, or, systems perspective, at three levels of analysis: (1) the person as a system unto itself, (2) the person as an open system within an environment or social milieu, and (3) as a longitudinal system integrated across time. Like an experimenter with two control groups, our goals for this essay are to provide a framework whereby personality pathology can be conceptually distinguished from both classical psychopathologies and normal personality.

Persons as Entities

Historically, psychologists have tended to locate personality within various content areas. From a behavioral perspective, personality can be viewed as a particular distribution of behaviors. From a cognitive perspective, personality can be viewed as a collection of cognitions or schemas. From a physiological perspective, personality is largely the result of one's temperament and genetic endowment. However, all of these are really just "parts" of the whole person. Persons do behave, think, and have impact on others, and they are likely born with particular predispositions or temperaments. All approaches to personality are necessary, but any one alone is not sufficient; that is, any single approach fails to exhaust all that a person is.

If persons are not "parts," what are they? Persons are natural entities, the only natural entities in the psychological milieu. Whatever "existence" behaviors, cognitions, attributions, and contexts possess is purely derivative of the essential unity of persons. Whether we work with "part functions," which focus on behaviors, cognitions, unconscious processes, and biological defects, or whether we address contextual systems that focus on the larger environment, the family, the group, or the socioeconomic and political conditions of life, the crossover point, the place that links parts to contexts, is the person, the individual, an intersecting, genuinely organic medium that brings both parts and contexts together and gives them substantive meaning (Millon, 1988).

Personality as a Totality

Unfortunately, the entity construct, because it is monadic, or internally undifferentiated, is also scientifically barren. For purely heuristic purposes, however, we can replace the idea of person-as-entity with person-as-totality. A totality, by definition, consists of discrete structures synthesized through discrete functions to form a single integrative gestalt. As a totality, persons are integrated both "horizontally" and "vertically."

Vertically, persons can be arbitrarily stratified as physical, biological, and psychological beings. Each higher level of analysis is to an extent dependent on those below it, so that, to our knowledge, there are no beings capable of cognitive operations who do not also possess biological and physical strata (unless, perhaps, one believes in ghosts). Moreover, new functions and structures can emerge at each higher level, so enabling that level to acquire a kind of functional independence from all those below it.

Horizontal integration is familiar at the biological level through the ideas of homeostasis and feedback loops. Relatively discrete psychological structures influence each other and the overarching gestalt, or pattern, through causal pathways that are circular rather than linear. We might say that causality is distributed throughout the system. Indeed, this interdependence is an essential feature of the totality construct: No single element can be abstracted from the whole and expected to reveal itself completely when studied in isolation. Conceptually, the totality forms a system of internal relations wherein the elements are contextually defined and possess no inner nature. They are genuine open concepts (Pap, 1953). These discrete structures and functions relevant to all personality patterns are presented in Table 3–1. These have been largely derived

TABLE 3–1 Structural and Functional Domains for a Clinical Science of Personology at Four Clinical Data Levels

	Functional Domains	Structural Domains
Behavioral	Expressive acts Interpersonal conduct	
Phenomenological	Cognitive style	Object relations Self-image
Intrapsychic	Regulatory mechanism	Morphologic organization
Biophysical		Mood/temperament

from traditional or historical approaches to the personality construct. Horizontally speaking, pathological personality patterns, in their pure form, are deviant integrations, wholes whose parts come together in an aberrant manner. In a very real sense, then, we could say that personality patterns do not so much characterize the person as they constitute the person; that is, if they are pathologies, they are pathologies of the entire person.

Distinction between Personality Patterns and Classical Psychopathologies

For the most part, the Axis I disorders are distinctively vertical phenomena—bottom-up pathologies. As one goes about one's daily business, the biophysical nature of one's existence can for all practical purposes be forgotten about. Occasionally, however, things go awry somewhere below the surface, in the physical substrates that form the infrastructure of the mind. The effects percolate upward, disrupting the horizontal integrity of the above levels. Indeed, the Axis I disorders are experienced as ego-dystonic, alien, unwanted, thrust upon the individual. The overt symptoms of schizophrenia, for example, quite possibly represent the psychological expression of essentially genetic abberations. Depression can be treated as a neurotransmitter imbalance and may also possess a genetic basis.

The distinction between vertical and horizontal integration is purely conceptual, but it is analogous to the distinction between the ''classical'' psychopathologies of Axis I and the so-called personality disorders of Axis II. In other words, the current multiaxial model can be deduced from the systems model. This means, then, that Axis I disorders can be understood only in the context of the structural and functional gestalt formed by the patient's premorbid personality pattern. Perhaps, for example, an individual possesses an inclination to major depression. Whatever clinical picture develops will emerge within the constraints and dispositions imposed by the premorbid personality pattern.

Persons as Open Systems

Having accomplished the first goal of this essay, we now extend the systems model three more tiers, ultimately seeking a conceptual framework for distinguishing normal and abnormal personality patterns. Thus far we have dealt with personality as a closed system, a system unto itself. However, the systems model can be extended to embrace the individual, family, and social milieu. At this level, individuals themselves are the structural units of analysis, and their interpersonal behaviors represent the functional units that synthesize these parts into a person-environment gestalt. Extension of the systems model to this level justifies the creation of a separate diagnostic axis, Axis IV. However, we will not consider purely interactional (horizontal) pathologies at this level, for which, say, family therapy might be required. Our focus is on person variance, the actor within the system.

Unhappily for the personality pathology patient, the social context is a dynamic milieu, presenting a variety of diverse challenges that vary both in quality and in intensity. Successful integration, or adaptation, requires the individual's responses be appropriate and proportional. Most individuals who possess mildly pathological personality patterns do find a niche for themselves in normal social life. Superficially, they may even seem to function adequately and even successfully. A careful assessment, however, will reveal the tenuous nature of their existence. Intense needs must be met. Extreme discomfort is experienced with certain situations or types of people. They are markedly distressed if conflicts and frustrations cannot be resolved quickly. Collectively, this set of characteristic manifests the pathological pattern's adaptive inflexibility. Strategies for dealing with others and with the environment are few and rigidly practiced, imposed ad nauseam on conditions for which they are ill-suited. Often this leads to what might be called *symptom disorders* (Millon, 1969). These are accentuations or distortions of the basic pattern that occur under conditions of stress when coping mechanisms fail. Regardless of how distinctive they may appear, they take on meaning and significance only in light of the patient's preclinical personality and should be described with reference to that pattern's articulation within the environmental milieu.

Personality as a Longitudinal Process

Inanimate systems unfold through efficient causal processes. Persons, however, are often motivated teleologically, by anticipations and goals, often not consciously realized, whose existence is as yet purely potential. Persons have the capacity to bring both the past and the future into the present and to alter their behavior accordingly. At any given moment, the individual possesses a variety of expectancies and goal-states, both long- and short-term. These must be balanced and flexibly managed to reduce that constellation of quantitatively and qualitatively different demands into a single behavioral vector in a multivariate space, the direction that accomplishes the most with the least, often serving many different ends at once.

Pathological personalities, however, have a tendency to foster vicious circles, that is, they tend to find themselves in the same situation again and again, and are unable to make progress. Some, such as the psychopath, are simply impulsive, and fail to think ahead. More often, however, consonant with the systems model, these vicious circles build on the patient's adaptive inflexibility. Narcissists, for example, are so consistently self-oriented that they inevitably alienate others. In contrast, the dependent is other-oriented almost to the exclusion of self and suffocatingly so. Thus, the individual perpetuates his difficulties, provokes new ones, and sets into motion self-defeating, vicious circles. Again, it is the personality pattern itself that is pathogenic.

Normality and Abnormality: A Continuum

We have kept quite close to the question that forms the title of this chapter. Elsewhere (Millon, 1991), this general line of reasoning has been developed into a three-polarity metapsychology, based on evolutionary principles, from which a theoretically grounded taxonomy, or system of types, for the *DSM* personality "disorders" can be deduced.

Nevertheless, a system of types does not allow one to draw the line between normal and pathological personality patterns. In fact, no such line exists. Personality pathology, indeed all psychopathology, can be thought of dimensionally, that is, as lying on a continuum from normality to severity, so that we can speak of normal personality patterns, mild personality pathologies, and severe personality pathologies. The dysfunctional variant of the normal "retiring" personality pattern, for example, would be the schizoid personality. The dysfunctional variant of the "gregarious" pattern would be the histrionic personality. Exaggeration of the basic pattern increases as one moves along the continuum from normality to pathology.

How can the notion of a continuum of pathology be incorporated in a systems model? The systems model reminds us that any single phenomenon, though perhaps somewhat cohesive unto itself, cannot be understood in and of itself. Much like any other paradigm, the systems perspective is not truth, it is simply a way of thinking, a kind of mental fiction. In short, the system can be expanded to include the observer. Whatever nature is when it is unobserved, the act of observation is itself a transformation of "whatever is" into the observer's own categories. This transformation is both selective and personal. Some things are ignored, others are highlighted, and the behavior of the thing observed is implicitly compared to one's own frame of reference.

Interestingly, such a scheme converges with the observation that personality pathologies are often ego-syntonic. That is, the individuals concerned, whose phenomenology is part and parcel of the personality pattern, using themselves as a reference point, may experience no subjective sense of dislocation from the pattern itself. Obviously, the distinction between normally and abnormally behaving systems is as much a matter of the observer's expectations as it is of the systems observed.

Does the inclusion of the observer in the system confound scientific "objectivity" with subjective "good-bad" judgments? Not really. In fact, inclusion of the observer gives insight only into how such judgments are possible at all—it does not tell one what judgments to make. Categorically speaking, it is likely that much like other diagnostic categories, normality and abnormality are polythetic, possessing no sufficient or necessary features (Cantor & Genero, 1986). If so, then it will be impossible for us to say, respectively, that a vicious circle is always evidence of a pathological personality pattern or that every personality pathology inevitably produces vicious circles. Again, it appears the individual is the *real* unit of analysis in the psychological milieu.

References

American Psychiatric Association. (1987). *Diagnostic and statistical manual of mental disorders* (3rd ed., rev.). Washington, DC: Author.

Cantor, N., & Genero, N. (1986). Psychiatric diagnosis and natural categorization: A close analogy. In T. Millon & G. L. Klerman (Eds.), *Contemporary directions in psychopathology: Towards the DSM-IV* (pp. 233–256). New York: Guilford Press.

Millon, T. (1969). *Modern psychopathology: A biosocial approach to maladaptive learning and functioning.* Prospect Heights, IL: Waveland Press.

Millon, T. (1988). Personologic psychotherapy: Ten commandments for a post-eclectic approach to integrative treatment. *Psychotherapy, 25,* 209–219.

Millon, T. (1991). *Toward a new personology: An evolutionary model.* New York: John Wiley and Sons.

Pap, A. (1953). Reduction-sentences and open concepts. *Methods, 5,* 3–30.

Annotated Bibliography

MacCorquodale, K., & Meehl, P. E. (1948). On the distinction between intervening variables and hypothetical constructs. *Psychological Review, 55,* 95–107.

This classic article gets at the essential distinction between "map" and "territory," "label" and "concept" as relevant to the philosophy of psychology.

Millon, T. (1981). *Disorders of personality: DSM-III, Axis II.* New York: Wiley.

This book provides a wealth of information on the nature of personality and abnormal personality patterns, historical formulations by major figures in psychology and psychiatry predating the *DSM-III,* and a detailed description of the manifestations, ontogeny, and prognostic considerations related to the major personality disorders.

Millon, T. (1990). *Toward a new personology: An evolutionary model.* New York: Wiley.

This book draws on principles inherent in the physical and biological sciences to fashion a metapsychology of personality and personality disorders grounded largely in evolutionary theory. This conceptual structure sees personality in terms of its basic survival and adaptive functions, pleasure-pain, active-passive, and self-other. Millon shows how this model undergirds much of psychology in general, as well as psychopathologic theory, assessment, and intervention.

Rejoinder to Mr. Davis and Professor Millon

Mark A. Mattaini

I am pleased that Mr. Davis and Professor Millon, on thoughtful reflection, find themselves agreeing that, "No, personalities cannot be disordered." We concur in many other areas as well, for example, that a line cannot be drawn between normal and pathological "personality patterns;" that the phenomena under consideration are, at base, dimensional rather than categorical; and that there is a need to think from a systems framework to understand human action.

We also have areas of profound, and critical, disagreement, however. Davis and Millon emphasize "pathology" throughout their discussion, despite initial caveats about overmedicalizing discussions of personality disorders. Most troubling is their assertion that pathological personalities are "pathologies of the entire person." They assert this very stark position based on a theoretical model for which no empirical support is offered. From a clinical perspective, perhaps the only more hopeless message than, "there is something wrong with your psychic structure" is that, "you, in your totality as a person, are pathological." This position is, if anything, potentially more damaging than the *DSM* notion of a person "having a disorder." I find this view disturbing, particularly when coupled with an emphasis on the subjectivity of the observer.

While the tone of the Davis and Millon argument seems, on the surface, quite humanistic, its endpoint is distinctly pessimistic and tends to draw a clear distinction between the pathological patient and the rest of us. The clinician cannot avoid communicating such an attitude to the patient. Given that there seem to be no more data to support the "pathological person" stance than that of the "personality disorder," I continue to assert that the most clinically sensitive and empirically based approach is to assume that behavior is behavior, and behavior can change. Within this view, a "person" is the nexus of biology, learning history and current environmental transactions, each of which is more or less lawfully related to action.

NO

MARK A. MATTAINI

Personality disorders, as commonly defined, have proven extremely good for clinicians. A person with a personality disorder has a mental illness that requires professional treatment, but by definition the disorder is expected to "continue throughout most of adult life," so little is expected of treatment. The problem, according to most theoreticians of the disorders, resides in invisible mental structures or cognitive schemas, which can be inferred, and treated, only indirectly. The diagnosis colors the treatment relationship, and justifies viewing the person with a personality disorder as qualitatively different than oneself. The concept of the personality disorder is an example of metaphor gone mad.

Several classes of issues need to be addressed. The first, and in some ways the most difficult, are definitional. In large part because of problems in defining the terms, substantial issues of reliability and validity are also present. Finally, and most importantly, there are critical issues about the clinical utility of these diagnoses. While "personality disorder" diagnoses may be good for clinicians (in the short term), I believe they can be profoundly iatrogenic for patients.

Issues of Definition

Personality

The Diagnostic and Statistical Manual of Mental Disorders (American Psychiatric Association, 1987) defines *personality* as "deeply ingrained patterns of behavior, which include the way one relates to, perceives, and thinks about the environment and oneself." Personality is seen as intrapersonal and relatively stable across time and situations. It is perhaps surprising how little this view takes into account decades of research in personality psychology. The notion that personality can be defined in terms of stable traits was largely discredited at least twenty-five years ago (Mischel, 1968). People act differently in different contexts. It is now clear that personality consists of the interactions of individual biology, learning history, and characteristics of the *situation.* In fact, one of the most prominent authorities indicates that human action cannot be understood or predicted without knowing "the personality of the situation" (Mischel, 1986).

Disorder

The definition of a *mental disorder* is also relevant to this discussion. In *DSM-III-R,* a mental disorder is a ''behavioral or psychological syndrome or pattern'' that is ''a manifestation of a behavioral, psychological, or biological dysfunction in the person.'' It is a condition that a person has. This primary locus of the issue ''in the person'' is the common feature linking problems as varied as Alzheimer's disease, bipolar disorder, and personality disorders.

There are several issues here. The first is that the definition of mental disorder mixes problems with a clear biological basis, which can unambiguously be defined as ''diseases,'' with life problems based on maladaptive learning. The meaning of the term therefore becomes diffuse. Wakefield (1992) has clarified that, if ''mental disorder'' is to have a precise meaning, the definition must include both an actual ''dysfunction'' (a failure of an organismic function) and significant harm to the individual in the given circumstances.

A psychiatric disorder is by definition a medical problem, a ''mental illness.'' Spitzer and Endicott (1978) indicate that an ''organismic dysfunction'' must be assumed to underlie every disorder. Note that expectable responses to difficult environmental conditions are excluded. It is also not adequate to suggest that behavior can be classified as ''disordered'' if it developed naturally in one context but then generalizes ''inappropriately'' to other situations. Generalization is a normal and predictable part of learning, about which we know quite a lot.

DSM is an official publication of the American Psychiatric Association, a professional organization of medical doctors. The extension of the medical metaphor found in *DSM* encourages emphasis on treatment of the individual, within whom the condition is defined to be, often with a biological focus. This may also prove to be true even for the expanded list of conditions that may be included in *DSM-IV,* such as family problems, physical violence, and acculturation difficulty (American Psychiatric Association Task Force on DSM-IV, 1991). But these are not diseases.

Personality Disorder

The heart of the matter is the definition of a *personality disorder.* Interestingly, *DSM-III-R* does not provide a definition, but states that ''when *personality traits* are inflexible and maladaptive and cause . . . impairment or subjective distress they constitute *Personality Disorders* [italics in original].'' Traits are defined as ''enduring patterns of perceiving, relating to, and thinking about the environment and oneself, and are exhibited in a wide range of . . . contexts.'' Given the breadth of these definitions, it is not surprising that the majority of adult patients in some mental health settings carry ''personality disorder'' diagnoses (e.g., Mattaini, 1990; also true in *DSM-III* field trials).

To receive a diagnosis of a specific personality disorder in *DSM* terms, a patient's behavior must fit a list of criteria. For example, a person with a pattern of unstable and intense relationships, who shoplifts and overspends, sometimes becomes quite depressed for a few days, threatens suicide several times, and reports a pervasive feeling of emptiness meets the criteria for "borderline personality disorder." A person who drinks too much and drives recklessly, is easily irritated, gets into recurrent physical fights, is uncertain about his sexual identity and choice of careers, and makes frantic efforts to avoid divorce from a wife on whom he is emotionally dependent *also* fits the criteria for "borderline personality disorder." Given this lack of specificity, it is perhaps not surprising that reliability issues, as discussed below, are so significant. It is also not surprising that there is little empirical evidence to support the efficacy of particular treatments for such a nonspecific "disorder."

Many clinicians and theoreticians believe that the *DSM* criteria for "personality disorders" are unsatisfactory. They offer alternatives based in theory and attempt to capture the essence rather than surface manifestations of the disorders. These approaches place heavy emphasis on cognitive "structures." Beck and Freeman (Beck, Freeman & Associates, 1990), for example, criticize the tendency to use diagnoses of "personality disorders" as "generic labels for difficult clients" (p. 178). They write about the need to assess "symptom structure (manifest problems) and underlying schema (inferred structures)." Psychoanalytic theorists, by contrast, emphasize unconscious structures, problems in object relations, and disorders of the self. Masterson (1980), for example, indicates that "the borderline syndrome is a stable diagnostic entity which is due to a failure of separation-individuation related to the mother's libidinal unavailability." Kernberg (1977) indicates that the organization of the "borderline structure" is characterized by identity diffusion ("and the related over-all quality of internalized object relations," p. 91), a "predominance of primitive defensive operations centering around the mechanism of splitting," and relatively intact reality testing. Considerable disagreement exists regarding the relationships among borderline conditions, borderline structures, borderline syndromes, and borderline personality disorders, but there is a core of agreement among the theorists. Relatively similar early developmental experiences are seen as contributing to damaged intrapsychic structures, and particular defensive styles (e.g., splitting, projective identification) are viewed as typical in cases characterized by borderline features, structures, and disorders.

Such descriptions sound profound. But to what extent does this profusion of mental entities and processes result in diagnoses specific enough that multiple observers can agree on evidence for their presence and distinguish them from other diagnoses (reliability and specificity)? Second, do these features distinguish a set of persons who are qualitatively different from the rest of us, who have a genuine *condition* (issues of validity and ontological reality)? And, finally, does the use of these diagnoses lead to enhanced clinical outcomes? Current evidence suggests that the answer to each of these questions is "no."

Issues of Reliability and Specificity

Studies of the reliability of diagnoses of specific personality disorders have consistently produced poor results (Kutchins & Kirk, 1986). In the *DSM-III* field trials, the level of agreement among trained clinicians as to whether a patient had *any* personality disorder was not high (kappas of .56 and .65 in two phases; according to the *DSM,* a kappa of .70 represents good agreement). But even this result obscures the true situation. These kappas reflect only agreement that a patient has some "personality disorder"; if one clinician diagnoses "borderline personality disorder" and another "obsessive compulsive personality disorder," this is regarded as perfect agreement. Kappas for specific "personality disorders" were reported to be "quite low," ranging from .26 to .75. New reliability data were not provided with *DSM-III-R,* in which some minor changes were made, nor for the three "clusters" of "personality disorders" that appeared in *DSM-III-R,* which may be dropped from *DSM-IV.*

Studies by other than the developers of *DSM* produce even poorer results. Mellsop and his colleagues (Mellsop et al., 1982) report overall agreement of .41, a very poor level, for personality disorders as a class, with kappas for specific disorders ranging from chance agreement to .49. Hanada and Takahashi (1983) report an Axis II (which includes personality and developmental disorders) kappa of only .33.

It is not surprising that clinicians agree to some extent that some patients manifest enduring behavior patterns that are "inflexible and maladaptive"; but the rather modest level of agreement, and their inability to agree on the specifics of just what these patterns might be, is troubling. The reliability data reported came, in general, from persons who knew they were part of a study and who had received specific training.

In my own experience in the world of day-to-day practice, patients are often inappropriately diagnosed as "personality disordered" by clinicians who tend to see the psychopathological world through that lens. Patients suffering from the aftereffects of severe child or sexual abuse, who meet the criteria for "post-traumatic stress disorder," are sometimes diagnosed as personality disordered instead. The same is true of persons suffering from depression, who can be dependent, angry, or demanding. It was once commonly believed that there was a specific "addictive personality," but the data indicate that personality disruptions are more likely to be effects of addictions than causes. Nevertheless, persons with substance abuse problems are often diagnosed as personality disordered based on precisely those features (e.g., impulsiveness). The clinical implications of over-diagnosing personality disorders, as will be seen below, are significant.

Issues of Validity

Does a diagnosis of a personality disorder refer to a real condition? Once again, this seems very doubtful. If a "personality" as a stable intrapersonal entity is a fiction, a disorder of this entity cannot be any more real. If reliability, which sets an upper limit for validity, is poor, validity cannot be any better. There is only limited agreement about the definition of a personality disorder, and the sands of diagnosis continue to shift. *DSM-III-R* included modifications of diagnostic criteria from *DSM-III* and introduced "clusters." *DSM-IV* will include additional changes and is likely to eliminate the clusters, and at least one *DSM-III-R* personality disorder may move to Axis I in *DSM-IV*.

The *DSM-IV* options book discusses the possibility of a dimensional approach rather than a categorical one, which could be an advance. This possibility is dismissed as "premature," however, because of lack of agreement on the relevant dimensions (a valid argument) and because of its "complexity." Complexity is a common difficulty the developers of *DSM* use to argue against alternative systems. But if reality is complex, a simplistic diagnostic system cannot capture it. How far would other branches of medicine have come if their diagnostic systems were driven by lack of faith in the sophistication of practitioners, rather than by empirical data?

What are we really talking about here? The majority of patients in many clinical settings are diagnosed as "personality disordered." Those who are harder to work with, who have deficits in interpersonal skills, or who appear to be "resistant" are almost uniformly diagnosed in this way. I have spoken with clinicians who have gone to supervisors and described difficult patients, patients who have trouble trusting, overreact interpersonally, and do things that are bad for them in the long run. When the supervisors pointed out that these patients sounded like "borderlines," the clinician often appeared to have an "Aha!" experience. Within a *DSM* framework, of course, such thinking is circular. The clinician describes the criteria, the supervisor provides the label based on and defined by those criteria, and the clinician believes this somehow "explains" the patient.

If, on the other hand, "personality disorders" are defined theoretically, as the object relations and self-psychology authors suggest, a new series of issues arises. No reliability or validity data are available for such diagnoses. They are based on large numbers of unseen and untestable mental "structures." There is, in fact, little objective reason to believe that these formulations are either accurate or clinically useful. Those who developed them sincerely believe they are correct; it is, therefore, no surprise that their clinical experience tends to support them. But supporting data have yet to be presented.

Clinical Utility

The reality is that a person with a personality disorder may be regarded as clinically interesting, but that the diagnosis itself often leads to barriers to genuine engagement. Most clinicians, though they may deny it, do not see a "borderline" as a person, like themselves, who is responding naturally and adaptively to his life experiences. Expecting lacunae in abilities to relate, therapists are likely to discover them; expecting few strengths, therapists probably will not find them.

A "personality disorder" is not a hopeful diagnosis. The *DSM* discussion suggests that it will persist throughout life; if improvements occur, these will be seen as "the manifestations . . . becom[ing] less obvious in middle or old age" (*DSM-III-R,* p. 335). No NIMH-funded clinical trials indicate that some forms of treatment are more effective than others in "curing" the disorder; in fact, defined as it is, no one expects "cures."

I suggest, recognizing that this statement will be controversial, that we have given up far too soon. Yes, some patients are difficult. Yes, some patients have grave difficulties in managing relationships and other aspects of their lives (although I think there are many different ways people have such troubles, which is why reliability is so poor when trying to fit the results of people's incredibly diverse learning histories into a few "disorders"). Perhaps their behavior can be understood in the same way as can everyone else's; there is no justification for giving up without trying.

An Alternative Framework

Let's start over for a moment. Let's assume that we are all, at base, very similar. Biology sets limits (and there are biological factors involved in some addictive and antisocial behaviors that are among *DSM* "personality disorder" criteria). Within those limits, using Occam's Razor, let's begin with a simple explanation: everyone's behavior is shaped by his or her learning history. Can we then account for the behaviors that are used to diagnose "personality disorders"?

Kohlenberg and Tsai (1991), for example, say, "Yes." They present examples of persons who might be diagnosed as having "narcissistic personality disorder," "borderline personality disorder," and "multiple personality disorder." Since space is limited here, I can only hint at a few points from their elegant discussion of why people might act in ways that might be called "borderline" and the treatment implications. The reader is encouraged to go to the original source for more detail and for discussions of the other conditions.

If a child grows up in an environment where his or her reports of emotional experience are invalidated, where the ease of controlling emotional states is oversimplified, and where he or she is punished (often rather covertly) for expressing preferences and beliefs different from the parent, the child is unlikely to develop a stable experience of "I." Private control of "I" responses (such as "I want," or "I feel") is not consistently reinforced and does not develop effectively. The individual becomes dependent on external cues (often varying with parental mood) to experience or describe internal events and fails to develop a consistent experience of self. If the child also experiences neglect or abuse (under which circumstances the significant other may be both crucial and punishing), it is natural that she learn to make alternating efforts to connect and distance.

In presenting their functional analytic psychotherapy (FAP), Kohlenberg and Tsai indicate that such persons are likely to begin treatment "being wary, overly attentive, and concerned about the therapist's opinion of them, and do not describe feelings, beliefs, wants, likes and dislikes." Note that these behaviors are seen as the results of specific learning histories, rather than disordered mental structures. Particular clinical tasks flow from this formulation, including reinforcing talking in the absence of external cues, shaping awareness of internal cues, providing opportunities to learn that one can learn to say what one wants (and request it without threatening), and so forth—in other words, providing a learning environment that evokes the development of the specific personal and interpersonal skills the patient has not yet learned. In some cases, action in the environment may also be needed to facilitate such learning, or help the patient move out of a situation with a "disordered personality."

The differences between therapy oriented to identifying dysfunctional mental structures and modifying them to the limited extent believed possible and treatment oriented to helping the person learn interpersonal and self-management skills (which previous history provided little chance to master) are subtle but crucial. The alternative framework suggests that everyone *can* (and does) adapt to life circumstances; in fact, the patient is experiencing difficulties not because he or she has a mental disorder, but because of prior learning experiences. Given new experiences, the therapist expects change. (This is not to say that change will be easy; overlearned behaviors may require powerful interventions over a substantial period.)

There are three crucial differences between the views of object relations theorists and the more hopeful FAP framework. Object relations theorists view mentalistic structures as the causes of behavior, whereas FAP sees environmental events as the ultimate forces shaping behavior. Object relations theory suggests that relatively immutable personalities are formed during specific developmental periods, whereas FAP indicates that behavior changes throughout life in response to changing events. Finally, the first group believe that certain behaviors, like splitting, are reflections of underlying pathology, and the second emphasize the contextual nature of behavior and suggest that the behaviors labeled *splitting, projective identification,* and so forth, are learned like any other.

Not only are personality disorders as currently conceptualized unreliable entities of questionable reality, but their wide application in clinical work is often iatrogenic. I believe it is more accurate and more useful to view human behavior as learned, contextual, and understandable, without recourse to inaccessible mentalistic structures that are defined as highly resistant to change.

References

American Psychiatric Association. (1987). *Diagnostic and statistical manual of mental disorders* (3rd ed. rev.). Washington, DC: Author.

American Psychiatric Association Task Force on DSM-IV. (1991). *DSM-IV options book: Work in progress.* Washington, DC: American Psychiatric Association.

Beck, A. T., Freeman, A., & Associates (1990). *Cognitive therapy of personality disorders.* New York: Guilford.

Hanada, K., & Takahashi, S. (1983). Multi-institutional collaborative studies of diagnostic reliability of DSM-III. In R. Spitzer, J. B. W. Williams, & A. Skodal (Eds.), *International perspectives on DSM-III* (pp. 273–290). Washington, DC: American Psychiatric Press.

Kernberg, O. F. (1977). The structural diagnosis of borderline personality organization. In P. Hartocollis (Ed.), *Borderline personality disorders* (pp. 87–121). New York: International Universities Press.

Kohlenberg, R. J., & Tsai, M. (1991). *Functional analytic psychotherapy: Creating intense and curative therapeutic relationships.* New York: Plenum.

Kutchins, H., & Kirk, S. A. (1986). The reliability of DSM-III: A critical review. *Social Work Research & Abstracts, 22*(4), 3–12.

Masterson, J. F., with Costello, J. L. (1980). *From borderline adolescent to functioning adult: The test of time.* New York: Brunner/Mazel.

Mattaini, M. A. (1990). *A study of the visual representation of quantitative data for ecosystemic research and practice.* DSW Dissertation, Columbia University.

Mellsop, G., et al. (1982). The reliability of Axis II of DSM-III. *American Journal of Psychiatry, 139,* 1360–1361.

Mischel, W. (1968). *Personality and assessment.* New York: Wiley.

Mischel, W. (1986). *Introduction to personality: A new look* (4th ed.). New York: Holt, Rinehart and Winston.

Spitzer, R. L., and Endicott, J. (1978). Medical and mental disorder: Proposed definition and criteria. In R. L. Spitzer & D. F. Klein (Eds.), *Critical issues in psychiatric diagnosis* (pp. 15–39), New York: Raven Press.

Wakefield, J. C. (1992). The concept of mental disorder: On the boundary between biological facts and social values. *American Psychologist, 47,* 373–388.

Annotated Bibliography

Kohlenberg, R. J., & Tsai, M. (1991). *Functional analytic psychotherapy: Creating intense and curative therapeutic relationships.* New York: Plenum.

This book provides an in-depth presentation of an approach to psychotherapy rooted in behavior analytic theory and identifies similarities and differences between behavioral and psychodynamic theory. The sections describing work with persons who might be diagnosed as "personality-disordered" are particularly strong.

Kutchins, H., & Kirk, S. A. (1986). The reliability of DSM-III: A critical review. *Social Work Research & Abstracts, 22*(4), 3–12.

This review and reanalysis of data regarding the reliability problem in psychiatric diagnosis succinctly summarizes the issues of changing standards and modest agreement among observers that characterize many *DSM* diagnostic categories.

Wakefield, J. C. (1992). The concept of mental disorder: On the boundary between biological facts and social values. *American Psychologist, 47,* 373–388.

In this important paper, Wakefield clarifies the weaknesses of the six most common accounts of mental disorder and argues for the need for a rigorous emphasis on both dysfunction as a failure of an internal mechanism and significant harm to the individual to provide an adequate definition.

Rejoinder to Professor Mattaini

ROGER D. DAVIS AND THEODORE MILLON

Several points in Professor Mattaini's essay deserve comment. Mattaini begins with definitional issues, noting that personality is usually defined in terms of stable traits, although persons behave differently in different contexts. The person-situation debate parallels the nature-nurture issue and, like the latter, has become rather tiresome, as it turns mainly on metatheoretical assumptions rather than empirical evidence.

Without a doubt, the personality construct pulls for constancy. In fact, therein lies its scientific utility. It means only that if one sums over various environments, as one might collapse over various factors of a multifactorial analysis of variance, a substantial amount of "variance" is left over that must be attributed to the persons themselves. Moreover, there are individual differences in whether behavior is typically driven more by person or situation. Some people respond to a range of environments flexibly, while others are inflexible and have only a small repertoire of coping behaviors. Yes, behavior is always the product of the person and (his appraisal of) the environment, but when the range of environments is large and "normative," yet adaptational difficulties persist, then it becomes clinically meaningful to ask what role the patient might play in creating and perpetuating these difficulties. Why does such a pattern emerge at all? Why is it this particular pattern rather than another?

Mattaini notes that the term ''personality disorder'' regards personality disorder as ''a condition that a person has,'' but which ''are not diseases.'' Mattaini's treatment of this point is laudable and we agree. The search for material causes is fundamental to the medical model and, in regard to personality, represents reification at its worst. Here Mattaini appears to be on the edge of a conceptualization of personality that does justice to it as a construct intended to inform scientific thought, rather than as a substantive entity in its own right.

Much of the remainder of Mattaini's essay consists of an indictment of personality disorders as they are represented in the *Diagnostic and Statistical Manual of Mental Disorders.* We hope the reader will distinguish the questions ''Can personality be disordered?'' and ''Can personality as given in the *DSM* be disordered?'' Though the choice of the terminology, ''personality disorder,'' is indeed unfortunate, the latter question is tied to a particular atheoretical dispensation. It does not address the relationship between abnormality and personality at an abstract level, which is the proper focus of our discussion.

Nowhere is this truer than with Mattaini's comments regarding the lack of interrater reliability and specificity of *DSM* personality disorders and criteria. Reliability and specificity of diagnostic criteria are simply irrelevant. All sciences distinguish between intervening variables and hypothetical constructs (MacCorquodale & Meehl, 1948). Not to defend the *DSM* personality criteria (which do, in fact, leave something to be desired), but if the conjunction of abnormality and personality is regarded as an abnormality of the matrix of the entire person, that is, as a multidimensional or multidomain problem with interpersonal, cognitive, behavioral, and biological aspects, then it quickly becomes apparent that the correct appraisal of personality ''disorder'' is a complex problem in pattern recognition. Because persons are genuine organic entities, the causality or ''ontological reality'' of these difficulties is borne by or distributed throughout the entire personality matrix. We might expect, then, that the interrater reliability of the Axis II ''disorders'' would be somewhat lower than many of those on Axis I.

Mattaini ends his essay with ''an alternative framework.'' Although it is difficult to appraise this framework because of the limited space in which it is offered, Mattaini appears to argue for a model that includes biological factors as well as individual learning history. As a multidomain perspective, such a model is not necessarily incompatible with the multidimensional, integrative conceptualization necessary for the personality ''disorders.''

References

MacCorquodale, K., & Meehl, P. E. (1948). On the distinction between hypothetical constructs and intervening variables. *Psychological Review, 55,* 95–107.

DEBATE 4

Should Human Diagnosticians Be Replaced by Automated Diagnostic Systems?

YES argues James G. Mazoué, who received his Ph.D. from Tulane University and has published in the areas of epistemology and metaphysics. His current research interests concern the social and ethical implications of using automated diagnostic systems.

NO says Randolph A. Miller, M.D., who received an A.B. from Princeton University in 1971 and an M.D. (cum laude) from the University of Pittsburgh School of Medicine in 1976. He is currently Professor of Medicine and Chief of the Section of Medical Informatics at the University of Pittsburgh School of Medicine. His research interests involve the application of computer technology to the clinical setting and to medical education. He is a Fellow of the American College of Physicians, a Fellow of the American College of Medical Informatics, and a member of the Board of Directors of the American Medical Informatics Association.

YES

JAMES G. MAZOUÉ

By both necessity and tradition, medicine has relied on human practitioners as diagnostic decision makers. Although technological advances have dramatically transformed modern medicine, the presumed need for clinicians skilled in interpreting the manifestations of illness has remained central to medical practice.

Throughout the history of medicine, diagnostic methods and criteria have changed and continue to evolve, but the conception of diagnosis itself as a distinctively human intellectual activity has remained essentially intact.

The advent and development of automated diagnostic systems now compel us, however, to reexamine the need for human diagnosticians. In a variety of well-defined diagnostic applications ranging from internal medicine to psychiatry, automated systems have consistently outperformed clinicians in the accuracy of their diagnoses. If it is reasonable to expect that improvements in research and design will lead to computer-based systems that surpass humans in diagnostic accuracy, should we continue to allow humans to diagnose patients?

We can distinguish between two competing views about how extensive a diagnostic role automated systems should have. The *weak thesis* (WT) holds that the use of computer-assisted diagnostic systems is limited to providing informational support and, perhaps, diagnostic recommendations to physicians. According to WT, the role of the physician as a polyfunctional practitioner in whom clinical and diagnostic reasoning skills are combined is essential to sound medical practice. The *strong thesis* (ST) holds that the diagnostic reasoning capabilities of humans are not inherently superior to those of automated systems. Because human reasoning capabilities are not indispensable, computer-based systems can be given greater responsibility for diagnosing patients even, perhaps, to the point of eventually replacing human diagnosticians altogether.

Most researchers involved in the development of automated diagnostic systems currently subscribe to the weak thesis. They believe that the notion that computer-based systems could replace physicians *as diagnosticians* can be dismissed as either naively optimistic or based on an unrealistically simplistic and flawed conception of clinical diagnosis. I argue that those who defend WT are mistaken. Conversion to computer-based diagnosis is not only possible, but there are good reasons to think that it would be preferable to practitioner-dependent diagnosis. I first consider some of the principal criticisms of ST given by those who think that a continuation of the present system would be best. I then consider the advantages of converting to automated diagnosis and explain why it would be more beneficial than retaining the existing practice of human-centered diagnosis.

Arguments against the Strong Thesis

The Defeasibility Condition

Perhaps the best way to demonstrate that ST is mistaken is to show that computer-based systems encounter intractable difficulties that can be effectively handled only by human diagnosticians. We can call this the *defeasibility condition* (DC). If DC were met, this would be sufficient to show that the ST is false. If there are good reasons, for example, to think that insurmountable technical limitations inherent in the design of diagnostic software programs exist, we would have sufficient reason to reject ST. The only limitations, however, that critics have cited as grounds for rejecting ST are those associated with the design of current prototypes. Yet, definitive conclusions about automated diagnosis cannot be justifiably drawn from the tentative nature of current research. Only if we were to know now that the design of computer-based diagnostic systems is technically impossible or too impractical to implement would we be justified in rejecting ST. To conclude, however, that ST should be rejected on the basis of assuming without further evidence that contingently true statements about the state of current research hold *categorically* would suppose that *presently* inhering limitations indicate the presence of *inherent* limitations. This sort of move clearly does not meet the burden of proof required to satisfy DC. If, however, we have no reason to accept DC, there is no reason to believe that *only humans* can diagnose or that the role of automated diagnostic systems is limited to assisting them.

Human Diagnosticians Are More Complete Sources of Information

Human practitioners have access to more, or at least different kinds of, information about patients than diagnostic programs. Because physicians operate out of a richer informational matrix, critics of ST conclude that they alone are competent to diagnose (Miller & Masarie, 1990).

Studies suggest, however, that patients' observations have far greater informational utility and decisional value than input from physicians (Lavelle & Kanagaratnam, 1990). Even if we were to grant, however, that physicians are more complete sources of information about patients, it wouldn't follow that this would make them definitive sources of diagnostic reasoning. Information that is diagnostically relevant needs to be distinguished from information that is useful in treating and managing patients. Typically, examples given in support of physicians' more complex understanding concern the social and ethical aspects of patient care, rather than information that is directly relevant to making a diagnosis. That software programs cannot represent every aspect of a patient's condition would be a drawback only if diagnostically relevant information could not be represented. Critics of ST have not shown, however, that diagnostic programs have any such inherent representational limitations.

Diagnosis Is a Process

Some critics of ST argue that its rejection follows from the definition of diagnosis as a *process* (Miller, 1990). Since obtaining clinically useful data from patients is a part of the diagnostic process, and only humans can elicit clinically useful information, it follows that automated systems cannot diagnose patients.

This argument does not, however, support WT. While it may demonstrate that the services of humans are needed, it does not in any way show that the diagnostic process requires practitioners in whom clinical information-gathering skills are combined with pathophysiological reasoning. To conclude that diagnosis requires the services of practitioners does not suffice to show that it depends on the services of *polyfunctional* practitioners. Since the argument that diagnosis is a process does not show that diagnosis depends on polyfunctional practitioners, it fails as a refutation of ST.

There's No Need to Fix What Isn't Broken

It is generally accepted that there is no need to change the present way of diagnosing patients. Medicine, by its very nature, is inexact and human diagnostic errors are to be expected as an inevitable consequence of acting under conditions of uncertainty.

Although nothing at all about the merits of converting to automated diagnostic systems follows from the mere fact that physicians make errors, the alarmingly high rate of human diagnostic error can hardly be cited by supporters of WT as a virtue of the present system. The Harvard Medical Practice Study, for example, found that in 8.1 percent of nonoperative hospitalizations adverse events were caused by diagnostic error (Brennan et al., 1991; Leape et al., 1991). Extrapolating from the 1 percent incidence of adverse events reported in the study, almost 2,800 patients in New York State died or were permanently disabled as a result of negligent diagnostic errors in 1984. The inadequacy of current levels of diagnostic performance contradicts the claim that the present system does not need serious remedial change.

Some advocates of WT have argued that computer-assisted training programs could be used to reduce the incidence of diagnostic error. The presumption that more knowledge and training will improve human diagnostic performance may not, however, be justified. One study, for example, found that there were no long-term residual benefits from the use of protocol-based computer reminders (McDonald, 1976). No "training effect" was noted and improvements lasted only as long as diagnostic protocols were being used. If, as the McDonald study suggests, errors of omission are not simply attributable to ignorance or correctable by training, then the gains from using diagnostic support systems to extend the limited information-handling capacities of humans would be negligible. Using computers as an educational resource simply does not go far enough. If we can entrust the training of physicians to automated diagnostic systems, why not use them to diagnose patients?

Arguments for the Strong Thesis

Accuracy

Automated diagnostic systems are more accurate than human diagnosticians. Computer-assisted decision support systems have consistently outscored unaided clinicians in diagnostic accuracy (Adams et al., 1986; Bankowitz et al., 1989; de

Bernardinis, et al., 1989; Boom et al., 1988; de Dombal et al., 1974; Kerkhof et al., 1990). The evidence strongly suggests that as the size of knowledge bases increases and diagnostic algorithms and heuristic models improve, the accuracy of automated diagnostic systems will also increase. The information-processing capacity of the human brain, on the contrary, is limited and prone to informational overload. Unlike computer-based systems, the human brain has inherent limitations on its ability to assimilate and process information. The greater computational power and precision of automated systems make them better suited to accurately analyze the diagnostic significance of complex informational relationships.

Cost

Automated diagnostic systems reduce health care costs. Computer-based algorithms have been effective in reducing the cost of screening patients for physical disease (Sox et al., 1989). They have also been used by the National Health Service of the United Kingdom to significantly lower expenditures by reducing the number of hospitalizations, unnecessary surgeries, and redundant procedures (Adams et al., 1986; de Dombal, 1990). Substantial long-term benefits would result from lower rates of misdiagnosis and earlier treatment. Savings from not having to teach humans how to diagnose could also be spent on primary care and basic research.

Efficiency

Psychological research indicates that formal methods of organizing probabilistic data are more efficient and consistent than informally derived clinical strategies (Elstein, 1976). Because diagnostic reasoning depends to a great extent on the ability to correctly calculate and effectively use statistical data, automated systems using formal decision criteria would be more efficient as information processors than human diagnosticians. Computers are simply much better at accurately estimating the prior probabilities of diseases and in taking conditional probabilities into consideration. A system of explicitly formulated decision rules can also be easily accessed and tested as well as rapidly revised. Building and maintaining a unified source of diagnostic expertise would be more efficient than having to continually train and retrain practitioners in whom expertise is unevenly distributed, disposable, and imperfectly replicated.

Reliability

Practitioner-based diagnosis is unreliable. A weakness of the present system is its dependence on inconsistent levels of diagnostic skill and competence that can vary widely among individuals and locations. Automated diagnostic systems, however, would ensure that recommendations for intervention are data-driven and uniformly applied. In addition to their greater consistency, computer-based systems would also better protect the diagnostic process from interpretational bias. The process of generating and selecting diagnostic hypotheses would be effectively freed from the influence of personal prejudices and institutional biases.

In conclusion, the arguments most often given as reasons for rejecting ST fail. They do not show that automated diagnostic systems are either impossible or impractical. There is, however, good inductive evidence to support the view that the health care system would be better served if human diagnosticians were replaced by automated systems. Using computer-based systems to diagnose patients would be more accurate, cost-effective, efficient, and reliable than the current practice of relying on human diagnosticians. It would be in the best interest of medicine to fully develop and use the diagnostic capabilities of automated systems.

References

Adams, I. D., Chan, M., Clifford, P. C., Cooke, W. M., Dallos, V., de Dombal, F. T., Edwards, M. H., Hancock, D. M., Hewett, D. J., McIntyre, N., Somerville, P. G., Spiegelhalter, D. J., Wellwood, J., & Wilson, D. H. (1986). Computer-aided diagnosis of acute abdominal pain: A multicentre study. *British Medical Journal, 293,* 800–804.

Bankowitz, M. D., McNeil, M. A., Challinor, S. M., Parker, R. C., Kapoor, W. N., & Miller, R. A. (1989). A computer-assisted medical diagnostic consultation service. *Annals of Internal Medicine, 110,* 824–832.

Boom, R., Chavez-Oest, J., Gonzalez, C., Cantu, M. A., Rivero, F., Reyes, A., Aguilar, E., & Santamaria, J. (1988). Physicians' diagnoses compared with algorithmic differentiation of causes of jaundice. *Medical Decision Making, 8,* 177–181.

Brennan, T. A., Leape, L. L., Laird, N. M., Hebert, L., Localio, A. R., Lawthers, A. G., Newhouse, J. P., Weiler, P. C., & Hiatt, H. H. (1991). Incidence of adverse events and negligence in hospitalized patients. *New England Journal of Medicine, 324,* 370–376.

de Bernardinis, M., Viola, V., Roncoroni, L., Montanari, M., & Peracchia, A. (1989). Automated selection of high-risk patients with acute pancreatitis. *Critical Care Medicine, 17,* 318–322.

de Dombal, F. T., Leaper, D. J., Horrocks, J. C., Staniland, J. R., & McCann, A. P. (1974). Human and computer-aided diagnosis of abdominal pain: Further report with emphasis on performance of clinicians. *British Medical Journal, 1,* 376–380.

de Dombal, F. T. (1990). Computer-aided decision support in acute abdominal pain, with special reference to the EC concerted action. *International Journal of Biomedical Computing; 12,* 183–188.

Elstein, A. S. (1976). Clinical judgment: Psychological research and medical practice. *Science, 194,* 696–700.

Kerkhof, P. L. M., Helder, J., Van Dieijen-Visser, M. P., Schreuder, J. J. A., De Bruin, H. G., & Gill, K. (1990). Evaluation of clinico-pathological conferences using a computer-supported diagnosis program with matrix structure. *Automedica, 13,* 45–51.

Lavelle, S. M., & Kanagaratnam, B. (1990). The information value of clinical data. *International Journal of Biomedical Computing, 26,* 203–209.

Leape, L. L., Brennan, T. A., Laird, N., Lawthers, A. G., Localio, A. R., Barnes, B. A., Hebert, L., Newhouse, J. P., Weiler, P. C., & Hiatt, H. (1991). The nature of adverse events in hospitalized patients. *New England Journal of Medicine, 324,* 377–384.

McDonald, C. J. (1976). Protocol-based computer reminders, the quality of care and the non-perfectability of man. *New England Journal of Medicine, 295,* 1351–1355.

Miller, R. A. (1990). Why the standard view is standard: People, not machines, understand patients' problems. *Journal of Medicine and Philosophy, 15,* 581–591.

Miller, R. A., & Masarie, F. E. (1990). The demise of the 'Greek Oracle' model for medical diagnostic systems. *Methods of Information in Medicine, 29,* 1–2.

Sox, H. C., Koran, L. M., Sox, C. H., Marton, K. I., Dugger, F., & Smith, T. (1989). A medical algorithm for detecting physical disease in psychiatric patients. *Hospital and Community Psychiatry, 40,* 1270–1276.

Annotated Bibliography

Mazoué, J. G. (1990). Diagnosis without doctors. *Journal of Medicine and Philosophy, 15,* 559–579.

A defense of the strong thesis. It is argued that automated diagnostic systems could effectively replace human diagnosticians.

Miller, R. A. (1990). Why the standard view is standard: People, not machines, understand patients' problems. *Journal of Medicine and Philosophy, 15,* 581–591.

A defense of the weak thesis. The author argues that automated diagnostic systems cannot replace human diagnosticians.

Miller, R. A., & Masarie, F. E. (1990). The demise of the 'Greek Oracle' model for medical diagnostic systems. *Methods of Information in Medicine, 29,* 1–2.

The authors argue that the creation of comprehensive computer-based diagnostic systems as replacements for human diagnosticians is not a viable research goal. Automated systems should only function as ''catalysts'' that assist physician-users in reaching diagnostic decisions.

Rejoinder to Dr. Mazoué

RANDOLPH A. MILLER

In his discussion, Dr. Mazoué presents arguments for what he calls the strong thesis (''the diagnostic reasoning capabilities of humans are not inherently superior to those of automated systems'' and ''computer-based systems can be given greater responsibility for diagnosing patients even, perhaps, to the point of eventually replacing human diagnosticians altogether'') and against what he calls the weak thesis (''the use of computer-assisted diagnostic systems is limited to providing informational support and, perhaps, diagnostic recommendations to physicians). While these arguments are sound from a logical viewpoint, they discuss a realm of theoretical possibilities that does not exist in the current-day world of medical practice and medical computing.

Dr. Mazoué states that the defeasibility condition has not been met by proponents of the weak thesis. Many aspects regarding the behavior of machines and human beings cannot be characterized by mathematical proofs. A large number of statements similar to that proposed in the strong thesis could be constructed but not disproved mathematically (e.g., ''Eventually, all possible lines of philosophical reasoning can be represented in computers, and since the logic of computer-based reasoning is impeccable, the profession of philosophy should be phased out in the near future''). Inability to mathematically construct a proof that shows that all lines of philosophical reasoning cannot be represented in a computer program should hardly cause the philosophers of the world to despair. No proof exists that a ''sufficient quantity'' of philosophical reasoning can be represented in current computer architectures, or ever will be.

In another highly theoretical position, Dr. Mazoué states that ''Although nothing at all about the merits of converting to automated diagnostic systems follows from the mere fact that physicians make errors, the alarmingly high rate of human diagnostic error can hardly be cited by supporters of WT as a virtue of the present system.'' Those of us who have developed and continue to develop diagnostic decision support systems certainly hope that our systems will improve the performance of human diagnosticians, but few if any of us extend this argument to stating that humans should not be allowed to practice medical diagnosis. Humans frequently make errors in performing mathematical calculations (some very costly); why not advocate the strong theory to propose legislation that forbids humans from ever adding or subtracting again? That McDonald et al. have demonstrated that "there is no training effect" does indicate a need for continued use of decision support systems for clinicians in certain busy settings, but this does not constitute a proof that the humans should be eliminated from such settings.

Dr. Mazoué's arguments for the strong thesis are weak. He states, "Automated diagnostic systems are more accurate than human diagnosticians." This is simply false. As a co-author of one of the studies Dr. Mazoué cites in support of this statement, I would like to point out that the study compared humans using a diagnostic decision support system to humans who were not using such a system on a limited number of carefully selected cases. Dr. Mazoué claims that "automated diagnostic systems reduce health care costs." While those of us developing decision support systems would like to believe that automated systems may eventually help physicians to deliver more cost-effective care, few if any convincing studies in the current medical literature carefully compare true health care costs in general medical practice with and without use of computer-based decision aids. The cost of the computers, training physicians, the time spent in using the computers, and the time required to build and maintain the computer software and knowledge bases must be taken into account as well as the actual health care costs. Limited studies in the literature document the potential impact of computers in carefully defined, narrowly constrained domains; success in such areas does not constitute a proof that use of computers will be cost-effective in other areas or overall.

NO

Randolph A. Miller

Introduction: Prerequisites for Automation

In an earlier thought-provoking article, Mazoué claimed, primarily on the basis that human medical diagnosis is fraught with error, that we should replace human diagnosticians with automated diagnostic systems (Mazoué, 1990). It is important to examine, at this juncture, the foundation for such claims and the circumstances that make any conclusion that humans are outmoded as diagnosticians untenable.

Most of the enterprises that humans undertake are subject to the phenomenon of "human error." While medical diagnosis is no exception (Voytovich, Rippey, & Suffredini, 1985; Dubeau, Voytovich, & Rippey, 1986; Dawson & Arkes, 1987), it does not follow that we should immediately replace human diagnosticians with automated systems (Yu, Fagan, & Bennet, 1983; Miller, 1984a; Miller & Masarie, 1990; Miller, 1990). Manual systems do not become outmoded simply because they may produce "mistakes." Furthermore, the current (and reasonably foreseeable) state of the art of automated diagnosis does *not* support such optimistic assessments and recommendations. This commentary explains why human diagnosticians should remain the "standard of practice" for diagnostic assessment of patients.

Existing diagnostic decision support systems represent a promising new technology that is in its infancy (Miller, Pople, & Myers, 1982; Kingsland, 1985; Miller, McNeil, Challinar, et al., 1986; Barnett, Cimino, Hupp, & Hoffer, 1987; Warner, Haug, Bouhaddou, et al., 1988; Bankowitz, McNeil, Challinor, et al., 1989; Miller & Masarie, 1989). The state of current technology makes speculation about diagnosis without human diagnosticians plausible science fiction, but not a realistic blueprint for the near-term future of medical practice. For the remainder of this century and the beginning of the next, humans will be the primary purveyors of medical diagnosis. Perhaps, at appropriate times, they will be assisted by diagnostic decision support software.

In any field of endeavor, certain criteria should be met before one proposes to replace humans with automata. This is particularly so in medicine (Miller, Schaffner, & Meisel, 1985). The following steps should be followed in automating any complex behavior now performed by humans—especially in medicine, where people's lives and well-being are at stake:

1. First, carefully define the scope and nature of the process to be automated. This is prudent because software systems often fail when forced to perform at or beyond design tolerance limits.
2. Next, study the existing state of affairs ("needs assessment") to determine how imperfect the pre-automation system is. The principle of *primum non nocere* ("first do no harm") should apply to systems as well as to patients—"if it's not broke, don't fix it."
3. Develop an understanding of the process to be automated, in order to reduce the process to an algorithm.
4. Once an algorithm is proposed, study it to determine the ways in which it might fail, both due to inherent theoretical limitations and due to flaws that might occur during the process of implementation.
5. Evaluate the automated system carefully, during each phase in its development and after completion of its development. By necessity, initial evaluations should be carried out "in vitro" using retrospective case data—outside of the patient care arena, with no risks to patients. Once warranted, "in vivo" evaluations must be completed—prospectively, employing the system on the front lines of actual patient care delivery. In vivo evaluations are required to determine if the automated system improves or promotes important outcomes that are not possible with the preexisting manual system (Bankowitz, McNeil, Challinor, et al., 1989; Bankowitz, Lave, & McNeil, 1992).

6. Demonstrate the practical utility of the system by showing that users (clinicians) can adopt it for daily, productive use. For example, automobile seat belts can save lives, but only do so when they are worn by drivers and passengers. An otherwise superb diagnostic system that is too cumbersome to be used by busy house officers may not help patients who are hospitalized in academic medical centers.

Unfortunately, few, if any, of the existing medical decision support systems have yet fulfilled these criteria. For that reason, developers of diagnostic decision support systems promote the ''standard view''—that these systems are valuable adjuncts to human decision making, but are not replacements for humans (Miller & Masarie, 1990; Miller, 1990).

Definition of Medical Diagnosis

It is important to define *medical diagnosis* before one proposes to automate it. A simplistic definition of diagnosis might be ''the placing of an interpretive, higher level label on a set of raw, more primitive observations.'' Under such a broad definition, it is easy to demonstrate circumstances where automated systems will outperform humans. For example, it is now commonplace for automated laboratory equipment to be able to specially flag all laboratory results falling outside the 95 percent confidence intervals for the ''normal'' values seen in that laboratory. The work of McDonald and his colleagues (McDonald, Hui, Smith, et al., 1984; Tierney, Miller, & McDonald, 1990) demonstrates the value of such systems by documenting that physicians perform better when given automated reminders.

Defining medical diagnosis as ''a mapping from patient data (normal and abnormal history, physical examination, and laboratory data) to a nosology of disease states'' might, at first pass, seem reasonable and sufficient. Yet, the *process of diagnosis* is far more complex than the foregoing definition, which focuses on the outcome of the diagnostic process, a label. *The Random House Collegiate Dictionary* defines diagnosis as ''the process of determining by examination the nature and circumstances of a diseased condition'' (Flexner & Stein, 1988, p. 366). The process of diagnosis elicits a portion of the patient's life story, an accounting of the patient's life situation before the illness began, how the illness has manifested itself, how it has affected the life situation, and the patient's understanding of and response to the illness. No responsible clinician would merely state, ''this is just another patient with AIDS,'' and wash his or her hands of the patient's situation. While automated systems may soon be helpful in identifying ''AIDS'' as an appropriate diagnostic label to use in a patient case, the elicitation of the circumstances of the patient and the illness cannot be performed by an automaton. No existing medical diagnostic system can successfully perform such a complex task.

Diagnosis is an ''art'' because it represents a sequence of interdependent, often highly individualized processes. The physician must initially elicit patient data. The data must be integrated into plausible scenarios regarding known disease processes. The physician then evaluates and refines the diagnostic hypotheses through selective elicitation of additional patient information. The physician must initiate therapy at appropriate points in time, often before a definitive diagnosis is established. Finally, the physician must evaluate the effect of both the illness and the therapy on the patient over time.

The process of diagnostic evaluation represents the essence of diagnosis. Statements such as, ''The crucial semantic issue is whether the practitioner who selects and identifies clinically relevant information can do so without possessing an understanding of its possible diagnostic significance'' (Mazoué, 1990) are untenable for two reasons. First, the process of gathering additional diagnostic information must be bounded or constrained by what is already known about a patient. Second, patients, their families, their life situations, and their preferences must be considered during the process of medical evaluation.

A person or automaton might be trained to mechanically elicit all possible historical, physical examination, and laboratory findings that might occur in any patient, just as a precocious five-year-old child might be taught to define and spell the majority of words in the English language. Yet, it would be unrealistic to expect the precocious five-year-old to generate Shakespearean-quality sonnets from a knowledge of word spellings and definitions. It would be just as unrealistic to expect an automaton to collect only the ''pertinent'' information for medical diagnosis based on a knowledge of all possible tests. The cost of mindlessly eliciting all possible patient data would be staggering—temporally, economically, and ethically (due to the large number of possible tests and the real risks of morbidity and mortality associated with many diagnostic procedures, such as liver biopsy or cardiac catheterization). Actual and rational diagnosis, as has been demonstrated in studies by Elstein (Elstein, Shulman, & Sprafka, 1978) and others, involves early hypothesis formation, which further directs and limits the elicitation of additional information about the patient. As noted by Blois, ''For a fact to be relevant, it must be relevant to something, and that would ordinarily be a diagnosis'' (Blois, 1980, p. 195). Given the impossibility and impracticality of gathering every conceivable piece of diagnostic information with respect to each patient, the ''art'' of diagnosis lies in the ability of the diagnostician to carefully evoke enough relevant information to justify all important and ultimately correct diagnoses in each case and to initiate therapies at appropriate points during the evaluation.

The knowledge of how to ''work up'' the patient depends critically on *concurrent* ability to procedurally evoke history, symptoms, and physical examination findings, as well as the ability to generate diagnostic hypotheses that suggest how to further refine or pursue the findings already elicited, or to pursue completely different additional findings. This must be done in a compassionate and cost-effective manner. Given current technology, no efficient man-machine system could be developed to instruct a human data-gatherer on how to go through this process, step by step.

An Unwarranted Sense of Optimism

Because peer-reviewed literature is biased toward reporting positive new results, one can easily develop an unwarranted sense of optimism regarding any promising new technology. Certainly, a superficial review of the literature on medical diagnostic decision support systems might lead to a conclusion that the technology has become well established. Most of the diagnostic decision support systems evaluated have attempted to support medical diagnosis in a carefully defined, artificially narrow domain. A few broad systems supporting diagnosis in general internal medicine have been evaluated with cautionary warnings about the preliminary nature of their results (Miller, Pople, & Myers, 1982, Bankowitz, McNeil, Challinor, et al., 1989; Barnett, Cimino, Hupp, & Hoffer, 1987; Warner, Haug, Bouhaddou, et al., 1988).

Even after encouraging evaluation results, systems must be viewed within the framework for which they were developed. For example, de Dombal's system for the diagnosis of acute abdominal pain (de Dombal, Leaper, Horrocks, et al., 1974; Adams, Chan, Clifford, et al., 1986) was developed to support triage of patients in an emergency setting to surgical versus nonsurgical therapy. A limited number of explicit diagnoses (fewer than twenty) are supported by the system; the majority of the diagnoses are surgical disorders such as acute appendicitis, acute cholecystitis, and acute diverticulitis. One of those diagnoses is "non-specific abdominal pain," which is intended as a catch-all category for conditions not requiring surgical intervention. While the performance of the system may be exemplary under the circumstances for which it was designed, consider the plight of a middle-aged male patient who comes to an emergency department with severe, colicky periumbilical abdominal pain and foot drop. If de Dombal's system works properly, the patient would be correctly assigned to the category "non-specific abdominal pain" (and not to a surgical diagnosis such as appendicitis). This would be of little consolation to the patient who is suffering from potentially life-threatening, yet treatable, lead poisoning related to occupational exposure, to the patient with trichinosis (also treatable), or to the patient with acute intermittent porphyria (a partially treatable, difficult to diagnose, recurrent disorder that is often mishandled). Because of the limited scope of de Dombal's system, it might not even be possible to enter the finding "foot drop," since it is not relevant to the diagnosis of surgical causes of acute abdominal pain. By contrast, a broad-spectrum medical diagnostic knowledge base developed by Dr. Jack Myers and colleagues at the University of Pittsburgh (Miller, Pople, & Myers, 1982; Masarie, Miller, & Myers, 1985; Miller, McNeil, Challinor, et al., 1986; Giuse, Giuse, & Miller, 1989; Miller & Masarie, 1989) lists more than 150 disorders that can be associated with acute abdominal pain and approximately 100 disorders associated with colicky abdominal pain. A diagnostic program that utilizes such a knowledge base can generate, within seconds, a list of more than 100 different ways in which a patient might have concurrent colicky periumbilical abdominal pain and foot drop. However, that system may not perform as well as de Dombal's system in triaging between surgical and nonsurgical causes of acute abdominal pain.

Even if diagnostic computer programs were to become an accepted component of medical practice, one must remember that the knowledge bases underlying diagnostic computer programs cannot be validated at only one point in time. Just as a physician who practices "state of the art" medicine in 1992 would be outmoded if he or she practiced in exactly the same manner in 2012, the knowledge bases of "validated" systems must be periodically reviewed and updated. Shortliffe's MYCIN program (Shortliffe, 1976) was developed as a research prototype to demonstrate the applicability of rule-based expert systems to the domain of medicine (specifically, for the recommendation of appropriate antimicrobial therapy for bacteremia or meningitis). It was a brilliant, pioneering effort in this regard. The evaluation of MYCIN in the late 1970s by Yu and colleagues (Yu, Fagan, Bennet, et al., 1979) demonstrated that the program could perform at the expert level (on paper problems) in recommending antibiotic therapy for a limited number of challenging cases. But MYCIN was never deployed for routine clinical use, and after 1979, lack of maintenance caused its antibiotic knowledge base to become out of date.

Substantial differences exist in the size and quality of medical knowledge bases required for "research prototype" systems that investigate new computational models of diagnosis, and actual "production" systems that are used in clinical practice. For example, CADUCEUS (Pople, 1982) and ABEL (Patil, Szolovits, & Schwartz, 1982) incorporated causal and temporal reasoning in the diagnosis of multiple disorders (Mazoué, 1990) but they had limited medical knowledge bases (Miller, 1990). Unfortunately, our understanding of pathophysiology across all areas of medicine is variable and subject to controversy among experts, making the feasibility of a general diagnostic system that reasons on a pathophysiological basis questionable (Parker & Miller, 1987). Similarly, there are no general methods for representing the time course of all illnesses that have been used by authors of the peer-reviewed literature describing patient cases. The data to support systems that reason temporally would therefore be anecdotal and difficult to maintain in the absence of standards. Even if the "ultimate diagnostic algorithm" were to be developed, if the effort required to develop and maintain its corresponding medical knowledge base required several hundred man-years of expenditure, then the system might never be tested or deployed in real-world clinical settings.

It is difficult to overestimate the work required to represent what is known about medicine in a computationally tractable manner. The INTERNIST-I/QMR Knowledge Base (Miller, Pople, & Myers, 1982; Pople, 1982; Masarie, Miller, & Myers, 1985; Miller, McNeil, Challinor, et al., 1986; Giuse, Giuse, & Miller, 1989), which is one of the largest and most general medical knowledge bases in existence, has required an estimated 30 person-years of work to date, is not yet complete, requires extensive ongoing maintenance efforts, and only covers diagnosis of previously untreated disorders in internal medicine. This system, like most existing general diagnostic systems, does not cover therapy of disease, does not provide information regarding patient-specific prognosis, and does not support temporal or pathophysiological reasoning to any great extent. Very few individuals are willing to undertake the arduous process of building and maintaining authoritative medical knowledge bases, and few institutions are willing to support such work beyond the initial phase of the research prototype. Construction of such knowledge bases has been compared to the process of cathedral building in Europe five centuries ago (Scherrer, 1990), and the analogy is an appropriate one.

Some optimists believe that diagnostic knowledge bases will become more common and of higher quality as the number of hospital information systems that capture and retain patient information increases over time. There are many potential problems with this strategy. First, the diagnostic labels currently placed on charts are used primarily for billing purposes. Discharge diagnoses are not verified with the same degree of rigor as, for example, the diagnoses of patients who are entered into clinical trials. No standardized criteria exist for how ''certain'' a diagnosis must be in order for it to appear on a discharge summary. While few physicians could be expected to actively falsify diagnoses, several recent studies have documented ''diagnosis-related group creep''—a tendency for discharge diagnoses with higher reimbursement rates to increase over time, compared to very similar, less well-paying diagnoses. Second, there are no widely accepted or commonly used terminologies for describing a patient's findings in hospital charts or outpatient records. (The ongoing Unified Medical Language System Project of the National Library of Medicine represents an attempt to combine a number of ''standard'' nomenclatures such as ICD-9 and SNOMED for clinical and research use, but this project is in its early stages.) In reviewing medical records, some patients might be described as having ''rusty sputum,'' while others are described as having ''blood-tinged sputum,'' and others ''hemoptysis.'' The range of variability of human expression (including the fact that busy physicians may fail to record on paper all the patient findings that they observe) makes it unlikely that one could accurately determine the frequency of ''blood-streaked sputum'' in pneumococcal pneumonia from a community hospital's database—unless all the hospital's patients with pneumonia had participated in a clinical trial that carefully stipulated what data to collect and how to record the data. Even if information about findings and diagnoses could be collected and recorded reliably, patients presenting with multiple diagnoses could threaten the accuracy of data collection on individual diagnoses. If a patient with a long history of cigarette smoking and emphysema presents with acute myocardial infarction complicated by congestive heart failure, the patient's subsequent dyspnea (shortness of breath) could be attributed to emphysema, to myocardial infarction, to congestive heart failure, or to a combination of these conditions. It is not easy to identify absolute causes for patients' findings. A hospital database that arbitrarily registered ''dyspnea'' as a finding of myocardial infarction (i.e., the admitting diagnosis) for such patients could potentially contain inaccurate data on frequencies of findings in diseases. For the several reasons mentioned, generating a medical diagnostic knowledge base by correlating patient findings with discharge diagnoses from an automated hospital information system is potentially fraught with error.

Conclusion: Human Diagnosis Remains the Standard of Care

There have been no clinical trials of practical, broad-spectrum diagnostic systems that suggest that ''we are fast approaching the point at which it would be more correct to refer to *human-assisted computer diagnosis* rather than computer-assisted diagnoses made by practitioners'' (Mazoué 1990). Machines do not directly examine patients and are dependent on human input for description of the history, physical examination, laboratory findings, and therapeutic interventions of a patient. Only a very small proportion of what is known about a patient can actually be transferred to a machine with the expectation that the automated system can internally represent the ''meaning'' or ''significance'' of the information conveyed (as opposed to simply remembering an arbitrary text string). Limitations in man-machine interfaces, and more importantly, in automated systems' ability to represent the broad variety of concepts relevant to clinical medicine, will prevent ''human-assisted computer diagnosis'' from being feasible for decades, if it is at all possible.

Time constraints, difficulty in judging what is ''relevant,'' and the often vague sense of familiarity with a patient physicians gain during years of interacting with the patient limit the physician's ability to record a comprehensive amount of data on a chart or to enter such data into a computer program. Only a small fraction of what is known about a patient can therefore be input into a computer program. However, the patient information, known by the physician, that is not entered into a diagnostic computer program, can significantly constrain the range of reasonable considerations and actions for a given case. Computer programs that generate a broad range of possible diagnoses (based on limited input data) require guidance from physicians to eliminate consideration of disorders that the physician knows to be irrelevant to the patient case. The physician who forgets to inform a computer program that a patient is male will most likely ignore a computer-generated diagnosis of pregnancy as a possible explanation for the patient's abdominal distention. Physicians who require diagnostic assistance are not globally incapable. Such physicians are likely to understand most of a patient's problems and to have only a limited number of focused questions. A computer program that can provide assistance on all aspects of a patient case potentially could waste valuable physician time in solving or explaining problems that the physician has already mastered. Computer programs require physician guidance to help focus on relevant questions of interest to the physician. Thus, automated systems cannot and will not replace human diagnosticians or human judgment in the foreseeable future.

What sort of role can diagnostic systems be expected to fulfill in the short term? The work of Perry Miller (Miller, 1984b) and others on computer-based "critiquing systems," and the work of McDonald and others (McDonald, Hui, Smith, et al., 1986; Tierney, Miller, & McDonald, 1990) on computer-based "reminder systems," indicate a useful role for computer-based consultant systems. While humans are an irreplaceable component of the diagnostic process (Miller & Masarie, 1990a), it is likely that computer-based diagnostic assistant programs can supplement human diagnosticians. Just as audible alarms based on computerized arrhythmia detectors help nurses in coronary care units to monitor patients' continuous ECG tracings, computer-based diagnostic systems may be able to help detect situations where human diagnosticians should exert more effort. Either when physicians recognize that they might benefit from diagnostic assistance (Bankowitz, McNeil, Challinor, et al., 1989) or when a computer system detects discrepancies between the diagnoses offered by humans and the data available in a case, critiquing or reminder systems can help the physician to select a correct course of action.

The existing health care delivery system is far from being perfect, but, until a better system for diagnosis than human diagnosticians has been developed and validated, it is counterproductive to reject the standard view. Software has not yet been designed that can safely replace human diagnosticians "without recourse to a case-by-case review by practicing physicians" (Mazoué 1990). Although people ultimately find the proper niche for each valuable new technology, new technologies are rarely all-powerful. Invention of the automobile did not make walking outmoded, and availability of commercial air travel has not resulted in our abandoning of cars. Traveling across a room does not require an automobile, and commuting twenty miles to work is better accomplished by car than by jet airplane. Human diagnosticians, when faced with a challenging problem, will often seek assistance—from textbooks, from the peer-reviewed literature, and from expert colleagues (Covell, Uman, & Manning, 1985). It is likely that computer-based diagnostic decision support systems will be added to the list of commonly used medical decision support modalities in the near-term future. The impact of computer-based diagnostic decision support systems is likely to be beneficial, but these systems will not completely replace textbooks, the peer-reviewed literature, or consultation with human colleagues. In the short-term future, human physicians will best know patients, their families, and their lifestyles. The greatest intellect to bring to bear during a diagnostic consultative session is that of a knowledgeable physician who understands the patient, not the "artificial intelligence" of a computer program.

Acknowledgments

The author thanks Kenneth F. Schaffner, Ph.D., M.D., for his insightful comments on earlier versions of this manuscript. The author thanks the Editor of the *Journal of Medicine and Philosophy* for allowing portions of a previous article (1990; 15:581–591) to be used as the basis for this chapter. Dr. Miller's work is supported in part by Grant R01 LM04622-04 and Contract N01-LM-1-3535 from the National Library of Medicine.

References

Adams, I. D., Chan, M., Clifford, P. C., Cooke, W., Dallos, V., de Dombal, F. T., Edwards, M. H., Hancock, D. M., Hewett, D. J., McIntyre, N., Somerville, P. G., Spiegelhaller, D. J., & Wilson, D. H. (1986). Computer aided diagnosis of acute abdominal pain: A multicentre study. *British Medical Journal, 293,* 800–804.

Bankowitz, R. A., McNeil, M. A., Challinor, S. M., Parker, R. C., Kapoor, W. N., & Miller, R. (1989). A computer-assisted medical diagnostic consultation service: Implementation and prospective evaluation of a prototype. *Annals of Internal Medicine, 110,* 824–832.

Bankowitz, R. A., Lave, J. R., & McNeil, M. A. (1992). A method for assessing the impact of a computer-based decision support system on health care outcomes. *Methods of Information in Medicine, 31*(1), 3–10.

Barnett, G. O., Cimino, J. J., Hupp, J. A., & Hoffer, E. P. (1987). DXplain: An evolving diagnostic decision-support system. *Journal of the American Medical Association, 258,* 67–74.

Blois, M. S. (1980). Judgement and computers. *New England Journal of Medicine, 303,* 192–197.

Covell, D. G., Uman, G. C., Manning, P. R. (1985). Information needs in office practice: Are they being met? *Annals of Internal Medicine, 103,* 596–599.

Dawson, N. V., & Arkes, H. R. (1987). Systematic errors in medical decision making. *Journal of General Internal Medicine, 2,* 183–187.

de Dombal, F. T., Leaper, D. J., Horrocks, J. C., Staniland, J. R., & McCann, A. P. (1974). Human and computer-aided diagnosis of abdominal pain. *British Medical Journal, 1,* 376–380.

Dubeau, C. E., Voytovich, A. E., & Rippey, R. M. (1986). Premature conclusions in the diagnosis of iron-deficiency anemia: Cause and effect. *Medical Decision Making, 6,* 169–173.

Elstein, A. S., Shulman, L. S., & Sprafka, S. A. (1978). *Medical problem solving: An analysis of clinical reasoning.* Cambridge, MA: Harvard University Press.

Flexner, S. B., & Stein, J. (Eds.). (1988). *The Random House Collegiate Dictionary, Revised Edition,* (p. 366). New York: Random House.

Giuse, N. B., Giuse, D. A., & Miller, R. A. (1989). Medical knowledge base construction as a means of introducing students to medical informatics. Proceedings of the International Symposium on Medical Informatics and Education, Victoria, BC, pp. 228–232.

Kingsland, L. C. III. (1985). The evaluation of medical expert systems: Experience with the AI/RHEUM knowledge-based consultant system in rheumatology. Proceedings of the Ninth Annual Symposium on Computer Applications in Medical Care, IEEE Computer Society Press, New York, pp. 292–295.

Masarie, F. E., Jr., Miller, R. A., & Myers, J. D. (1985). INTERNIST-I Properties: Representing common sense and good medical practice in a computerized medical knowledge base. *Computers and Biomedical Research, 18,* 458–479.

Mazoué, J. G. (1990). Diagnosis without doctors. *Journal of Medicine and Philosophy, 15,* 559–579.

McDonald, C. J., Hui, S. L., Smith, D. M., Tierney, W. M., Cohen, S. J., Weinberger, M., & McCabe, G. P. (1984). Reminders to physicians from an introspective computer medical record. *Annals of Internal Medicine, 100,* 130–138.

Miller, R. A., Pople, H. E., Jr., & Myers, J. D. (1982). INTERNIST-I, an experimental computer-based diagnostic consultant for general internal medicine. *New England Journal of Medicine, 317,* 468–476.

Miller, R. A. (1984a). INTERNIST-I/CADUCEUS: Problems facing expert consultant programs. *Methods of Information in Medicine, 23,* 9–14.

Miller, P. L. (1984b). A critiquing approach to expert computer advice: ATTENDING. Boston: Pittman.

Miller, R. A., Schaffner, K. F., & Meisel, A. (1985). Ethical and legal issues related to the use of computer programs in clinical medicine. *Annals of Internal Medicine, 102,* 529–536.

Miller, R. A., McNeil, M. A., Challinor, S. M., Masarie, F. E., Jr., & Myers, J. D. (1986). The INTERNIST-I/Quick Medical Reference Project: Status report. *Western Journal of Medicine, 145,* 816–822.

Miller, R. A., & Masarie, F. E., Jr. (1989). Use of the Quick Medical Reference (QMR) program as a tool for medical education. *Methods of Information in Medicine, 28,* 340–345.

Miller, R. A., & Masarie, F. E., Jr. (1990). The demise of the Greek Oracle model for medical diagnostic systems. *Methods of Information in Medicine, 29,* 1–2.

Miller, R. A. (1990). Why the standard view is standard: People, not machines, understand patients' problems. *Journal of Medicine and Philosophy, 15,* 581–591.

Parker, R. C., & Miller, R. A. (1987). Using causal knowledge to create simulated patient cases: The CPCS project as an extension of INTERNIST-I. Proceedings of the Eleventh Annual Symposium on Computer Applications in Medical Care, (pp. 473–480). New York: IEEE Computer Society Press.

Patil, R. S., Szolovits, P., & Schwartz, W. B. (1982). Modeling knowledge of the patient in acid-base and electrolyte disorders. In P. Szolovits (Ed.), *Artificial intelligence in medicine* (AAAS Symposium Series, no. 51). (pp. 191–226). Boulder, CO: Westview Press.

Pople, H. E., Jr. (1982). Heuristic methods for imposing structure on ill-structured problems: The structuring of medical diagnosis. In P. Szolovits (Ed.), *Artificial Intelligence in Medicine* (AAAS Symposium Series, no. 51), (pp. 119–190). Boulder, CO: Westview Press.

Scherrer, J. R. (1990). Personal communication. Geneva, Switzerland, May 1990.

Shortliffe, E. H. (1976). *Computer-based consultations: MYCIN,* New York: American Elsevier.

Tierney, W. M., Miller, M. E., & McDonald, C. J. (1990). The effect on test ordering of informing physicians of the charges for outpatient diagnostic tests. *New England Journal of Medicine, 322*(21), 1499–1504.

Voytovich, A. E., Rippey, R. M., & Suffredini, A. (1985). Premature conclusions in diagnostic reasoning. *Journal of Medical Education 60,* 302–307.

Warner, H. R., Haug, P., Bouhaddou, O., Lincoln, M., Warner, H., Jr., Sorensen, D., Williamson, J. W., & Fan, C. (1988). ILIAD as an expert consultant to teach differential diagnosis. Proceedings of the Twelfth Annual Symposium on Computer Applications in Medical Care, (pp. 371–376). New York: IEEE Computer Society Press.

Yu, V. L., Fagan, L. A., Bennet, S. W., Wraith, S. M., Clancey, W. J., Scott, A. C., Hannigan, M. S., Blurn, R. L., Buchanan, B. G., & Cohen, S. N. (1979). Antimicrobial selection by a computer: A blinded evaluation by infectious disease experts. *Journal of the American Medical Association, 242,* 1279–1282.

Yu, V. L. (1983). Conceptual obstacles in computerized medical diagnosis. *Journal of Medicine and Philosophy, 8,* 67–75.

Rejoinder to Dr. Miller

JAMES G. MAZOUÉ

In the eighteenth and nineteenth centuries the introduction of new techniques of clinical investigation, such as percussion and auscultation, initially met with skepticism and resistance. The stethoscope, now standard issue in the armamentarium of medical practitioners, was viciously lampooned in medical journals as a device that would dehumanize the physician-patient relationship. Today a similar skepticism concerning the role of automated diagnostic systems threatens to forestall the development of technological innovations that could revolutionize health care.

What is at issue is not whether physician-based diagnosis should be *immediately* abolished and replaced with automated systems. The issue, rather, is whether we should allow future research to be bound by needlessly restrictive assumptions about the diagnostic capabilities of automated systems. By dismissing an interest in pursuing the strong thesis as a viable research goal, Miller and other supporters of the standard view advocate a position that imposes unfounded methodological constraints on what should be left as a matter for vigorous empirical investigation. The failure to produce automated systems that could effectively replace humans *as diagnosticians* may very well turn out to be a self-fulfilling prophesy if those who are currently involved in the research and development of diagnostic decision support systems adopt the weak thesis as a working hypothesis built into their assumptions about the inherent limitations of automated diagnostic systems. To the extent that the outcome of future research will be determined by researchers' present assumptions, progress could be unduly impeded if what are only tractable limitations are prematurely classified as intractable. We should not let a hasty and uncritical acceptance of the weak thesis bias our assessments of the validity of embarking on projects that go beyond the limited parameters of current research prototypes.

It would appear, however, that just such a peremptory conclusion has already been reached by Miller and others involved in the design of computer-based medical diagnostic decision support systems. This is unfortunate because they have yet to make a convincing case against the strong thesis. It is one thing to accept Miller's claim that current prototypes fall short of the clinical diagnostic skills of human practitioners. It is quite another, however, to conclude that this in any way demonstrates that the diagnostic reasoning capabilities of human practitioners are an indispensable feature of medical practice.

We might just find out that the acceptance of physician-centered medicine is as unfounded as a geocentric world view. Just as Copernicus radically transformed our conception of the solar system by showing the inadequacy of a humanocentric view of the universe, might not computer diagnosis revolutionize medical practice by displacing physicians from their time-honored role as diagnostic decision makers? We shall never know the answer to this question if proponents of the standard view prevail. The only way we shall ever find out is if researchers take the strong thesis seriously enough to test it by pushing automated diagnostic systems to their theoretical and practical limits.

DEBATE 5

Is Primary Prevention the Best Use of Funds Allocated for Mental Health Intervention?

Arguing YES are George W. Albee, Ph.D., and Kimberly D. Ryan-Finn. Dr. Albee is Professor Emeritus at the University of Vermont. He is past President of the American Psychological Association (1969–1970) and is the founder and President of the Vermont Conference on Primary Prevention of Psychopathology (VCPPP). He chaired the Task Panel on Prevention for President Carter's Commission on Mental Health and was a member of the Commission of Prevention of the National Mental Health Association. Professor Albee has published extensively in the area of primary prevention for the past thirty years.

Kimberly Ryan-Finn was named Honorary Undergraduate Fellow of the New England Psychological Association in 1991 and graduated summa cum laude from the University of Vermont. She is the Conference Coordinator for the 1993 Vermont Conference on Primary Prevention of Psychopathology. Her research and writing has focused on the identification and prevention of child sexual abuse. Her honors thesis examined the protocols for reporting suspected child sexual abuse in Vermont elementary schools. Ms. Ryan-Finn is the coauthor with George Albee of "An Overview of Primary Prevention" (*Journal of Counseling and Development,* in press) and "Prospects for Primary Prevention in the American Indian Population" (APA Task Force report on American Indian Mental Health).

Arguing NO is Jack G. Wiggins, Jr., Ph.D., a member of the National Academies of Practice. Dr. Wiggins is centennial President of the American Psychological Association and is well known for his leadership in obtaining access to psychotherapy for the public through freedom of choice laws. He is the founder of the Psychological Development Center, an interdisciplinary group serving primarily working and middle class populations. He has been a prime mover in obtaining psychological services for the medically indigent in Medicaid, the vocationally impaired through the federal Vocational Rehabilitation Act, and the physically and mentally impaired in Workers Compensation programs.

YES

GEORGE W. ALBEE AND KIMBERLY D. RYAN-FINN

Reducing the Incidence of Mental Disorders

If we are to avoid an endless treadmill of treatment, with all the problems associated with insufficient numbers of therapists and overwhelming numbers of people in distress, we must shift our priorities and expand efforts at the primary prevention of mental and emotional disorders. It is well-established public health doctrine, proven repeatedly, that no mass disorder afflicting humankind has ever been eliminated, or even brought under control, by attempts at treating affected individuals. Elimination, or significant reductions, of the great plagues that have afflicted humanity over the centuries continues to emphasize the critical point: prevention succeeds, treatment fails, in reducing incidence. This fact is not clearly understood by many persons in the fields of both health and mental health. High-technology medical intervention continues to be featured in the popular press. Kidney transplants, artificial hearts, baboon hearts, and promising cures for all kinds of diseases and disorders are constantly presented to the public as the best way of spending health care dollars. Since the early 1980s this trend has been increasingly apparent in the mental health field as well. Unfortunately, stories of the effective forms of public health intervention and successful primary prevention programs do not carry the same exciting appeal, because in public health and prevention successes, no one knows who has been saved.

The strategies of primary prevention of mental and emotional disorders are essentially the same as the strategies of prevention of physical illness and disease. One of the effective strategies is to *discover the noxious agent* and take steps to eliminate it or reduce it. A second strategy is to *strengthen the resistance of the host* to the noxious agent. In the field of mental health the noxious agent frequently is excessive stress. Often the stress results from powerlessness, exploitation, poverty, and hopelessness. Strengthening the resistance of the host can involve building a greater degree of social competencies in high-risk groups or improving self-esteem, or providing support systems and networks.

Unfortunately, too many of the recent primary prevention programs have focused exclusively on individual resistance to stressors at the expense of societal reforms, and some programs would be more aptly viewed as early intervention. For instance, a review of the current primary prevention literature on child sexual abuse points to the increasing popularity of victim-focused programs that teach children to recognize and escape sexually abusive situations. Clearly, this preparation serves only to shorten the sexually abusive occurrence. True prevention must focus instead on the factors that predispose individuals to the emotional and psychological disorders that can lead to aggression and abuse (e.g., stress, deficient parenting skills, confusion and discomfort regarding sexuality, unemployment). Many of the primary prevention strategies require educational reform, redistribution of social power, and a reduction in societal exploitation and victimization (Ryan-Finn, 1992).

The Futility of Individual Treatment

One of the popular career choices currently for young professionals-to-be is the field of counseling, psychotherapy, or case work. Graduate programs in clinical psychology, the new professional schools of psychology, and training programs in social work are all busy preparing people to be one-to-one therapists. Gurus of the middle-brow culture (like Ann Landers) regularly recommend individual help for people with relationship problems. The suburbs of America have more and more visible signs advertising the private offices of psychotherapists. Despite the growing numbers of individual therapists, the problem of getting help to people who most need it seems insurmountable. Kiesler and Morton (1987) have done a careful study of the availability of therapists for people with mental and emotional problems. They established with great clarity and precision the unbridgeable gap between the small number of professionals available to treat and the large numbers needing treatment. Those with the most serious mental and emotional problems (the poor) are not covered by health insurance and cannot afford therapy. One of the major barriers is the length of time (in number of visits) demanded by mental and emotional sufferers. This has led insurance companies and other third-party payers to try to reduce or eliminate mental health services from health care coverage. New corporations offering to provide mental health coverage to insured groups have stressed a strictly limited number of office visits and resistance to hospitalization and have recruited modestly trained therapists who will accept lower fees. In spite of all these restrictions the cost of providing mental health intervention threatens to overwhelm health care coverage.

It is also an incontrovertible fact that the groups with the most prevalent mental health problems are those least likely to avail themselves of psychotherapy. The group in the United States with the highest rate of emotional disturbances is the five million migrant farm workers (Task Panel on Migrant and Seasonal Farmworkers, 1978). Larson, Doris and Alvarez (1990) found that as a group migrant workers also had significantly higher rates of reported child abuse than the general population or even nonmigrant groups of the same socioeconomic status. Indeed, a body of research suggests that exposure to such abject conditions as chronic poverty, social isolation, inadequate education, and weak cultural ties, common in exploited groups such as migrant farm workers, increases the risk of all forms of psychopathology including child abuse and neglect (Galston, 1964; Garbarino, 1976). Therapeutic intervention can do little to alleviate the effects of these stressors, and it will never reduce the incidence of psychopathology in this and other have-not groups (such as inner-city minorities, Native Americans, Alaskan natives, and Hispanics). In fact, it is useless to speak of the efficacy of therapeutic intervention when these groups are simply not covered for treatment despite their high levels of emotional distress. Recent surveys (Mays and Albee, 1992; Albee and Ryan-Finn, [in press]) make clear the unavailability of treatment for minority groups. (The same thing can be said of millions of poverty level Anglo-Saxon people living in Appalachia.)

Availability of individual treatment is also influenced by the fact that more than half of the total number of psychiatrists and psychologists are to be found in five states and the District of Columbia. There are large regions of the country where almost no mental health professionals are available. This is particularly true of such rare groups as child psychiatrists and professionals speaking Spanish, Aleut, and Navajo.

It is also clear that individual treatment of physical and mental disorders is far more costly in the long run than preventive measures. The cost of treating individuals with AIDS or cardiovascular disease far exceeds the cost of educating the public with regard to sexuality, condoms, diet, and exercise. Similarly, the price tag for treating infants born prematurely, infants born to drug-addicted mothers, and infants with preventable birth defects currently strains an already overburdened medical system. In the mental health field the crisis is no less severe, and prevention is equally effective. An illustrative example of the cost differential in treating versus preventing emotional and psychological disorders can be seen in the results of the High Scope/Perry Preschool Program (Schweinhart & Weikart, 1988). At age nineteen the children exposed to this prevention program were less likely to be on welfare, to be classified as mentally retarded, to drop out of school, or to be arrested; and they were more likely to be literate, to be employed, and to attend college than their cohorts in a control group. Furthermore, a cost-benefit analysis revealed that this prevention program would save taxpayers $28,000 per child over the nineteen-year period due to the reduction in intervention services at an original cost of $5,000 per child.

Epidemiology of Disorders

We know that distress is far more common (85%) in persons below the national median income level (Mirowsky & Ross, 1989). We know that the rates of schizophrenia, alcoholism, drug abuse, delinquency, mental retardation, lead poisoning, premature and damaged infants, and so forth are associated with poverty and minority status. Every immigrant group who occupied for a time the lowest rung on the socioeconomic scale had the highest rates of ''idiocy and lunacy.'' In turn, the Irish, the Scandinavians, the Russia Jews, and the Italians (and currently, the Blacks, Puerto Ricans, Chicanos, and Native Americans) have had high rates of children with school learning problems and of adults with severe mental and emotional disorders. But as each group in turn made it into the economically more secure middle class their rates declined dramatically (Albee, 1986).

In 1986 the United States Secretary of Health Task Force on Black and Minority Health (Heckler, 1986) reiterated many of these same facts, although many indicators of both health and mental health have grown worse. This Task Force found that among African-Americans, approximately 42 percent to 47 percent of total deaths were calculated to be excess deaths. Accidental death and homicide made up some 35 percent of these excess deaths in African-Americans under the age of forty-five years, and 19 percent in the under seventy group. Although not quite so high, a similar pattern was found for Hispanics, and the situation was more ominous for Native Americans. No other cause of mortality so clearly differentiated African-Americans from other Americans as did homicide. Although, technically, homicide is often reported in the health context, the prevention of violence and altering the nature of violence clearly also fall within the realm of psychological intervention.

Healthy People 2000 (1990) cites a whole range of data supporting the decline in the health and mental health of most ethnic minorities. African-Americans have significantly higher rates of coronary deaths; African-American women, Hispanic women, Native American women, and men with high blood pressure (mostly African-American men) were reported to have a high prevalence of obesity from poor diets. Motor vehicle crash deaths are startlingly higher among Native American men, and cirrhosis of the liver is high among this group as well as African-American males. Heavy use of alcohol and other drugs is also more common among ethnic minorities. Premature pregnancy, usually unplanned, is especially high among African-American and Hispanic adolescent girls. Overall infant mortality, fetal deaths, maternal mortality, low birth weight infants, and failure to thrive infants all affect minority groups disproportionately, often because of the failure to receive any prenatal care. African-American women and Hispanic women are also less likely to receive breast exams, mammograms, or pap tests. Smoking during pregnancy, which results in more fetal deaths and lower birth weight, is more common among ethnic minorities, as is the use of smokeless tobacco. In addition, growth is retarded among low-income children and is much more common among African-American, Hispanic, Asian, and Pacific Islander children. Without question, chronic disabling conditions (mental and physical) and reduced life expectancy are problems associated with ethnic minorities' status in the United States.

The Evidence Supporting Primary Prevention

One of the most common arguments advanced against efforts at primary prevention holds that "there is no evidence that it works." This statement invariably comes from someone unfamiliar with the literature that has accumulated over the past twenty-five years. Ample evidence of the effectiveness of primary prevention in reducing the incidence of mental and emotional disorders is available to anyone interested in reading the literature. A detailed review in the *Annual Review of Psychology* (Kessler & Albee, 1975) covered prevention efforts up to that time. The carefully composed Report of the Task Panel on Prevention of the President's (Carter) Commission on Mental Illness (1978) reviews subsequent evidence that primary prevention works. The Report of the National Mental Health Association's Commission on Prevention (1986), chaired by Beverly Long, includes testimony about effective prevention at various levels of life span development. The published final report is a model of organization and clarity. A companion volume contains the verbatim papers prepared for the Commission by the experts who testified.

There are now seventeen volumes summarizing primary prevention programs published by the Vermont Conference on Primary Prevention of Psychopathology. The five Prevention Centers established by the National Institute of Mental Health have all produced voluminous reports on effective prevention programs. A number of states (e.g., Michigan, California, Georgia, Virginia) have active statewide prevention programs with carefully evaluated results. The American Psychological Association has published *Fourteen Ounces of Prevention* (see Price, Cowen, Lorain, & Ramos-McKay, 1989) and the *American Journal of Community Psychology* has a special issue edited by Emory Cowen (1982) detailing prevention programs that work. In short, the evidence is clear for those that want to find it.

Opposition to Prevention

Opposition to efforts at primary prevention comes from several groups. The first of these are the clinicians who subscribe to the common illusion that eventually we will have enough therapists to reach everyone through individual treatment. The facts are sufficiently clear to refute this notion, but many of these people apparently have not considered all the facts.

A second source of opposition is from political conservatives who argue strongly that all mental and emotional disorders are biological or genetic. These conservatives have been in control of the federal mental health agencies for well over a decade. Indeed, they have declared the 1990s to be the "Decade of the Brain" during which time, they predict, will be found the organic causes of most forms of mental disorders—all inside people's heads. Conservatives greatly favor an "inside the skin" explanation of people's mental problems, for this means that nothing has to be done about injustice, discrimination, sexism, racism, and other social causes of distress.

Understandably, too, most people attracted to the field of one-to-one intervention were self-selected originally to be interested in the highly visible mainstream activities of one-to-one therapy. The history and kinds of intervention that characterize the field of public health are simply not available or visible to most college students and fledgling mental health workers. The appeal of psychotherapy, or of psychiatric drug treatment, is far more visible than public health approaches, so understandably a large proportion of people in the field are uninformed, uninterested, and even resistant to the prevention message. This situation is changing. Social work has a long history, since Jane Addams—particularly in the Settlement Houses and in Community Organization—to concentrate on prevention approaches. Community psychology, while always underfunded, still attracts a goodly number of dedicated social change agents. The clarity and logic of primary prevention eventually will disburse the confusion and obfuscation of the conservative leaders of the present day mainstream.

However, it is quite clear that the improvements in community mental health that occurred in the 1960s and 1970s were not carried over into the decades of the 1980s and 1990s. The safety nets were removed after 1980. The sharp increase in the number of homeless and the growing numbers of persons classified as poor show that things have only gotten worse. In addition, it is obvious that there are significantly higher rates of psychopathology, poor health, and early death among ethnic minorities, particularly those who are poor and powerless. Inasmuch as we have evidence that these forms of pathology could be prevented with adequate diet, health care, and decent jobs, it seems fair to ask whether this whole situation may not reflect a subtle form of genocide.

References

Albee, G. W. (1986). Advocates and adversaries of prevention. In M. Kessler & S. E. Goldston (Eds.), *A decade of progress in primary prevention* (pp. 309–332). Hanover, NH: University Press of New England.

Albee, G. W., & Ryan-Finn, K. D. (in press). An overview of primary prevention. *Journal of Counseling and Development.*

Cowen, E. L. (Ed.). (1982). Research in primary prevention in mental health [Special issue]. *American Journal of Community Psychology, 10*(3).

Galdston, R. (1965). Observations on children who have been physically abused and their parents. *American Journal of Psychiatry, 122,*(4), 440–443.

Garbarino, J. (1976). A preliminary study of some ecological correlates of child abuse: The impact of socioeconomic stress on mothers. *Child Development, 47*(1), 178–185.

Healthy People 2000. (1990). (Report of the Public Health Service, U.S. Department of Health and Human Services). Washington, DC: U.S. Government Printing Office.

Heckler, M. M. (1986). *Report of the Secretary's Task Force on Black and minority health.* (Publication of U.S. Department of Health and Human Services). Washington, DC: U.S. Government Printing Office.

Kessler, M., & Albee, G. W. (1975). Primary prevention. In M. R. Rosenzweig and L. W. Porter (Eds.), *Annual Review of Psychology.* Volume 2 (pp. 557–591). Palo Alto, CA: Annual Review.

Kiesler, C. A., & Morton, T. (1987). Responsible public policy in a rapidly changing world. *Clinical Psychologist, 40*(2), 28–31.

Larson, O. W., Doris, J., & Alvarez, W. F. (1990). Migrants and maltreatment: Comparative evidence from central register data. *Child Abuse & Neglect, 14,* 375–385.

Mays, V. M., & Albee, G. W. (1992). Psychotherapy and ethnic minorities. In D. K. Freedheim (Ed.), *History of psychotherapy: A century of change* (pp. 552–570). Washington, DC: American Psychological Association.

Mirowsky, J., & Ross, C. E. (1989). *Social causes of psychological distress.* New York: Aldine de Gruyter.

National Mental Health Association. (1986). *The prevention of mental-emotional disabilities. Report of the Commission on Prevention.* Alexandria, VA. Author.

Price, R. H., Cowen, E. L., Lorain, R. P., & Ramos-McKay, J. (1988). *Fourteen ounces of prevention.* Washington, DC: American Psychological Association.

Ryan-Finn, K. D. (1992). *Primary prevention of child sexual abuse: A societal issue.* Manuscript submitted for publication.

Schweinhart, L. J., & Weikart, D. P. (1988). The High/Scope Perry Preschool program. In R. H. Price, E. L. Cowen, R. P. Lorain, & J. Ramos-McKay (Eds.), *Fourteen ounces of prevention: A casebook for practitioners* (pp. 9–23). Washington, DC: American Psychological Association.

Task Panel on Migrant and Seasonal Farmworkers. (1978). *Report to the President's Commission on Mental Health.* Volume III, Appendix. Washington, DC: U.S. Government Printing Office.

Task Panel on Prevention. (1978). *Report to the President's Commission on Mental Health.* Volume IV, Appendix. Washington, DC: U.S. Government Printing Office.

Annotated Bibliography

Albee, G. W. (1985). The answer is prevention. In P. Chance and T. G. Harris (Eds.), *The best of Psychology Today* (pp. 197–202). New York: McGraw-Hill Publishing Company.

An argument for the importance of prevention over treatment, with commentary on the latest major epidemiological study of mental disorders.

Albee, G. W. (1990). The futility of psychotherapy. *The Journal of Mind and Behavior, 11*(3), 369–384 and *11*(4), 123–138.

In these articles George Albee explains why psychotherapy is an ineffective means of reducing the incidence of psychopathology. He argues that social and economic factors such as poverty, unemployment, racism, and sexism are the causal agents in many of the so-called mental illnesses and that only primary prevention leading to social change can reduce the incidence of psychopathology.

Albee, G. W., Joffe, J. M., & Dusenbury, L. A. (1988). *Prevention, powerlessness, and politics: Readings on social change.* Newbury Park, CA: Sage Publications.

This volume of readings is one of the seventeen books published in cooperation with the Vermont Conference on the Primary Prevention of Psychopathology. Primary prevention programs that facilitate the redistribution of power and the reduction of victimization are described.

Kessler, M., & Albee, G. W. (1975). Primary prevention. In M. R. Rosenzweig and L. W. Porter (Eds.), *Annual Review of Psychology.* Volume 2 (pp. 557–591). Palo Alto, CA: Annual Review.

This is the only extensive review of the prevention literature up to the early 1970s.

Price, R. H., Cowen, E. L., Lorain, R. P., & Ramos-McKay, J. (1988). *Fourteen ounces of prevention: A casebook for practitioners.* Washington, DC: American Psychological Association.

This is a well-organized casebook conceived and published by the American Psychological Association's Task Force on Prevention, Promotion and Intervention Alternatives in Psychology. It presents descriptions of effective model prevention programs that can be used by practitioners and local communities nationwide.

Rejoinder to Dr. Albee and Ms. Ryan-Finn

Jack G. Wiggins

It is surprising to have primary prevention of mental and emotional disorders justified by the means of the medical model when the senior author has argued strenuously for over a quarter century against using the medical model for psychological treatments. Nevertheless, we do agree that excessive stress is harmful to the mental health of those who otherwise function normally in everyday life. The medical concept of strengthening the resistance of the host to the noxious agents, such as stress, unfortunately results in blaming the victim and stigmatizing those who suffer mental and physical effects of stress. There is no question that socioeconomic problems such as poverty, paucity of political power, and lack of social purposefulness create stress that can lead to psychological disorders. However, psychological treatment is not designed to overcome either socioeconomic conditions or social injustices. Even though workers who receive psychotherapy tend to increase their incomes by an average of 20 percent, this will not correct poverty or overcome an economic recession (Reiss, 1967). Holding psychotherapy accountable for correcting the socioeconomic conditions causing stress does not follow the rules of logic. The authors do not explain how primary prevention of mental health conditions would correct poverty, political powerlessness, social exploitation, and other social stressors. Other sociopolitical action must be taken to modify the societal sources of stress.

The problem of access to psychological treatment is more a matter of financing or, precisely, a lack of financing, resulting from the social stigma placed on individuals who do not learn by traditional means. Individualized instruction is a generally accepted corrective intervention in the educational system; yet, when education of the public is termed "prevention," individual instruction afforded through psychotherapy is attacked as being wasteful. The problem of access to psychotherapy is not that there are insufficient counselors, as the authors assert, but rather that there are insufficient well-trained counselors. There is a growing trend for states to allow individuals with minimum credentials to be licensed to provide mental health and alcoholism services. The statutory qualifications are being lowered to provide services at lesser cost regardless of the quality of the services rendered.

Authors presenting for prevention and I agree that those who argue for a biological or genetic basis of mental conditions are content to develop new medications to address mental conditions. That these biologically oriented interventions tend to discourage preventive efforts based on an educational model is not surprising. They also tend to discount psychotherapy as well. What is not appreciated about psychotherapy either by the geneticists or behavioral preventionists is that successful psychotherapy with a parent or primary community leader has broader effects than just mental stability of that individual. The lessons learned in psychotherapy can be and are transmitted to others through a transfer of training process. Thus, advancing the mental health and psychological insights of a corporate manager can be transmitted to all those who report to that manager. The case of psychotherapeutic interventions with leaders may be tertiary in our present intervention hierarchy but is a *primary prevention* for those with whom the leader interacts. Thus, psychotherapy/prevention of mental conditions cannot be an either-or proposition, rather it must be a joint venture using the methods of both science and practice to focus on the psychological needs of our nation.

References

Reiss, B. (1967). Changes in patient income concomitant with psychotherapy. *Journal of Consulting Psychology, 31,* 130.

NO

Jack G. Wiggins, Jr.

When considering the controversy over the proper balance in allocation of funds for psychotherapy versus prevention, I am reminded of Munich's Glockenspiel clock. Each quarter hour its figures twirl to the tinkling sounds depicting a charming peasant dance designed to ward off the plague of 1517. Effective rituals used to avoid misfortunes are familiar human behaviors to psychotherapists. The concept of prevention is as appealing a concept as the forty-three bells of the clock's carillon but requires the same close scrutiny that psychotherapy receives in managed care.

The Poor Richard admonition of "an ounce of prevention is worth a pound of cure" is so embodied in our folk wisdom that it is difficult to be objective when an action plan is labeled "prevention." Interventions, whether labeled as preventive or therapeutic, are not without cost or risk. The value of interventions must be weighed against costs and risks. To the extent that prevention is not held to the same standards of cost-benefit analysis and risk assessment that therapy is, we inadvertently create a sacred cow of good intentions. Committing resources to prevention without measuring outcomes is a folly to which the Glockenspiel clock's measured tones should serve as fair warning.

It is difficult to argue psychotherapy versus prevention funding in the abstract for the terms are too imprecise to be measurable. It is necessary to have the same criteria by which both prevention and psychotherapy can be measured. The current mental health crisis in the workplace can serve as a contextual example with measurable criteria. In 1991, a group of workers were surveyed by Northwestern National Life (NWL) (Northwestern National Life, 1991). These results were compared with the 1985 National Health Interview Survey of the general population (National Center for Health Statistics, 1985). In 1985, 20 percent of the population reported feeling highly stressed. In 1991, 46 percent of the workers reported feeling highly stressed. In 1985, 13 percent of the general population reported multiple stress-related illnesses, whereas in 1991, 25 percent reported the same conditions. Thus, in a period of six years, disabling stress appears to have doubled.

The job stress data suggest that one of four workers is either receiving personal assistance for stress related problems or else is taking over-the-counter medications to reduce the effects of exhaustion, anxiety, muscle pain, headaches, inability to sleep, respiratory illness, ulcers, intestinal disorders, or depression. This frequency of stress would be considered an epidemic if these same conditions were due to some bacterium or virus. The fact that symptoms are reported due to ''mental stress'' depreciates their significance. Individuals who are unaffected tend to look at those who report these kinds of stress symptoms as being weak or suffering the consequences of imprudent behavior. Some way must be found to alleviate these conditions rather than ignoring the situation by passing judgment on those affected.

The stigmata of psychological reactions to stress require that we look at mental and emotional conditions differently from other health conditions that are not stigmatized. Psychotherapy carries the stigma of the conditions it attempts to alleviate, whereas prevention tends to be seen as a rational course of action. *Counseling* is a more acceptable term to the general public and is preferred over *psychotherapy.* Psychotherapy is even sold to corporations under the guise of prevention. For example, corporations often use stress management programs to reduce job stress as a preventive measure. Actually, these programs train people to use techniques discovered and employed in psychotherapy that have group applicability. Psychotherapy is an extremely adaptable method that allows the therapist to tailor interventions to the unique circumstances of the patient. Through psychotherapy we learn what technique works under what kind of circumstances, how long it takes, and with what degree of success. Thus, psychotherapy serves as the research laboratory for prevention.

Prevention uses a broad-gauge approach of the educational model, which applies to many but does not deal with extreme cases. With the recognition that we are experiencing a mental health crisis or epidemic in the workplace, it is only prudent to provide treatment interventions and not try to teach fire safety in a school house that is already burning. According to the NWL study, 34 percent of employees expect to ''burn out'' on the job. Seventy-two percent of all workers experienced three or more stress-related illnesses either somewhat or very often. Workers tend to hold employers responsible for stress problems. They also felt their health plan should cover stress illnesses and that individuals who were disabled because of stress were entitled to some sort of compensation. Employee assistance programs are useful in identifying highly stressed workers and dysfunctional families. However, they indicate that what is needed is more counseling services to deal with the problems at hand. Having a health benefit to reimburse psychological conditions was the single most effective method of reducing worker stress according to the NWL study.

Employers tend to look at job stress differently and make it the responsibility of the employee. Employers often feel they have fulfilled employee needs by offering stress management courses to prevent stress reactions. The question should not be whether to use preventive techniques or psychotherapeutic techniques to deal with our stress-induced psychological epidemic in the workplace. What is needed is to have psychological prevention and psychological treatment measured by the same yardstick. To do this, there must be ways of measuring stress in the workplace. It is my judgment that what is needed is a work-related psychological diagnostic system. The International Classification of Diseases 9 (ICD-9) and the *DSM-III-R* diagnostic systems are based on development patterns of psychopathology. These diagnostic methods are based on clusters of symptoms and tend to omit the stressors that may precipitate the symptom patterns of diagnosis. Until we can measure the effects of the stressors at work on worker health and productivity, we will not be able to clearly identify the causation factors that are leading to the disturbances seen in workers. When we can pinpoint these work-related stressors, we will have a means of designing jobs to simultaneously increase productivity and reduce inflated health costs.

Sauter, Murphy & Hurrell (1990) have studied stress at work and advocate that treating employee tensions at the worksite is a cost-efficient way to prevent worker stress. Manuso (1978) demonstrated a cost-benefit of three dollars of increased productivity for each dollar spent for stress intervention at work, even though the employee was already undertaking psychotherapy privately. We must stop looking at workers as simply patients but rather as victims of job stress. To better serve companies, management and workers, it is necessary for psychologists to get out of their offices and ivory towers to view firsthand the conditions of work that employees experience to provide a livelihood for themselves and their families. This means we will have to train our students to take a more global view of psychological problems in the future. A psychosocial-ecological approach of dealing with psychological problems redefines both psychotherapy and preventive efforts. A psychosocial-psychological approach can be employed only when management and unions take a portion of enlightened self-interest to obtain measurable results. As long as employees are preoccupied with their own stress-related symptoms, they do not "listen up" to educational messages. Until we can demonstrate the interaction between stressors and stress responses by large-scale psychotherapeutic studies, it will be necessary to keep focusing on the reduction of the victims of stress and see that adequate health services are available to them.

At the present time, many corporations tend to ignore the psychosocial environments that lead to higher rates of stress reactions among their workers. Managers are often inclined to find scapegoats other than the working conditions themselves to avoid their responsibility of providing adequate psychological health care benefits for workers. It is the responsibility of psychotherapists to identify the effects of stress and include the work environment as part of the treatment endeavor. To some people this may be called prevention, and to others it is merely part of the psychotherapeutic challenge. We do not serve the public well by arguing the semantics of prevention versus psychotherapy. We need to redefine our mental health mission by devising a work-related psychological diagnostic system to apply interventions to achieve the desired results at a price we can afford.

References

Manuso, J. J. S. (February, 1978). Benefits from mutual health services. The President's Commission on Mental Health. Vol. 2, Appendix. Washington, DC: Supt. of Documents, U.S. Printing Office.

National Center for Health Statistics. (1985). Health Interview Survey of the general population. Washington, DC: U.S. Department of Health and Human Services.

Northwestern National Life. (1991). Northwestern National Life survey of working Americans on workplace stress. Minneapolis: Author.

Sauter, S. L., Murphy, L. R., & Hurrell, J. J. (1990). Prevention of work-related psychological disorders. *American Psychologist, 45*(10), 1146–1158.

Rejoinder to Dr. Wiggins

George W. Albee and Kimberly D. Ryan-Finn

Our opponent does not show an understanding of the primary prevention literature. When Wiggins says "prevention . . . does not deal with extreme cases," it is clear that he does not understand that prevention deals only with people who have *not* shown any disturbance but who are known from epidemiological research to be at high risk. Furthermore, to compare prevention to Munich's clock designed to ward off the plague of 1517 also demonstrates a lack of familiarity with the history of public health. The plagues of smallpox, cholera, childbed fever, and the deadly childhood diseases have all been eliminated or greatly reduced by effective prevention programs firmly rooted in scientific interventions.

Wiggins's argument also ignores the findings of numerous prevention programs for mental and emotional disorders that have included a systematic evaluational component. The evidence for effective preventive interventions developed over the past two decades in the field of emotional disorders is readily available in the seventeen volumes of the Vermont Conference on the Primary Prevention of Psychopathology, in Cowen's (1982) special issue of the *American Journal of Community Psychology,* in APA's volume *Fourteen ounces of prevention* (Price, Cowen, Lorion, & Ramos-McKay, 1988), in the Report of the Prevention Task Force of the President's (Carter) Commission on Mental Health (1978), and in the National Mental Health Association Report from the Commission on Prevention of Mental-Emotional Disabilities (1986), to mention just a few.

The fact that we are experiencing "a mental health crisis or epidemic" is used by our opponent as an urgent argument for treatment and as an argument against teaching "fire safety (prevention) in a school house that is already burning." The point we have tried to emphasize is that one-to-one treatment has absolutely no effect on future incidence (new cases). Therefore, if our goal is to reduce the incidence of future disorders, then prevention is the only hope we have.

If we can only hope to reduce workers' stress through (health-insured) counseling then the situation is bleak indeed. Most stressed workers (to say nothing of the hourly workers, part-time workers, and the involuntarily unemployed) do not have counseling benefits. Even if the entire population had such benefits, however, nothing would change in the area of causation. To reiterate, the field of public health offers clear evidence as to the futility of treatment strategies in reducing the incidence of disease and disorder. A primary prevention program would seek to correct the major sources of work-related stress and strive to reduce unemployment.

We are unwilling to conclude with a typical compromise statement that settles for a middle ground position. Unless we devote most of our resources to prevention, we walk endlessly on a treadmill to nowhere.

References

Cowen, E. L. (Ed.). (1982). Research in primary prevention in mental health [Special issue]. *American Journal of Community Psychology, 10*(3).

Commission on Prevention of Mental-Emotional Disabilities. (1986). National Mental Health Association Report. *Journal of Primary Prevention, 7*(4), 175–241.

Price, R. H., Cowen, E. L., Lorion, R. P., & Ramos-McKay, J. (Eds.). (1988). *Fourteen ounces of prevention: A casebook for practitioners.* Washington, DC: American Psychological Association.

Task Panel on Prevention. (1978). *Report to the President's Commission on Mental Health.* Volume IV, appendix. Washington, DC: U.S. Government Printing Office.

DEBATE 6

Is Mental Illness a Cause of Homelessness?

Irwin Garfinkel says YES. He is the Mitchell I. Ginsberg Professor of Contemporary Urban Problems at the Columbia University School of Social Work. He was the Director of the Institute for Research on Poverty (1975–1980) and Director of the School of Social Work (1982–1984) at the University of Wisconsin. Professor Garfinkel is co-author with Sara McLanahan of *Single Mothers and Their Children: A New American Dilemma* and author of *Assuring Child Support: An Extension of Social Security.* He has recently begun to do research on homelessness.

James D. Wright, an author, educator, and the Charles and Leo Favrot Professor of Human Relations in the Department of Sociology at Tulane University, argues NO. After receiving his Ph.D. from the University of Wisconsin in 1973, he taught at the University of Massachusetts for fifteen years and went to Tulane University in 1988. He has written twelve books and 150 publications dealing with such topics as American politics, gun control, natural disasters, health policy, and homelessness. He is the author of *Homelessness and Health,* which received a commendation from the National Press Club. His most recent book, *Address Unknown: The Homeless in America,* is a comprehensive review and synthesis of studies on all facets of homelessness. His current research includes a large national study of firearms acquisition and use among juveniles, a three-year study of alcohol and drug treatment programs for homeless people, and a study of health problems of homeless street children in Honduras.

YES

IRWIN GARFINKEL

Mental illness is one of the causes of the current American episode of homelessness. Estimates of the proportion of the homeless who suffer from severe mental illness range from about 20 percent to 40 percent. The consensus estimate is about one-third, which means that on an average night in the early 1990s, about 200,000 to 250,000 severely mentally ill individuals are homeless (Interagency Council on the Homeless, 1992). There is no doubt that at least some of these individuals would not be homeless if it were not for their mental illness. In that sense, given the world we live in, mental illness is clearly a cause of homelessness.

On the other hand, it is easy to conceive of a world in which mental illness did not lead to homelessness. Imagine a world in which anyone who sleeps in a public place and otherwise acts in a bizarre fashion is committed to a state mental hospital. All of the homeless individuals who suffer from severe mental illness would no longer be homeless. They would be involuntarily committed patients in mental hospitals. Whether mental illness leads to homelessness therefore depends on how society provides for the mentally ill.

During the 1950s, before the advent of the deinstitutionalization of the mentally ill, the United States more closely resembled the above described imaginary world than it does now. For the most part, individuals who suffered from serious mental illness were not afforded the opportunity to become homeless. If their families were unwilling to house and care for them, they were placed in large state mental institutions. In 1955, there were 560,000 patients in state mental hospitals. As a result of deinstitutionalization, by 1969 the number had dropped to 339,000. As of 1986, there were only 111,000. (National Institute of Mental Health, 1990).

Deinstitutionalization of the mentally ill is also a cause of homelessness. For if we followed the institutionalization practices of the 1950s, the 200,000 to 250,000 severely mentally ill individuals who are now homeless would be involuntarily committed patients in large state mental hospitals.

Of course, advocates of deinstitutionalization of the mentally ill imagined a better world than the one we now inhabit. They did not assume that deinstitutionalization would lead to homelessness. When deinstitutionalization began, there was a more plentiful stock of cheap rooms in boarding houses, single room occupancy (SRO) hotels, and flophouses. Moreover, advocates envisioned a world in which mental health services would follow the mentally ill from the large state mental hospitals to local communities. What actually happened is that the costs of housing soared and the stock of SROs and flophouses declined. Mental health resources did not follow the mentally ill. And, as a consequence, deinstitutionalization, along with a diminution in the supply of cheap housing and the failure to provide adequate mental health services on the local level, led to homelessness.

So far we have argued both that (1) given the unique conditions that pertained in the United States, mental illness and deinstitutionalization led to homelessness and (2) neither mental illness nor deinstitutionalization by itself inevitably lead to homelessness. In logical terms the second argument means that neither mental illness nor deinstitutionalization is sufficient to explain homelessness. In view of the fact that the bulk of the homeless are not mentally ill, it follows that mental illness is also not a necessary condition for homelessness. If mental illness is neither a necessary nor a sufficient condition for homelessness, how can it be said to be a cause of homelessness? First, that mental illness is not the only cause of homelessness, is not to say that it is not one of the causes. Some people who never smoke get cancer. But that does not mean that smoking is not a cause of cancer. Second, that mental illness would not lead to homelessness if the world were different than it is, is not to say that given the world we live in, it did not lead to homelessness. That many people who smoke do not get cancer does not mean that smoking is not a cause of cancer. The role of mental illness and deinstitutionalization in homelessness is more than a philosophical or semantic issue. To cure homelessness we must have a clear understanding of its causes. That mental illness and deinstitutionalization of the mentally ill are implicated in the growth of homelessness suggests that services for the severely mentally ill must be a part of the solution to homelessness. To deny that the mental illness and deinstitutionalization are implicated suggests the opposite: that services for the mentally ill are unimportant to the solution of homelessness. Would anyone seriously make this argument?

References

Interagency Council on the Homeless. (1992). *Outcasts on Main Street: Report of the Federal Task Force on Homelessness and Severe Mental Illness* (p. x). Washington DC: U.S. Department of Health and Human Services.

National Institute of Mental Health. (1990). *Mental Health, United States, 1990* (p. 57, table 1.13). R. W. Manderscheid & M. A. Sonnenschein (Eds.). DHHS Pub. No. (ADM) 90–1708. Washington, DC: Superintendent of Documents, U.S. Government Printing Office.

Annotated Bibliography

Burt, M. R. (1992). *Over the edge: The growth of homelessness in the 1980's.* New York: Russell Sage Foundation.

This is a useful discussion of the numbers of homeless and a different view about the role of mental illness and deinstitutionalization in causing homelessness.

Mechanic, D., & Aiken, L. H. (1987). Improving the care of patients with chronic mental illness. *New England Journal of Medicine 317*(26), 1634–1638.

This article places homelessness among those suffering from severe mental illness within the broader context of mental health policy.

Interagency Council on the Homeless. (1992). *Outcasts on Main Street: Report of the Federal Task Force on Homelessness and Severe Mental Illness.* Washington DC: U.S. Department of Health and Human Services.

This is a very good government report on homelessness and severe mental illness.

Rossi, P. (1989). *Down and out in America: The origins of homelessness.* Chicago: The University of Chicago Press.

This is an excellent historical discussion of homelessness and the relationship between poverty and homelessness.

Rejoinder to Professor Garfinkel

JAMES D. WRIGHT

My argument that mental illness is not a cause of homelessness is not intended to deny or belittle the often profound psychiatric disabilities suffered by many homeless people. Any capable services program for the homeless must necessarily address these psychiatric difficulties. Many homeless people are also undernourished, and a capable services package would also include food. That homeless people need to eat, however, does not mean that they are homeless *because* they are hungry. Likewise, many battered women prove, on detailed examination, to be mentally ill; any program of services for battered women would, of course, include psychiatric counseling. But their need for psychiatric service surely does not imply that these women are battered *because* they are mentally ill.

It is misleading and incorrect to confuse the needs of homeless people with the reasons why they are homeless. The former are many and varied and inhere principally in the individuals involved. The latter are also many and varied—a severely restricted and still diminishing supply of low-income housing, widespread joblessness and underemployment, a "minimum" wage that is in fact a subpoverty wage, inadequate welfare provisions for the needy and dependent, and on through a long list. These factors, however, do *not* inhere in individuals but rather in the large-scale structure of the society and its economy and in specific policies of the federal government and state and local jurisdictions. In the end, the emphasis on mental illness as a cause of homelessness individualizes what is truly a *social* problem.

Psychiatric disorder is one among many disabilities that make certain people more vulnerable than others to the vicissitudes of economy, society, and polity. Alcohol and drug abuse, physical disability, estrangement from family and social networks, extreme poverty, illiteracy, and so forth are others. No sensible person would dispute these facts. But to say that people become homeless *because* of these vulnerabilities is much the same as saying that bad luck is the reason why people lose their money in Las Vegas. The *rules of the game* ensure that the house always comes out ahead—that, not bad luck, is why people lose their money. And, likewise, the rules of the housing ''game'' now ensure that some will be homeless. Finding the *causes* of homelessness requires investigation of the rules of that housing game, not further analysis of the needs, personal defects, or other characteristics of those who have crapped out.

NO

JAMES D. WRIGHT

The argument is frequently made that homelessness is largely a mental health problem, one caused in substantial measure by inadequate discharge planning during the process of deinstitutionalization and by other related changes in society's treatment of the mentally ill. The argument advanced here, instead, is that homelessness is fundamentally a housing problem and that the emphasis on mental illness as a causative factor diverts attention from more basic issues of political economy that lie at the heart of the homeless dilemma.

Supporting the view of homelessness as a mental health issue is the now commonplace finding that the rate of psychiatric disorder is sharply elevated among the homeless compared with the domiciled population. Although I do not dispute this finding in general, it must nonetheless be said that the measurement (or diagnosis) of mental illness among the homeless is a formidable challenge and that the published estimates of the rate of mental illness among the homeless vary from about 10 percent to more than 90 percent.

Estimates toward the low end of this range are usually based on the records of mental health service providers, on cases of psychiatric hospitalization, and on related archival or documentary sources of data. It is therefore important to stress that not all psychiatrically impaired people come at one or another point into the mental health care system. This may be even truer of the mentally ill homeless than of the mentally ill in general; it is almost certainly more true today, where hospitalization or institutionalization for psychiatric problems is assiduously avoided and where involuntary commitment to treatment is virtually impossible unless the person is an obvious ''danger to self or others,'' than at any previous point in the nation's history. It is also important to stress that not everyone who *does* come under care leaves a discernible or identifiable trace in agency records, especially not in outpatient or crisis intervention programs.

Estimates toward the upper end of the range cited above are usually based on some sort of diagnostic protocol contained within a larger questionnaire administered to homeless people. But many of the questions often used in these standardized assessment protocols could not in any realistic sense be construed as indicating "mental illness" within a homeless context—for example, "Do you feel unhappy about the way your life is going?" or "Do you feel discouraged and worried about your future?" or "Do you feel so tired and worn out that you cannot enjoy anything?" Nearly any *sane* homeless person would have to answer yes to all of these—not because of mental disorders but because of the material conditions of their existence. Many of the apparently "crazy," "bizarre," or "abnormal" behavioral patterns observed among the homeless are adaptations to the rigors and dangers of street or shelter existence and should not be taken as signs of psychiatric impairment.

Lay people routinely mistake coping behavior among the homeless for mental illness. Rummaging in garbage cans for something to eat would strike most people as bizarre, or "situationally inappropriate" to say the very least, but it is very sensible behavior if it is the only alternative to hunger. Urinating in public is repulsive and, again, bizarre to most, but in a nation that (unlike most civilized nations) does not routinely provide public restroom facilities, where else are the homeless to go? Lack of options accounts for as much, or more, of the apparently "crazy" behavior observed among the homeless as clinical psychiatric impairment.

Finally, concerning the inference of mental illness from a history of psychiatric hospitalization, it has become something of a truism among care providers for the homeless that the "never-institutionalized" mentally ill are now much more common that the "ever-institutionalized" mentally ill. It is often overlooked that the first waves of deinstitutionalization of the mentally ill in this country occurred in the 1950s and accelerated in the 1960s; by the middle 1970s, almost all of the people who were ever destined to be "deinstitutionalized" already had been. Homeless mentally ill persons in their twenties or early thirties are very unlikely to have been institutionalized in the first place and, therefore, equally unlikely ever to have been deinstitutionalized. Their lack of prior psychiatric treatment, however, speaks more to large-scale societal developments of the past three decades than to their level of psychiatric functioning.

Given the measurement problems to which I have alluded, what can be said with some certainty about the proportion of homeless persons who are indeed "mentally ill" in some clinically significant sense? The consensus figure that has emerged in the literature is that about a third of the homeless are chronically mentally ill. And while a one-third rate is high, indeed astonishingly high, compared to the general population, it also leaves two-thirds who are not mentally ill and whose homelessness must therefore result from other factors altogether. It is obviously misleading to suggest that homelessness is mainly a mental health problem if, in fact, the majority of the homeless are not mentally ill.

One might therefore usefully rephrase the issue and ask whether mental illness is not the cause of homelessness at least for the third who *are* mentally ill. But I believe that even this proposition is fundamentally misleading. I think it is wrong, in other words, to conclude that mentally ill homeless people are homeless because of their mental illness. The better conclusion is that many mentally ill people have housing needs that are not being adequately addressed, and they are therefore homeless.

Obviously, the housing needs of mentally ill homeless people are very different from the housing needs of other homeless persons or of the poor in general, as was recognized at the beginning of the deinstitutionalization movement. The initial plan was to provide a large network of halfway houses, supported housing options, and community-based mental health centers to address the unique needs of the deinstitutionalized population. Although deinstitutionalization itself proceeded apace, and even accelerated in subsequent decades, very little of this intended network was ever put in place. As a consequence, many former mental patients were "returned" to families and communities only to find that their families were unwilling or unable to provide for their care and that their communities lacked adequate provisions for their unique housing and other needs.

The housing problem posed by the existence of large numbers of mentally ill homeless people is that the current supply of supported transitional and extended-care housing for the mentally disturbed is insufficient or, in many places, simply nonexistent; the absence of an ample supply of such housing is exactly why so many mentally ill people are homeless in the first place.

The housing problems faced by the mentally ill homeless cannot be addressed by the simple expedient of more flophouses or public housing projects. Adequate housing for this group requires on-site supportive social and psychiatric services, and since few could afford to pay rent, the necessary subsidies would be deep ones. These points, of course, only specify the nature of the housing problem that mentally ill homeless people face; they do not imply that people are homeless because of their mental illness.

Stated simply, people do not become homeless just because they are mentally ill. Mentally ill people become homeless because housing that satisfactorily meets their needs is in very short supply and because they do not have sufficient financial resources to translate their evident needs into a housing demand that would stimulate additions to the supply. In the absence of capable advocacy and case management, the homeless mentally ill fall easily through the cracks—and the housing "crack" is one that they have fallen through in distressingly large numbers. It is, of course, correct to say that the mentally ill homeless require more than just housing, but it is also correct to say that the absence of acceptable housing lies at the base of their problems.

Indeed, it is a fair judgment that until the housing situations of homeless mentally ill persons are stabilized, efforts to address their many other problems will be largely fruitless. By themselves, counseling, therapy, and psychotropic medication cannot compensate for the psychic anguish and mental disordering that results from life on the streets. The point is that in the absence of acceptable housing options along the lines sketched above, we cannot even adequately address the mental health problems of the homeless mentally ill, much less their housing, financial, and other problems.

Homeless people themselves readily identify the lack of housing and money as the source of their troubles. Ball and Havassy (1984) asked a sample of mentally disturbed homeless people in San Francisco to identify "the most important issues you face or problems you have trying to make it in San Francisco or generally in life." The most common responses had nothing to do with mental health services, crisis intervention, or psychiatric counseling. The leading responses, rather, were "no place to live indoors" (mentioned by 94%), followed by "no money" (mentioned by 88%). No other response was chosen by as much as half the sample.

Housing and money are by no means the only problems homeless mentally ill people face. Many of the homeless mentally ill are also chemically dependent, some are physically disabled, and most are profoundly estranged from family and friends. And, of course, they are among the poorest of the poor, surviving on a mere fraction of the poverty-level income in most cases. These characteristics are of critical importance in specifying exactly what kind of housing problem homelessness is, but they do not negate the principal conclusion: that the most fundamental need, even among the mentally ill, is for housing.

The last decade has witnessed a virtual decimation in the low-income housing supply and a sharp increase in the urban poverty population. Data reported by Wright and Lam (1987) have shown that in a sample of twelve of the nation's twenty largest cities, the poverty population *increased* by 36 percent between the late 1970s and the early 1980s. In the same period, the supply of low income housing *decreased* by 30 percent. Given these facts, it was inevitable that the trend lines would cross, sooner or later, or in other words, that a time would come when there were more poor people than housing for them. The rise of the "new homeless" is a direct and largely indisputable consequence of these structural developments. Rephrased, it is quite clear that the nation would now be facing a very serious homelessness problem *even if* there were no mentally ill people, no alcohol or drug abuse, indeed, no personal "pathologies" of any sort.

The general trends in the political economy of the country, in short, have created a housing "game" that increasing numbers are predestined to lose. That point alone, however, says little or nothing about who, specifically, loses at the game; and it would be remarkable indeed if the "losers" turned out to be anyone other than the most vulnerable segments of the urban poverty population. It is also true that there are many different vulnerabilities that might cause one to compete poorly for a dwindling supply of housing and, surely, mental illness is prominent among them. But to conclude that people are homeless because of their mental illness is to mistake the characteristics of the losers for the nature of the game itself.

References

Ball, J. F., & Havassy, B. E. (1984). A survey of the problems and needs of homeless consumers of acute psychiatric services. *Hospital and Community Psychiatry 35,* 917–921.

Wright, J. D., & Lam, J. (Spring, 1987). Homelessness and the low income housing supply. *Social Policy 17*(4), 48–53.

Annotated Bibliography

Interagency Council on the Homeless. (1992). Report of the Federal Task Force on Homelessness and Severe Mental Illness. *Outcasts on Main Street.* Washington DC: U.S. Department of Health and Human Services.

Mental illness is the most heavily researched aspect of the homeless problem, and so the research literature on the topic is truly vast. An exceptionally useful overview is provided in this report.

Wright, J. D., & Rubin, B. A. (1991). Is homelessness a housing problem? *Housing Policy Debate 2*(3), 937–956; see also the Wright and Lam reference.

This article provides a more extended analysis of homelessness as a housing problem.

Burt, M. R. (1992). *Over the edge: The growth of homelessness in the 1980s.* New York: Russell Sage Foundation.

The stunning increase in homelessness in the 1980s is documented and analyzed in this book. Burt points out that while mental illness is widespread among the homeless, it is difficult to maintain that the increasing number of the homeless in the 1980s was the result of an increasing rate of psychiatric disability in the at-risk population.

Rejoinder to Dr. Wright

Irwin Garfinkel

Although Professor Wright and I are arguing the opposite sides of the proposition that "mental illness is a cause of homelessness," our agreements should not be overlooked. With respect to facts, we agree that about one-third of the homeless are severely mentally ill.

Professor Wright argues that the major cause of homelessness is the intersection of two economic trends: (1) a decline in real incomes at the bottom of the income distribution and (2) an increase in rents at the bottom of the housing market. Even if there were no mentally ill individuals, a continuation of these two trends was bound to produce homelessness at some point. I agree. And, if I had written on his side of the debate I would have made this point. With respect to the overall problem of homelessness, it is the most important point to keep in mind.

Finally, Professor Wright and I agree that the solution to homelessness among severely mentally ill individuals must involve a combination of special housing and services.

Where Professor Wright and I disagree is with respect to the narrower question of whether mental illness is a cause of homelessness. If we miraculously rid individuals who suffer from severe mental illness of their mental illness, homelessness would decline. For surely the distribution of capabilities of the population as well as the levels of incomes and rents determines the levels of homelessness within the population. If the homeless who suffer from severe mental illness were no longer mentally ill, they would be more capable of earning enough to afford housing. If they couldn't find work, they would be more capable of amicably sharing a residence with family or friends. To deny these facts is to deny that severe mental illness incapacitates.

DEBATE 7

Is the Emphasis on Genetics Distorting our Approaches to Mental Disorders?

YES argues Jill Littrell. Dr. Littrell received her M.S.S.W. from the University of Wisconsin at Madison in 1972 and her Ph.D. from Arizona State University in 1981. She has been employed as a social worker in a state hospital system, as a clinician at CIGNA Health Plan's Alcohol and Drug Dependency Department, and as a child protective services worker. In 1991, she published a two-volume work on alcoholism. She has taught at Arizona State University's School of Social Work and is currently on the faculty at Georgia State University in Atlanta.

Rita B. Black says NO. Dr. Black, M.S., D.S.W., is an Associate Professor at Columbia University School of Social Work. Her graduate training was in both genetic counseling and social work. She has written and conducted research on the psychosocial impact of reproductive genetic and infertility technology on women and couples, collaboration between professionals and consumers in the delivery of genetic services, and the impact of chronic illnesses and disabilities on families.

YES

JILL LITTRELL

The emphasis on genetics is distorting our approaches to mental disorders. This is not because genetic information is inherently misleading. Rather, the problem stems from a specific set of improper inferences that are sometimes gleaned from the genetic findings. The unwarranted inferences from this area of research are the following:

1. Genes exert an ineluctable influence in the development of a disorder. The physical process underlying the disorder is fixed by events happening at conception.
2. Since the genes produce protein products that influence the occurrence and rate of chemical reactions, the best approach to altering the process dictated by the gene products is through some type of chemical intervention.
3. Because the occurrence of a mental disorder is determined by genetic events, neither the individual manifesting a disorder nor that individual's environment can be held accountable (i.e., made to feel guilty) for the occurrence of the disorder.

It will be argued here that none of the above implications necessarily follow from the empirical findings supporting the genetic case.

Twin, adoption, and genetic linkage studies are the paradigms that are presently used to support a genetic basis for a disorder. Unfortunately, these paradigms supply no information about the mechanism through which genes provide a diathesis increasing the probability of the emergence of a disorder. Without knowledge of the mechanism it is impossible to know whether environmental factors could override the genetic predisposition. A cogent illustration is available. Albino rats are genetically predisposed to behave in a neurotic fashion. When placed in an open field, the albino rats defecate more often, hover more, and explore less. The basis for the apparent neurosis does not reside in neuronal structural abnormalities of the albino rats, nor is it attributable to differential rates of neurotransmitter production or hormonal influences. What might have looked like a temperament difference or a neurosis gene is in fact a light-sensitivity issue. When fitted with the proper spectacles (red tinted ones), the albino rats no longer behave in a neurotic fashion (Plomin, DeFries, & McClearn, 1990, p. 54). A genetic problem, in this case, has an environmental solution.

Only when the mechanism through which genes influence the occurrence of a particular behavior disorder is known will it be possible to estimate the extent to which volitional action and environmental influences can moderate the mechanism. For example, although hereditary factors in alcoholism are suggested by the research, the nature of the mechanism by which increased consumption is mediated has not been identified. Perhaps alcohol provides a more exciting, pleasurable experience for the genetically predisposed? This enhanced pleasure could be attributable to differences in brain structure or differences in the rate of chemical process occurring in the central nervous system. Or, as an alternative explanation, perhaps the genetically predisposed, when sober, are in a more uncomfortable state than are the nonpredisposed and therefore have a greater need to escape from or alter their normal level of functioning. As a third possibility, perhaps the genetically predisposed do not experience greater pleasure when they drink, nor do they differ from others in terms of the subjective quality of their sober states, but rather they are less able to experience danger or alarm. Because they do not experience alarm, they would not have a built-in deterrent when acting in a fashion that could have potential deleterious consequences. These three possible scenarios through which genetic products might exert an influence on the emergence of crapulous consumption imply differing intervention strategies. Further, the magnitude of the compulsion toward the expression of the disorder may vary among the pathways. When the mechanism toward drinking specified by the genetic recipe is illuminated, it is possible that volitional behavior could be identified capable of counteracting or overriding the genetic mechanism.

It might be argued by those who do research in population genetics that the extent to which environment can override or ameliorate the genetic recipe can be estimated by their research. It is true that population genetic studies can sometimes provide an estimate of the proportion of variance accounted for by genetics, by environmental factors that are shared by siblings, and by environmental factors that are encountered outside the home environment. It is well to remember, however, that these studies provide an estimate of the influence of environmental factors and genetic factors as they operated in determining the phenomenon under investigation *in the particular study* (Plomin et al., 1990, p. 365–366). The findings from any specific study can offer misleading information on potential relative influences of environment or heredity. An example will help to make this difficult point clear.

Phenylketonuria (PKU) is a type of retardation that has a genetic basis. Those exhibiting PKU have a single genetic mutation on a chromosome. They do not have the nucleotide blueprint that specifies the production of phenylalanine-hydroxylase, the enzyme that converts the amino acid phenylalanine to tyrosine. Without the converting enzyme, phenylalanine accumulates in the brain where it destroys tissue. Since discovery of the mechanism by which genes contribute to PKU, the practice of limiting the consumption of phenylalanine in the diet has developed for those known to lack the enzyme. Retardation is no longer inevitable. Thus, an environmental practice was identified that could override the impact of the gene.

With knowledge of the mechanism, it is retrospectively possible to consider the results of how outcomes in population genetic studies might have varied depending on the range of environmental variables represented in the study. Within the context of the American culture, in which phenylalanine is a component of the standard diet of every American, genetic factors would emerge as large determiners of the occurrence of PKU. However, were the consumption of phenylalanine to vary dramatically across particular home environments, which themselves vary with sociocultural and economic factors, then a population genetics study of PKU might suggest that environmental factors were very important determiners of the phenomenon. Most studies estimating the impact of heredity and environment on the emergence of a phenomenon use samples for which the represented range of environmental variables are limited. It is therefore difficult, and in some cases impossible, to determine the potential impact of environmental factors. The fact that the percentage of variation attributable to heredity versus environmental effects can only be estimated as it occurs for the particular subjects in the particular study may explain some rather puzzling findings. For example, the magnitude of the influence of genes on intelligence has been found to vary across cultures (Plomin et al., 1990, p. 302).

An additional unwarranted conclusion from the fact that heredity is a contributing factor in the emergence of a disorder is the belief that chemical interventions are implied by support for genetics. A genetic basis does imply that chemicals are somehow involved in the expression of a phenomenon. However, the conclusion that a chemical intervention is appropriate, from the recognition of a genetic disorder, can be a non sequitur. There are genetically determined problems for which chemicals are ineffective. For example, Down syndrome generally does not respond to chemical intervention. Conversely, there are environmentally caused problems for which chemical intervention might be useful. Post-Traumatic Stress Disorder (PTSD) illustrates how environmental stress can be sufficiently severe to disrupt an individual's physiology and chemical reactions. Psychotropic medications can ameliorate the symptoms of PTSD. Thus, there are environmentally induced problems that can be ameliorated by medications. Some genetic problems are refractory to medications. There is no necessary connection between the etiology of a problem and the classes of potential strategies for treating the problem.

There is a second lack of association as well. It might be argued that if an individual is known to have a chemical imbalance, regardless of etiology, chemical interventions constitute the best treatment for this imbalance. This is also untrue. Brain chemicals as well as chemicals elsewhere in the body respond to behavioral manipulations. In rats, exposure to particular types of learning paradigms can turn on the genes for particular chemical products (Plomin et al., 1990). Stress can activate hormonal release. Although provision of exogenous chemicals can also influence body chemistry, environmental manipulation is an alternative pathway. In each particular case, evaluation of which pathway constitutes the more pragmatic intervention is necessary.

Particular chemicals can influence behavior in all persons whether the behavior in question has a genetic basis or some other type of etiology. Chemicals often exert the same effect on persons known to have genetic disorders as on persons without the disorder. For example, Rapoport, Buchsbaum, Zahn, Ludlow, Weingartner, and Mikkelse (1980) demonstrated that ritalin has the same impact on all children whether they are hyperactive or not. Ritalin, in low to moderate doses, enhances the attention span of most individuals. Drug consumption for those with a disorder or drug consumption by persons free of disorder should be dictated by efficacy considerations (will the drug effect a desired outcome) and the importance of achieving the desired outcome, balanced against concerns regarding side effects. The genetic basis of a disorder then has limited implications regarding psychotropic medication treatment.

Some have argued that establishing a disorder as inherited lifts the stigma of guilt from the individual and family members (Johnson, 1987). Empirical investigation has shown how the presumed etiology of a disorder affects assignment of blame and positive regard toward a person exhibiting the disorder. With respect to the disorder of alcoholism, Rule and Phillips (1973) found there is little difference in liking and admiration for an individual with an alcohol problem as a function of whether his problem was viewed as a disease or a behavioral problem. The major factor determining positive evaluation toward the individual was whether evaluators believed that the problem could be ameliorated. Sobell and Sobell (1975), in a public survey, found that portraying the perpetrator of a nonspecified violent crime as alcoholic resulted in more severe sentencing despite the fact that half of the sample endorsed the disease concept of alcoholism. Sommer, Burstein, and Holman (1988) demonstrated that labeling the perpetrator of eccentric behavior as a schizophrenic had little impact on tolerance ratings. These findings suggest that even when a problem is seen as a disease, punishment is not necessarily attenuated, nor is positive regard enhanced.

Although explaining a problem as genetically based may not decrease the negative stigma associated with the problem, emphasizing a genetic basis may convince people they are more limited in finding solutions to their problems than they actually are. Fisher and Farnia (1979) demonstrated that when individuals are told that their emotional problems have a genetic basis, such individuals feel less personally able to influence their problems, they rely more on alcohol and drugs, and they are less willing to invest energy in identifying environmental precipitants to their distress. For some reason, a genetic-physiological explanation for a difficulty carries a connotation of inevitability and lack of responsivity to behavioral control, which may not be justified. Further, believing that one has a genetic problem may engender a sense of fragility and vulnerability precluding reasonable risk taking, which can extend into unrelated areas of life. Clinicians should avoid constraining a client's options through inculcation of a self-fulfilling prophecy of limitations that the available research findings cannot justify. Madanes' (1981) advice to define a problem in such a way that it will have a solution should be heeded. Even if such a definition is invalid, the belief may have a salubrious impact.

References

Fisher, J. D. & Farnia, A. (1979). Consequences of beliefs about the nature of mental disorders. *Journal of Abnormal Psychology, 88,* 320–327.

Johnson, H. C. (1987). Biologically based deficits in the identified patient: Indications for psychoeducational strategies. *Journal of Marital and Family Therapy, 13,* 337–348.

Madanes, C. (1981). *Strategic family therapy.* San Francisco: Jossey-Bass.

Plomin, R., DeFries, J. C., & McClearn, G. E. (1990). *Behavioral genetics: A primer.* New York: W. H. Freeman and Company.

Rapoport, J. L., Buchsbaum, M., Zahn, T., Ludlow, C., Weingartner, E., & Mikkelse, E. (1980). Dextroamphetamine: Cognitive and behavioral effects in normal and hyperactive children and normal adult men. *Archives of General Psychiatry, 37,* 933–946.

Rule, B. G., & Phillips, D. (1973). Responsibility versus illness models of alcoholism: Effects on attitudes toward an alcoholic. *Quarterly Journal of Studies on Alcohol, 34,* 489–495.

Sobell, L. C., & Sobell, M. B. (1975). Drunkenness, A ''special circumstance'' in crimes of violence: Sometimes. *International Journal of Addictions, 4,* 869–882.

Sommer, R., Burstein, E., & Holman, S. (1988). Tolerance of deviance as affected by label, act, and actor. *Deviant Behavior, 9,* 193–207.

Annotated Bibliography

Brickman, P., Rabinowitz, V. C., Karuza, J., Coates, D., Cohn, E., & Kidder, L. (1982). Models of helping and coping. *American Psychologist, 37,* 368–384.

This article outlines how views on the etiology of a problem imply models of intervention and are related to outcome.

Littrell, J. (1991). *Understanding and treating alcoholism, Vol. II: Biological, psychological, and social aspects of alcohol consumption and abuse.* Hillsdale, NJ: Lawrence Erlbaum Associates.

The first section in this volume reviews the empirical research pertinent to how alcoholism might be inherited. The limits on inferences from twin and adoption studies are discussed.

Reiss, D., Plomin, R., & Hetherington, E. M. (1991). Genetics and psychiatry: An unheralded window on the environment. *American Journal of Psychiatry, 148,* 283–291.

This article focuses on empirical support for the role of environmental factors in influencing the emergence of pathological states.

Plomin, R., DeFries, J. C., & McClearn, G. E. (1990). *Behavioral genetics: A primer.* New York: W. H. Freeman & Company.

This work explains the process of research in molecular genetics and behavioral genetics. The bottom lines on the contributions of genetics to particular behaviors are reviewed.

Rejoinder to Dr. Littrell

RITA BECK BLACK

Dr. Littrell provides a clear and enlightening overview of principles of gene-environment interaction and population genetics. Indeed, I found Dr. Littrell's discussion a most helpful elaboration of many of the points that I raised in my own argument. Unfortunately, Dr. Littrell's statement does not directly address the growing body of research findings on genetic factors in mental illness.

Dr. Littrell emphasizes her concern that stigma and lack of hope will be associated with genetic findings. I share her concern but disagree with the conclusions she draws. The only solution she seems to offer is to redefine genetics out of mental health problems, even if the "definition is invalid." I do not find ignoring or sidestepping research evidence an acceptable strategy. A correct understanding of genetic principles, as so beautifully reviewed by Dr. Littrell, demands aggressive efforts to identify etiological factors and treatment strategies in the realms of both biology and the environment.

For patients and families, who must live today with our very imperfect understanding of how genes and environments interact in shaping mental illnesses, I suggest that honesty and education are the best policies. This means open discussion of all pertinent research findings about etiology and treatment, supported by collaborative educational projects in which patients, families, and mental health professionals come together to learn about and consider the potential implications of new findings in gene-environment research.

NO

RITA B. BLACK

My answer to this question is "no." However, I find it hard to stay with a simple response when the question itself raises many other questions that bear on my otherwise straightforward reply. A simple yes or no answer requires me to gloss over the vague language used in the question and ignore the slant it gives to the issue. Therefore, I will explain my answer in the context of considering the issues raised by the ambiguous terms *emphasis* and *distorting.*

First, the question asks us to assume that there currently is some (unspecified) emphasis on genetics in the field of mental health. But what exactly does it mean if we say we are or are not emphasizing genetics? Are we to assume that emphasizing genetics really means *over*emphasizing genetics? If we emphasize genetics, does that imply we necessarily ignore or give insufficient attention to other factors? Perhaps most important, given the growing research evidence for a genetic contribution to many forms of mental illness, what is the alternative to emphasizing genetics?

Some acquaintance with the research findings is an essential prerequisite for judging whether mental health professionals are placing too much emphasis on genetics. Although early psychiatric genetic studies concentrated on schizophrenia, inquiry in recent decades has broadened to include the affective disorders, alcoholism, and panic disorder, along with many other conditions. Family studies often provide the first evidence to suggest that genetics plays some role in an illness. Although family aggregation (a greater than expected number of relatives with the same disorder) can result from shared environment rather than shared genes, it raises the question of whether genes play some role. For example, family studies have shown that first degree relatives (parents, siblings, and offspring) of patients often are at increased risk compared to the general population: twenty four times higher for bipolar affective disorder; eighteen times higher for schizophrenia; ten times higher for alcoholism; and nine times higher for panic disorder (Pardes, Kaufmann, Pincus, & West, 1989). While the exact levels given for increased risk often vary across studies (Plomin, 1990), first degree relatives consistently have been found at increased risk for these disorders.

Twin studies compare rates of illness for monozygotic (identical) and dizygotic (fraternal) twins. This line of research is based on the assumption that while both types of twins share very similar prenatal and postnatal environments, monozygotic twins share the same genes whereas dizygotic twins, on average, have only half their genes in common. Adoption studies similarly seek to separate contributions of "nature" versus "nurture" by examining children raised apart from their biological parents and comparing rates of illness in biological and adoptive relatives. Again, findings from both twin and adoption studies have contributed evidence for genetic influences on schizophrenia, bipolar affective disorder, alcoholism, and panic disorder (Pardes et al., 1989; Plomin, 1990).

Molecular biology now is moving psychiatric genetic research to the new frontier of attempting to specify and localize in the human genome those genes involved in the development of certain mental illnesses. Although results remain tentative, success in defining the location of genes implicated in the pathogenesis of a certain illness can open doors for additional research and treatment. This approach has already been successful in studies of familial Alzheimer's disease (Pardes et al., 1989). Investigators were able, in a series of steps, first to locate the gene for β-amyloid protein (which accumulates in the brains of patients with Alzheimer's disease and Down syndrome) to chromosome 21 and then to identify the gene for familial Alzheimer's disease, which was found to be near the β-amyloid gene (St. George-Hyslop, Tanzi, Polinsky, et al., 1987). Similarly, the gene for Huntington's disease has been identified as residing on chromosome 4.

This brief overview certainly is not meant in itself to prove the involvement of genetic factors in mental illness. Interested readers are urged to turn to primary sources and major literature reviews for more in-depth presentations and examination of a wider range of disorders (see, for example, Biederman, Faraone, Keenan, Knee, & Tsuang, 1990; Ciaranello & Ciaranello, 1991; Crowe, 1990; Johnson, 1989; Pardes et al., 1989; Plomin, 1990; Vandenberg, Singer, & Pauls, 1986). However, the evidence is strong and consistent that ''genetic influence is nearly ubiquitous for both animal and human behavior'' (Plomin, 1990, p. 186). Thus the question of *emphasis* on genetics is not the critical issue in this debate. More important is whether the attention placed on genetic influences, however real and important those influences might be, is somehow *distorting* our approaches to research and services in the field of mental health.

Let us look then at what it might mean if genetics did *distort* our work. The most likely distortions result from two main types of misunderstandings of genetic principles. I will call these errors: (1) the assumption that genetic influence means no environmental influence and (2) the assumption that genetic influence equals destiny.

The first erroneous assumption arises out of an overly simplistic view of genetic modes of inheritance. Thousands of medical illnesses, including many that affect mental functioning, have been shown to have monogenic roots (caused by a single major gene) and be transmitted according to traditional Mendelian principles (dominant, recessive, X-linked). However, the appearance of any one of these illnesses tends to be rare (e.g., Huntington disease). Much more common are disorders that result from what is called multifactorial inheritance. As the name suggests, this is inheritance that is based on the combined effects of a number of major and minor genes interacting with environmental influences. Current evidence suggests that many psychiatric disorders fall into the category of multifactorial inheritance (Pardes et al., 1989; Plomin, 1990; Reiss, Plomin, & Hetherington, 1991). If we read the genetics research literature using the lens of multifactorial inheritance, we cannot help but notice that the growing body of evidence for genetic influences also supports the statement that ''nongenetic sources of variance are at least as important as genetic factors'' (Plomin, 1990, p. 186). For example, one large study of schizophrenia showed twin concordances (both have illness) of 30.9 percent for 164 pairs of identical twins compared to 6.5 percent for 268 pairs of fraternal twins (Plomin, 1990, p. 188). Data such as these, which clearly show the important role of genetic factors, show the equally critical role of nongenetic factors.

The preceding evidence also helps to correct the second erroneous assumption, that genetic influence equals destiny. Identical twins, who share a common genetic heritage, do not always grow up to have all the same physical or behavioral characteristics. In fact, the presumption of shared environmental experiences, on which twin studies have been based, is coming under closer scrutiny as genetic studies highlight the enormous individual variation in people's prenatal and postnatal environmental experiences (Reiss, Plomin, & Hetherington, 1991).

Equally important, even when genetic influences are monogenic and strong, environmental manipulation may prove stronger. The most powerful example of this combination is provided by phenylketonuria (PKU), an autosomal recessive disorder. Without a special diet, the normal intelligence of babies with PKU is ravaged by their bodies' failure to metabolize the basic protein phenylalanine. However, a special diet (an environmental intervention) that eliminates this protein can prevent the otherwise marked intellectual decline. That we do not yet know the environmental interventions to prevent or effectively treat most forms of mental illness does not make environment any less important than genetics.

I return then to the question before us in this debate. Genetic influences do play an important role in the development of many types of mental illness. Yet, careful study of genetic principles and of findings in psychiatric genetic research does not point toward an exclusive or all-powerful role for genetics in psychiatry. To the contrary, psychiatric genetic research, by confirming and specifying the important contributions of nongenetic factors, is providing an "unheralded window on the environment" (Reiss, Plomin, & Hetherington, 1991). Researchers are being challenged to learn more about both genetic and environmental influences and to sharpen their inquiry into the important individual differences in the environments experienced by members of the same biological family.

But there is an equal challenge to mental health clinicians to learn about and understand the place of genetics in psychiatry. Clinicians have a responsibility to assist patients and families with their spoken or perhaps unspoken genetic questions and fears. A woman called me recently in what was proving to be a difficult search for a mental health professional who could help her understand the possible genetic implications that her father's manic-depressive illness carried for her and for the children she would like to have in the future. She was not overemphasizing genetics or distorting its possible significance in her life. However, mental health professionals will be distorting their practice if they ignore genetic factors or remain ignorant about the complex ways that genes and environment work together in forming each individual's pattern of development.

References

Biederman, J., Faraone, S. V., Keenan, K., Knee, D., & Tsuang, M. T. (1990). Family-genetic and psychosocial risk factors in DSM-III attention deficit disorder. *Journal of the American Academy of Child Adolescent Psychiatry, 29,* 526–533.

Ciaranello, R. D., & Ciaranello, A. L. (1991). Genetics of major psychiatric disorders. *Annual Review of Medicine, 42,* 151–158.
Crowe, R. R. (1990). Panic disorder: Genetic considerations. *Journal of Psychiatric Research, 24* (supplement 2), 129–134.
Johnson, H. C. (1989). Disruptive children: Biological factors in attention deficit and antisocial disorders. *Social Work, 34,* 137–144.
Pardes, H., Kaufman, C. A., Pincus, H. A., & West, A. (1989). Genetics and psychiatry: Past discoveries, current dilemmas, and future directions. *American Journal of Psychiatry, 146,* 435–443.
Plomin, R. (1990). The role of inheritance in behavior. *Science, 248,* 183–188.
Reiss, D., Plomin, R., & Hetherington, E. M. (1991). Genetics and psychiatry: An unheralded window on the environment. *American Journal of Psychiatry, 148,* 283–291.
St. George-Hyslop, P. H., Tanzi, R. E., Polinsky, R. J., Haines, J. L., Nee, L., Watkins, P. C., Myers, R. H., Feldman, R. G., Pollen, D., Drachman, D., Growdon, J., Bruni, A., Foncin, J. F., Salman, D., Frommelt, P., Ameducci, L., Sorbi, S., Placentini, S., Stewart, G. D., Hobbs, W. J., Conneally, P. M., & Gusella, J. F. (1987). The genetic defect causing familial Alzheimer's disease maps on chromosome 21. *Science, 235,* 885–890.
Vandenberg, S. G., Singer, S. M., & Pauls, D. L. (1986). *The heredity of behavior disorders in adults and children.* New York: Plenum Medical Books.

Annotated Bibliography

Pardes, H., Kaufman, C. A., Pincus, H. A., & West, A. (1989). Genetics and psychiatry: Past discoveries, current dilemmas, and future directions. *American Journal of Psychiatry, 146,* 435–443.
Reiss, D., Plomin, R., & Hetherington, E. M. (1991). Genetics and psychiatry: An unheralded window on the environment. *American Journal of Psychiatry, 148,* 283–291.

These articles provide a lively contrast of positions. The authors present their views and supporting evidence for the prominence that should be given to nature and nurture in current psychiatric research.

Rejoinder to Dr. Black

Jill Littrell

In response to the question, "Is the emphasis on genetics distorting our approaches to mental disorders?" Dr. Black asks, "What is the alternative to emphasizing genetics?" She seems to assume that if information pertinent to a hereditary basis for a problem is available, the clinician is obligated to discuss this information with a client and perhaps use the information in some fashion in treatment. The decision to focus on genetic information constitutes a choice of strategy. Professional behavior is purposeful. What could be the purpose of discussing or focusing on the hereditary basis of a mental disorder? Several possible purposes for such a discussion are suggested. These specific purposes are associated with particular tasks:

1. When the task is to assist a client in making family planning decisions, discussion of genetic information has a purpose. Accurate information about the probability of an offspring developing a condition that has been manifested by a parent can influence the decision of whether to bear a child. People decide on varying courses of action by taking into account the risks and benefits associated with each course. There is a purpose for discussing and focusing on genetics in the process of reproductive planning.

2. At some future time, facts regarding inheritance of particular problems may be useful in enabling the design of more effective prevention programs. Hence, a focus on genetics might assist in the task of prevention program development. To be useful in the development of prevention programs, knowledge of the mechanisms through which genes operate to predispose to a particular disorder must be available. Further, there must be understanding of how genetic predisposition interacts with environmental factors. Only when such understanding is attained will genetic research have reached a state permitting its use in the development of prevention programs that are targeted toward those at risk by virtue of their heritability. Presently, genetic research offers little information for how people at risk might conduct their lives so as to prevent particular problems.

Environmental risk factors for specific problems have been identified for the general population. These environmental risk factors do suggest behaviors and environmental conditions associated with a decrease in the probability of developing a particular problem. Prevention programs are designed so as to encourage salubrious behavior and environmental conditions. There is not yet enough understanding specific to how genetic predisposition interacts with environment to suggest whether different types of prevention programs should be designed for those at genetic risk versus those in the general population. Given the present state of genetic knowledge, this reservoir of information is not yet helpful in the development of better prevention programs for those with genetic liability for many heritable conditions.

3. When the task is the treatment of mental disorders, a case for a purpose in presenting information pertinent to the role of genetic factors in the etiology of a disorder must be made. What is the impact of the provision of genetic information? If a client believes that he or she inherited a condition, does he or she feel less guilty or ashamed? So far, evidence is lacking. There is evidence that clients who are provided with a genetic explanation for the development of behavioral problems feel more out of control and rely more on drugs and alcohol. Clinicians may wish to avoid a strategy that could result in such an impact when treating clients.

4. Even if a clinician elects to avoid a discussion of genetics in the course of provision of treatment for mental conditions, clients often come into treatment already knowing about genetic contributions to their particular problems. Clients may have jumped to the conclusion that they were doomed by their genes, believing that environmental factors (or other factors under their control) played no role in the development of their problems. There may be some benefit in disabusing clients of their erroneous fatalistic conclusions.

The purpose of treatment of mental disorders is to change behavior and ameliorate distress; the purpose is not the provision of information. However, sometimes clients want information. Clients do have a right to information, probably even when the impact of the information might be harmful. Clinicians should possess accurate information on topics that are likely to be highly salient for their clients so as to satisfy their clients' right to know.

Deemphasizing genetics among behavioral clinicians does not mean that molecular biologists should discontinue conducting laboratory research. Genetic research promises the future possibility of genetic engineering, that is, changing one's genes. Further, biochemical research promises the specification of those protein sequences that underlie particular processes that manifest in specific behavioral conditions. Once the chemistry is mapped out, it may be possible to take a pill to change the chemistry at the level of the DNA. At such a juncture, the behavioral problem may no longer exist in the population. At the present time, however, the current fund of information is a long way from allowing this.

If a decision is made by behavioral clinicians to focus on genetics there should be some purpose in so doing. With regard to each particular task, the question of the purpose to be served in raising the issue of genetics should be evaluated. Is there evidence that a focus on genetics will achieve the purpose? Is there reason to believe that some untoward side effects may result even when the purpose is achieved? The fact that a fund of information on a topic exists does not necessarily mean that conveying the information is useful to the objective of changing behavior and relieving distress.

DEBATE 8

Is Psychoanalytic Therapy Relevant for Public Mental Health Programs?

Dr. Carl C. Bell, M.D., says YES. Dr. Bell is the Executive Director of the Community Mental Health Council. He received his medical degree from Meharry Medical College in 1971 and trained in Psychiatry at the Illinois State Psychiatric Institute from 1971 to 1974. He is a Fellow of the American Psychiatric Association and a member of the American Association of Community Psychiatrists.

Taking the NO position is Bruce A. Thyer. Dr. Thyer is Professor of Social Work and Adjunct Professor of Psychology at the University of Georgia and Clinical Associate Professor with the Department of Psychiatry and Health Behavior at the Medical College of Georgia. Dr. Thyer received his Ph.D. in social work and psychology from the University of Michigan in 1982. His major professional interest is in promoting an empirical approach to social work practice and research.

YES

CARL C. BELL

From the perspective of clinical need, the question of whether psychoanalytic therapy is relevant for public mental health programs is ridiculous. The purpose of this article should make this assertion abundantly clear.

Reading Freud's works, especially his work with Breuer on *Studies on Hysteria* (Freud & Breuer, 1955) and the *Interpretation of Dreams* (Freud, 1957), and actually using psychoanalytic therapy or psychoanalytically based psychotherapy to resolve psychic symptoms that originate in psychic trauma and unconscious defense mechanisms makes it clear what the relevancy should be. The problem is that few practitioners read Freud's works starting with his first book with Breuer (Freud & Breuer, 1955) and, as a result, do not thoroughly understand the empirical observations on which Freud based his theories and his psychoanalytic technique. Rather, many practitioners read Freud's later works (which assume familiarity with his earlier empirical observations and theoretical underpinnings) or, worse yet, they read about Freud's theories from another source other than Freud. The result is that very few people actually understand what Freud was writing about and, unfortunately, very few have had the opportunity to make the same empirical observations that he made because they do not know what they are seeing.

Having worked in public mental health programs for the past twenty years, I have found that many of my patients have experienced psychic trauma or traumatic stress that overwhelmed their ability to cope with their experience and who, as a result, repressed their memory of their experience; this resulted in symptoms of anxiety that were psychic derivatives of their repressed memory. Further, when I used an earlier Freudian psychoanalytic technique of what I refer to as "symptom tracing" (this is essentially what Freud and Breuer did in their first reported studies on hysteria [Freud & Breuer, 1955]), the patients recovered the repressed memory of their trauma and their symptoms were alleviated.

A brief case history may illuminate the use of this psychoanalytic therapeutic technique, which I first used in a City of Chicago Department of Mental Health Clinic (Bell, 1979). A middle-aged African-American female presented with complaints of low self-esteem presumably due to the early abandonment of the patient by her mother. I was seeing her to establish if her low self-esteem was in fact a symptom of major depression, and if so, whether it could be alleviated with antidepressant medication. A trial of this medication showed that it was poorly tolerated by the patient. In the process of my evaluation, which extended through several medication evaluation sessions, I also learned she suffered from migraine headaches. Having realized antidepressants were not the answer, I was talking to the patient about what to consider next, when she informed me she was having a migraine while she was there in my office. I found this difficult to accept as her affect was pleasant and affable, and, as a result, I became suspicious of the origin of her symptoms. I asked when she first had begun to have migraines. She told me they began when she had found some pictures of her deceased mother. In fact, when she found the pictures, she became paralyzed on one side of her body and had gone blind for a week. She had not seen a doctor, but recovered spontaneously. I pressed her further about when symptoms of migraine began, as she noted they had occurred before she found the pictures, but she couldn't recall when; she said it seemed a "wall" was keeping her from remembering. I "commanded" her to remember, and she recalled that her headaches began at her mother's funeral. Apparently, her mother had breast cancer that metastasized to her brain, causing the mother to have headaches, blindness, and paralysis of one side of her body. The patient had reunited with the mother later in life and was trying to resolve her feelings of abandonment when this illness occurred. The patient had "sick nursed" her mother. With the recollection of this memory, which the patient remarked she'd not thought of in years, her headaches went away. This case was remarkably similar to Freud's and Breuer's earlier cases. The patient remained symptom free for six years until her husband nearly got killed, which caused her to re-repress her care of her mother and her mother's illness and death. She returned for one session, and it was very easy for me to show her how similar her husband's near-death experience was to the loss of her mother. With this insight, her headaches went away again. This case is a clear example of psychoanalytic technique helping patients resolve psychic trauma. While it can be argued, as Freud later learned, that more needs to be done for complete treatment, this case illustrates the need that poor patients have for this form of treatment. Certainly, poor patients who use public mental health facilities are subject to psychic trauma just the same as are middle class patients and should have this treatment modality available to them.

Another case history will show the relevance of psychoanalytic technique to resolve traumatic stress that results in anxiety symptoms. A middle-aged African-American female came to the clinic complaining of having had her home broken into while she was home. Despite the fact she had not been physically harmed by the three men responsible for her robbery, since her victimization she had begun to experience symptoms of acute anxiety: she had sleep onset insomnia, she was jumpy and fearful, and she felt she was no longer safe in her own apartment. In addition, she reported symptoms of tremulousness, intrusive recollection of the event, headaches, and gastrointestinal disturbances. I felt that her management should involve some very clear crisis intervention techniques, and so I helped to assist her in establishing a safer milieu (i.e., adding locks on her doors and window guards on her windows). I had her thoroughly ventilate her concerns and suggested concrete actions to correct her vulnerable areas of concern. Finally, I prescribed a minor tranquilizer to aid in reducing her sleep and anxiety problems in an effort to allow her the opportunity to reestablish her psychic equilibrium. After three or four brief sessions, the patient was improved and released from my care with a caveat to return if the need arose.

Five months later the patient returned because of another victimization that caused her to be even more anxious than during her first visit. Apparently, while on her way to work one morning, a stranger grabbed her in the vestibule of her apartment and put a knife to her throat. When she asked what he wanted, the stranger just laughed. Fortunately, another tenant in the building was also leaving for work and scared the attacker away. Again, although not physically harmed, the patient reported being extremely anxious as a result of this assault. The evidence of her anxiety was apparent in her lack of eye contact, her visible tremulousness, her irregular respirations, and her report of symptoms of anxiety. Because it had worked before, I asked her to ventilate her feelings, but unlike the previous treatment contact, when I asked her what she was thinking during her attack, she said, ''Nothing.'' I became suspicious and told her this wasn't possible, and, since the fellow had the knife to the throat for such a long time (she said it seemed like five minutes), she must have been thinking something. She told me her mind had been blank. I began to press her, and finally she said she was thinking she was glad her daughter wasn't with her. This didn't make sense to me, but it occurred to me she didn't want her daughter to have witnessed something, possibly a sexual assault. As a result, I asked if she'd ever been raped. She replied that she could not remember. As I continued to press her, the patient dropped to the floor from her chair and said she couldn't remember and there was a ''barrier'' in her way. I ''commanded'' her to remember, and she recalled being raped in the snow while on her way home from work by two men when she was eighteen years old. After a thorough report of her victimization, the patient got off the floor, took a deep breath, looked me in the eyes, and said, ''You know, I had forgotten that that had happened.'' Her demeanor had changed drastically and her symptoms of anxiety (i.e. cracking voice, tremulousness, and irregular respirations) were gone. After turning to a resident, who was in the room with me, and asking her to close her mouth, I turned back to the patient who mused that maybe her rape victimization explained why she had always noticed herself being more anxious in winter when it snowed. This case clearly underscores issues discussed by Fenichel (1954) in his text, *The Psychoanalytic Theory on Neurosis,* as it highlights psychoanalytic dynamics of traumatic stress. I have written extensively on issues of victimization and traumatic stress in poor, inner-city children and patients who use public mental health facilities (Bell, Taylor-Crawford, Jenkins, & Chalmers, 1988; Bell & Jenkins, 1991). Surely, recognizing the extent of this victimization and traumatic stress, and being cognizant of how these issues impacted on troops in war exposed to violence, would cause us to realize psychoanalytic therapy or a variant is relevant for public mental health programs. Clearly, this is an important treatment modality to have in one's armentarium in a public mental health setting because the levels of victimization are greater in poorer communities.

A last brief case highlights the use of dream interpretation to assist public mental health clinic patients in getting relief from psychic symptoms. A middle-aged black male reported difficulty with impotence. After several sessions, he reported a dream that he was in the Garden of Eden surrounded by dinosaurs and trees. He looked outside the fence surrounding the garden, and he saw a red Volkswagen Beetle driving away. I asked the patient to give me his associations to various elements in the dream. We discovered the garden represented the rural environment he had been in as a child, and the dinosaurs were representative of the cows on his parents' farm. The fence represented the fence around the farm, but there were no associations to the red Volkswagen Beetle. I offered my own associations of red being associated with blood and Volkswagen Beetle being affectionately referred to as pregnant rollerskates. Thus, I wondered about any occurrences of pregnancy while he was a child. He recalled that at age five, his mother had been pregnant but miscarried. He had to summon the doctor, on foot, in the dark, late at night while his father stayed with his mother. Despite a long, scary walk, he was able to get the doctor to come in an ambulance, and his mother was taken away to the hospital. He recalled, despite her recovery, his resolve to never get a woman pregnant because of his horror of having seen his parents' bed with all the bright red blood in it. His deduction was that getting women pregnant could kill them. With this recovery of a repressed memory, which had been unaccessible for years, his impotence improved considerably.

I trust my three case examples make the point that psychoanalytic therapy is relevant to public health settings. Not to have this form of therapy available is really offering a second-class array of treatment options. The real issue of debate isn't whether such therapy is relevant because a Jewish, European, middle-class physician developed a theory and technique that some feel couldn't possibly apply to an African-American, poor class group. The real issues are the assumptions that the application of psychoanalytic theory and technique require current formal psychoanalytic treatment contexts to work (i.e. visits five days a week on a couch). Clearly, establishing such a treatment context is a costly procedure that drains resources of time and money. However, my experience is that appropriate modifications of the technique do work in public mental health settings. Further, there may be additional concerns about the validity and utility of the theory and the techniques, but from the perspective of practicing community psychiatry for twenty years, I believe the theory and techniques have merit. I suspect the question of relevancy of psychoanalytic therapy for inclusion in public mental programs isn't so much the issue as the problem that in our society that the most needy often get the least because they can't afford the best. Thus, patients in public mental health programs are deprived of this relevant treatment modality, and staff are not trained in how to apply this modality. The reality is that many of the professionals most capable of providing this form of treatment or training to public mental health staff prefer to be in private offices or well-resourced private facilities instead of where the need may actually be greater.

References

Bell, C. C. (1979) The need for psychoanalysis is alive and well in community psychiatry. *Journal of the National Medical Association, 71*(4), 361–368.

Bell, C. C. & Jenkins, E. J. (1991) Traumatic stress and children. *Journal of Health Care for the Poor and Underserved, 2*(1), 175–188.

Bell, C. C., Taylor-Crawford, K., Jenkins, E. J., & Chalmers, D. (1988). The need for victimization screening in a black psychiatric population. *Journal of the National Medical Association 80*(1), 41–48.

Fenichel, O. (1954). *The psychoanalytic theory of neurosis.* New York: W. W. Norton.

Freud, S. (1957). Interpretation of dreams (1901). In Strachey, J. (Trans. and Ed.), *Complete psychological works,* Vol. 4 and 5. London: Hogarth Press.

Freud, S. & Breuer, J. (1955). Studies on hysteria (1893–1895). In Strachey, J. (Trans. and Ed.), Complete psychological works. London: Hogarth Press.

Rejoinder to Dr. Bell

Bruce A. Thyer

On Relevant Evidence and Irrelevant Claims: A Response to Bell

Dr. Bell is a fine advocate for psychoanalytic therapy (PAT), and he continues the one hundred year long tradition of this field by attempting to persuade the reader solely on the basis of his personal experience and by appeal to authority (Freud) of the value of this approach. Indeed, he states this clearly: "My experience is that appropriate modifications of the technique do work in public mental health settings" and ". . . I believe the theory and techniques have merit." By illustrating this approach through several superficially compelling case studies, the case is made that PAT is a valuable modality. I have no doubt of the sincerity with which Dr. Bell adheres to this belief, but I also am aware that the strength of such convictions carries absolutely no weight in scientific discourse. The history of science, and of psychology in particular, is replete with examples of reasonable and well-educated people who were convinced of the value of some worthless treatment: Wilhelm Reich and his orgone therapy; insulin shock therapy or lobotomies for schizophrenia; Dr. Battey and his ovariectomies for cranky women, and so forth. For each supposedly successful case presented by Dr. Bell, we need to know how many unsuccessful ones there were. We also need to know the improvement and deterioration rates of people who did not receive such treatment. Assessment of improvement is best done using valid indicators by persons unconnected with providing treatment. Only when all such relevant empirical data are available can relatively strong conclusions be drawn regarding the efficacy of any particular treatment. When such studies have been conducted on psychoanalytic therapy (and many have been), it has been shown *not* to be helpful (see, for example, the review by Rachman &

Wilson, 1980, pp. 50–76, whose conclusions have not appreciably changed in over a decade).

Dr. Bell employs a non sequitur argument when he contends that our recognition of victimization and traumatic stress and of the effects of exposure to violence, should ". . . cause us to realize psychoanalytic therapy or a variant is relevant for public mental health problems." No one denies the pain experienced by clients and the need for effective care, but it simply does not logically (or empirically) follow that PAT is thereby indicated. A variety of psychosocial and medical treatments may be indicated, but there is little evidence beyond that of carefully selected clinical anecdote that PAT should be among these options. Torrey (1992) makes an excellent case regarding the pernicious effects of PAT and of psychoanalytic theory in general. Clinicians get railroaded by their training programs into the dead end siding of PAT, and clients end up not receiving effective care.

References

Rachman, S. J., & Wilson, G. T. (1980). *The effects of psychological therapy* (second edition). Elmsford, NY: Pergamon.

Torrey, E. F. (1992). *Freudian fraud: The malignant effect of Freud's theory on American thought and culture.* New York: HarperCollins.

NO

Bruce A. Thyer

> "The tenacity in which these theories were kept alive in the analytic community . . . despite the fact that their therapeutic application did not improve the patient's condition, reflects the strength of an ideological structure disregarding clinical facts." (American Psychiatric Association, 1989, p. 511)

I am pleased to take the "no" position for this statement since psychoanalytic therapy (PAT) and its numerous progeny (psychodynamic psychotherapy, and others) are so pervasive within mental health practice and in professional education, despite compelling evidence that this position is ill-deserved. My response is centered around two main themes: (1) PAT is not therapeutically beneficial and is often dangerous and (2) the general approach of PAT is unethical. I will present each of these points in turn. Space does not permit addressing a third contention, namely, that psychoanalytic/psychodynamic theories are simply incorrect and reflect invented knowledge that does not correspond with human development or functioning.

Psychoanalytic Therapy Is Not Helpful

Quite simply, I know of no well-controlled study that demonstrates that psychoanalytic therapy is of benefit for any disorder currently listed in *DSM-III-R* (or in its prior versions). Furthermore, I know of no well-controlled study that documents the efficacy of this approach in helping clients who present with other types of problems commonly seen in the public mental health setting, such as spouse abuse, child abuse or neglect, the treatment of rape or incest victims, of the perpetrators of sexual crimes, marital or family problems, interpersonal skills deficits, and the like—*not one*. I challenge the defenders of the ''yes'' position to cite and describe such studies. If such citations are not forthcoming the ''yes'' position would seem to be untenable.

Mainstream psychology and psychiatry grudgingly acknowledge these facts. Referring to the training of clinical psychologists, Peterson (cf. Buie, 1989, p. 22) noted that ''any faculty made up entirely or predominantly of people whose main stock in trade is dynamic personality assessment and long-term individual psychotherapy will not produce students who work effectively with tough problems in public agencies,'' and training in intensive dynamic psychotherapy is clearly waning in the education of United States psychiatrists (Altshuler, 1990). Freud himself was apparently not an effective therapist (Goleman, 1990), and prospective patients are voting with their feet (and checkbooks), leaving many psychoanalytically oriented therapists alone with their couches. ''In the '80s, the reality is that psychoanalysis is 'starved' for patients'' (Gelman, 1988, p. 62). In Great Britain, training in psychodynamic psychotherapy is no longer required of psychiatrists, and similar proposals have surfaced in the United States.

The issue is not merely the lack of evidence to support the efficacy of PAT in the treatment of various disorders, but of considerable research which shows that these forms of treatment are *not* helpful. In their recent review of psychodynamic treatments for schizophrenia, Mueser and Berenbaum (1990) report that both well-controlled and naturalistic studies evaluating this approach have failed to support its efficacy and, indeed, found significant evidence indicating *deleterious* effects. In an earlier and more comprehensive review of the effects of individual psychotherapies, Parloff, London, & Wolfe (1986) noted that ''these findings do not encourage the view that intensive psychotherapy will soon reestablish itself as the 'treatment of choice' for schizophrenia'' (p. 330). With respect to alcoholism, ''Three controlled studies of insight-oriented psychotherapy . . . showed a high dropout rate, and the levels of improvement were either limited or simply equivalent to those in alternate treatments. . . . No more recent controlled investigation using psychotherapy as a treatment for alcoholics was found'' (Parloff et al., 1986, p. 332). Generally, PAT is conspicuously absent when the empirical literature on evaluating psychosocial treatments is reviewed. In a review of 223 such studies pertaining to child and adolescent psychotherapy, psychoanalysis and psychodynamic therapies formed only 5.4 percent of the available studies published between 1970 and 1988 (Kazdin, Bass, Ayers, & Rodgers, 1990).

Psychoanalytic Therapy Is Seriously Ethically Flawed

Clients have a right to be provided with empirically supported therapies as a first "treatment of choice" whenever clinical research provides such guidance. Failure to be guided by this "right to effective treatment" poses grave ethical implications. Take, for example, the sad case of Dr. Rafael Osheroff, admitted to the Chestnut Lodge hospital near Washington, DC, in 1979. He was provided with individual psychodynamic therapy four times a week for seven months. During this time he lost forty pounds and grew considerably worse. After seven months of inpatient treatment his family had Dr. Osheroff discharged from Chestnut Lodge and admitted him to another hospital, where he was diagnosed with major depression (apparently his original condition). After being treated with medication he greatly improved and resumed his medical practice. In 1982 he initiated a lawsuit against Chestnut Lodge, claiming that their failure to provide him with proper drug therapy for his condition represented malpractice. The litigants eventually settled out of court, in favor of Dr. Osheroff (see summary by Klerman, 1990). Klerman notes the absence of scientific evidence in support of the psychoanalytic therapy provided to Dr. Osheroff and the extensive evidence in favor of pharmacotherapy and behavioral treatments in the treatment of major depression, options Dr. Osheroff was in effect denied. As Klerman (1990) noted, even if a respectable minority of qualified practitioners (e.g., psychodynamic therapists) hold that a given treatment is an acceptable one, such views are not tenable if they contradict scientific evidence. Furthermore, it is now the responsibility of mental health practitioners to provide patients with accurate information about alternative treatments, including facts regarding their efficacy, safety, and likely outcomes. Forcefully put by Klerman, "The psychiatrist has a responsibility to use effective treatment. The patient has the right to the proper treatment. Proper treatment involves those treatments for which there is substantial evidence" (1990, p. 417). By these ethical standards, psychoanalytic therapy cannot be considered "proper treatment" for any client in either the public or the private mental health arena.

Psychoanalytic therapy is perhaps the most sexist treatment model available. As documented by Sward (1980), Freud held a number of pejorative views of women, including the "facts" that they are less ethical than men, more narcissistic, more emotional and hysterical, less rational, lack a full-fledged sexuality of their own, have faulty super-egos, lack creativity, and are unsuited for intellectual or professional pursuits, and Freud favorably commented on "the man's right to exclusive possession of a woman" (p. 19). Penis envy and the castration complex were highly salient features in female development, according to this theory. I will mention only in passing the obviously homophobic nature of psychoanalytic "insights" into the nature of gay and lesbian individuals, in favor of a few sentences on recent evidence which apparently finds that Freud clearly and unambiguously suppressed or distorted facts that contradicted his theories (see Raymond, 1991). Masson's (1992) *The Assault on Truth: Freud's Suppression of the Seduction Theory* amply documents that when Freud revised his views on the seduction theory (in the face of serious opposition by the medical establishment) along the lines that patient reports of incest/sexual abuse were merely *fantasies,* and not real, he (Freud) was perfectly aware that many of these reports *were* true, but made this revisionist claim that they were imagined to promote the acceptability of psychoanalytic theory. Imagine the incalculable harm caused by succeeding generations of incest and rape victims whose legitimate claims of being assaulted were dismissed as "Oedipal fantasies"!

If the theoretical foundations on which a therapeutic edifice are based can be seen in contemporary light as unethical, sexist, and homophobic, how can succeeding generations of practitioners escape the baleful influence of these views? To be a woman is virtually, by definition, to be a lesser species of human being. To be homosexual is to be disordered. If the clinical data do not fit the theory, alter them to support your views! If conventionally accepted scientific methods of research do not yield supportive findings, either repudiate the scientific method as unsuitable for research into your "special" area, or simply cease conducting research.

I have followed the editors' instructions to "combine a simple, direct writing style with clear, forceful substance." The seriousness of the issue requires the unembellished truth without the usual platitudes about respecting all orientations. I believe that the ongoing use of psychoanalytic therapy and its derivatives in the public mental health sector represents a clear disservice to clients and is both ethically and scientifically unjustified. Not only is there no role for this approach, it is time for it to roll over and get out of the way of empirically supported treatments.

References

Altshuler, K. Z. (1990). Whatever happened to intensive psychotherapy? *American Journal of Psychiatry, 147,* 428–430.

American Psychiatric Association. (1989). *Treatment of psychiatric disorders, Volume I.* Washington, DC: Author.

Buie, J. (1989, October). Increase in therapists could help severely ill. *The APA Monitor,* p. 22.

Gelman, D. (1988, June 27). Where are the patients? *Newsweek,* pp. 62–65, 67.

Goleman, D. (1990, March 6). As a therapist, Freud fell short, scholars find. *The New York Times,* B5, B9.

Kazdin, A. E., Bass, D., Ayers, W. A., & Rodgers, A. (1990). Empirical and clinical focus of child and adolescent psychotherapy research. *Journal of Consulting and Clinical Psychology, 56,* 729–740.

Klerman, G. L. (1990). The psychiatric patient's right to effective treatment: Implications of *Osheroff v. Chestnut Lodge. American Journal of Psychiatry, 147,* 409–418.

Masson, J. M. (1992). *The assault on truth: Freud's suppression of the seduction theory.* New York: HarperCollins.

Mueser, K. T., & Berenbaum, H. (1990). Psychodynamic treatment of schizophrenia: Is there a future? *Psychological Medicine, 20,* 253–262.

Parloff, M. B., London, P., & Wolfe, B. (1986). Individual psychotherapy and behavior change. *Annual Review of Psychology, 37,* 321–349.

Raymond, C. (1991, May 29). Study of patient histories suggests Freud suppressed or distorted facts that contradicted his theories. *Chronicle of Higher Education,* A4–A6.

Sward, K. (1980). Self-actualization and women: Rank and Freud contrasted. *Journal of Humanist Psychology, 20*(2), 5–26.

Annotated Bibliography

Grunbaum, A. (1984). *The foundations of psychoanalysis: A philosophical critique.* Berkeley, CA: University of California Press.

A well-articulated review of the serious flaws of psychoanalytic theory and therapy from the perspectives of both science and of philosophy.

Giles, T. R. (1990). Bias against behavior therapy in outcome reviews: Who speaks for the patient? *The Behavior Therapist, 13,* 86–90.

Giles discusses the fraudulent nature of the "equivalence of therapies hypothesis" which is so commonly bandied about these days. In each and every one of the published meta-analyses, investigation of the effect sizes obtained by various forms of treatment shows that the behavioral therapies are vastly superior to the psychodynamic psychotherapies. Reasons why this striking finding is never elaborated on by the authors of these meta-analyses are discussed.

Prioleau, L., Murdock, M., & Brody, N. (1983). An analysis of psychotherapy versus placebo studies. *Behavioral and Brain Sciences, 6,* 275–285.

An extremely well-conducted meta-analysis, limited to a review of experiments in which the effects of psychotherapy were contrasted with credible placebo treatment. Psychotherapy and placebo yield equivalent effect sizes, suggesting that conventional psychotherapy is not a viable professional modality.

Rejoinder to Dr. Thyer

CARL C. BELL

As the "no" position is based on only two main themes, I will respond only to these two flawed propositions.

The first, that is, that psychoanalytic therapy is not helpful, just has not been apparent to me in my twenty years of frontline clinical practice of community psychiatry in public mental health programs. The case histories presented clearly document the empirical observation that various aspects of psychoanalytic therapy, when applied to appropriate cases, can be helpful to patients in public mental health programs. Regarding the challenge to cite a well-controlled study documenting the efficacy of psychoanalytic therapy in helping patients in public mental health settings with problems commonly seen in these settings, there are two flaws with the notion that unless such citations are forthcoming the "yes" position is untenable. The first flaw is that this treatment modality is available only to patients who can afford it and, as a result, is not practiced in public mental health settings. The second flaw can be found in the American Psychiatric Association's Commission on Psychiatric Therapies book (1984), which devotes an entire chapter to psychotherapy outcome research. This chapter points out that well-controlled studies are currently being done and that "unequivocal conclusions about causal connections are never possible in psychotherapy research because psychotherapy is not a simple stimulus that produces a simple response." So the demand is unrealistic, and, as such, does not debunk my proposition. Lastly, on the "no" position that psychoanalytic therapy is dangerous, I would agree in the same way that I would agree that any treatment misapplied is harmful. Freud himself warned that his method was not meant for schizophrenia or serious affective disorders. Simply because it has not been shown to be effective in treating schizophrenia or alcoholism does not mean psychoanalytic theory and technique are useless for all psychiatric problems. Such a reductionistic approach is "throwing the baby out with the bath water."

The second point, that psychoanalytic therapy is seriously ethically flawed, totally escapes me. Dr. Thyer cites an example in which the technique was misapplied—of course it did not work and was harmful. By this logic, if I gave haloperidol to a patient with panic disorder and the patient got worse by developing tardive dyskinesia, then physicians should no longer use haloperidol even where it is indicated (e.g., for schizophrenia). Regarding the sexist nature of the treatment model, I would again suggest that we not throw out the baby with the bath water. The cultural context in which the theory was developed was sexist and antihomosexual. In addition, the etiology of the source of the early psychoanalytic patients' traumatic stress was in error, that is, it was not from fantasy but actual sexual abuse. However, that does not negate the basic psychoanalytic empirical observation (made by Freud and by numerous mental health professionals treating patients in extremely stressful environments such as war) that traumatic stress overwhelms the psyche's means of stability, thereby causing memory loss and psychic symptoms. Further, helping the patient recall those traumatic stressors in supportive environments relieves those symptoms.

Finally, I maintain that, while psychoanalytic theory and techniques are not perfect, Freud was a shrewd observer of human behavior. Certain core concepts of psychoanalytic theory are essential in helping patients in public mental health settings resolve their experiences with traumatic stress.

Reference

American Psychiatric Association Commission on Psychiatric Therapies. (1984). *The psychiatric therapies.* Washington, DC: American Psychiatric Press.

Debate 9

Should ECT Be Prohibited?

Leonard Roy Frank emphatically argues YES. In 1962, Mr. Frank was involuntarily committed to a psychiatric facility and later forcibly administered thirty-five electroshocks in combination with fifty insulin coma shocks. He has been active in the psychiatric survivors' movement since 1972 when he joined the staff of *Madness Network News.* Two years later he cofounded the Network Against Psychiatric Assault (NAPA). In 1978 he edited and published *The History of Shock Treatment.* He has lived in San Francisco for thirty-three years.

Arguing NO are Susan L. McNeill and André Ivanoff. Ms. McNeill is a social worker on the Inpatient Psychiatry Unit of the University of Washington Medical Center. She has worked in psychiatric and emergency room social work since receiving her M.S.W. from the University of Washington in 1984. Her thesis was "Suicidal Behavior, Alcohol Use, and Emergency Room Disposition." Recently she helped develop a managed care plan for dual diagnosis psychiatric inpatients.

Dr. André Ivanoff is an Associate Professor at Columbia University School of Social Work. She received her M.S.W. and Ph.D. from the University of Washington and worked as a mental health practitioner in Outpatient Psychiatry at the University of Washington Medical Center. She has written articles and chapters on mental health and suicidal behavior, particularly in prison populations, and is coauthoring a book entitled *Research-Based Practice with Involuntary Clients.* Her research interests include the concomitants of suicidal behavior and the development and testing of prevention-focused interventions for populations at high risk for health and mental health problems.

YES

LEONARD ROY FRANK

Electroshock Is a Crime against the Spirit

Electroshock (also known as shock treatment, electroconvulsive therapy, and ECT) is a procedure used in psychiatry as a treatment for people diagnosed as "mentally ill."

Since its introduction in 1938, electroshock has been administered to between 10 and 15 million people worldwide. In the United States alone, about 100,000 people are now being electroshocked yearly, and the number appears to be growing. Recent media accounts report a resurgence of ECT interest and use.

About two-thirds of those undergoing ECT are women. About 95 percent of those administering ECT are men. A 1978 American Psychiatric Association (APA, 1978) survey showed that 22 percent of its members used ECT. Based on this figure and the current APA membership, there are now more than 8,000 ECT practitioners in the United States.

Except for infants, individuals from all age groups have been subjected to ECT. In the 1940s psychiatrist Lauretta Bender, best known as the originator of the Bender Gestalt Test, supervised a program in which 100 children (all under twelve years of age, the youngest being just under three) were electroshocked at New York's Bellevue Hospital (Bender, 1947; 1955). ECT practitioners continue to shock children and adolescents. Young and middle-aged adults had born the brunt of ECT until recent years when the trend shifted toward the elderly. A growing proportion of ECT subjects, now estimated at 50 percent, are 65 years of age and older. According to a 1989 report in a professional journal, persons over 100 are being electroshocked (Alexopoulos, Young & Abrams, 1989).

Most ECT is now being administered in the psychiatric wards of general hospitals and in private psychiatric facilities. Formerly, state hospitals were the centers of ECT activity. Currently, the most common diagnosis of ECT subjects is depression; a much smaller percentage bear the diagnosis of schizophrenia and mania. A relatively small number of ECT practitioners in the 1978 APA survey cited above reported using the procedure recently in cases of "anorexia nervosa, drug or alcohol abuse, intractable pain, personality disorder, toxic dementia, and sexual dysfunction (APA, 1978).

Electroshock is usually given in a series, which in cases of depression ranges from six to fifteen individual seizures administered three times a week. In cases of schizophrenia, the series ranges from fifteen to thirty-five seizures. The procedure usually entails three to four weeks of hospitalization, but a small proportion of subjects are treated as outpatients at hospitals and in the offices of ECT specialists. Some of these outpatients return for individual ECTs periodically as a preventive measure in what is called "maintenance ECT." Others return for individual ECTs at the first sign of a recurrence of symptoms.

Electroshock involves the production of a grand mal convulsion, similar to an epileptic seizure, by passing from 100 to 400 volts of electric current through the brain for from 0.5 to 5 seconds. Before application, ECT subjects are typically given anesthetic and muscle-paralyzing drugs to reduce fear, pain, and the risk—from violent muscle spasms—of fracture (particularly of the spine, a common occurrence in the earlier history of ECT when muscle-paralyzers were not used). These drugs carry their own risks and also raise the individual's convulsive threshold so that more current is needed to induce the convulsion. Because electricity is the most destructive component in the ECT procedure, the more current used, the greater is the risk of injury.

The electrically induced convulsion usually lasts between thirty and sixty seconds and may produce life-threatening complications, such as apnea and cardiac arrest. The convulsion is followed by a period of unconsciousness lasting several minutes. On awakening, the subject experiences a number of effects, including disorientation, confusion, grogginess, headache, nausea, delirium, amnesia, apathy or euphoria, and physical weakness. Most of these effects subside after a few hours or days, but amnesia, learning difficulties, and decreased creativity, emotionality, and energy may continue for weeks or months. Very often, one or more of these residual effects are permanent; the amnesia always is. The intensity, number, and spacing of the individual electroshocks in a series, together with the subject's physical condition, influence the severity and persistence of these effects.

In a 1983 letter printed in a professional periodical, neurologist Sidney Sament described the clinical picture of someone who has undergone ECT:

> I have seen many patients after ECT, and I have no doubt that ECT produces effects identical to those of a head injury. After multiple sessions of ECT, a patient has symptoms identical to those of a retired, punch-drunk boxer. After one session of ECT the symptoms are the same as those of a concussion (including retrograde and anterograde amnesia). After a few sessions of ECT the symptoms are those of a moderate cerebral contusion, and further enthusiastic use of ECT may result in the patient functioning at a subhuman level. (p. 11)

ECT's effects, as described in the two previous paragraphs, point clearly to what in medicine is called *organic brain syndrome,* or in lay terms *brain damage,* which by its very nature is irreversible. Brain cells—unlike skin cells, for example—do not renew themselves: destroyed once is destroyed forever. Although there is a large body of evidence (including human autopsy reports, animal and brain-wave studies, and clinical observations) in the professional literature, psychiatrists have yet to acknowledge, at least publicly, the causal relationship between electroshock and brain damage. What they think privately is another matter. In the above cited 1978 APA survey, 41 percent of psychiatrist-respondents, who were anonymous, agreed with the statement, "It is likely that ECT produces slight or subtle brain damage." Only 26 percent disagreed.

Some of the most striking evidence of brain damage from electroshock was revealed in psychiatrist David Impastato's 1957 study of 254 ECT-related deaths (Impastato, 1957). Based mainly on previously published reports which included autopsy findings, Impastato, a leading electroshock proponent, identified sixty-six "cerebral deaths."

Ironically, brain damage is one reason the procedure supposedly "works." As in other cases of serious head injury, ECT causes amnesia, denial, euphoria, apathy, mood swings, helplessness, and docility. Amnesia victims, having forgotten some problems, tend to complain less. As a result of denial, other problems are minimized or no longer recognized as such. With euphoria, the subject's depression seems to lift. With apathy, the subject's "agitation" (if that had been a factor in the original diagnosis) seems to diminish. Dependency and submissiveness tend to make what may have been a resistive, hostile subject more cooperative and friendly. In hailing the wonders of electroshock, psychiatrists have simply redefined the symptoms of psychiatrogenic brain damage as signs of improvement or recovery.

The theory that electroshock "works" by damaging the brain has been corroborated by Paul H. Hoch, an outspoken defender of both electroshock and lobotomy, who in 1948 stated at a professional meeting, "This brings us for a moment to a discussion of the brain damage produced by electroshock. . . . Is a certain amount of brain damage not necessary in this type of treatment? Frontal lobotomy indicates that improvement takes place by a definite damage of certain parts of the brain."

One of the surest indicators of brain damage is memory loss, which, not surprisingly, is the most common effect of ECT reported by ECT survivors. The loss stretching backward in time from the treatment period is called *retrograde amnesia* and may cover many months or years. The memory loss from the treatment period forward in time is called *anterograde amnesia* and usually covers several months, often including the treatment period itself. The amnesia may be global or patchy; some memories return, others are permanently lost. These losses can have a devastating effect on one's entire personality and are often experienced as a diminution of self. They not only impair one's ability to function in everyday affairs but also in the higher realms of spiritual and creative activity.

If electroshock is as destructive as portrayed here, how can its growing use be explained? Indeed, how can its ever having been used be explained? The answer is complex. Here are some factors that should be considered (Frank, 1976; 1978; 1990).

1. At a time when insurance companies are increasingly reluctant to pay for other psychiatric services, they almost always cover electroshock costs without serious questioning. In more than 70 percent of ECT cases, insurance companies pay the cost, which runs upwards of $35,000 per series. Twenty-five to thirty days of hospitalization ($600 to $800/day) for a series of 8 to 12 individual ECT treatments ($800 to $1000/treatment, including the ECT specialist's and anesthesiologist's fee, treatment-room rental, cost of premedications) is routine. Five or six people can be easily shocked in a couple of hours, at $300 per treatment for the psychiatrist. The yearly earnings of psychiatrists specializing in ECT may be twice that of other psychiatrists. In short, for psychiatrists and hospitals alike, ECT is an important money-maker: overall a $2 to $3 billion a year industry.

2. For more than fifty years the psychiatric profession has been promoting one of the biggest frauds in medical history. Through lies, distortions, and omissions it has completely misrepresented the truth about electroshock and, in so doing, has duped almost everyone, themselves included, into accepting the notion that ECT is a beneficial procedure.

By way of illustration, in 1990 the American Psychiatric Association published a 186-page Task Force Report entitled, ''The Practice of Electroconvulsive Therapy: Recommendations for Treatment, Training, and Privileging'' (APA, 1990). This authoritative report, whose publication was announced with much fanfare, including a press conference uncritically reported by the Associated Press, informed psychiatrists that ''in light of available evidence, 'brain damage' need not be included as a potential risk [in the informed consent form for ECT].'' Such ''available evidence'' as the Impastato study, cited above, reporting sixty-six ''cerebral deaths'' following ECT; the 1978 APA survey, also cited above, showing 41 percent of the responding psychiatrists agreeing that ECT produces some brain damage; and psychiatrist Peter Breggin's fully documented studies of electroshock as a brain-damaging procedure (Breggin 1979, 1991, 1992) are nowhere mentioned in the report. Breggin and Impastato are also excluded from its bibliography of 342 references.

In another instance of deception, the same report, referring to Freeman and Kendell's frequently cited 1980 follow-up study of ECT patients in Scotland, concluded that ''a small minority of patients . . . report persistent [memory] deficits'' (APA, 1990). In this study, about which the report had nothing further to say, 64 percent of 166 patients interviewed one to seven years following ECT reported ''memory impairment'' from ECT (25 percent ''thought symptom severe,'' 39 percent ''thought symptom mild''). Twenty-eight percent agreed with the statement that ''ECT causes permanent changes to memory.'' An appendix to the APA report included an example of an ECT consent form, which stated, ''A small minority of patients, perhaps 1 in 200, report severe problems in memory that remain for months or even years'' (p. 158). Thus the report grossly understated the risk of memory loss following ECT and then added to its deceit by referring to both the 28 percent in the Freeman and Kendell study and the 0.5% in its own consent form as ''a small minority.''

3. Electroshock is useful as a method of social control. Individuals who fall or step out of line become troublesome to themselves or others. Not only does the use or threatened use of ECT usually bring them back into line, but the knowledge of its availability has an intimidating effect on many other people as well. At some level of their consciousness the message has come home: stay in line—or else (Warren, 1986)!

4. Last, electroshock reinforces the biological model of ''mental illness.'' Under this model, which dominates contemporary psychiatry, mental illness is seen as a brain, hormonal, metabolic, or genetic disorder. Biological psychiatrists, as those psychiatrists who have adopted this model are usually called, regard people as objects to be manipulated and fixed. But human beings are much more than that. Biology is not destiny. Character is. And character is shaped primarily by the manner in which individuals choose to conduct themselves and by what is done for and to them throughout their lives. By reducing the individual's ability to function spiritually, intellectually, emotionally, and physically, electroshock undermines character and, along with it, freedom and responsibility. It has no place in a free society; wherever it is used, society cannot be truly free.

In conclusion, if the body is the temple of the spirit, the brain may be seen as the inner sanctum of the body, the holiest of holy places. To invade, violate, and injure the brain, as electroshock unfailingly does, is a crime against the spirit and a desecration of the soul.

References

Alexopoulos, G. S., Young, R. C., & Abrams, R. C. (1989). ECT in the high-risk geriatric patient. *Convulsive Therapy, 5:* 75–87.

American Psychiatric Association (1978). *Electroconvulsive Therapy.* Task Force Report 14. Washington DC: Author.

American Psychiatric Association (1990). *The practice of electroconvulsive therapy: Recommendations for treatment, training, and privileging.* Task Force on Electroconvulsive Therapy. Washington, DC: Author.

Bender, L. (1947). One hundred cases of childhood schizophrenia treated with electric shock. *Transactions of the American Neurological Association, 72:* 165–168.

Bender, L. (1955). The development of a schizophrenic child treated with electric convulsions at three years of age. In G. Kaplan (Ed.), *Emotional problems of early childhood.* New York: Basic Books, pp. 407–425.

Breggin, P. R. (1979). *Electroshock: Its brain-disabling effects.* New York, Springer.

Breggin, P. R. (1991). *Toxic psychiatry: Why therapy, empathy, and love must replace the drugs, electroshock, and biochemical theories of the ''new psychiatry.''* New York, St. Martin's Press.

Breggin, P. R. (1992). The return of ECT. *Readings, 7,* 12–17.

Frank, L. R. (1976). The Frank papers. In J. Friedberg, *Shock treatment is not good for your brain* (pp. 62–81). San Francisco, Glide Publications.

Frank, L. R. (1978). *The history of shock treatment.* San Francisco, Frank.

Frank, L. R. (1990). Electroshock: Death, brain damage, memory loss, and brainwashing. *Journal of Mind and Behavior, 11,* 489–512 (Reprinted in R. F. Morgan, ed. (1991). *Electroshock: The case against.* Toronto, IPI Publishing.)

Freeman, C. P. & Kendell, R. E. (1980). ECT: 1. Patients' experiences and attitudes. *British Journal of Psychiatry, 137:* 8–16.

Impastato, D. (1957). Prevention of fatalities in electroshock therapy. *Diseases of the Nervous System, 18* [supplement], 34–75.

Hoch, P. H. (1948). Discussion and concluding remarks. *Journal of Personality, 17:* 48–49.

Sament, S. (1983, March). Letter. *Clinical Psychiatry News 11* (3): 11.

Warren, C. A. B. (1986). Electroconvulsive therapy: ''New'' treatment of the 1980s. *Research in Law, Deviance and Social Control, 7,* 41–55.

Rejoinder to Mr. Frank

SUSAN L. MCNEILL AND ANDRÉ IVANOFF

ECT is one of the most controversial treatments in psychiatry. Although the arguments against ECT are cogent and compelling, they fall short of convincing us that ECT should never be used. The rhetoric of fear based on reports twenty to fifty years old must be separated from the current standards, procedures, and protections surrounding the use of ECT. Philosophically and pragmatically, the decision to ban this medical procedure is a complex one, raising many questions. Do some people benefit from the procedure? Is ECT used primarily to hurt, control, and abuse? Do the side effects outweigh the benefits? From a critical perspective, what does the outcome research say?

Case study reports and standardized mental health measures document marked improvement in depression among geriatric populations as a result of ECT. The current use of ECT in the United States is regulated in each state; its primary purpose here is as treatment. Misuse of ECT clearly has occurred in the past. In some countries, ECT is used as political torture and is misused on vulnerable and institutionalized populations. In the United States however, ECT is no more an instrument of social control than the use of psychotropic medications and institutionalization; few advocate totally abolishing these. Important larger issues of psychiatry's role in defining mental health or illness and the ascendancy of biologic psychiatry are not appropriately focused on this single procedure.

Measurement of permanent and significant memory dysfunction has not been documented in research. Blaine's (1986) summation of current use reports ECT to be an extremely safe procedure and shows no evidence that ECT produces brain damage. The rates of amnesia resulting from properly administered ECT are not known (Martin, 1986). Those who speak out against the procedure, however, are those who feel they have been harmed by it and attest to these dysfunctions.

Research examining the outcome of ECT with depressed geriatric individuals has found significant improvement in the commonly accepted vegetative and affective symptoms associated with depression. Investigations of ECT and many other psychiatric treatments are often limited to case study reports and small or nonrandomized samples of patients; methodologically, better research is needed.

A pervasive suggestion throughout Frank's arguments is that current ECT procedures and safeguards are no different than those of thirty to fifty years ago. This is not the case. The work of Frank and others has been in large part responsible for establishing the regulations that currently govern the use of ECT in all fifty states. These regulations were developed in direct response to the misuses described. The arguments presented here against ECT contain numerous minor exaggerations. Positioned to incite anger and fear, they interweave fact with experiential interpretation and result in a politically and personally frightening picture. Just one example is the suggestion that ECT is disproportionately used on women by male psychiatrists. Unfortunately, this is true of all psychiatric and psychotherapeutic interventions, not just ECT.

ECT is usually not a treatment of first choice; however, with geriatric patients suffering from depression there is evidence that it is an effective treatment. Protecting the rights of patients unable to advocate for themselves is a paramount concern. Part of protecting patient rights, however, is ensuring the widest availability of treatment options. The deterioration of spirit and body resulting from refractory depression is horrible to witness in a loved one. When a course of ECT results in an individual reconnecting with family, deciding to eat, and regaining, after many months, an interest in a favorite object or pastime, the procedure seems both humane and worthwhile.

The decision to use ECT must be made carefully with the informed involvement of family members and, to the fullest extent possible, the patient. Our positive experiences with clients, patients, and loved ones have created a willingness to include ECT among the range of treatment options. Mental health practitioners, whether opposed to or in favor of ECT, cannot defer these decisions solely to medical colleagues. We are responsible for educating those involved and helping them weigh, with intelligence and compassion, the possible side effects of the procedure against its potential benefits. The unfortunate use of frightening images may prevent informed consideration by those who might benefit from the procedure.

References

Blaine, J. D. (1986). Electroconvulsive therapy and cognitive dysfunction. *Hospital & Community Psychiatry, 37,* 15–16.

Martin, B. A. (1986). Electroconvulsive therapy: Contemporary standards of practice. *Canadian Journal of Psychiatry, 31,* 759–771.

NO

Susan L. McNeill and André Ivanoff

Electroconvulsive therapy (ECT) has been a controversial treatment since it was first used in Italy in 1933. It is an inelegant and invasive procedure, frightening to think about, and the reasons why it is effective remain poorly understood. There is no doubt that there has been inappropriate use of ECT in the past and that some current usage may be questionable. We do not attempt to defend all uses of ECT. The efficacy of ECT with children, adolescents, or patients suffering from psychotic disorders is not well established. Data do support the effectiveness of ECT, however, in the treatment and management of refractory depression when more conservative treatments have failed.

ECT was used before the advent of psychotropic medications and before patients' rights to information and to refuse treatment were recognized. Reports suggest that, even during this time, when ECT was used in a less knowledgeable and less discriminating manner, it was more effective at reducing the physical symptoms of depression than no treatment at all (Martin, 1986). During this early period, anesthesia and muscle relaxants were not used during ECT. Patients were not only terrified, they suffered complications such as memory loss, fractures, and even death. Informed consent was not obtained and patients were often subjected to ECT involuntarily and without regard for civil liberties. Considering how barbaric the procedure was and the lack of understanding about how ECT actually changed things, it is not surprising that strong biases developed against its use. When these biases are coupled with evidence of overuse, misuse, and abuse, they become even stronger and fear-based. Nightmare images of ECT used to control uncooperative patients (as portrayed, for example, in Kesey's "One Flew Over the Cuckoo's Nest") and the use of ECT to punish political dissidents have led to lasting negative impressions. The argument for not abolishing ECT, however, is the same as for other controversial, potentially overused and abusive methods of treatment that have proved useful (e.g., hysterectomy, cesarean section deliveries, drugs with high abuse potential such as cocaine and heroin): The prohibition of ECT would be to the detriment of those individuals who can truly benefit from the procedure.

Because of the increasing use of psychotropic drugs to treat depression and ECT's misuse and subsequent bad reputation, use of ECT declined through the 1970s. During the 1980s, however, ECT regained some acceptance as a relatively safe, low-risk, and effective treatment for depression. This increased use may be attributed to three developments: (1) new techniques for administering ECT; (2) recognition of the limitations of medications for some patient groups; and (3) data demonstrating its effective use in the treatment of suicidal and geriatric patients.

Administration

A first priority in the ethical use of ECT is informed consent of the patient. Although individual rules vary across the country, all states have regulations governing the use of ECT. This is a general model of how informed consent is obtained. First the details of the ECT procedure, including anticipated risks and benefits, are explained to the patient and to the family. They are then shown a video demonstrating the procedure. Patients are given time to consider their options and ask questions. A second physician opinion is usually required. Last, the patient must sign an informed consent form, acknowledging an understanding of the procedure and its risks, before ECT can be performed. In the case of a patient who may not be competent to make decisions about his or her medical care, a court hearing is required before administering ECT. A guardian or other individual with power of attorney cannot make the decision for the patient.

The patient receives a thorough medical examination to ensure that there are no contraindications for the procedure. On ECT administration days, the patient is not allowed oral intake after midnight because a general anesthetic is used. An operating room or special unit prepared for anesthesia and ventilation is used for ECT. A short-acting anesthetic and a muscle relaxant are administered to prevent injury and provide for patient comfort. Cardiac monitoring continues throughout treatment and recovery. The electrical stimulus is administered and adjusted so that the patient has a seizure lasting twenty-five or more seconds. A brief pulse sine wave current is used. This method of triggering seizures results in fewer side effects than the use of continuous sine wave current which was formerly used. Treatments are given two or three times per week, and the average number of treatments ranges from seven to twelve. The patient remains in the recovery room until he or she recovers from the effects of the anesthesia and then returns to the regular unit.

Side Effects

Immediately after treatment, and lasting for several hours, the most common adverse reactions are a transient headache and some nausea, which can be symptomatically treated. Post-treatment confusion is common, but not long-lasting, and usually clears in a matter of hours or a few days. Memory loss is the most widely reported and controversial side effect of ECT. Many, but not all, patients report amnesia for a period of time immediately surrounding the treatment. Recovery of memory begins in a few weeks and is completely restored in three to six months. Permanent memory loss that occurs as a result of current ECT administration procedures cannot be objectively documented (Pearlman, 1991). The procedure is remarkably safe, with a mortality rate of three to five patients per 100,000 treatments, which is similar to that of outpatient dental surgery.

Effectiveness

The efficacy of ECT in treating major depression has been demonstrated. Rates of improvement are reported at 70 percent to 80 percent. This is particularly impressive when one considers that most of today's ECT patients have failed medication trials and other more conservative treatments. ECT has been shown to be as effective as or superior to medications and to sham ECT in controlled, double-blind studies with patients suffering from diagnosed major depression (Pearlman, 1991).

In cases of severe depression, the risk of suicide is always present. Because ECT provides more rapid response than medication or psychological treatments, it may more directly reduce suicide risk. At least one study reports reduced suicidal behavior and improved survival rates in ECT versus drug-treated patients (Tanney, 1986). ECT has also been successfully used on an outpatient maintenance basis to prevent relapse to major depression and psychiatric rehospitalization (Thienhaus, Margletta, & Bennett, 1990).

ECT is frequently the treatment of choice for geriatric patients. The very elderly often have medical conditions that make the use of antidepressants problematic. These medications also have side effects that are very poorly tolerated in the geriatric population. For this patient group, ECT is a relatively safe and effective treatment that can add much to the quality of life for the older patient. Older patients respond well, and as their depression lifts, memory, rather than being impaired, often also improves (Martin, 1986). Not surprisingly, complications may occur at a higher frequency among the very old and those in poor health, but the risks of complication have not been found to outweigh the benefits of treatment (Burke, Rubin, Zorumski, & Wetzel, 1987).

Case Study

Ms. R. is a 72-year-old woman who was admitted to the psychiatric unit of an urban hospital following four years in a nursing home. The reason for this long stay was unclear as she had recovered from the bowel resection that initially necessitated the placement and had no other major or ongoing medical problems. She was severely depressed and would not eat, drink, or respond to questions. She stayed in bed all day with her eyes closed except to use the bathroom. Although a feeding tube was in place, she was starving herself to death; her skin was breaking down and wasting was evident. ECT was initiated. After her second ECT treatment, Ms. R. was opening her eyes and giving the nurse orders. After the third treatment she began eating a bit and complained about the food. After a few more treatments she improved enough to participate in physical therapy and independently went into the day room and interacted with other patients. By the end of treatment she was joking and telling the nurses that she looked forward to physical therapy because the therapists were "such hunks." At the time of her discharge, her son reported his mother had not looked so well in over five years.

Dramatic? Yes. Unusual? No. The use of ECT as a treatment for serious refractory depression is adequately established as safe, effective, and appropriate. It can prolong and improve the quality of life. Data on current methods support the use of ECT. To abolish it based on overuse and misuse would deny treatment to a subset of persons for whom no other equally effective treatment exists.

References

Burke, W. J., Rubin, E. H., Zorumski, C. F., & Wetzel, R. D. (1987). The safety of ECT in geriatric psychiatry. *Journal of the American Geriatric Society, 35,* 516–521.

Martin, B. A. (1986). Electroconvulsive therapy: Contemporary standards of practice. *Canadian Journal of Psychiatry, 31,* 759–771.

Pearlman, C. (1991). Electroconvulsive therapy: Current concepts. *General Hospital Psychiatry, 13,* 128–137.

Tanney, B. (1986). Electroconvulsive therapy and suicide. *Suicide and Life Threatening Behavior, 16,* 117–131.

Thienhaus, O. J., Margletta, S. & Bennett, J. A. (1990). A study of the clinical efficacy of maintenance ECT. *Journal of Clinical Psychiatry, 51,* 141–144.

Annotated Bibliography

Martin, B. A. (1986). Electroconvulsive therapy: Contemporary standards of practice. *Canadian Journal of Psychiatry, 31,* 759–771.

This article reviews the history and effectiveness of ECT with a variety of disorders and identifies knowledge gaps.

Pearlman, C. (1991). Electroconvulsive therapy: Current concepts. *General Hospital Psychiatry, 13,* 128–137.

This article reviews recent developments in the practice and theory of ECT. It describes treatment procedures in detail and medical considerations.

Taub, S. (1987). Electroconvulsive therapy, malpractice, and informed consent. *The Journal of Psychiatry and Law, 15,* 7–54.

This is an excellent overview of the use of, research on, and legal issues concerning ECT. It addresses malpractice and patients' rights.

Rejoinder to Ms. McNeill and Dr. Ivanoff

LEONARD ROY FRANK

In presenting their case for electroshock, Ms. McNeill and Dr. Ivanoff have made many serious errors. This brief rebuttal addresses a few of the most important ones.

The authors discuss the early period of ECT (for example, "how barbaric the procedure was," implying that it no longer is) and comment that there was "evidence of overuse, misuse, and abuse." If the procedure was barbaric, as it undoubtedly was, its wrongful use was not the issue: it shouldn't have been used at all. While there have been minor, mostly cosmetic, changes in the method of administration, electroshock—as commonly used today with higher doses of electricity and longer seizures—is usually more damaging to the brain, and thus more barbaric, than it was previously.

The authors talk about informed consent as "a first priority in the ethical use of ECT." What ECT practitioners try to obtain from their subjects would be better called *misinformed* consent. The possibility of brain damage, the single most obvious and significant effect of ECT, is rarely if ever mentioned in consent forms. These forms also grossly understate the risk of permanent and severe memory loss from electroshock. Moreover, the inherent coerciveness of psychiatric wards, where most ECT is administered, and the threat of forced treatment (masquerading as legitimate court-ordered treatment for persons ruled incompetent or incapable of giving consent) render free choice impossible.

Memory loss is not "completely restored in three to six months," as the authors assert. In addition to the findings of permanent amnesia from ECT in the Freeman and Kendell study (1980), there is the three-year follow-up study by research psychologist Larry Squire (1983). He found that of thirty-one people who had been electroshocked three years before testing, seventeen (55 percent) still had memory difficulties that they attributed to ECT.

The authors state that ECT's effectiveness in "treating major depression has been demonstrated." The standard way to test for ECT effectiveness is by comparing real ECT and sham ECT (the subject is anesthetized but not shocked) in controlled double-blind studies. At the First European Symposium on ECT in Graz, Austria, in March 1992, two psychiatrists from England, Graham P. Sheppard and Saad K. Ahmed, delivered a paper entitled, "A Critical Review of the Controlled Real Versus Sham ECT Studies in Depressive Illness." Sheppard and Ahmed concluded that the thirteen such studies under review and analysis "do not offer significant evidence that real ECT is more therapeutically effective than sham ECT in depressive illness." (p. 80) The Crowe and Johnstone review published in the *Annals of the New York Academy of Sciences* (1986) drew the same conclusion from a smaller number of studies.

Given the reports cited above, the absence of solid double-blind studies showing long-term effectiveness, and electroshock's demonstrated harmfulness, one must conclude that there is no scientific justification for using ECT.

McNeill and Ivanoff echo the claims of ECT specialists that for those elderly who respond poorly to antidepressant drugs ECT is a "relatively safe and effective treatment." While it is true that antidepressants carry serious risks for the elderly, particularly the infirm and those with heart disease, the very ones who tolerate these drugs least are the most vulnerable to ECT's damaging effects. ECT is a more invasive procedure than the antidepressants. It is for this reason that biological psychiatrists generally use antidepressants before resorting to ECT. It should also be noted that Impastato (1957) estimated that the ECT death rate for the elderly was five times higher than for the young.

The authors go on to say that ECT often improves the memory of the elderly. The notion that ECT, with its resultant brain damage, improves memory is preposterous. What happens is that some individuals, previously mute or taciturn, are more responsive to questions after undergoing ECT. This does not signify that the ECT has improved their memory. It merely indicates that they are more motivated to answer questions following ECT than they had been before.

The quality of life for the elderly is crucially linked to memory. It is often their most valued possession. And well it should be, for memory is the soul's companion and a bulwark of human dignity. As Emerson once wrote, "[To remember] what is best in our experience is our splendid privilege." Whether or not they talk about it, many elderly people are deeply troubled by their loss of memory, whatever the cause. To claim, as McNeill and Ivanoff do, that electroshock, a known memory destroyer, "can add much to the quality of life for the older patient" is shameful.

References

Crow, T. J. & Johnstone, E. C. (1986, March 14). Controlled trials of electroconvulsive therapy. *Annals of the New York Academy of Sciences, 462:*12–29.

Freeman, C. P., & Kendall, R. E. (1980). ECT: Patients' experiences and attitudes. *British Journal of Psychiatry, 137:* 8–16.

Impastato, D. (1957). Prevention of fatalities in electroshock therapy. *Diseases of the Nervous System, 18* [supplement], 34–75.

Sheppard, G. P. & Ahmed, S. K. (1992, March). A critical review of the controlled real versus sham ECT studies in depressive illness. Presented at the First European Symposium on ECT, Graz, Austria.

Squire, L. R. (1983). Electroconvulsive therapy and complaints of memory dysfunction: A prospective three-year follow-up study. *British Journal of Psychiatry, 142:* 1–8.

DEBATE 10

Should the Use of Neuroleptics Be Severely Limited?

YES argues Peter R. Breggin, M.D., who is a psychiatrist in private practice in Bethesda, Maryland, and the author of two recent books, *Toxic Psychiatry: Why Therapy, Empathy and Love Must Replace the Drugs, Electroshock and Biochemical Theories of the "New Psychiatry"* (St. Martin's Press, 1991) and *Beyond Conflict: From Self-Help and Psychotherapy to Peace-Making* (St. Martin's Press, 1992). Dr. Breggin is Director of the Center for the Study of Psychiatry in Bethesda and a Professor of Conflict Analysis and Resolution at George Mason University in Fairfax, Virginia. He frequently writes, lectures, and consults on a wide variety of subjects in psychiatry and has been a medical expert in landmark lawsuits on behalf of patient rights.

Steven A. Mitchell says NO. Dr. Mitchell first became interested in psychopharmacological issues while working in the Neurosciences Program at the University of Alabama in Birmingham where he was a graduate student in psychology. After completing a master's degree he went on to do further research there, publishing several papers on topics related to psychopharmacology, and obtained a Ph.D. in physiology and biophysics. He subsequently completed an M.D. at the University of South Alabama and currently is in private practice in psychiatry in Seattle, where he also works at the Department of Psychiatry, University of Washington.

YES

PETER R. BREGGIN

In 1954 chlorpromazine (Thorazine) broke like a tidal wave across the state mental hospitals of the Western world. Within a year or two, most mental hospital patients in Europe and North America were being forced to take the drug. Over the next several years, a dozen new neuroleptics were introduced into the market, and their use became focused on the psychoses, especially schizophrenia and acute mania. Several hundred million people worldwide have now received them, often involuntarily.

The Claims

The neuroleptics drugs gradually became promoted as agents with a specific "antipsychotic" effect on schizophrenic symptoms. Meanwhile, psychosocial approaches fell into disrepute among many psychiatrists. Patients were often instructed to remain on neuroleptics for a lifetime and were told that it was safe to do so. Later the public was told that the "miracle" drugs had emptied the hospitals and returned millions of patients to normal lives.

The Reality

In 1973, psychiatrist George Crane gained the attention of the medical community by disclosing that many, and perhaps most, long-term neuroleptic patients were developing a largely irreversible, untreatable neurological disorder, tardive dyskinesia (Crane, 1973). The disease, even its mild forms, is often disfiguring, with involuntary movements of the face, mouth, or tongue. Frequently, the patients grimace in a manner that makes them look "crazy," undermining their credibility with other people. In more severe cases, patients become disabled by twitches, spasms, and other abnormal movements of any muscle groups, including those of the neck, shoulders, back, arms and legs, and hands and feet (American Psychiatric Association, 1992; Breggin, 1983, 1990, 1991). The muscles of respiration and speech can also be impaired. In the worst cases, patients thrash about continually.

The rates for tardive dyskinesia are astronomical. The latest estimate from the American Psychiatric Association (1992, p. 68) indicates a rate for all patients of 5 percent per year, so that 15 percent of patients develop tardive dyskinesia within only three years. In long-term studies, the prevalence of tardive dyskinesia often exceeds 50 percent of all treated patients and is probably much higher. The disease affects people of all ages, including children, but among older patients rates escalate. In a controlled study, 41 percent of patients age 65 and older developed tardive dyskinesia in a mere twenty-four months (Yassa, Nastase, Camille, & Belzile, 1988). Hundreds of thousands of older people receive these drugs in nursing homes and state hospitals.

Other closely related, untreatable neurological disorders have now been recognized as variants of tardive dyskinesia. Tardive akathisia involves painful feelings of inner tension and anxiety and a compulsive drive to move the body. In the extreme, the individual undergoes internal torture and can no longer sit still. Tardive akathisia often develops in children who have been treated for "hyperactivity," ironically and tragically subjecting them to permanent inner torture. Tardive dystonia involves muscle spasms, frequently of the face, neck, and shoulders, and it too can be disfiguring, disabling, and agonizing.

There are no accurate surveys of the total number of patients afflicted with tardive dyskinesia. There are probably a million or more tardive dyskinesia patients in the United States today, and tens of millions have been afflicted throughout the world since the inception of neuroleptic treatment (Breggin, 1991). Despite this tragic situation, psychiatrists too often fail to give proper warnings to patients and their families. Often psychiatrists fail to notice that their patients are suffering from tardive dyskinesia, even when the symptoms are flagrant (Brown & Funk, 1986; Breggin, 1991).

In 1983 I published the first in-depth analysis of the vulnerability of children to a particularly virulent form of the tardive dyskinesia that attacks the muscles of the trunk, making it difficult for them to stand or walk. This is now an established fact. In the same medical book, I offered the first detailed documentation showing that many or most tardive dyskinesia patients also show signs of dementia—an irreversible loss of overall higher brain and mental function. Indeed, it was inevitable that these losses would occur. The basal ganglia, which are afflicted in tardive dyskinesia, are richly interconnected with the higher centers of the brain, so that their dysfunction almost inevitably leads to disturbances in cognitive processes (for the functional neuroanatomy, see Alheid, Heimer, Lennart, & Switzer, 1990). Since my observations, a multitude of studies have confirmed that long-term neuroleptic use is associated with both cognitive deterioration and atrophy of the brain (Breggin, 1990; Gualtieri & Barnhill, 1988). While defenders of the drugs sometimes claim that this mental and neurological deterioration is caused by schizophrenia itself, their position is untenable. More than a hundred years of autopsy studies of patients labeled as schizophrenic failed to show any such deterioration, until the recent advent of neuroleptics.

Growing evidence indicates that these drugs produce tardive psychoses that are irreversible and more severe than the patients' prior problems. In children, permanent behavioral or mental disorders frequently develop as a result of the drugs (Gaultieri & Barnhill, 1988). Furthermore, drug withdrawal often causes rebound of the anticholinergic neurotransmitter system, resulting in a flu-like syndrome that includes emotional upset, insomnia, nausea, and vomiting. Many patients find themselves unable to stop taking the drugs, suggesting that we should consider them addictive (Breggin, 1989a, 1989b).

Shocking as it may seem, this brief review can only scratch the surface of neurological disorders associated with these drugs, let alone the vast number of other potentially serious side effects. For example, in a small percentage of patients the neuroleptic reaction goes out of control, producing neuroleptic malignant syndrome. The disorder is indistinguishable from an acute inflammation of the brain comparable to lethargic encephalitis (Breggin, 1990, 1991) and can be fatal.

Given that these are exceedingly dangerous drugs, what about their advantages? How do they "work"? It is well-known that these drugs suppress dopamine neurotransmission in the brain, directly impairing the function of the basal ganglia and the emotion-regulating limbic system and frontal lobes and indirectly impairing the reticular activating system as well. The overall impact is a chemical lobotomy—literally so, since frontal lobe function is suppressed (Breggin, 1983, 1991). The patient becomes de-energized or de-enervated. Will or volition is crushed, and passivity and docility are induced. The patient complains less and becomes more manageable. Despite the claims made for symptom cure, multiple clinical studies document a nonspecific emotional flattening or blunting effect (reviewed in Breggin, 1983, 1991).

There is no significant body of research to prove that neuroleptics have any specific effect on psychotic symptoms, such as hallucinations and delusions. To the contrary, those remain rather resistant to the drugs. The neuroleptics mainly suppress aggression, rebelliousness, and spontaneous activity in general. This is why they are effective whenever and wherever social control is at a premium, such as in mental hospitals, nursing homes, prisons, institutions for persons with developmental disabilities, children's facilities, and public clinics, as well as in Soviet and Cuban psychiatric political prisons. Their widespread use for social control in such a wide variety of people and institutions makes the claim that they are specific for schizophrenia ridiculous. They are even used in veterinary medicine to bend or subdue the will of animals. When one of our dogs was given a neuroleptic for car sickness, our daughter observed, "He's behaving himself for the first time in his life."

The neuroleptics are supposedly most effective in treating the acute phase of schizophrenia, but a recent definitive review of controlled studies showed that they perform no better than sedatives or narcotics and even no better than placebo (Keck, Cohen, & Baldessarini, 1989). One psychiatrist (Turns, 1990) responded to these revelations with anguished questions: "Has our clinical judgment about the efficacy of antipsychotics been a fixed, encapsulated, delusional perception. . . . Are we back to square 1 in antipsychotic psychopharmacology?"

That the neuroleptics emptied the mental hospitals is myth. The drugs were in widespread use as early as 1954 and 1955, but the hospital population did not decline until nearly ten years later, starting in 1963. That year the federal government first provided disability insurance coverage for mental disorders. The states could at last relieve themselves of the financial burden by refusing admission to new patients and by discharging old ones. The discharged patients, callously abandoned by psychiatry, received a small federal check for their support in other facilities, such as nursing or board and care homes. Some patients went home as dependents while others went onto the streets. Follow-up studies show that very, very few patients became independent or led better lives following these new policies (Mosher & Burti, 1989; Breggin, 1991).

But are there better psychosocial alternatives? Yes, there are. Controlled studies by Loren Mosher have shown that patients diagnosed with acute schizophrenia improve better without medication in small home-like settings run by nonprofessional staff who know how to listen and to care (Mosher & Burti, 1989). The patients become more independent, and do so at no greater financial cost, because nonprofessional salaries are so much lower. As an enormous added benefit, the drug-free patients do not get tardive dyskinesia or tardive dementia, as well as other drug-induced and sometimes life-threatening disorders.

Controlled studies by Karon & Vandenbos (1981) indicate that even in traditional psychiatric facilities psychotherapy is the treatment of choice for patients labeled as schizophrenic. My own experience in psychiatry began as a college student volunteer in a state mental hospital. We proved that untrained college students, with only minimal supervision, could work as case aides to help nearly all of our chronic patients leave the hospital (Breggin, 1991).

But isn't schizophrenia a biochemical and genetic disease? In reality, there's no convincing evidence that schizophrenia is a biochemical disorder. While there are a host of conjectures about biochemical imbalances, the only ones we know of in the brains of mental patients are those produced by the drugs. Similarly, no substantial evidence exists for a genetic basis of schizophrenia. The frequently cited Scandinavian genetic studies (Kety, Rosenthal, Wender, Schulsinger & Jacobsen, 1975; reviewed in Breggin, 1991) actually confirm an environmental factor while disproving a genetic one. My conclusions may seem incredible to readers who have been bombarded with psychiatric propaganda, and I can only hope they will personally review the literature and read *Toxic Psychiatry* for a review and analysis. But even if schizophrenia were a brain disease, it would not make sense to add further brain damage and dysfunction by administering neuroleptics.

If the neuroleptics are so dangerous and have such limited usefulness, and if psychosocial approaches are relatively effective, why is the profession so devoted to the drugs? The answer lies in maintaining psychiatric power, prestige, and income. What mainly distinguishes psychiatrists from other mental health professionals, and of course from nonprofessionals, is their ability to prescribe drugs. To compete against other mental health professionals, psychiatry has wed itself to the medical model, including biological and genetic explanations, and physical treatments. It has no choice; anything else would be professional suicide. In providing psychosocial therapies, psychiatry cannot compete with less expensive, more helpful nonmedical therapists, so it must create myths that support the need for medically trained psychiatrists.

After falling behind economically in competition with psychosocial approaches, psychiatry formed what the American Psychiatric Association now admits is a "partnership" with the drug companies (Sabshin, 1992). Organized psychiatry has become wholly dependent for financial support on this unholy collaboration with the pharmaceutical industry (Breggin, 1991). To deny the effectiveness of drugs or to admit their dangerousness would result in huge economic losses on every level from the individual psychiatrist who makes his or her living by prescribing medication, to the American Psychiatric Association which thrives on drug company largesse.

If neuroleptics were used to treat anyone other than mental patients, they would have been banned a long time ago. If their use wasn't supported by powerful interest groups, such as the pharmaceutical industry and organized psychiatry, they would be rarely used at all. Meanwhile, the neuroleptics have produced the worst epidemic of neurological disease in history. At the least, their use should be severely curtailed.

Beyond the specific issue of the neuroleptics, there is a much broader one—how are we to understand and to show care for people who undergo emotional pain and anguish (Breggin, 1991, 1992; Mosher & Burti, 1989). Are we to view them as defective objects or as human beings struggling with emotional and social problems and personal conflict? Are we to drug them into oblivion, or are we to understand and empower them? Giving a drug disempowers the recipient. It says, "You are helpless in the face of your problems. You need less feeling and energy, and less brain function." The true aim of therapy should be to strengthen and to empower the individual. People, not pills, are the only source of real help.

References

Alheid, G. F., Heimer, L. & Switzer, III, R. D. (1990). Basal ganglia. In G. Paxinos (Ed.). *The human nervous system* (pp. 483–582) New York: Academic Press.

American Psychiatric Association (1992). *Task force on tardive dyskinesia.* Washington, DC: American Psychiatric Association.

Breggin, P. R. (1983). *Psychiatric drugs.* New York: Springer Publishing.

Breggin, P. R. (1989a). Addiction to neuroleptics? [letter]. *American Journal of Psychiatry, 146,* 560.

Breggin, P. R. (1989b). Dr. Breggin replies [follow-up letter on addiction to neuroleptics]. *American Journal of Psychiatry, 146,* 1240.

Breggin, P. R. (1990). Brain damage, dementia and persistent cognitive dysfunction associated with neuroleptic drugs: Evidence, etiology, implications. *Journal of Mind and Behavior 11,* 425–464.

Breggin, P. R. (1991). *Toxic psychiatry.* New York: St. Martin's Press.

Breggin, P. R. (1992). *Beyond conflict.* New York: St. Martin's Press.

Brown, P., & Funk, S. C. (1986). Tardive dyskinesia: Barriers to professional recognition of an iatrogenic disease. *Journal of Health and Social Behavior, 27,* 116–132.

Crane, G. (1973). Clinical psychopharmacology in its 20th year. *Science, 181,* 124–128.

Gualtieri, C. T., & Barnhill, L. J. (1988). Tardive dyskinesia in special populations. In M. E. Wolf and A. D. Mosnaim (Eds.), *Tardive dyskinesia* (pp. 135–154). Washington, DC: American Psychiatric Press.

Karon, B., & Vandenbos, G. (1981). *The psychotherapy of schizophrenia.* New York: Jason Aronson.

Keck, P. E., Jr., Cohen, B. M., & Baldessarini, R. (1989). Time course of antipsychotic effects of neuroleptic drugs. *American Journal of Psychiatry 146,* 1289–1292.

Kety, S., Rosenthal, D., Wender, P., Schulsinger, F., & Jacobsen, N. B. (1975). Mental illness in the biological and adoptive families of adopted individuals who have become schizophrenic. In E. Fieve, D. Rosenthal, & H. Brill (Eds.), *Genetic research in psychiatry,* (pp. 157–163). Baltimore: Johns Hopkins.

Mosher, L. R., and Burti, L. (1989). *Community mental health.* New York: Norton.

Sabshin, M. (1992, March 10). To aid understanding of mental disorders. *New York Times A,* 22.

Turns, C. N. (1990). Effects of sedatives and neuroleptics [letter]. *American Journal of Psychiatry 147,* 1576.

Yassa, R., Nastase, C., Camille, Y., & Belzile L. (1988). Tardive dyskinesia in a psychogeriatric population. In M. D. Wolf & A. D. Mosnaim (Eds.) *Tardive dyskinesia.* Washington, DC: American Psychiatric Press.

Rejoinder to Dr. Breggin

STEVEN A. MITCHELL

Reading through Dr. Breggin's article, rebuttal, and book, *Toxic Psychiatry,* one is struck by the deep concern that he brings to the topic of what constitutes optimal care for psychiatric patients. In addition, he has clearly invested an enormous amount of time and energy in investigating this issue and in pursuing what sounds like nothing so much as a crusade against all biological therapies used in psychiatry. For example, in his book he states, "While I was able to prevent the wholesale return of psychiatric surgery. . . ." For a more realistic account of the factors that have influenced the decline of psychosurgery, see Elliot Vallenstein's excellent review, *Brain Control* (1973).

Unfortunately, in his zeal to advance his views Dr. Breggin appears to have gone beyond scholarly review and dispassionate, balanced analysis of available scientific data to create a blanket diatribe against virtually anyone who has chosen psychiatry as a profession. What he seems to have lost sight of is that he is not the only psychiatrist who has empathy and compassion for the suffering of psychiatric patients. What he chooses not to address is the successful alleviation of symptoms obtainable by medications. Not content to attack antipsychotic medications, he blasts away at all biological therapies currently used in psychiatry to alleviate symptoms.

Throughout his article, and in more detail in his book, Dr. Breggin asserts that there has developed a vast, sinister conspiracy to mislead, misinform, and harm psychiatric patients. Indeed, by characterizing psychiatric patients as "survivors of psychiatry" and repeatedly referring to them as "victims," he reflects his not so subtle bias. His characterization of the distinction between psychiatrists and their patients as "the mad are inarticulate poets, psychiatrists are articulate know nothings" reflects somewhat the flavor of his underlying view. Reading through his article and book shows his clear tendency to minimize therapeutic benefits of biological therapies and to overestimate side effects. For example, much of Dr. Breggin's attack on antipsychotic medications focuses on tardive dyskinesia. After admitting that there are no definitive data on the incidence of this disorder he proceeds to provide an opinion that "many and perhaps most" patients on antipsychotic medications have tardive dyskinesia and that it is "largely irreversible." The widely accepted estimate that twenty to twenty-five percent of individuals chronically treated with antipsychotic medications demonstrate tardive dyskinesia is disregarded, as is the finding that patients with tardive dyskinesia who stop medications experience a fifty percent reduction in symptoms spontaneously within eighteen months.

Dr. Breggin also undermines his argument by expressing doubt as to the existence of schizophrenia, asserting that psychiatric patients have been "abandoned" by psychiatry, that antipsychotic medications are "addictive" and that they constitute a "chemical lobotomy," that psychiatry is involved in producing "iatrogenic helplessness" in patients, and by stating that "all of the major psychiatric treatments exert their primary or intended effect by disabling normal brain function."

Psychiatrists are not going to abandon the only effective treatment of psychotic symptoms. To do so would be as irresponsible as Dr. Breggin asserts they currently are. In my view it is both more realistic and more helpful to insist that the choice to use antipsychotic medications be made rationally, for a specific and well-documented psychotic disorder and at the minimal effective dose to maximize benefits and minimize side effects. I and most other psychiatrists who actively work treating patients with psychotic symptoms would join Dr. Breggin in this goal.

Reference

Breggin, P. R. (1991). *Toxic psychiatry.* New York: St. Martin's Press.
Vallenstein, E. S. (1973). *Brain control.* New York: John Wiley.

NO

Steven A. Mitchell

Antipsychotic medications are the only currently effective treatment for individuals with psychotic symptoms. It is the view of this essay that antipsychotic medications are essential in the treatment of disorders such as schizophrenia, but that a more relevant issue is how to ensure that these indispensable medications are used appropriately.

In 1954, before the introduction of antipsychotic medications in this country, approximately 550,000 inpatients, primarily individuals with schizophrenia, resided in mental hospitals. Twenty years later, in 1975, that number had fallen to about 150,000, despite an increase in the overall population of this country by approximately one-third. Thus, over that time period there was a reduction in the per capita hospitalization rate by a factor of about five, which was largely attributable to the use of antipsychotic medications.

Before the advent of antipsychotic medications, attempts to demonstrate the effectiveness of long-term, intensive, psychodynamically oriented psychotherapy of psychotic patients had begun at Chestnut Lodge Hospital in Maryland and at the McLean Hospital in Massachusetts. Careful review of the results clearly shows that psychotherapeutic interventions are not effective in treating psychotic symptoms. Indeed, in reviewing the available literature on the topic it would appear that, at best, the addition of psychotherapeutic treatment to antipsychotic medication can contribute to a reduction in the recurrence rate of psychotic symptoms of approximately 10 percent (Hogarty, 1973).

Anyone who has had more than a cursory experience with patients experiencing psychotic symptoms is vividly aware of the intense psychological distress caused not only to the patient themselves, but also to those around them. It is difficult to overstate the emotional costs involved in untreated psychotic illness. In addition, there are clear, though poorly understood, increases in both morbidity and mortality in individuals with psychotic symptoms. For example, individuals with schizophrenia experience a mortality rate that is approximately twice that of the general population, with approximately 10 percent dying by suicide (Talbott, 1988). On a more mundane level, the financial costs are also enormous. In 1984 it was conservatively estimated that the costs related to the 2.5 million individuals with schizophrenia totaled $73.2 billion, with two-thirds of this in lost productivity and one-third in the costs of treatment (Talbott, 1988).

Much of the confusion and misuse regarding antipsychotic medications arises from lack of appreciation of a number of essential aspects of antipsychotic medications. One of the unfortunately more common inappropriate uses of antipsychotic medications involves the mistaken impression that they should be used for their sedative or antianxiety effects. To do this exposes the patient unnecessarily to the risks of both short- and long-term side effects, particularly when other medications, such as antidepressants and benzodiazapines, which have more specific effects, are available.

Another potential problem involves ensuring that a correct diagnosis has been made before beginning treatment with antipsychotic medications. Over the past several years it has become increasingly clear that in this country there has been a pronounced tendency to overdiagnose schizophrenia and, correspondingly, to underdiagnose affective disorders with a psychotic component. Because of this past trend, in these cases, less than optimal treatment has been provided to individuals with affective disorders, sometimes over extended periods with antipsychotic medications when antidepressants or lithium would have provided a more specific and appropriate treatment for the underlying disorder. An additional issue is that there is some evidence that individuals with affective disorders may possibly be at higher risk for tardive dyskinesia, a long-term side effect consisting of an involuntary movement disorder associated with antipsychotic medication, than individuals with schizophrenia (Gardos & Casey, 1984).

A frequent source of confusion involves misunderstanding the rate at which psychotic symptoms remit during treatment with antipsychotic medications. It is not widely recognized that the typical time course of response of psychotic symptoms to antipsychotic medications involves a fairly rapid onset with the initial effect occurring within days after beginning treatment, but with a delay of several weeks, or in some cases even several months, before the full benefit of these medications are obtained. Unless this is appreciated, excessively high dosages may be prescribed and the patient will be overmedicated and placed at unnecessary risk for side effects. Unless clinicians are aware of this pattern they may also use p.r.n., or as needed, dosing schedules which have no clear rationale, unless, again, one is attempting to use antipsychotic medications for sedation.

Over the past several years there has been clear evidence that clinicians have been making more rigorous attempts to limit dosage of antipsychotic medication to the minimally effective amount when treating individuals with psychotic symptoms (Talbott, 1988). Admittedly, some of this concern comes from an increasing appreciation of the risks of long-term side effects, such as tardive dyskinesia, but another significant factor is the accumulating evidence that there may well be dosages of antipsychotic medication that are optimal, with additional amounts of medication not providing any additional benefit but only additional side effects. For example, there is recent evidence that there may exist a therapeutic range for Haldol, one of the most commonly used antipsychotic medications, between 9 and 15 ng/ml (Perry, 1988). Using this information it would be possible to make clinical decisions about what type of therapeutic intervention would be most appropriate if a patient exhibits an exacerbation of symptoms or does not appear to be responding to usually effective dosages. If an individual were found to be below this therapeutic range, either decreased absorption of the medication or, more likely, noncompliance with the medication would be factors to investigate.

One of the most significant variables that accounts for a high proportion of apparent treatment failures with antipsychotic medications, as well as a large percentage of hospital readmissions, is that of noncompliance with medication. Reviewing the available literature on the subject reveals that between 20 to 82 percent (with a mean of about 50 percent) of patients prescribed antipsychotic medication were significantly noncompliant with treatment (Klein, 1980). When these rates are compared with other groups of patients treated with medications for a variety of disorders, it can be seen that individuals treated with antipsychotic medication have a higher rate of noncompliance than any other group, except asymptomatic hypertensives.

When these data are considered along with evidence from studies of relapse rates, which show that patients who are on no effective antipsychotic medication relapse at a rate of between 8 and 15 percent per month while those who are on effective doses relapse at a rate of 1.5 to 3 percent per month (Linden, et al., 1984), it is clear that noncompliance with antipsychotic medication can cause as much as a fivefold increase in the rate of recurrence of psychotic symptoms. With the advent of depot preparations of antipsychotic medications, which are given by intramuscular injection on a once or twice monthly basis, the issue of compliance with treatment becomes a much less significant variable, and this form of antipsychotic medication has contributed to a much more consistent therapeutic benefit for patients with psychotic symptoms (Linden, et al., 1984).

In summary, antipsychotic medications have clearly been shown to be the most and indeed the only effective treatment available for individuals experiencing psychotic symptoms. At present there is simply no alternative form of treatment available that will alleviate psychotic symptoms. Given these facts the major issue then becomes how to effectively and safely use these medications, while minimizing side effects. Optimal use of these medications involves careful monitoring of both therapeutic and side effects and a consistent attempt to use only minimum effective dosages. Considerable patience on the part of both patient and clinician is required to observe symptom changes over a period of weeks, or sometimes even months, after any given dosage adjustment. The use of depot medication can dramatically reduce the variability in apparent efficacy of treatment of antipsychotic medications, especially in individuals who have a pattern of noncompliance, and can help reduce the regrettable pattern of repeated hospital admissions which taxes a system already overburdened and underfinanced. Reducing noncompliance by means of depot preparations would make possible, at least to some degree, a shift away from the crisis-oriented cycling in and out of the hospital of patients who drain a disproportionate share of available resources. In addition, new testing techniques are now available, based on dopamine receptor binding of antipsychotic medications, which show promise in providing a more precise determination of medication effects on the brain and may ultimately provide a more rational basis for optimal prescribing of antipsychotic medication.

References

Gardos, G., & Casey, D. (1984) *Tardive dyskinesia and affective disorders.* Washington DC: American Psychiatric Press.

Hogarty, G. E., et al., (1973). Drugs and sociotherapy in the aftercare of schizophrenic patients. *Arch Sen Psych 32,* 375–380.

Klein, D. F., et al., (1980). *Diagnosis and drug treatment of psychiatric disorders: adults and children* (2nd ed.). Baltimore: Williams & Wilkins.

Linden, R., et al. (1984). Antipsychotics in the maintenance treatment of schizophrenia. In H. C. Stancer, et al. *Guidelines for the use of psychotropic drugs.* New York: Spectrum Publications.

Perry, P. J., et al. (1988). The relationship of haloperidol concentrations to therapeutic response. *J. Clin. Psychopharmacol (8)* 1:38–43.

Talbott, J. A., et al. (1988). *Textbook of psychiatry.* American Psychiatric Press.

Annotated Bibliography

Bernstein, J. (1988). *Handbook of drug therapy in psychiatry.* Littleton, MA, PSG Publishing.

A thorough review of clinical psychopharmacology as it pertains to psychiatry. Very clear and readable style with much valuable clinically relevant information.

Hollister, L. (1983). *Clinical pharmacology of psychotherapeutic drugs.* New York, Churchill, Livingson.

Succinct overview, focusing on pharmacological issues relevant to clinical treatment.

Strayhorn, J. (1982). *Foundations of clinical psychiatry.* Chicago, Year Book Medical Publishers.

Easily understandable overview of major issues in psychiatry.

Rejoinder to Dr. Mitchell

PETER R. BREGGIN

Although I didn't have an advance look at Dr. Mitchell's arguments in favor of neuroleptic drugs, my presentation deals with and disproves much of what he claims.

First, antipsychotic drugs are not "the only currently effective treatment" for patients labeled as schizophrenic. As I documented, psychosocial approaches are more effective, are no more expensive, and don't cause permanent brain dysfunction and damage.

Second, the drugs had little to do with the reduction in the patient population in state mental hospitals between 1955 and 1975. The reduction began in 1963 as a result of changes in fiscal policy which switched the cost from state budgets to the federal disability programs. The states could then transfer their patients to private facilities, such as nursing homes and board and care homes, where patients' *continued institutionalization* would be paid for by the federal government. These private facilities are often more oppressive than the state hospitals.

Third, although Dr. Mitchell is correct about the suffering of many patients while "experiencing psychotic symptoms," their suffering is often made worse by the drugs. He acknowledges that many or most patients refuse to take the prescribed neuroleptics, but he doesn't explain why. Studies show that patients refuse to take neuroleptics because the drugs *cause* so much suffering, including a feeling of mental and emotional suppression and a high rate of akathisia, an intense anxiety that drives the patient to move about in an effort to relieve the tension. These drugs cause much more emotional pain than they relieve.

Fourth, Dr. Mitchell points to a high mortality rate in schizophrenia, indirectly suggesting or hinting that the drugs reduce it. There is no evidence that neuroleptics reduce mortality and much evidence that they increase it. The neuroleptics produce a sudden unexplained death syndrome, cause a sometimes lethal neuroleptic malignant syndrome, and increase suicide among disheartened tardive dyskinesia patients. These drugs cause more deaths than they prevent.

Typical of too many drug advocates, Dr. Mitchell gives only passing mention to tardive dyskinesia. The reader would have no way of knowing that millions of patients worldwide are afflicted with the disease, that it is largely irreversible and untreatable, and that it is frequently disfiguring and sometimes disabling. The reader of Dr. Mitchell's presentation would not realize that rates are astronomical: 5 percent per year in younger adults and 20 percent or more per year in older ones (Breggin, 1991). After taking the drugs for five years, one-quarter of younger patients will develop the disease and nearly all of the older patients (Breggin, 1991). To present the drugs in a good light, a virtual epidemic of drug-induced brain disease is ignored.

Dr. Mitchell illustrates the extremes to which drug advocates will go to perpetuate tired old myths about the neuroleptics and to ignore their devastating effects. He further illustrates how doctors fail to inform potential patients or the public about the dangers of the drugs.

Reference

Breggin, P. R. (1991). *Toxic psychiatry.* New York: St. Martins Press.

DEBATE 11

Is the Remedicalization of Psychiatry Good for the Mental Health Field?

Dr. Robert O. Pasnau, M.D., argues YES. Dr. Pasnau is Professor of Psychiatry in the UCLA School of Medicine, Department of Psychiatry and Biobehavioral Sciences. He is also Assistant Dean for Student Affairs and Director of the Mental Health Service for Physicians-in-Training. He is a past president of both the American Psychiatric Association and the American College of Psychiatrists. He is currently president of the Pacific Rim College of Psychiatrists. His major area of research and clinical practice is Consultation-Liaison Psychiatry, the area of psychiatric practice that is concerned with the psychological effects of physical illness, consultation for patients with psychosomatic disorders, and education of primary care physicians. "Psychiatry in Medicine: Medicine in Psychiatry" was the theme of the 1987 Annual Meeting of the American Psychiatric Association and the title of his Presidential Address to that meeting.

NO is David A. Levy's answer to the debate question. Dr. Levy has extensive experience as a teacher, psychotherapist, and researcher. He received his Ph.D. in psychology from UCLA and is an Associate Professor of Psychology at Pepperdine University. He has served as a Visiting Professor of Psychology at Leningrad (now St. Petersburg) State University. He works in both inpatient and outpatient clinical settings as a psychologist and a marriage, family, and child counselor. His numerous theoretical and empirical research studies on social cognition, media psychology, and social influence have been published in scientific journals and presented at professional conferences. He has also appeared on a number of television and radio programs (including CNN and PBS), where he was interviewed on his research findings, as well as on current issues and trends in the field of psychology.

YES

Robert O. Pasnau

From the very beginning of psychiatry in America, the integration of psychiatry with the rest of medicine has been a distinctive feature and a cherished goal. Benjamin Rush, M.D., honored as the Father of American Psychiatry undertook the task of coordinating psychiatric and medical care and teaching in the United States. His textbook on psychiatry, published in 1812, was the first American medical textbook, and it influenced generations of physicians. Unlike the traditions in Europe, psychiatric wards in general hospitals had been present since 1756. During the thirty years he served as Professor of Medicine at the University of Pennsylvania, he taught the unity of body and mind and the importance of mental functions in understanding and treating physical illness (Pasnau, 1987b).

By the time Adolph Meyer, M.D., arrived from Switzerland at the turn of the twentieth century, psychiatric practice had declined to the primarily institutional and legal level. In his attempts to revitalize psychiatry, he fought against the narrow mechanistic medical models of the nineteenth century which he found to obstruct his vision. Instead, he led psychiatry into an era of concern with all aspects of human life, and he formulated his psychobiological model. In this model he viewed the human being as a dynamically adapting *and* biologically developing organism throughout life. In summary, he taught that the central focus of psychiatry was the individual patient first, the illness second. His academic work led to the formation of the Mental Hygiene Movement, the formation of the multidisciplinary team, and the foundation of the present-day curriculum for psychiatric residency training. Indirectly, his example led to both modern community and child psychiatry, with an emphasis on social and psychological issues. For this he has been honored as the Father of Modern American Psychiatry.

The examples of these two great psychiatrists highlight the tension in the swing of the psychiatric pendulum over the years between the narrower view of psychiatry as a medical specialty and of psychiatry as a part of the mental health community. The boundary issues have never been completely settled because the swing is influenced by broader social and political interests. In the 1930s, for example, the first remedicalization of psychiatry in this century occurred in response to the collapse of support for community psychiatry as a result of the unfulfilled promises of prevention of mental illness. Psychoanalytic training became limited to physicians, and many organic treatments were promulgated, including ECT, insulin, and psychosurgery. During this period, the American Board of Psychiatry and Neurology was founded.

The present remedicalization began in the 1970s, partially as a response to the perceived failure of the community mental health centers and deinstitutionalization of psychiatric patients during the 1960s; partly out of development of consultation-liaison psychiatry in medical centers during the 1960s; partly from the increased development of the techniques, methodologies, and findings in neuroscience; and largely from the economic pressures brought about by the need to reduce expenditures for mental health care. Whether the challenge to psychiatry is for the cost of mental health care to be included in health care insurance coverage or a national health service, by the mid-1980s it was felt to be in the interest of psychiatry to publicize its scientific and medical base and to narrow its boundaries.

Sabshin noted that:

> There is an opportunity for gradual circumscription and delineation of our field so that: (a) we can more easily be differentiated from other specialties in medicine and from other mental health fields; (b) we don't need to be everything to everybody; (c) we are not perceived as a ''bottomless pit'' by decision makers and the relevant public; (d) we can emphasize the scientific rationale for our boundaries and our priorities; and (e) we can distinguish normality from psychopathology in a more rational manner. (Sabshin, 1989)

In his role as medical director of the American Psychiatric Association he has been a strong advocate for what he terms *structural remedicalization,* concentrating on etiology, diagnosis, treatment, and epidemiology (Sabshin, 1977, 1986).

Economics have accelerated the remedicalization, and to a large extent the success of the remedicalization will determine whether or not psychiatry survives as a clinical specialty. The corporatization of the mental health field, managed care, and focus on outcomes has driven psychiatry to attempt to demonstrate cost effectiveness of treatments. This is relatively easy in psychopharmacotherapy research; it is relatively difficult in psychotherapeutic and behavioral research. The erosion of the mental health clinician authority, the focus on increasing the capacity of the individual to function in the workplace, and, above all, the need to cut the costs of mental health treatment have led to a narrower definition of the role of the psychiatrist in the mental health field. This has also led to the increased role that psychiatry plays in alcohol-related illness, one of the major concerns of corporations. Alcoholism impedes productivity, increases absenteeism, increases corporate liability, destroys general health, leads to serious accidents and escalating medical and surgical costs, and complicates the treatment of other mental and physical illnesses. The aging of the population has also enhanced the role of psychiatrists in treating the mental disorders of the elderly, most of whom are suffering from physical disabilities or illnesses as well, requiring the combined medical-psychiatric collaboration.

As noted in the opening paragraph, American psychiatry has always been ''medicalized.'' Thus, the term *remedicalization* may be misleading. In my view, the current period of remedicalization signifies a slight, but important, swing of the pendulum—a redefinition of the boundaries of psychiatry that help distinguish its unique place in the mental health field. This is necessary for psychiatry's survival, and it is a matter of focus rather than ideology.

Whether or not psychiatry should remedicalize is not the issue. Make no mistake about it, remedicalization has occurred. One has only to read the latest summary of the field in the July 15, 1992, issue of the *Journal of the American Medical Association* to learn how far the pendulum has swung. Highlights listed include the advances in 5-hydroxytryptamine pharmacology, the epidemiology of obsessive-compulsive disorder (some experts consider OCD as a model of "grooming behavior out of control"), and the failure of controlled studies to demonstrate fluoxetine-induced violence. Behavior therapy is mentioned only once in combination with pharmacotherapy; psychotherapy is not referenced at all (Freedman & Stahl, 1992).

It is important to note that most psychiatrists who favor remedicalization have warned of the attendant dangers. As Freedman observed a decade ago:

> Medicines, whether penicillin or tricyclics, can be trivialized as conveniences (or, worse, technologies). They can, in ignorance, be overestimated, either as menaces or as the sole magical ingredient of therapeutics—but medicines are only a part of the management of illness. They can be too rapidly and mindlessly implemented. (Freedman, 1982)

In his discussion of psychiatry's central agenda in his Adolph Meyer Lecture before the American Psychiatric Association ten years later, Freedman acknowledged the ebbing and flowing of psychiatry's relationship with medicine:

> Now, whether all this to and fro is a part of the natural tides of history and simply a response to evolving discovery and socioeconomic necessities is difficult to determine. Amnesias about intrinsic purpose, about what we serve for, recur in all collectivities chartered for special societal services—the church, the law, the university, or medicine. But psychiatry has a special fuel for some of these oscillations. Thus, for our forefathers as for us, the core issue is no more or less than the nature of human nature. Psychiatry, then, intrinsically embraces both broad concerns and their pragmatically narrower derivatives, since we deal with impairments in the very psychobiological tools with which humans attend to, express, and effect their personal purposes. (Freedman, 1992)

While recognizing the danger of reductionism in diverting attention from the person who is the patient, at the same time he regards the reason for psychiatry's focus on biology as *not* a matter of ideology but because new insights are now feasible. He doubts if remedicalized psychiatry will lose either its mind or its brain (Freedman, 1992).

Sabshin was also clear in his warning of the attendant hazards of remedicalization:

> Circumscription and increased objectification of our field are often accompanied by biological reductionism. We need to avoid reductionism for many reasons, including the dangers of trivialization, dehumanization, and loss of clinical vitality. (Sabshin, 1989)

In an earlier paper on the remedicalization of psychiatry, I also attempted to outline what the remedicalization of psychiatry was not (or ought not to become):

1. The remedicalization of psychiatry is not a return to the reductionistic biomedical model with its focus on disease while ignoring the patient.
2. The remedicalization of psychiatry is not a renunciation of psychoanalysis, psychotherapy, or psychodynamics.
3. The remedicalization of psychiatry is not a return to nineteenth century neuropsychiatry.
4. The remedicalization of psychiatry is not the detachment of our commitment to the families of our patients, to the communities in which they live, to the public hospitals and clinics in which they are treated, or to the social problems and policy issues that have an impact on the mental health of our patients.

In summary, I argued, and still do argue, that the firm identity of psychiatry as a specialty of medicine and its improved image and visibility provide promise and opportunity for vitality in the coming century. Thus, the remedicalization of psychiatry is good for psychiatry (Pasnau, 1987a).

The larger issue is whether what is good for psychiatry is necessarily good for the mental health field. I believe that a strong, scientifically based, public-supported psychiatric profession, working together with other mental health professionals, will ensure that our patients receive the very best mental health care that the society is willing to provide.

The mental health field, like psychiatry, is about patients. The discoveries in neuroscience will lead to better and more humane treatment of the mentally ill, which will lead to benefits to the entire field. Already, teams of psychiatrists, nurses, social workers, and psychologists are working together in employee assistance, affective disorder, and anxiety disorder treatment programs, providing cost-effective and focused treatment based on medical research. The psychiatric research agenda today is largely biological and neuroscience oriented. But epidemiology, nosology, and combined treatments are also important. Thus, neuroscience with its open agenda complemented by research focused on specific mental disorders is the order of the day.

The role of consultation-liaison psychiatry will continue to expand as a result of remedicalization. Efforts will increase in the evaluation and treatment of patients with alcohol and substance abuse (the major contributor to hospitalization in general hospitals), AIDS, oncology, and organ transplantations, and they will contribute to the progress in meeting the psychological needs of the physically ill.

Consultation-liaison psychiatry will continue to provide academically based training for mental health professionals who devote their careers to the psychological care of the physically ill. Psychiatrists, working with their colleagues in the rest of medicine, will help to educate other physicians in diagnosis, treatment, and referral of the mentally ill who are first encountered in primary care medicine.

The special role of the psychiatrist with the rest of medicine in quality assurance, peer review, physician impairment, ethics, and professional liability will also expand as a result of remedicalization. This will lead to improved relations between the rest of medicine and the mental health field, which will benefit our patients and the field.

Perhaps some feel that the mental health field might be better off without psychiatry. A medical colleague recently shared with me his fantasy that some all-embracing clinical neuroscientist would eventually replace the psychiatrist. Again, Freedman has the last word: "If we abolish psychiatrists, a race of 'psychiatroids' would have to emerge to replace us!" (Freedman, 1992).

References

Freedman, D. X. (1982). Science in the service of the ill. *American Journal of Psychiatry, 139,* 1087–1095.

Freedman, D. X. (1992). The search: Body, mind, and human purpose. *American Journal of Psychiatry, 149,* 858–866.

Freedman, D. X., & Stahl, S. M. (1992). Psychiatry. *Journal of the American Medical Association, 268,* 403–405.

Pasnau, R. O. (1987a). The remedicalization of psychiatry. *Hospital and Community Psychiatry, 38,* 145–151.

Pasnau, R. O. (1987b). Psychiatry in medicine: Medicine in psychiatry. *American Journal of Psychiatry, 144,* 975–980.

Sabshin, M. (1977). On remedicalization and holism in psychiatry. *Psychosomatics, 18,* 7–8.

Sabshin, M. (1986). The future of psychiatry: Coping with "new realities." In J. A. Talbott (Ed.), *Our patients' future in a changing world.* Washington, DC: American Psychiatric Press.

Sabshin, M. (1989). What is our field? In J. A. Talbott (Ed.), *Future directions in psychiatry.* Washington, DC: American Psychiatric Press.

Annotated Bibliography

Freedman, D. X. (1992). The search: Body, mind, and human purpose. *American Journal of Psychiatry, 149,* 858–866.

This paper, which was presented as the Adolph Meyer Lecture at the 1991 Annual Meeting of the American Psychiatric Association, articulates the author's concern with the need to preserve the "scientific agenda" in modern psychiatry and his belief that the fear of "biological reductionism" that plagues the current era of remedicalization of psychiatry is groundless. He argues persuasively that psychiatry begins and ends with patients and that, in studying their mental illnesses, psychiatry will borrow from and contribute to all the life sciences, including medical, psychological, and social sciences.

Freedman, D. X., & Stahl, S. M. (1992). Psychiatry. *Journal of the American Medical Association, 268,* 403–405.

This article, outlining the advances made in psychiatry during the 1991–1992 period, is as remarkable for what it omits as for what it includes. Highlighting the discoveries made in the psychobiology of the anxiety and obsessive-compulsive disorders and demonstrating the importance of 5-hydroxytryptamine (5-HT) pharmacology in modifying previously held theories, almost no mention is made of the more traditional therapies, including psychotherapy. This paper supports my assertion that the focus of present-day psychiatry is primarily on the biomedical rather than the psychosocial dimension of psychiatry.

Pasnau, R. O. (1987). The remedicalization of psychiatry. *Hospital and Community Psychiatry, 38,* 145–151.

This was the first paper in which I outlined my views on what the "remedicalization" of psychiatry does *not* mean, including the renunciation of the biopsychosocial model, psychotherapy, and psychodynamics or a return to a mindless, biological reductionism. In this paper I outlined what I believed to be the need for redefining the boundaries of the specialty, the role of consultation-liaison psychiatry, and the need for more research. Five years later, I am astounded that I did not foresee the economic forces that have propelled the remedicalization so much faster than I anticipated.

Sabshin, M. (1989). What is our field? In J. A. Talbott (Ed.), *Future directions in psychiatry.* Washington, DC: American Psychiatric Press.

In this three-page account of the opportunities and obstacles facing psychiatry in the decade of the nineties, the author, who has been the medical director of the American Psychiatric Association for the past two decades and one of the most ardent supporters of psychiatry's role in organized medicine, argues that psychiatry has outgrown its ideological disputes and seems firmly grounded in neuroscience. While noting the danger of an "overcorrective" biological exclusivity, which he warns could lead to "trivialization, dehumanization, and loss of clinical vitality," he believes that survival of the field is linked to the public image of psychiatry as a rational, empirical, and scientific medical specialty.

Rejoinder to Dr. Pasnau

DAVID A. LEVY

In his essay in favor of the remedicalization of psychiatry, Dr. Pasnau presents a brief but interesting chronology of psychiatry's development in America. He also neatly spells out what he believes remedicalization is not or ought not to become. Further, he provides several very cogent and persuasive arguments—with which I find myself in complete agreement—*against* the remedicalization of psychiatry, including the dangers of reductionism, trivialization, dehumanization, loss of clinical vitality, and the overestimation of medication as a menace or a panacea.

Where then do I disagree? To begin with, Pasnau makes a number of assertions that are totally unsubstantiated. For example, he declares that "discoveries in neuroscience will lead to better and *more humane* [italics added] treatment of the mentally ill" and that remedicalization "will lead to improved relations between the rest of medicine and the mental health field, which will be of benefit to our patients and to the field." Although Pasnau's enthusiastic spirit is admirable, he offers no evidence whatsoever to support these claims.

Pasnau also makes a common mistake of medical reification by equating alcohol-*related* illness with alcoholism *as* an illness. As I discuss in my NO argument, psychiatry typically but erroneously confuses physical disease with social norms. Cirrhosis of the liver due to chronic alcohol intake, for example, is a proven medical illness; it is *not,* however, equivalent to a person's behavior (or misbehavior) in the workplace.

But my major problem overall with Pasnau's essay is not so much with what he does say, but rather with what he doesn't say. Specifically, he fails to provide a clear definition and explanation of what remedicalization *is.* He also does not differentiate remedicalization as a unique theoretical or clinical approach, nor does he present a convincing case as to why it is good for the mental health field. For example, Pasnau states that remedicalization stands for a commitment to more scientifically based research. Here we have an excellent example of a "one-size-fits-all" pseudo-issue. It is akin to an educator taking a stand for more knowledge, a minister for more faith, or a politician for more justice, liberty, or family values. These all are pseudo-issues because no one really opposes them. Yet the implication here is that a position in support of scientific research somehow distinguishes remedicalization from other professional orientations—which it does not.

Similarly, Pasnau states that remedicalization stands for increasing the role of consultation-liaison psychiatry, that is, helping people to cope with physical illness. This certainly is an important endeavor, but not one that is unique to psychiatry, remedicalized or otherwise. In fact, it is a primary focus of many other scientific and professional disciplines, most notably the rapidly emerging field of health psychology.

I certainly would not quarrel with Pasnau's conviction that "the remedicalization of psychiatry is good for psychiatry." But, as I indicated in my NO essay, what's good for psychiatry isn't necessarily what's good for the patient. Here again, Pasnau makes no convincing argument that remedicalized psychiatry, by narrowing its boundaries and priorities along biological lines, is superior to nonremedicalized, unremedicalized, or contraremedicalized mental health orientations in meeting the needs of patients.

In his effort to describe remedicalization, Pasnau states that it is not a renunciation of psychotherapy, psychoanalysis, psychodynamics, and the biopsychosocial model, or a return to mindless biological reductionism. He supports his argument that remedicalization has already occurred by citing a recent journal article that summarizes the latest advances made in the field. Yet, the article focuses almost exclusively on biological phenomena while essentially disregarding all psychosocial dimensions of psychiatry, particularly psychotherapy.

Given this striking contradiction, what are we left to conclude? At best, there is a fundamental confusion as to what remedicalization in psychiatry really means. At worst, remedicalization purports to stand for something that, in fact, it does not. Under this unsettling scenario, lip service is paid to the importance of psychological and social factors and to the needs of the patient's family, the community, and society at large, while psychiatry continues on its myopic hunt to explain and treat human distress solely in terms of neurochemical disease.

Pasnau apparently concurs with Sabshin's view that "the survival of the field is linked to the public image of psychiatry as a rational, empirical, and scientific medical specialty." True enough. But perhaps psychiatry should concern itself less with image and more with substance.

NO

DAVID A. LEVY

Is the remedicalization of psychiatry good for the mental health field? The answer to this question depends on which side of the prescription pad one happens to be. From the vantage point of the doctor, enormous profits are to be reaped by the systematic medical diagnosis and treatment of various forms of human misery. But from the perspective of the patient—on whose behalf these diagnoses and treatments are ostensibly fashioned—it is quite a different matter. And because the greatest priority should be given to the needs of the patient, it is from this perspective that I oppose the remedicalization of psychiatry in the mental health field.

My objections are founded on three major grounds: conceptual, utilitarian, and moral. First, medical model thinking in psychiatry typically is conceptually confusing, misleading, and fallacious. Second, it has limited usefulness. Third, it is morally unjustifiable.

Conceptual Objections: Errors in Understanding

A great deal of psychiatric thinking rests on faulty premises, poor logic, and erroneous conclusions. Perhaps the most basic mistaken belief is that disorders are either *physical* (biological/neurochemical/physiological/organic) or *mental* (psychological/psychogenic/functional). In fact, in clinical practice, this is the primary diagnostic question: "Is the patient's problem physical or mental?" This question is fundamentally flawed for two reasons. First, in this context, *physical* and *mental* are linguistically noncomparable terms. That is, we are mistakenly attempting to compare a concrete event to a theoretical construct (see Szasz, 1974). This error in thinking occurs whenever we create an abstract concept (such as "the mind") and then delude ourselves into believing that it actually exists as a concrete thing. The brain is a thing; the mind is a concept. Apples and oranges are things; existentialism is a concept. Thus, asking the question, "Is the patient's problem physical or mental?" is a profound error in reification that is as senseless as comparing apples and existentialism.

Second, the question implies that mental phenomena are somehow not physical. This notion is, of course, patently absurd. *Every* mental event has some corresponding physical correlate. Thinking, happiness, and creativity are no more or less biochemical than delusions, depression, or schizophrenia. They are all reflected or "mapped" in some form physically (biochemically/neurologically/anatomically), whether or not we know how to measure them. But, in the course of clinical diagnosis, when we are not able to locate a physical malfunction, we almost invariably jump to the erroneous conclusion that "since the person's problem isn't physical, it therefore must be mental." As you can see, this is a foolish leap in logic.

This artificial dichotomy does not take into account the principle that there are *multiple levels of description.* At one level, phenomena can be described as physical events; at another level, the same phenomena can be described as theoretical constructs. For example, at the physical level "anxiety" involves specific neurochemical events, while at the conceptual level it involves the perception of apprehension or fear. Thus, neurochemistry doesn't cause anxiety, and anxiety doesn't cause neurochemistry; they are *equivalent* and *simultaneous* phenomena, simply described at two different levels of analysis. The same is true for all psychological phenomena, pathological or otherwise: the relationship between physical and mental is, by definition, not causal but correlational.

Why is this important? Because we must not allow ourselves to be seduced into believing that once we have located a biological correlate to a psychological process, we have therefore discovered its biological cause; or even worse, we must not equate biological cause with biological disease. For example, if we find neurological differences between those persons whom we label as psychotic as compared to those whom we consider normal, it should come as no great surprise. After all, we are also equally likely to discover neurological differences between those persons whom we call creative versus those whom we do not. But what does this prove? Only that we've located the biological correlate or map for different types of psychological processes. However, this criterion alone doesn't prove that psychosis is a medical disease any more than it proves that creativity is not. Even if we were to find the physical correlates to every psychological phenomenon, we would still have the formidable and complex task of defining and differentiating illness from health (see Wakefield, 1992, for the one such attempt). In other words, evidence of physical *difference* is not per se scientifically valid proof of medical *disease.* All things considered, it isn't surprising that the ''physical or mental'' question hasn't been answered. What's surprising is that it's still being asked.

Why, then, does traditional psychiatric thinking persist in the face of such conceptual confusion? Although there are many reasons, one of the most insidiously influential is a common mistake of medical misattribution, the *treatment-etiology fallacy.* This flaw in logic refers to arriving at the erroneous conclusion that a positive response to medical *treatment* proves that there was a medical *cause.* as counterintuitive as it may seem, a favorable response to medication is not proof of disease. Specifically, if a psychotropic drug is effective in alleviating a so-called mental disorder, many people would (and do) falsely conclude that the disorder therefore must have been caused by (or is) a biological illness.

Let's say, as an example, that after an extremely stressful day, you develop a splitting headache. So, you take a couple of aspirin and within minutes your headache vanishes. What caused the headache to disappear? Clearly, the aspirin. But what caused the headache to appear in the first place? A *lack* of aspirin? Of course not. We cannot, on the basis of its response to medication, attribute the etiology of your headache as being due to a biological disease. Rather, the aspirin has influenced a biochemical process that is neither the cause nor the effect of the headache—in point of fact, it *is* the headache. Let's take another example. Suppose that we observe someone with a diagnosis of schizophrenia who displays hallucinations, delusions, and bizarre affect. After several doses of a powerful antipsychotic drug, his hallucinations diminish, his delusions abate, and his affect stabilizes. Did the medication reduce his symptoms? Yes. But can we take this result as incontrovertible proof that schizophrenia is a biological disease? Using the same line of logic as in the above example, the answer is no. Even if one were to hypothesize that all so-called mental disorders are rooted in biological pathology, don't make the mistake of assuming that their response to medication provides the proof.

To summarize my arguments thus far: First, everything that is mental is also physical, depending on one's level of description. Second, evidence of biological differences is not per se a scientifically valid criterion of medical disease. Third, positive response to medical treatment does not prove medical illness as the etiology of the problem. Unfortunately, mainstream psychiatry's failure to recognize and appreciate the importance of these principles does not bode well for the future of the mental health field.

Utilitarian Objections: Errors in Application

When evaluating any theoretical orientation, it isn't a question of which position is true or false, right or wrong, correct or incorrect. Instead, the key question is one of utility: What is the relative usefulness—in practical, applied, real-world terms—of one approach as compared to another? In this context, the question should be, "How *useful* is it to conceptualize and treat psychopathology as a medical problem?" One way to examine this question is by the principle of *multiple pathways of causation,* by which I mean that the same event may spring from different causes.

To illustrate this concept, laughter may be produced by many independent pathways, such as humor, nervousness, happiness, embarrassment, or physical tickling. Tears may be caused by sadness, joy, frustration, anger, allergies, or ocular irritation (exposure to onions, soap, or smog). Male genital erection may be the result of direct physical stimulation, visual exposure to erotic photographs, sexual fantasies, as a correlate of the REM sleep cycle, as a side effect of some antidepressant medications, or by being hanged by a rope from the neck until dead.

The notion of multiple pathways of causation can be applied to the etiology of many types of psychopathology. Depression, for example, may be produced by numerous independent routes, including the ingestion of drugs (such as barbiturates), withdrawal from drugs (such as amphetamines), vitamin deficiencies (such as thiamine), starvation, physical illness (such as mononucleosis), as well as "psychological" (but of course, no less physical) phenomena, such as faulty belief systems, loneliness, helplessness, loss, failure, trauma, or a sense of existential futility and meaninglessness.

And just as there are multiple pathways to a problem, there are multiple pathways to its solution. In terms of psychopathology, there exist numerous valid routes to treatment. For example, depression may be alleviated by psychopharmacology (such as heterocyclic antidepressants), electroconvulsive therapy, cognitive psychotherapy, insight-oriented psychotherapy, emotional catharsis, success experiences, supportive interpersonal relationships, or finding meaning and purpose in life.

I am not, therefore, arguing against the medical model as a useful approach to addressing some of life's problems. But we must remember that it is one route—not the *only* route—to etiology and treatment. I advocate, instead, the utilization of *multiple* avenues of understanding and application. If we allow ourselves to become fixated at the psychomedical stage of conceptualization and treatment, we run the risk of severely limiting our choices and thereby overlooking solutions that could be of tremendous usefulness.

Which is the best pathway? That is a matter of personal choice, and does not (nor should not) lie solely in the hands of the medical practitioner. It is, in fact, this confusion between medical and moral choices that forms the basis of my third major objection to the remedicalization of psychiatry.

Moral Objections: Errors in Judgment

Some people believe things that other people don't believe, feel things that other people don't feel, see things that other people don't see, or hear things that other people don't hear. And in many cases these people might irritate, offend, confuse, or frighten us. But just as differences in biology are not per se a valid criterion of medical disease, neither are differences in people's attitudes, emotions, or behaviors.

Unfortunately, however, the mixing of objective descriptions with subjective value judgments continually plagues psychiatric thinking. This is especially evident when psychiatry equates what is *different* with what is *bad.* Although psychiatry purports to be a medical science, it typically employs pseudomedical terminology, justified in pseudoscientific theory, as a means of judging and controlling other people. In other words, psychiatry confuses medicine with morality.

Nowhere is this confusion more evident than in psychiatry's use of diagnostic labeling. The problems associated with psychiatric diagnoses are numerous and well documented. They are often unreliable and dehumanizing (Rosenhan, 1973), stigmatizing (Page, 1977), and frequently reveal more about the person assigning the label than about the person to whom the label is affixed (see Levy, 1992, for a satirical perspective on this point). Specifically, they are a better reflection of sociocultural and political values and creeds and mores than of objective, medical science.

A vivid case in point is the American Psychiatric Association's shifting attitudes toward homosexuality. In the first and second editions of the *Diagnostic and Statistical Manual of Mental Disorders* (better known as the DSM), homosexuality was listed as a mental disorder (APA, 1952, 1968). In 1973 the Board of Trustees of the American Psychiatric Association voted to remove homosexuality from the DSM. There was strong minority opposition to this action, however, and the following year a referendum was introduced to reinstate homosexuality as a diagnostic category. The referendum was defeated by a vote of 5,854 to 3,810. Thus, homosexuality was eliminated as an officially recognized mental disorder. But a new diagnosis, sexual orientation disturbance, was devised to classify people who experienced distress due to their homosexuality. Six years later, with the publication of the *DSM-III* (APA, 1980), the name of this diagnosis was changed to ego-dystonic homosexuality. In the revised version of *DSM-III* (APA, 1987), the category was eliminated entirely. In essence, homosexuality as a mental disorder was alternately voted in and then out of existence.

Can you imagine the same sort of thing happening with any *real* medical illness? How likely is it, for example, that the American Medical Association one day will declare by vote that tuberculosis, diabetes, or leukemia is no longer a disease? Yet, this idea is no less preposterous than psychiatry's application of a medical model perspective to personal and social problems.

Perhaps the most serious moral consequence of medical model psychiatric thinking, however, is that it undermines the principle of personal responsibility (Szasz, 1974) by encouraging people to assume the role of passive, helpless patient rather than of active, responsible human being. Irrespective of the situation, it is a relatively easy task to absolve oneself of personal responsibility simply by hiding behind one's psychiatric diagnosis-of-choice: "Well, what do you *expect* from someone who's got oppositional defiant disorder/antisocial personality disorder/borderline personality disorder/self-defeating personality disorder/intermittent explosive disorder/kleptomania/pyromania/frotteurism? I can't help it. I can't control myself. *I am not responsible.*"

Where will it end? With someone claiming that he is helpless because he's got pervasive helplessness syndrome, or that he cannot be held responsible for his behavior because he's got pervasive helplessness syndrome, or that he cannot be held responsible for his behavior because he's got irresponsible personality disorder? The more we accept medical explanations and excuses for our problems in living, the more we relinquish our own personal responsibility, free will, and choice—in short, the very qualities that are the essence of our humanity.

References

American Psychiatric Association. (1952). *Diagnostic and statistical manual of mental disorders.* Washington, DC: APA.

American Psychiatric Association. (1968). *Diagnostic and statistical manual of mental disorders* (2nd ed.). Washington, DC: APA.

American Psychiatric Association. (1980). *Diagnostic and statistical manual of mental disorders* (3rd ed.). Washington, DC: APA.

American Psychiatric Association. (1987). *Diagnostic and statistical manual of mental disorders* (3rd ed., rev.). Washington, DC: APA.

Levy, D. A. (1992, Winter). A proposed category for the *Diagnostic and Statistical Manual of Mental Disorders (DSM):* Pervasive labeling disorder. *Journal of Humanistic Psychology, 32*(1), 153–157.

Page, S. (1977). Effects of the mental illness label in attempts to obtain accommodation. *Canadian Journal of Behavioral Science, 9,* 84–90.

Rosenhan, D. L. (1973). On being sane in insane places. *Science, 179,* 250–258.

Szasz, T. S. (1974). *The myth of mental illness: Foundations of a theory of personal conduct* (rev. ed.). New York: Harper & Row.

Wakefield, J. C. (1992). The concept of mental disorder: On the boundary between biological facts and social values. *American Psychologist, 47*(3), 373–388.

Annotated Bibliography

Cooper, D. (1967). *Psychiatry and anti-psychiatry.* London: Paladin & Tavistock Publications.

In this extremely penetrating book, David Cooper presents his insightful and compelling criticisms of classical psychiatry.

Frankl, V. E. (1963). *Man's search for meaning: An introduction to logotherapy.* New York: Simon & Schuster.

Viktor Frankl outlines his acclaimed theory of logotherapy, which focuses upon mankind's fundamental pursuit of a higher meaning in life, emphasizing that existential and spiritual distress are not tantamount to mental disease.

Haley, J. (1986). *The power tactics of Jesus Christ and other essays* (2nd ed.). Rockville, MD: Triangle Press.

Jay Haley's brilliant collection of provocative, stimulating, and satirical essays provides a potent alternative to medical model thinking in the mental health field.

Laing, R. D. (1967). *The politics of experience.* New York: Pantheon Books.

R. D. Laing presents his unique blend of social phenomenology, existentialism, and psychoanalysis in this captivating book which challenges our most basic assumptions of sanity, normality and madness.

Szasz, T. S. (1987). *Insanity: The idea and its consequences.* New York: Wiley.

Thomas Szasz, one of the most influential, distinguished, revolutionary, and controversial thinkers of our time, delivers his carefully constructed and devastating criticisms of the medical model of mental illness, the nature of the psychiatric profession and the moral implications of its practices.

Rejoinder to Dr. Levy

Robert O. Pasnau

In his argument opposing the remedicalization of psychiatry, Dr. Levy is actually arguing a different agenda. His position could best be described as one that asserts that "psychiatry is bad for the mental health field." I believe that his argument is wrong, unfair, and divisive.

He defines the remedicalization of psychiatry as the application of "medical model thinking" in psychiatry. He then characterizes "psychiatric thinking" as dualistic, which he finds flawed, conceptually confusing, misleading, and fallacious.

In fact, it is Dr. Levy who confuses the "medical model" and "remedicalization." The medical model has always been a part of psychiatry; psychiatry is a specialty of medicine. Some controversy may exist as to what is the current "medical model," but most authorities agree that at its heart is the concept of the physician's responsibility to the patient and the application of scientific diagnosis, treatment, and prognosis to patient care based on careful observation and clinical research. The remedicalization of psychiatry, on the other hand, as I have described, is not the return to a medical model that it never left, but it is a *slight* shift in emphasis toward the biological focus of psychiatry and a significant shift in the political focus closer to the rest of medicine.

I agree with Dr. Levy that the belief that disorders are either physical or mental is mistaken. But he unfairly alleges that modern psychiatric thinking rests on this premise. The biopsychosocial model, which is embraced by almost all contemporary psychiatrists, is a major reformation of the older biomedical model which was largely dualistic. Thus, Dr. Levy's dispute appears to be with other medical practitioners, not psychiatrists. Yet, he persists in attacking psychiatry and psychiatrists using this "straw man." I know of *no* psychiatrists who subscribe to the idea that medical treatment proves there is a biological cause. By using these and other attributions to psychiatry and psychiatrists, he betrays a lack of understanding of modern psychiatry and is unfairly spreading misinformation.

A strong argument could be made against remedicalization by mental health professionals, including many psychiatrists, who fear that remedicalization may lead to the trivialization of psychotherapy and of the mental health field in general. This is not based on "which side of the prescription pad one happens to be." There is far more economic benefit to be derived from providing long-term intensive psychotherapy, whether or not one is an M.D., R.N., M.S.W., or

Ph.D., than from brief, prescription pad oriented medical visits. Congress knows this, the insurance companies know this, and managed care companies know this. All mental health professionals need to work in a concerted way together to stem the insidious tide of rationing of mental health care based on this form of dualistic thinking.

Far more danger threatens the mental health field from such divisive attacks on psychiatry and psychiatrists than from the remedicalization of psychiatry.

DEBATE 12

Should Non-Physician Mental Health Professionals Be Allowed to Prescribe Medicine?

Patrick H. DeLeon argues YES. Dr. DeLeon received an M.S. and Ph.D. in clinical psychology from Purdue University, an M.P.H. from the University of Hawaii, and a J.D. from Catholic University. Since 1973 he has served on the staff of U.S. Senator Daniel K. Inouye of Hawaii, where he is now an Administrative Assistant. He serves on the boards of numerous public policy and professional organizations. A recipient of many awards, he has been very active in the American Psychological Association and is currently on the editorial boards of several psychology journals.

Ronald W. Pies, M.D., argues NO. Dr. Pies is Director of Psychopharmacology at the Harry Solomon Mental Health Center (Lowell, MA) and Associate Clinical Professor of Psychiatry at Tufts University School of Medicine. He is the author of *Psychotherapy Today: A Consumer's Guide to Choosing the Right Therapist* (Manning-Skidmore-Roth) as well as a chapbook of poetry, *Riding Down Dark* (Nightshade Press). He is a contributing editor to *The Psychiatric Times* and the coauthor (with Andrew Weinberg, M.D.) of a booklet on geriatric psychopharmacology.

YES

PATRICK H. DELEON

Currently a wide range of non-physician health care providers (including mental health specialists) *are* prescribing medications and are doing so in a competent and responsible manner. Contrary to the allegations of their specialty competitors within organized medicine, these professionals do not represent a ''public health hazard.'' At the public (and health) policy level the decision of whether any profession should prescribe medications represents both training and political considerations—that is, can the profession's educational institutions develop credible training modules, provide appropriate objective evidence of competence (i.e., credentials), and, in conjunction with their clinical colleagues, convince the public (and their elected officials) that the potential societal benefits outweigh any possible clinical (and political) risks?

A review of the relevant health professions literature makes clear that the obtainment of prescription privileges by non-physicians has always been a slow and evolutionary process (Burns, DeLeon, Chemtob, Welch, & Samuels, 1988). In 1935 the Indiana State Legislature enacted legislation that the state's attorney general eventually ruled authorized optometry to utilize medications for both diagnostic and therapeutic purposes. More than fifty years later optometry finally completed its fifty-state quest, with the passage of legislation in Maryland providing that state's optometrists with the authority to utilize medications for diagnostic purposes. However, once the underlying public policy issue had been decided, the process of ''upgrading'' their statutes to include, for example, therapeutic use, progressed remarkably rapidly. For example, in 1991 only four states allowed optometrists to utilize drugs for therapeutic purposes; today, thirty-one states have modified their optometry ''scope of practice'' act to authorize this clinical responsibility. Other nonphysicians who possess medication authority include dentistry and podiatry in all states, nurse practitioners in thirty-five states, physician assistants in thirty-two states, and clinical pharmacists in five states.

The fundamental decision of whether any profession should be deemed ''competent'' to utilize medications (and under what conditions) must ultimately be made at the individual state level, where it has frequently been accomplished by the adoption of a binary statutory approach under which the state's pharmacy act provides a listing of those professions that are allowed to prescribe medications, and the individual professional practice acts set the specific legal parameters for each profession. The various state medical practice acts may also contain additional restrictions on prescriptive authority, even as it applies to non-physician disciplines.

It is commonly thought that only physicians and dentists have traditionally been able to prescribe medications. Yet, in early Western history, pharmacy and medicine were so intertwined that, in effect, they were the same profession. In colonial America the medical and pharmaceutical functions of both professions were interchangeable. It was not until the twentieth century that pharmacists in America lost the right to prescribe. And, it was only in 1951 that the Durham-Humphrey amendments to the Food, Drug, and Cosmetic Act (P.L. 82–215) defined whether a particular drug was to be made available over the counter or by prescription only. Although the federal government thereby asserted the authority to determine which drugs were to require a prescription, the various states retained the authority to decide which professions were authorized to write prescriptions and under what conditions. Central to the underlying policy debate is the federal government's residual responsibility and experiences in determining the clinical responsibilities appropriate for federal non-physician health care providers.

From a conceptual frame of reference the broad plenary authority granted to physicians in the prescription arena contrasts sharply with that generally granted to the various non-physician providers. Dentists, optometrists, and podiatrists are generally defined as "limited practitioners" and are restricted to specific body parts or clinical conditions affecting those body parts. They are also generally afforded independent status (i.e., their "scope of practice" does not require physician supervision or direction in the use of the medications). Physician assistants, nurse practitioners, and, surprisingly, clinical pharmacists are generally considered "physician extenders," and therefore their "scope of practice" acts usually require predetermined arrangements that call for either: (a) prearranged protocols or agreements between the non-physician provider and a supervising physician, including a list of predetermined approved drugs and guidelines, or (b) drug formularies established by a state Drug Formulary Commission that determines the list of authorized drugs and also provides specific guidelines for their use. Non-physician providers who are authorized to prescribe by formulary are viewed as limited but "independent" providers, whereas those who use protocols are considered "dependent" providers because they actually prescribe only under the supervision of an attending physician. Although nurse practitioners are generally considered under the category of "physician extender," that profession has recently begun a national effort to enact "substitution" legislation (for example, as is the case in Alaska and the State of Washington), under which there is no statutory requirement of physician involvement.

The health professions literature makes it quite clear that not only do non-physicians prescribe in a competent and safe manner, but also that, further, nurse practitioners in particular tend to be more conservative than their medical colleagues in using this clinical modality. In fact, one study comparing the prescription recommendations of pediatricians and pediatric nurse practitioners found that there was significant clinical disagreement in less than 1 percent of the cases (OTA, 1986). Further, although not generally appreciated by most mental health professionals (or their traditional educational institutions), our individual state governments have a long history of experimenting with innovative health delivery systems. In 1982 the State of California reported on utilizing its broad health manpower demonstration authority to "test out" whether non-physicians in that state should be authorized to prescribe medications. California's Office of

Statewide Health Planning and Development reported on ten separate pilot prescription projects and concluded that:

> None of the projects, to date, have received the intense scrutiny that these 10 prescribing and dispensing projects have received. Over 1 million patients have been seen by these prescribing and dispensing (non-physician) trainees over the past three years. At least 50 percent of these patients have had drugs prescribed for them or dispensed to them by these professionals'' (State of California, 1982, p. 1).

Of considerable interest was that aspect of the State's report which indicated that the principal teaching methods employed were lectures and seminars, varying from sixteen hours to ninety-five hours in length. The report further noted that only 56 percent of the trainees had previously graduated from academic programs with a bachelor's degree or higher. The patients were clearly comfortable with the trainees' performance (99.5 percent indicated as such), as were the supervising physicians, 98 percent of whom expressed their support for non-physicians being granted this clinical responsibility.

There really should no longer be any serious question as to whether each of our nation's core mental health disciplines could, if they so desired, train their practitioners to competently and safely utilize psychotropic medications. Already a wide range of non-physician mental health providers *are* competently prescribing. This is being done legally within the various federal agencies, such as the Department of Defense, Indian Health Service, and Veterans Administration, and ''informally'' within the private sector (always, we would note, with the knowledge and consent of supportive physicians).

Within professional psychology two independent efforts were recently made to develop comprehensive prescription training modules that could then be recommended for integration into traditional doctoral training programs (Fox, Schwelitz, & Barclay, 1992). The proposed courses of study consisted of approximately thirty-nine quarter credit hours and were essentially identical. On closer examination, it was reported that many of the current programs would only have to expand their present curriculum by adding no more than three additional courses—a conclusion subsequently reiterated by a number of psychology professional school deans. We further note that the contemplated trainees did not include licensed/practicing (i.e., experienced) clinicians.

In our judgment, the key to obtaining clinical competence with psychotropic medications will be obtaining systematic hands-on supervised experience with real-life patients. For experienced practitioners, we project that this could be accomplished with six to eight weeks of training, on a continuing education basis. We further suggest that the appropriate method is to train experienced clinicians to feel comfortable in using the most up-to-date computer software available ''off the shelf,'' and not—as many of our professional colleagues have suggested—to ensure that the aspiring clinician knows all there is to possibly know about developing his or her own computer programs, including perhaps building his or her own computer.

Within professional psychology several additional significant developments have occurred in the prescription arena (DeLeon, Folen, Jennings, Willis, & Wright, 1991). In the mid-1980s members of the Hawaii Psychological Association were successful in having legislation introduced in their state legislature that called for a detailed study of the possibility of psychologists prescribing. No fewer than nine separate bills were introduced on the topic, and extensive hearings were held in both the House and Senate chambers. At the direction of the legislature, the Hawaii Center for Alternative Dispute Resolution ultimately conducted a series of roundtable meetings and submitted a formal report to the legislature. As might be expected, throughout that process organized psychiatry expressed considerable opposition to even considering the possibility.

One might view the policy developments within professional psychology as having three distinct thrusts. Within the various state associations, considerable interest in obtaining this clinical privilege continues to evolve. Today, eleven state and county psychological associations have joined Hawaii in establishing formal task forces to explore various legislative and educational opportunities. The Executive Committee, for example, of the California State Psychological Association voted unanimously to seek the introduction of appropriate legislation during their 1993 legislative session. At the national association level, the APA Board of Directors and its Council of Representatives voted to establish a formal APA task force on prescription privileges. That body is expected to complete its deliberations soon and, we understand, will issue a supportive report. Finally, within the federal sector, an increasing number of federal psychologists have begun reporting that they do, in fact, already issue prescription orders and, further, that a number of federal hospital facilities, such as those within the Indian Health Service, have modified their bylaws to formally recognize this practice.

Perhaps most interesting, however, has been the recent decision by the Department of Defense (DoD) to initiate, at Congressional direction, a pilot psychology prescription training program. During its deliberations on the Fiscal Year 1989 DoD Appropriations bill, the House-Senate conferees included language directing the Department to develop a "... demonstration pilot training project under which military psychologists may be trained and authorized to issue appropriate psychotropic medications under certain circumstances." The DoD is implementing the program. However, the intensity of organized psychiatry's vitriolic attacks has caused various delays and required additional Congressional pressure. The initial trainees were assigned to the DoD physician assistant training program to begin their studies. As one might imagine, this positive action by DoD resulted in intensified political vigilance by psychiatry—always alleging that the trainees represented a "public health hazard" to military personnel and their families.

Eventually, a formal two-year training program was initiated—as was originally contemplated by the Congress—and four military psychologists are currently participating in the program. On completion of their training, and an independent evaluation by the American College of Neuropsychopharmacology, additional trainees are expected to be enrolled. Of particular interest, it now appears that specific educational modules are being developed *to complement* the psychologists' expertise, rather than continuing to rely on traditional medical school course work. This development in itself truly represents a qualitative shift in the debate. Can professional psychologists be taught to responsibly prescribe? The "hows" and "how nots" *are* currently being developed.

Although we have primarily focused on professional psychology, as we indicated earlier, within professional nursing a very significant prescription agenda continues to evolve, with the express goal of obtaining autonomous, fully substitutive models of practice. Within psychiatric nursing, progress is being made in developing both a model curriculum and special prescription "centers of excellence," with increasing evidence of active financial support from the drug industry. Although professional social work has been admittedly somewhat hesitant to address this issue, the recent issuance of a special NIMH contract to the Council on Social Work Education to support an interactive video conference on psychopharmacology clearly suggests that considerably more interest within social work may soon surface.

One might reasonably ask: Is there a true societal need for our nation's non-physician health care providers to move into the prescription arena? In our view there definitely is (DeLeon, 1988; DeLeon, Fox, & Graham, 1991). Depending on the target population that one seeks to serve—those in rural America, the chronically mentally ill, the elderly, or hyperactive children—a demonstrable need exists for improved quality of care. When the HHS Inspector General reports that currently 40 percent of our nation's elderly residing in nursing homes receive psychoactive medications, even though most do not possess mental health diagnoses, something beyond "more of the same" must be done. In our judgment, there is a particular societal need for a fundamentally psychosocial/behavioral orientation to the use of psychotropic medications, and we are confident that the evolution of the various non-physician mental health disciplines into this arena will, in the long run, fundamentally revolutionize our nation's mental health programs and will do so in a manner that simply cannot be predicted today. Fundamental changes in the status quo are always unsettling; however, they are sometimes very necessary.

REFERENCES

Burns, S. M., DeLeon, P. H., Chemtob, C. M., Welch, B. L., & Samuels, R. M. (1988). Psychotropic medication: A new technique for psychology? *Psychotherapy: Theory, Research, Practice, and Training, 25,* 508–515.

DeLeon, P. H. (1988). Public policy and public service: Our professional duty. *American Psychologist, 43,* 309–315.

DeLeon, P. H., Folen, R. A., Jennings, F. L., Willis, D. J., & Wright, R. H. (1991). The case for prescription privileges: A logical evolution of professional practice. *Journal of Clinical Child Psychology, 20*(3), 254–267.

DeLeon, P. H., Fox, R. E., & Graham, S. R. (1991). Prescription privileges: Psychology's next frontier? *American Psychologist, 46,* 384–393.

Fox, R. E., Schwelitz, F. D., & Barclay, A. G. (1992). A proposed curriculum for psychopharmacology training for professional psychologists. *Professional Psychology: Research and Practice, 23*(3), 216–219.

State of California, Office of Statewide Health Planning and Development, Division of Health Professions Development. (1982, November). *Prescribing and dispensing pilot projects* (Final report to the legislature and to the healing arts licensing boards). Sacramento, CA: Author.

U.S. Congress, Office of Technology Assessment (OTA). (1986). *Nurse practitioners, physician assistants, and certified nurse-midwives: A policy analysis.* (Health technology case study #37; OTA-HCS-37). Washington, DC: U.S. Government Printing Office.

Rejoinder to Dr. DeLeon

RONALD PIES

Dr. DeLeon's essay in favor of ''prescribing'' privileges for psychologists contains too many non sequiturs to rebut in so little space. The most obvious of these is his ''piggybacking'' the political agenda of psychologists onto the expanded privileges of podiatrists, dentists, nurse practitioners, and clinical pharmacists. I deliberately avoided dealing with these other professions in my argument precisely because they have nothing whatsoever in common with clinical psychology. Dr. DeLeon seems to reason that (1) if non-physician A has been granted ''prescribing privileges'' and is apparently prescribing competently, then (2) non-physician B (i.e., a clinical psychologist) should also be granted these privileges, even in the absence of any credible empirical evidence that this second type of non-physician can prescribe competently. (Credible evidence, by the way, does not consist of anecdotal reports from Indian reservations; it consists of many large-scale, controlled studies of several hundred psychologists under a variety of real-life clinical conditions.)

Dr. DeLeon also looks back to ''colonial America,'' when pharmacists and physicians were both allowed to prescribe medication, implying that in some sense this practice was laudable and a potential model for the expansion of psychologists' privileges. Dr. DeLeon should also be aware that ''Barbers, beard trimmers, bath attendants, and similar functionaries were ubiquitous in medieval society, where they performed a variety of services, some of which were medical'' (McGrew, 1985). I doubt that Dr. DeLeon would utilize this fact in support of his arguments. Indeed, the progress of medical care since the Middle Ages has depended on the further refinement of ''who should do what,'' not on the blurring of critical distinctions. It is precisely for this reason that allergists (who are, of course, physicians) do not practice brain surgery. The ''distinctions'' to which I allude are part of what I have termed the ''deep structure'' of a particular discipline. Though different in many important respects, the fields of medicine and dentistry have very similar deep structures—so, too, have medicine and nursing. In contrast, the field of clinical psychology has never been grounded in biomedical science and hands-on clinical practice (D'Afflitti, 1991). Dr. DeLeon thinks that such hands-on experience could be acquired ''with six to eight weeks of training, on a continuing education basis.'' Medical interns will attest to their profound perplexity even after a year of intensive hands-on clinical experience; Dr. DeLeon's estimate can only send nervous shivers down the spines of his potential patients. But then, Dr. DeLeon's argument from its inception assumes that we are merely discussing ''the right to prescribe.'' Nowhere does he appreciate that we are really addressing the right to practice medicine—to take full medicolegal responsibility for life-and-death issues. He sees prescribing privileges for psychologists in the context of ''a long history of experimenting with innovative health delivery systems.'' Characteristically, he cites no ''experimental'' evidence that psychologists per se are now, or could be in the future, equipped to practice medicine competently, absent a medical degree. The public may be understandably reluctant to serve as guinea pigs in Dr. DeLeon's bold experiment.

References

D'Afflitti, J. P. (1991). Profoundly different professions: Commentary on prescribing privileges for psychologists. *Journal of Clinical Psychiatry 52,* 11–12.

McGrew, R. E. (1985). *Encyclopedia of medical history* (p. 30). London: Macmillan Press.

NO

Ronald W. Pies

The short and flippant response to the question of whether psychologists should be allowed to prescribe psychotropic medications is this: Yes, psychologists should be granted prescribing privileges—once they have gone through medical school. Physicians in general and psychiatrists in particular would then have no basis for complaint; indeed, psychologists so trained would be in a remarkably strong position from which to make decisions about psychotropic medications—a powerful and potentially hazardous group of drugs. But to suggest that a year or two of "course work" in psychopharmacology will sufficiently prepare anyone to "prescribe" is to misunderstand radically the nature of medication, medical science, and—above all—medical responsibility.

Let us at once get down to cases: A 35-year-old man walks into the office of a "prescribing psychologist" and describes what sounds like symptoms of generalized anxiety (e.g., feeling "uptight," "shaky," and "like I'm gonna explode"). The man gives a history of a "break-up," three days previously, of a long-standing relationship. He has been unable to sleep since then, and his appetite has been poor. The psychologist takes a routine history and concludes that the patient is undergoing an "adjustment reaction with anxious mood." He arranges to see the man in brief psychotherapy and prescribes diazepam (Valium) 5 mg twice daily. Unbeknownst to the psychologist, the individual also had a history of chronic active hepatitis and episodic alcohol abuse. He had been drinking heavily two days before evaluation and was beginning to develop signs of alcohol withdrawal. One week before evaluation, the patient had received a prescription for cimetidine (Tagamet), an anti-ulcer medication. On taking two diazepam tablets, the patient initially felt better, but ten hours later found that he was extremely groggy. He stopped taking the diazepam; one day later, he suffered a grand mal seizure and was taken to the emergency room.

What precisely happened here? First, the diagnosis of alcohol withdrawal was missed, and no blood pressure or pulse rate was taken to evaluate this possibility. Second, no medical history was obtained, and thus the patient's markedly impaired liver function was not appreciated. Third, a long-acting benzodiazepine was prescribed, which—partly because of the patient's compromised liver function—was not metabolized normally. The cimetidine further slowed metabolism of the drug, and the resultant accumulation made the patient transiently groggy. Cessation of the diazepam then left the patient vulnerable to full-blown delirium tremens and seizure.

Psychologists clamoring for "prescribing privileges" will no doubt cry "foul." "Hold on, doctor," they are likely to say, "you deliberately stacked the deck in your case vignette. First of all, how many patients are going to come in with hepatitis and alcohol withdrawal, not to mention some drug that affects liver metabolism? More important, a good clinical psychologist would certainly have obtained a substance abuse history. Furthermore, as we psychologists envision prescribing privileges, we would have some form of 'medical backup.' We would have gotten this individual checked out first by a GP. Finally, appropriate course work and internship experience would have prepared your hypothetical psychologist to prescribe a shorter-acting agent, such as lorazepam (Ativan)."

These arguments are plausible, but specious. First of all, as many as one in twenty patients presenting with so-called emotional problems turn out to have a physical basis for their complaint (e.g., cerebrovascular problems, viral illness, endocrine disease, or substance abuse). Many of these patients are receiving concomitant medication from family or general practitioners, and these agents often interact with psychotropic medications. While it is true that a "good" clinical psychologist would have obtained a substance abuse history, patients often distort or conceal such facts. Unlike physicians, clinical psychologists are not—and under current proposals will never be—trained to detect signs of physical illness such as jaundice, ascites, or tell-tale "spider angiomata" (tiny vascular malformations) in the chronic alcoholic. Naturally, if every imagined "prescribing psychologist" worked hand-in-glove with a readily available "backup physician," some of these difficulties could be mitigated. But—contrary to the "set-and-forget" mentality that underlies the notion of "prescribing"—the patient is not a static system. His or her metabolic, nutritional, and neurologic status changes from week to week and even hour to hour. The concept of the eternally available "backup physician" is a self-serving fantasy that will never materialize in the disadvantaged regions psychologists propose to serve. Even in medically well-endowed areas, I seriously doubt that many physicians will wish to assume the nebulous legal responsibility entailed in "backing up" psychologists. (And who, by the way, will deal with the frantic call at two in the morning from the patient having "a weird side effect" from the medication? The "prescribing psychologist" or the "backup physician"?) I will concede that a sophisticated course in psychopharmacology would have prepared our hypothetical psychologist to prescribe a shorter-acting benzodiazepine; but then, benzodiazepines are among the most benign and "prescriber-friendly" medications administered in psychiatry. What about antidepressants, antipsychotics, or lithium, with their myriad side effects and potential toxic reactions?

"We wouldn't seek to prescribe complicated agents like that," some psychologists might respond. "We would restrict our practice to more straightforward and benign agents." To which the psychopharmacologist replies: "Dream on." In the first place, no agent of any use in psychopharmacology is entirely benign—even a benzodiazepine can be lethal to, say, an individual with sleep apnea. More important, the clinician whose practice is limited to one or two types of psychotropic agents will be under considerable (unconscious?) pressure to use precisely those agents—when all you have is a hammer, everything tends to look like a nail.

Both the popular press and some psychologists and psychiatrists like to portray the debate over prescribing privileges as merely a "turf war." This catastrophic misreading stems from the failure to understand what I have called (borrowing Noam Chomsky's term) the "deep structure" of clinical medicine. Surely no one would call it a "turf war" if psychologists demanded the right to perform brain surgery after "sufficient course work" and a brief internship. Rather, we would call it either insanity or fraud. The systematic refusal to understand what is really involved in "prescribing" has led some to the erroneous conclusion—to quote one prominent psychologist—that "it's no big deal." To the experienced physician, nothing more need be said to discredit the psychologists' position.

Psychiatrists and psychologists need not get caught up in an endless adversarial position. There is room for cooperative endeavors, such as a combined M.D.-Ph.D. program that integrates clinical medicine and clinical psychology. Psychiatrists and psychologists share an honorable and humane history of helping troubled individuals. They do not share, however, the skills necessary to prescribe medication.

Annotated Bibliography

DeLeon, P. H. (1990). Psychotherapeutic medications. *Register Report, 16,* 5–12.

A synopsis of the prescribing controversy from one of the leading proponents of privileges for psychologists.

Pies, R. W. (1991). The "deep structure" of clinical medicine and prescribing privileges for psychologists. *Journal of Clinical Psychiatry, 52,* 4–8.

I have outlined the concept of "deep structure" and how it reveals critical differences between seemingly related professions.

LaBruzza, A. L. (1981). Physical illness presenting as psychiatric disorder: Guidelines for differential diagnosis. *Journal of Operational Psychiatry 12,* 24–31.

Describes the myriad conditions that can mimic "psychological" problems, thus laying the foundation for a medical approach to "prescribing privileges."

Rejoinder to Dr. Pies

Patrick H. DeLeon

The notion that all any non-physician mental health specialist has to do to responsibly prescribe is to "go to medical school" sadly reflects the extent to which those in opposition to the prescription movement really do not understand, nor appreciate, the complexities and maturation of our current mental health educational system. First, one should never forget that organized medicine, and psychiatry in particular, has a long history of actively opposing *any* expansion in the scope of practice of each of the core mental health disciplines. This has been the case surrounding the issue of providing autonomous outpatient care, becoming a licensed/certified profession, obtaining third-party reimbursement, and most recently in the inpatient and prescription arenas. And, notwithstanding the "public health hazard" argument that is always proffered, today each of the mental health disciplines is, in fact, authorized at the state (and federal level) to function autonomously, including having their practitioners independently "diagnose and treat."

This is a very critical point. If a profession is authorized to independently diagnose and treat patients/clients, its state licensure act does not limit that clinical responsibility to only certain types of diagnoses. The "straw person" argument proffered by Dr. Pies clearly ignores this fundamental fact. Clinical psychologists (as well as members of each of the other mental health disciplines) are already authorized to diagnose (and on rare occasions, unfortunately, to misdiagnose) his hypothetical patient—including ascertaining *all* pertinent facts and making appropriate referrals when necessary.

Medicine possesses a long history of seeking to be the "captain of the ship." In its collective judgment, the other disciplines are "necessary and valuable" but, of course, must always "know their place." Above all else, only medicine has been trained to know what is "truly best" for the patient. Clinical findings (or objective evidence) suggested by others as to what really is best for the patient must never interfere with the captain's clinical judgment—for only medical school teaches the "truth." If this sounds a little harsh, one should take a close look at the realities of our current health (and mental health) delivery system. As indicated earlier, the excessive utilization within our nation's nursing homes of psychotropic medications for behavior control is a national tragedy; similarly, the continuing evidence that 60 to 80 percent of those hospitalized for mental health reasons should not be, is equally unacceptable. In both incidences, the inappropriate clinical decisions were made by licensed physicians. We simply suggest that those who claim that "others" cannot learn their particular clinical expertise either have very little respect for our educational system or, more likely, simply do not want to have to face the personal and professional competition that is evolving. To cite psychology as an example, after approximately fifteen years of being eligible for outpatient reimbursement under the Department of Defense CHAMPUS program, in 1985 psychology surpassed psychiatry in the number of outpatient visits being provided. And, today, a similar trend is evolving within the inpatient market.

In our judgment the key to each of the non-physician mental health disciplines responsibly obtaining prescription privileges is for their educational institutions to develop relevant training modules that complement their present core mental health expertise. Interestingly, the "public health hazard" horrors that medicine predicted at every stage in the maturation of the non-physician professions simply do not seem to happen.

DEBATE 13

Are There Sufficient Foundations for Mental Health Experts to Testify in Court?

Stanley L. Brodsky argues YES. He is Professor of Psychology and coordinator of the Psychology-Law specialty at the University of Alabama, where he teaches graduate courses in forensic psychology and clinical psychology applied to legal problems. He is Associate Editor of the *American Psychologist* and was the founding Editor of *Criminal Justice and Behavior*. Dr. Brodsky is a frequent contributor to scholarly journals in psychology and is editor or author of nine books. He is coauthor with H. O'Neal Smitherman of the *Handbook of Scales for Research in Crime and Delinquency* (1983), and he is author of *Testifying in Court: Guidelines & Maxims for the Expert Witness* (1991).

Arguing NO is David Faust who is Professor, Department of Psychology, University of Rhode Island, and holds an affiliate appointment in the Department of Psychiatry and Human Behavior, Brown University Medical School. He was formally the Director of Psychology at the Rhode Island Hospital. Dr. Faust has published widely on such topics as clinical decision making, psychology and the law, and philosophy of science. He has received various awards and honors in psychology, including the National Academy of Neuropsychology's annual Award for Excellence in Research.

YES

STANLEY L. BRODSKY

The annual conventions of the American Psychological Association are pretty tame events. Occasional excitement does arise from talks by renowned figures in psychology and from debates in the elected council. One additional source of volcanic heat that erupts every year is found in symposia about the scientific foundations of testimony in court.

The critics in these disputes are Jay Ziskin and David Faust, who have also published about court testimony and research foundations of the mental health professions, most notably in a book for attorneys titled *Coping with Psychiatric and Psychological Testimony* (Ziskin & Faust, 1988), and in a critical article in *Science* (Faust & Ziskin, 1988). They have asserted that substantial unreliability and lack of validity exist in diagnoses related to legal matters and, furthermore, that mental health professionals are not any better than lay persons in the most important clinical-legal judgments. They have concluded that expert opinions are overly subjective and waste vast amounts of money and time in court proceedings.

At scholarly conventions these assertions sometimes have been met by red-faced, passionate rebuttals and angry, ad hominum, pejorative attacks. The issue is of sufficient importance that the president and president-elect of the American Psychological Association wrote a reply in *Science* to Faust and Ziskin (Fowler & Matarazzo, 1988). These association presidents asserted that the Faust and Ziskin article ". . . disregards a wide body of more recent research that demonstrates acceptably high reliability for many psychological and psychiatric diagnoses" (p. 1143) and that clinical conclusions can be imperfect while still being valuable for many practical purposes.

But are there in fact sufficient foundations for psychologists to testify in court? In one sense this is an easy question to answer. The answer is *yes* when the experts speak in court with sound knowledge about the specific issue at hand. The answer is *no* when the experts testify without sound knowledge. The assessment of whether the specific knowledge bases are sound is the key point at which the strongest critics and the strongest defenders of mental health testimony differ. Is the body of professional knowledge in mental health consistent and accurate enough to contribute to the legal process? Faust and Ziskin argue "no." In contrast, my view is that mental health knowledge can offer a source of clinical information about human behavior that is extraordinarily useful in the courtroom. This knowledge is the result of systematic observations by professionals who are trained to go beyond the understandings of lay persons. And they are accepted in essence by every court in this country on the bases that experts in every scientific field are accepted: because the professionals have education, training, and skills that allow them to offer their opinions. From the landmark *Jenkins v. United States* decision rendered by the distinguished jurist David Bazelon in 1965 to the more recent U.S. Supreme Court *Barefoot v. Estelle* (1983), courts have thoughtfully considered the depth and breadth of psychological knowledge and, while recognizing the limitations, have affirmed psychologists as appropriately admitted as expert witnesses.

However, the fit is not always easy between what mental health professionals do and know and what the court demands. Sometimes I think we need a translator. The language differences and the underlying differences in concepts between the law and mental health seem as far apart as the villagers speaking Kanada to me when I was living in the Indian state of Karnataka and me replying in my northeastern American version of English. Communication was difficult. In the same sense, the law uses terms and operating assumptions far removed from what mental health professionals use in their work. Because it is the mental health professionals who appear in the legal setting, and not vice versa, the strain we find is considerable and often uncomfortable. As a consequence, particularly serious hazards faced by mental health witnesses are the pull toward legal conclusions and the potential for compromising professional judgments to the affiliative influences of the adversarial system. Just such a Procrustean bed is often found when mental health professionals appear in court. For example, every time a mental health expert is insistently asked by the court whether an individual is insane, the witness should (and most often does) decline to offer an opinion. ''Insanity'' is a legal term.

The law expects truth to emerge from an adversarial process and admits only selected pieces of information that meet predetermined rules. In contrast, the mental health field proceeds like all sciences. Any information is admissible, provided it meets standards of scientific merit. In the law, material may be ruled out of consideration because it does not meet standards generated from past cases or legislative statutes.

Mental health experts who testify in court are admitted as expert witnesses, a special status granted under the law. Expert witnesses are permitted to give opinions in their areas of expertise, unlike lay witnesses who may only testify about what they have seen or heard (or, less frequently, what they have smelled, tasted, or touched). As a result, the psychological expert witness is allowed to do what otherwise would be the province of the judge or jury: to put together facts and to draw conclusions. This privilege appears explicitly when attorneys ask witnesses questions that begin with the phrase: ''Doctor, in your opinion, is it true that . . .?'' In turn, many witnesses, myself included, often begin answers with the prefix that, ''In my best professional judgment. . . .'' That phrase is important because it clarifies that the witnesses are making judgment calls, based on their particular professional skills or scientific knowledge. The issue of the substantive contributions of such professional knowledge may be clarified by considering first one of the most common areas of mental health testimony—competence to stand trial—and then a civil case about which extensive documentation has been published: the Buffalo Creek disaster.

To be mentally competent to stand trial, defendants must be able to understand the nature of the proceedings and charges against them and be able to aid in their own defense. Trained mental health professionals use standardized procedures to make inquiries into these issues and then offer reports or testimony to courts about the underlying psychological abilities related to these legal issues. A comprehensive review of competency assessments by Grisso (1986) concluded that the Competency To Stand Trial Assessment Instrument (the most frequently used interview schedule) is highly reliable, and that the validity research is insufficient and mixed, but the research results "... generally are consistent with legal presumptions about pretrial competency as a construct" (p. 83). My own observations coincide with the Grisso analysis: consistent and replicable patterns of interviewing are utilized in forensic centers. The clinical evidence presented to the court provides more organized, pointed, and psychologically meaningful data than otherwise is available.

We move from criminal to civil cases as we consider the Buffalo Creek lawsuit. The slag dam built by the Pittston Coal Company in Buffalo Creek, West Virginia, collapsed in the early morning of February 26, 1972. A massive wave of mud and water swept through the valley below the dam, killing 125 people and destroying the homes and property of thousands more. When attorney Gerald Stern (1976) sued the mining company on behalf of the survivors, he set out to prove that the losses of family, friends, homes, and community were psychologically injurious. To study the presence, nature, and extent of the psychological damage, psychiatrist James Titchener of the University of Cincinnati led a team of psychiatrists, psychologists, and social workers that interviewed a sample of 178 families and a total of 611 individuals. Gleser, Green, and Winget (1981) described these procedures, including the standardized interview schedules that were used. A symptom checklist asked about forty-eight specific problem areas, including somatic concerns, obsessive-compulsive behaviors, anxiety, hostility, and depression. Family disruption and sleep problems were quantified. General clinical impairment was measured. Twenty additional areas were assessed in a Psychiatric Evaluation Form, which looked into areas such as alcohol abuse and suicide attempts. Scales that did not have adequate reliability or validity in this study were dropped. Some of the most important data were counts of frequency of psychiatric symptoms, increases in alcohol and drug use, and disruptions in sleep.

The experts prepared their psychological evidence in the suit filed by the survivors against the Pittston Coal Company and were prepared to testify in court about their professional evaluations of the totality of the survivors' experiences, over and beyond what individual survivors could describe. While the out-of-court settlement yielded generous payments for the survivors, and negated the need for formal court testimony, the final outcome of a trial is not a measure of witness usefulness and desirability. Rather, this case illustrates the fundamental role of expert mental health evidence: observations were made and psychological conclusions drawn from a foundation of generally systematic, objective procedures. In his reviews of the consistency and validity of psychological assessments in general, Matarazzo (1978, 1990, 1991) has concluded that massive research findings support the reliability and validity of evaluations of intelligence, neuropsychological impairment, and psychiatric diagnoses.

As we examine the controversy over mental health testimony, the underlying questions are: who is right, and for what kinds of cases? Are Faust and Ziskin and the other few voices of protest like Ignaz Semmelweiss, the nineteenth century Austrian physician who cried out that doctors should not go with unwashed hands directly from autopsies on diseased bodies to delivering children and performing surgery? Semmelweiss was initially ridiculed by his fellow physicians: ". . . they laughed at him, they castigated him, they lied about him, they took his job away from him and eventually he had to flee from Vienna. . . ." (McConnell, 1969, p. 68), and, of course, eventually, Semmelweiss was unequivocally vindicated. Or are these lonely voices more like Wilhelm Fleiss, Freud's intimate correspondent, who in isolation argued that sexual and psychological disturbances arose in the mucous membranes of the nose? His psychological theory is remembered as an idiosyncratic, historical quirk, incorrect in its theory, far-fetched in its assumptions, and harmful in its surgical practices.

The view of the majority of clinicians who speak and write on this issue is that Faust and Ziskin are more Fleissian than Semmelwiessian. From my view, Faust and Ziskin are correct on one essential point: many clinicians do testify on matters well beyond their real knowledge. However, Faust and Ziskin oversimplify and their work is not incorporated by most practitioners, largely because of their perceived commitment to the adversarial process of aiding attorneys in dismissing most psychological evidence. In their *Science* article, for example, they make this attack: it is impossible for mental health experts to ever verify the statement, "I just knew what she was thinking when she committed suicide" (p. 34). That assertion, like so many others in their rhetoric, is setting up a straw target, easy to knock down. Clinicians rarely make such absurd statements. When such statements are made, they indeed should be fiercely attacked in the courtroom.

I lead frequent workshops on testifying in court for mental health professionals. When inept clinicians complain about their experiences of being embarrassed and their testimony made ineffectual as a result of cross-examination, these processes affirm for me the self-correcting mechanisms of court testimony. Incompetent professionals should be embarrassed on the witness stand. Testifying in court is a dramatic way of getting their attention about how much more they have to learn. The aggressive cross-examination of incompetent professionals serves in part as a check on the abuses so feared by Faust and Ziskin. The sweeping assertions that psychologists or psychiatrists are not qualified to testify in court are themselves founded on incomplete information. Some experts should and some should not be permitted to testify in the courtroom, and that is determined in part, and reasonably, by their credentials and experience. Judges do not always admit individuals presented as experts. Over and beyond that admittedly coarse judicial screening, the cross-examination serves the purpose of bringing light and accountability to mental health experts. The Ziskin and Faust books for attorneys on how to examine expert witnesses in psychiatry and psychology are flawed but also terrifically important; they help screen out the less knowledgeable from future court appearances and encourage other witnesses to be more academically responsible. In my own workshops I emphasize the same thing. The fundamental issue in court testimony is "how do you know what you know?" Polished courtroom demeanor is never a substitute for solid knowledge of the research roots of one's practices.

In her poem describing a snake in her garden, Emily Dickinson used the phrase "zero at the bone." I have come to think of that phrase as capturing the sense of rightness in a personal function, from hitting a golf ball to being in tune with the environment. Being zero at the bone on the tennis court occurs when one sees the spin on the approaching ball, and time slows down preceding the perfect cross-court return. And zero at the bone on the witness stand are the times when there is an effortless unification of scholarly and professional roles in the interests of offering constructive and objective psychological evidence. I am encouraged by seeing attention to and enhancement of expert witnesses who are indeed zero at the bone.

References

Faust, D., & Ziskin, J. (1988). *Coping with psychiatric and psychological testimony.* Volumes 1–3. Venice, CA: Law and Psychology Press.

Faust, D., & Ziskin, J. (1988). The expert witness in psychology and psychiatry. *Science, 241,* 31–35.

Fowler, R. D., & Matarazzo, J. D. (1988). Psychologists and psychiatrists as expert witnesses. *Science, 241,* 2.

Gleser, G. C., Green, B. L., & Winget, C. (1981). *Prolonged psychological effects of disaster: A study of Buffalo Creek.* New York: Academic Press.

Grisso, T. (1986). *Evaluating competencies: Forensic assessments and instruments.* New York: Plenum.

Matarazzo, J. D. (1978). The interview: Its reliability and validity in clinical diagnosis. In B. B. Wolman (Ed.), *Clinical diagnosis of mental disorders: A handbook.* (p. 47–96). New York: Plenum.

Matarazzo, J. D. (1990). Psychological assessment versus psychological testing: Validation from Binet to the school, clinic, and courtroom. *American Psychologist, 45,* 999–1017.

Matarazzo, J. D. (1991). Psychological assessment is reliable and valid: Reply to Ziskin and Faust. *American Psychologist, 46,* 882–883.

McConnell, J. V. (1969). A psychologist looks at the medical profession. In A. G. Sugarman (Ed.), *Examining the medical expert: Lectures and trial demonstrations.* Ann Arbor: Institute of Continuing Legal Education.

Stern, G. M. (1976). *The Buffalo Creek disaster.* New York: Vintage.

Ziskin, J., & Faust, D. (1988). *Coping with psychiatric and psychological testimony, Fourth Edition.* Volumes 1–3. Venice, CA: Law and Psychology Press.

Rejoinder to Dr. Brodsky

DAVID FAUST

I agree with Brodsky's standard that expert testimony should be based on "sound knowledge about the issue at hand." Unfortunately, his commentary does not meet this test or establish such a basis for expert testimony.

Although acknowledging that courtroom and scientific standards may differ, Brodsky nevertheless cites the court's acceptance of evidence, noting Barefoot, Jenkins, and Judge Bazelon. I discuss the Barefoot case in my NO argument and would add here that subsequent to Jenkins, as is well documented, Bazelon became disillusioned with mental health testimony. Also, Bazelon himself has been supportive of *our* work, stating in a letter to my coauthor, Jay Ziskin, that our text "should be required reading for judges as well as students and practitioners."

Brodsky presents two examples to support the value of expert evaluation, the Buffalo Creek disaster and a competency assessment inventory (CAI). We are not told that the Buffalo Creek plaintiffs were evaluated by plaintiff *and* defense experts and that the two groups often reached directly conflicting conclusions, thereby providing a compelling demonstration of bias or problems in psychiatric evaluations (Zusman & Simon, 1983). Brodsky cites Grisso (1986) as indicating that the CAI is highly reliable and that the validity research is mixed and insufficient but seems to correspond with legal definitions of competency. Here and elsewhere, Brodsky cites his personal observations or impressions, apparently to bolster his arguments.

However, Brodsky has badly misrepresented Grisso's stated views on the CAI. Grisso does describe a single positive study on reliability, but then notes its limitations and states, "Published details of standard administration will be necessary *before* meaningful studies of interrater reliability can be performed" (p. 82, italics added). In regard to validity, which essentially refers to a technique's accuracy and is the most critical feature, Grisso qualifies an initial positive statement by adding, "This is based on only one study. . . . Courts' acceptance of CAI results . . . clearly has not been based on demonstrated empirical validity of the instrument" (p. 83). Even ignoring this distortion of Grisso, Brodsky first presents the requirement for sound knowledge, but then provides this supposed exemplar in which the validity research is mixed or insufficient and in which there is only the most flimsy supportive scientific evidence. Note that in complex areas such as competency evaluations, proper examination of validity often requires many studies. In sum, the "supportive" evidence appears to be little more than Brodsky's favorable impression. The standard thus seems to be that even if the scientific evidence is clearly inadequate and the evidence that does exist on accuracy is mixed, an unproved belief that the method works is good enough. And if unproved beliefs are treated as good enough, it is no wonder that someone believes in the value of mental health testimony. Of course, subjective impression is no substitute for scientific evidence, and numerous studies examining the accuracy of subjective belief or clinical judgment have yielded negative results, so there is informed reason to doubt the faith.

Various other examples of mistakes, unsound reasoning, and misrepresentations exist in Brodsky's commentary, but I must limit myself to one more. He seems to suggest that our views are idiosyncratic, comparing us to Fleiss, a speculative theorist. But are we out there on our own? Zusman (1990) has stated: "The scientific foundation of mental health expert testimony is seriously deficient. . . . Just about all of the reviewers who have set out to examine the quality of scientific support seem to have come to the same conclusion [which is that] the issues on which mental health experts usually testify are lacking sufficient scientific support" (pp. 6–7). We have merely reported what is in the scientific literature. Brodsky has misrepresented the state of the literature, disregarded a huge body of evidence, and cited unverified subjective impressions that sometimes fly in the face of considerable research evidence. As Fleiss might tell him, "Now that's speculating!"

References

Grisso, T. (1986). *Evaluating competencies. Forensic assessments and instruments.* New York: Plenum.

Zusman, J. (1990, August). *Abolish the expert witness: A modest proposal.* Paper presented at the Annual Meeting of the American Psychological Association. Boston, MA.

Zusman, J., & Simon, J. (1983). Differences in repeated psychiatric examinations of litigants to a lawsuit. *American Journal of Psychiatry, 140,* 1300–1304.

NO

David Faust

Question: "Is it possible to fool a mental health expert into thinking someone is mentally ill?"

Answer: "Although it's possible, given the specific pattern of symptoms presented in this case, I feel confident that Smith is psychotic."

Question: "Did Jones show unusual inconsistency in her performance on the Wechsler Adult Intelligence Scale subtests?"

Answer: "Yes. Jones showed a six-point spread, or sometimes performed normally and sometimes at an impaired level, further strengthening the evidence for brain damage."

Question: "Were Smith to be released from prison, what is his potential for acting violently?"

Answer: "It is very likely he would act violently again."

In deciding such matters as the truthfulness of defendants in insanity cases, the presence of brain damage in personal injury cases, or the propensity for violence in the sentencing phase of a murder case, mental health experts have frequently offered testimony of the above type. In the area of violence prediction alone, mental health experts have testified thousands of times, and the evidence they present may decide whether another's life is ended by execution.

In theory, the role of the expert in legal cases is to help the trier of fact—judge or jury—reach sounder decisions than they could have otherwise. And, in fact, experts' authoritative testimony on such matters as malingering, IQ subtest patterns and their relation to brain damage, and the propensity for violence are sometimes received positively. The courts are satisfied, justice is served, and the expert has represented himself, and the profession, with distinction—or so it seems.

The problem with all this is that when the scientific lens is focused on these clinical judgments or pronouncements, this happy picture shatters. Studies directly examining psychologists' and psychiatrists' capacity to detect malingering have generally shown very low accuracy levels (see Faust, 1988). In the famous Rosenhan (1973) study, no individual faking psychosis was detected by the professional staff. Other research shows that inconsistency in performance that is often judged to be indicative of abnormality on the Wechsler Intelligence Scales is typical of *normal* individuals (Matarazzo, Daniel, Prifitera, & Herman, 1988). And studies examining clinicians' ability to predict violence often show accuracy levels no better than tossing coins, and sometimes worse. (For further coverage of research on these and other topics discussed in this chapter, see Faust & Ziskin, 1988 and Ziskin & Faust, 1988, 1991.)

These examples are meant to be illustrative, not probative, and to raise five essential points. First, sincere belief in a method may be misplaced and is weak evidence for the method's effectiveness. Palmists and fortune-tellers may sincerely believe in their powers, but I doubt many mental health experts would argue for their inclusion in courtroom proceedings, so long as they *really* believe in what they are saying.

Research shows that the confidence of decision makers, mental health experts included, often exceeds their level of accuracy, sometimes substantially.

In some studies, individuals who are highly confident are frequently wrong, and the *most* confident are among the *least* accurate. Problems adjusting confidence are not difficult to understand. Experts often do not discover whether their judgments were correct, thereby making appraisal of accuracy problematic. It is like trying to determine your proficiency in a ring toss game when someone shuts off the lights after every throw. Further, the feedback that is received tends to be distorted in such a way that it seems one is correct more often than is actually the case, thereby inflating confidence. The clinician who tells the worried person that her memory slips are normal will probably be believed, as he would have been had he said these problems were abnormal, when, of course, both judgments cannot be correct. Thus, patient agreement with interpretation typically exceeds interpretive accuracy.

Second, the initial examples provided here of misplaced faith in clinical judgment are not isolated. There is a long list of mistaken beliefs in the history of medicine and psychology, such as the notion that bleeding individuals with leeches was a medical panacea or that swinging mental patients from wicker baskets suspended from the ceiling or injecting them with malaria were treatments of choice. Further, there is an enormous body of current research that casts doubt on the basis of mental health testimony. In some areas, the literature is predominantly negative (e.g., efficacy of clinical judgment versus alternate [actuarial] judgment methods; capacity to identify malingerers using interview or subjective methods); in other areas supportive literature is lacking (e.g., capacity to perform psychological autopsies or to determine the more suitable parent in a custody dispute); and in other areas the literature is mixed (e.g., the reliability or consistency of psychiatric diagnoses). Where the literature is mixed and there is no clear superiority in the quality of evidence supporting either position, then typically the profession has been unable to resolve the issue. How can one expect a jury of laypeople to resolve an issue in the course of a trial that professionals have not been able to resolve themselves? None of this is to deny the existence of positive literature in some areas (see below).

Third, the court's decision to accept *or reject* mental health evidence does not establish the scientific merit of that evidence and should not be confused with what is scientifically established. When the court rejects evidence, or does not allow it in, experts may be quick to criticize the court's wisdom. When the court accepts evidence, these same critics may turn around and argue that this shows the evidence is useful (that is, the court's judgments serve as a standard when they are favorable, but not when they are unfavorable). Experts are fond of citing *Barefoot v. Estelle* to help justify their courtroom involvement. In this case, despite the formal *protest* of the American Psychiatric Association that testimony on violence is not trustworthy, the Supreme Court ruled to admit such evidence, based on the rationale that these judgments are not always wrong, this on a dichotomous (yes-no) decision task in which, in order to always be wrong, one would always have to know the correct answer in order to keep from providing it.

The ruling also set a very low standard for expert testimony (that it is not always wrong) and became a basis for executing Barefoot, a result that many citing *Barefoot* as a triumph probably would not support given the low accuracy of violence predictions. Amazingly, the court's acceptance of evidence in this case, despite psychiatry's opposition, is sometimes cited as support for the merit of expert testimony. (And it is not as if legal scholars have uniformly embraced the court's decision and reasoning in *Barefoot.*)

Fourth, because sincere belief in a method is not a sufficient basis for determining its merit, some substitute is needed, scientific testing being the obvious choice. A major function of science is to test belief. Preston (1981) quotes Aldous Huxley: "The tragedy of science is that frequently a beautiful hypothesis is slain by an ugly fact." Scientific testing, of course, will sometimes disconfirm, and sometimes support, a belief. I am not arguing for blind adherence to scientific outcomes or that scientific findings are never in error, only that, when it comes to developing trustworthy knowledge, the scientific method is clearly the best game in town (see Faust & Meehl, 1992).

Fifth, our basic position on mental health expert testimony follows from the first four points and can be simply stated. Where there is a sufficient body of supportive research (pertaining to the legal determination at issue), it seems reasonable to argue for the value of expert testimony. Where such evidence is lacking, then given the frequency with which subjective beliefs in methods have proven faulty and the large body of related negative evidence, the accuracy of methods should not be presumed but rather viewed as questionable and in need of verification through proper scientific testing. Short of sufficient supportive evidence, or until such evidence is forthcoming, the accuracy of experts could be determined through independent, formal examination with an adequate number of cases, perhaps as part of a credentialing process (in contrast to current credentialing procedures). Satisfactory results would provide support for the value of that expert's testimony.

One might have trouble specifying what a phrase such as "sufficient body of scientific research" means exactly, for at the boundaries, distinctions of this type are almost always fuzzy. However, agreement often should not be too difficult to achieve. For example, when there is virtually no supportive research or the research is predominantly negative (and the contrary studies are not far superior methodologically), it should be obvious the standard has not been satisfied. *Experts often testify on matters in which it is clear the standard of sufficient scientific evidence has not been met.*

Individuals who testify despite negative evidence or lack of adequate supportive research often believe that their powers of clinical judgment, or their clinical experience, compensate for scientific shortcomings. Research challenges such beliefs. A large body of evidence casts doubt on the effectiveness and accuracy of clinical judgment (see Chapter 5 of Ziskin & Faust, 1988). Additionally, numerous studies have examined mental health professionals' experience and judgmental accuracy. Anyone who has a detailed familiarity with this research should recognize that the great bulk of past and present studies run counter to the notion that more experienced clinicians reach more accurate diagnoses or predictions. As with confidence and accuracy, lack of feedback and distorted feedback are probably prime explanatory factors—if errors are not seen or recognized, accuracy is unlikely to improve.

Experts may claim that they are exceptions to the general research findings. The consistent outcomes across studies on experience and accuracy, despite the considerable diversity in diagnostic tasks, judgments, and clinicians, should make us cautious about such claims. Many of the clinicians who participated in the studies probably believed they were exceptions, only to have it shown otherwise. The clinician should be required to back claims for judgmental powers with sound evidence, as did Dr. Ralph Reitan (1964) by conducting a formal, scientific test of his ability to diagnose brain damage. Short of a proper scientific demonstration, exemption from the general research should not be presumed based on self-belief.

The expert who disregards the scientific evidence and continues to defer to his or her experience and subjective judgment might consider the words of the eminent clinical psychologist P. E. Meehl (1992), who said, ''One who considers 'my experience' a valid reply to research studies is self-deceived, and must never have read the history of medicine, not to mention the psychology of superstitions. It is absurd, as well as arrogant, to pretend that acquiring a Ph.D. somehow immunizes me from the errors of sampling, perception, recording, retention, retrieval, and inference to which the human mind is subject.'' One who overvalues their subjective judgment in this manner may not only fool themselves, but, unfortunately, their courtroom audience as well, who depends on the professional's flawed deliverances in deciding matters of vital human interest.

None of this is a general criticism of psychology, nor does it devalue mental health professionals' efforts to help troubled people or their other worthwhile activities. Further, where the scientific evidence is adequate, experts may help the trier of fact, although at present this is far more likely to involve testimony on scientific findings or principles (e.g., methods of statistical sampling or research design) as opposed to clinical evaluations of individuals. My argument is not with psychology's *potential* to develop knowledge that will form an adequate basis for expert testimony, for on that score I am highly optimistic. It is rather that much of current expert testimony is premature and misrepresented, mostly inadvertently, as sounder or better established than is scientifically justified.

As to the argument that despite such limits, expert testimony still helps the court resolve legal matters and thus nervousness about scientific merit or truth value is misplaced, one must ask what information that is falsely overvalued helps to settle. I have heard experts argue that the courts are not regulated by such ideals as truth and justice, even in principle, and rather serve to resolve conflict.

Resolution of conflict, by itself, is not necessarily desirable. The need to reach a conclusion may be satisfied by deciding to execute an innocent person, but such a decision, of course, is not to be sought after. Despite potential abuses and pragmatic difficulties, justice and truth remain regulative ideals. I dare any expert to face the judge and say, "What I am about to present distorts the truth and may foster an injustice, but I think, your honor, you will find it useful in resolving the case."

References

Faust, D. (1988). Psychologists' and psychiatrists' capacity to detect malingering. *Texas Health Law Reporter, 5,* 41–46.

Faust, D., & Meehl, P. E. (1992). Using scientific methods to resolve questions in the history and philosophy of science: Some illustrations. *Behavior Therapy, 23,* 195–211.

Faust, D., & Ziskin, J. (1988). The expert witness in psychology and psychiatry. *Science, 241,* 31–35.

Matarazzo, J. D., Daniel, M. H., Prifitera, A., & Herman, D. O. (1988). Intersubtest scatter in the WAIS-R standardization sample. *Journal of Clinical Psychology, 44,* 940–950.

Meehl, P. E. (1992, June). *Philosophy of science: Help or hindrance?* Paper presented at the Fourth Annual Convention of the American Psychological Society, San Diego.

Preston, T. P. (1981). *The clay pedestal.* Seattle: Madrona.

Reitan, R. M. (1964). Psychological deficits resulting from cerebral lesions in man. In J. M. Warren & K. Akert (Eds.), *The frontal granular cortex and behavior* (pp. 295–312). New York: McGraw-Hill.

Rosenhan, D. L. (1973). On being sane in insane places. *Science, 179,* 250–258.

Ziskin, J., & Faust, D. (1988). *Coping with psychiatric and psychological testimony* (Vols. 1–3, 4th ed.). Los Angeles: Law and Psychology Press.

Ziskin, J., & Faust, D. (1991). *1990 Supplement to coping with psychiatric and psychological testimony* (Vols. 1 and 2). Los Angeles: Law and Psychology Press.

Rejoinder to Dr. Faust

Stanley L. Brodsky

"I dare any expert to face the judge and say, 'What I am about to present distorts the truth and may foster an injustice, but I think, your honor, you will find it useful in resolving the case.' " What Faust failed to include in this surrealistic scenario is the additional comment, "I respectfully offer this opinion from the perspective of an ignorant and dense-headed troglodyte." Such flights into self-flagellating fantasy aside, experts can and often do choose a response that is second cousin to the Faust proposal; that is, to say "I don't know" more often in the courtroom. As I pointed out in my book *Testifying in Court* (Brodsky, 1991), ''I don't know'' is one of the most appropriate, important, and honest replies an expert can make when questioned about an area of limited information.

Faust essentially argues that in most areas of testimony mental health expert witnesses (1) are not knowledgeable, (2) do not know they are not knowledgeable, and (3) therefore cannot and do not maintain a fundamental integrity in their courtroom testimony. Each of these assumptions may be examined separately.

First, are mental health experts knowledgeable? When Faust presents the David Rosenhan study (1973) ''On being sane in insane places'' as proof that psychologists and psychiatrists cannot make accurate diagnoses, he is attempting a long stretch. The ten-minute interviews by minimally trained psychiatric residents with Rosenhan's rehearsed confederates have little to do with the detailed and careful assessments of clients in most court matters. Testimony about competency to stand trial and about psychological impairments from industrial accidents are examples of sound knowledge.

Second, are mental health professionals aware when they are not knowledgeable? The best answer is that some professionals are aware and some are not. However, compelling ethical mandates (e.g., American Psychological Association, 1992) require that professionals do know the current scientific and professional information in their fields. Much as in medicine, as in the law, and as in the most rigorous areas of physical science, a wide range of awareness of current knowledge exists among mental health professionals. Faust damns these professionals as engaged in a ''see no evil'' nearsightedness. I see a normal distribution of awareness and applaud the commitment of so many professionals to be conscientious consumers of current knowledge.

Finally, is there integrity? Faust argues that essentially there is not, because expert conclusions are overvalued or misrepresented. Indeed, this is sometimes the case. However, integrity comes from the accumulation of knowledge, the awareness of the limitations on that knowledge, and the willingness to be modest on the witness stand when modesty about knowledge is called for. By those standards, I see much integrity now, and more emerging with the distribution of scientific knowledge and the mastery of mental health professional roles in the courtroom. Rather than being trogolytes hiding in the caves of professional provincialism, psychologists and psychiatrists are instead practicing and testifying in the intentionally open air of professional challenge and knowledge.

References

American Psychological Association (1992). Ethical principles of psychologists and code of conduct. *American Psychologist.*

Brodsky, S. L. (1991). *Testifying in court: Guidelines & maxims for the expert witness.* Washington, DC: American Psychological Association.

Rosenhan, D. L. (1973). On being sane in insane places. *Science, 179,* 250–258.

DEBATE 14

Do Mental Health Professionals Basically Offer Clients the Same Service?

YES says Shirley Cooper, M.S., L.C.S.W., formerly Child Clinical Services Director for Mount Zion Hospital, Department of Psychiatry, who is a Clinical Professor in the Department of Psychiatry, University of California, San Francisco. She is a past President of the American Orthopsychiatric Association. Her numerous publications include *Children in Treatment: A Primer for Beginning Psychotherapists, A Casebook of Child Psychotherapy,* and a monograph, *The Treatment of Children and Parents: A Validation of Social Work Thesis.*

NO argues Carol H. Meyer, D.S.W., who is a Professor at the Columbia University School of Social Work, where she teaches social work practice and family and children's services. Her writing has been about practice theory and issues, and her experience is primarily in family and child welfare agencies and in public welfare. Her current book is entitled *Assessment in Social Work* (Columbia University Press, in press).

YES

SHIRLEY COOPER

I argue that mental health professionals basically provide clients with similar services, when they offer the common core element in such services—psychotherapy or counseling. All clinical efforts, no matter how the presenting complaint is phrased, are committed to help clients achieve, as fully as they can, a greater sense of autonomy and affiliation, greater competence, mastery, and coherence; a widened sense of self-esteem; and a more integrated sense of identity and purpose. Moreover, clinical work proceeds under the aegis of a purposeful, professional relationship in which maximum partnership and self-determination are valued and created.

The concepts of partnership and self-determination are ideals, modified in reality by many factors, among which are the character style, reality circumstances, skill of the practitioner, and the degree of "fit" between therapist and client. It is in this sense that every psychotherapy relationship remains distinctive and tailor-made. Hilde Bruch comments that despite the mastery of complex bio-psycho-social concepts, in the final analysis each therapist "meets each client as a stranger whose anguish and problems remain unprecedented and unique" (Bruch, 1974).

To argue the case for similarities among mental health professionals, I stress the educational needs and aims for those who practice psychotherapy. My assumption rests on the perspective that although basic and early teaching and learning experiences set the outlines, conceptions, philosophy, and style for most psychotherapists, some do and will change their orientation and practice. My experience suggests that most psychotherapists retain the basic stance learned as they were inducted into their profession. This does not imply that further learning and experience are unimportant in altering practice.

Of course, different mental health disciplines have particular skills. Psychiatrists can provide psychotropic medications and a more educated biological perspective; psychologists are particularly skillful in diagnosis through their use of standardized tests (although this emphasis seems to be receding in many training programs); and social workers are particularly trained to address interactional processes in psychotherapy and in the interaction between the person and the environment. There are, of course, other mental health personnel, such as nurses, who are each fashioned by differences in training emphasis. When each offers psychological assistance, however, the differences tend to blur and recede or arise from differences in practice experience, theoretical persuasion, native endowment, levels of artfulness, or institutional constraints (Bergen & Strupp, 1972).

I make these assertions based on thirty years of experience in a department of psychiatry that provided postgraduate training to many cohorts of the "big three" psychotherapy disciplines in a truly interdisciplinary setting. Seminars, supervision, and other learning experiences were commonly provided for all trainees.[1]

Let me concede, at once, that true interdisciplinary training and practice were, even in the best of times, not so readily developed or found. Today, however, interdisciplinary training is very much an endangered species. Interdisciplinary training flourishes in a climate of optimism, confidence, and enlightened self-interest, with a recognition of the common attributes in clinical practice and a respect for the differing emphasis, heritage, and values each of the disciplines brings to its work. Such a climate rests heavily on a sense that there are sufficient resources that a society feels obliged to render to all of its citizens. It rests on the proposition that those who teach can convey, implicitly as well as explicitly, that competence, diversity, and shared power are more valued than labels, turf, hierarchy, or compliance. It rests further on the recognition that practice competence cannot be learned exclusively in a classroom and must be matched by sufficient experiential experience in the field.

This is hardly such a time! In these days of extremely limited resources for human services, "biological and psychosocial theorists are receding even from each other's peripheral vision" (Cain, 1989).

Multidisciplinary is often mistaken for interdisciplinary preparation for psychotherapeutic practice. In the former, various mental health professionals are taught in the same facility, but each is typically taught and supervised by members of one's own profession. At times, seminars and consultations are offered by psychiatrists to their "lesser" colleagues, social workers. This maintains a hierarchical system of training, a model that is antithetical to the teaching and practice of psychotherapy, which values partnership over "expertness" and compliance over creativity. Parenthetically, psychologists have always tended to find their own way, resisting being fit into a tilted training arrangement. Lacking equality and contiguity, a richly textured training experience, paradoxically fed by more openly conflicted struggles and strains, is a loss to all three disciplines.

Several important (albeit not all-inclusive) constructs underpin the work of all psychotherapists. These include the following:

1. No one discipline or group has a monopoly on any sector of human knowledge. There is simply no way to fence off knowledge for the exclusive use of one profession. All psychotherapists must have knowledge about human development along the life span, including familiarity with the exciting and emerging field of infant development, an appreciation for constitutional and temperamental givens, a complex understanding of the psychosocial problems and environments that both undermine and facilitate growth, a base for competent assessment and diagnosis at the outset of the treatment—later to be modified as the work unfolds—the complex ways in which people evolve relationships and duplicate earlier ones in the present, coping and defensive styles, practice theory and skill, an awareness of one's own limits and how one's own personality is engaged in the psychotherapeutic effort, ethics and values, and some understanding of special populations and their needs. Put another way, all therapists need to understand developmental, cognitive, and interpersonal processes and how personality functions and evolves in various contexts throughout the life space, influenced by political and socioeconomic trends (Cooper, 1977).

2. The perspective—increasingly recognized by most—that the person/situation matrix is the domain and concern of all who treat clients. Inner and outer reality are inextricably woven and can be made discrete only in concept, rather than in reality. Put another way, this premise rests on the view that the bio-psycho-social perspective is the lens through which most clinicians look and make sense of their observations, both diagnostic and therapeutic—no matter what their discipline. The American Psychiatric Association, through its publication of *DSM-III,* has officially and implicitly endorsed and explicated this perspective, although it has not embraced interdisciplinary training. Clearly, however, the clinician who subscribes to the biological perspective exclusively will see little commonality with others in training or in service.

3. As indicated, the view that no matter what the client's presenting complaint, most clinicians commonly aim at helping clients achieve, as fully as they can, a greater sense of autonomy and affiliation, enlarged competence and mastery, better self-esteem, and a more cohesive sense of identity and reality. Naturally, the particular aims and goals presented by the client form the more precise concerns for both partners.

4. The recognition that all clinical work proceeds under the aegis of a professionally purposeful relationship, in which, as indicated, maximum partnership and self-determination are essential.

5. The view that diversity in training pathways and values and receptivity to differing discipline emphasis can and do add richness and complexity, in spite of taxing the development of a cohesive professional identity. Put differently, discipline insularity tends to create a more narrow view of the world, people, and their circumstances and prepares less well for differential treatment.

6. Learning for all clinicians is marked by gradual, episodic, fragmentary and chaotic leaps, regressions, and plateaus. Concepts are slowly integrated, worked, and reworked repeatedly before a solid, usable, and stable grasp is achieved. Clinical learning proceeds along a trajectory, typically beginning with an initial stage of acute self-consciousness and moving (if all goes well) toward that stage when the clinician has enough knowledge and skill to teach others (Reynolds, 1942).

7. All mental health clinicians must divest themselves of sharply ingrained cultural premises to take on a professional culture, values, and styles. For example, clinicians must learn to be curious (nosey) instead of minding their own business. We must ask highly personal questions, frowned on in polite society. There must be a purpose to our inquiries, other than idle curiosity. Chit-chat is rarely useful in a clinical interchange, and clinicians must learn to tolerate and understand the multiple meanings of silence and to detect the highly complex and hidden meanings in a client's presentation, while becoming able to tolerate and ''stay with'' intense feelings. Charlotte Towle (1954) observed: ''A profession's traditions, its rationale, ethical system, body of knowledge, vocabulary, and its special function tend to make it a culture within a culture. . . . Professional education, as a re-educational process, has to fulfill a task which is essentially equivalent to a change in culture.'' (p. 10)

8. And, finally, each of the disciplines must yield some of its often recently acquired and prized learning. Folk wisdom has it and my experience confirms that the psychiatrist must yield the white coat and stethoscope, symbols of authority as well as expertise; the psychologist must come out from behind the books and test paraphernalia while providing psychotherapy; and social workers are advised to yield their ''candy,'' often masking grandiose rescue drives, if each is to engage in a true partnership with clients—in most instances, a more productive effort than the hierarchical one.

Interdisciplinary learning helps this process immeasurably. Nonetheless, I remain aware that such thinking cannot easily flourish in these harsh and uncivil times.

The practice of psychotherapy itself is today at risk. It is certainly changing rapidly as managed care and self-help groups become more central to the provision and delivery of mental health services. Some changes may be productive; others may reveal the American impatience with slow processes and partial solutions, a proper fear about rising health costs, and a turning away from disadvantaged groups in our society who require help of all sorts, of which psychotherapy may be a part.

Endnote

1. It may be important to note that I served in various capacities, under various titles, but almost from the outset, I engaged in direct practice, the development of a Postgraduate Training Program for Advanced Social Workers supported for over two decades by NIMH, along with other program developments, and taught interdisciplinary seminars, while I supervised perhaps hundreds of trainees of all disciplines. Later, when the department initiated and participated in designing and implementing a Doctorate in Mental Health (drawing on the strengths of each of the more traditional disciplines), I taught in the classroom at the University of California, Berkeley, during the first two years of that curriculum. For a description of the rise and demise of this pioneer program, see Wallerstein, R. (Ed.) (1991). *The Doctorate in mental health: An experiment in mental health education.* New York: University Press of America.

References

Bergen, A. E., & Strupp, H. H. (1972). *Changing frontiers in the science of psychotherapy.* New York: Aldine, Atherton.

Bruch, H. (1974). *Teaching psychotherapy.* Cambridge, MA: Harvard University Press.

Cain, A. C. (1989). In parting. *American Journal of Orthopsychiatry, 59,* 4–5.
Cooper, S. (1977). Social work: A dissenting profession. *Social Work, 22*(5), pp. 360–367.
Reynolds, B. (1942). *Learning and teaching in the practice of social work.* New York: Farrah and Rinehart.
Towle, C. (1954). *The learner in education for the professions.* Chicago: Chicago University Press.

Rejoinder to Professor Cooper

CAROL H. MEYER

This book must have been created for Shirley Cooper and me, for we represent in our debate, the prevailing arguments on the nature of mental health services. As stated in my NO argument, when mental health services are defined as psychotherapy, it is likely that clinical skills will appear similar. That is the fundamental distinction between the two views—that mental health services are (or are not) definable as psychotherapy, where the parameters are expressed in the professional, psychotherapeutic relationship between patient and clinician.

What then of intake decisions and discharge planning? Under what rubric would fall arrangements with families for their visiting and engagement with the patient or negotiations with activities therapists and other mental health specialists? What of the clinician's role in helping the patient to adapt to the institutional rules and to take his or her medication? Where would one locate the necessary connections with the patient's former or potential job, housing, financial, and social supports? And would the narrow (psychotherapeutic) definition of mental health services allow for the clinician to advocate for needed services? If we view all of these services as purely "relational" in psychotherapeutic sense, then the term is so generic that it loses definitional power.

Professor Cooper's commitment to the unified approach of separate professional disciplines cannot be discounted in view of her long and widely recognized experience in both the practice and teaching of clinical methods. Her well-reasoned arguments only underline two questions remaining: Are mental health services to be equated with *clinical* practice (across disciplines), or are they to be viewed as a *field* of practice, with identifiable legal sanctions, funding sources, organizational structures, and services? Further, as Professor Cooper laments the failure of interdisciplinary training (the Fifth Profession?) to achieve credibility, does this not leave us with the question of why there are distinctive professions, each with a mission, albeit often with blurred boundaries? Given the long history and traditions inherent in all disciplines, and the elaborate training and credentialing enterprise in which each profession is involved, can we really reduce their distinctiveness to mere turfdom?

As all professions open their minds to new information, of course they will rely on the same knowledge base as regards child development, for example. Yet, each discipline has a unique perception of its own interventive repertoire, and should enter cases in distinctive, professionally defined ways. This may be fortuitous for the patient, because it ensures that there will be a second or third opinion. There is value in diversity, and difference more than likeness can create light and push us all to give evidence to our arguments.

NO

Carol H. Meyer

Mental health professionals once were called psychiatrists, psychologists, and social workers.[1] Even despite their separate domains and training, there has been a blurring in the perception of differences among them. Typically, in a mental hospital or a mental health clinic, cases often are assigned arbitrarily, not according to which discipline is most appropriate to treat the defined problem; in interdisciplinary teams, contributions to the clinical conference often are made in accordance with the experiences of the clinician with the patient, rather than out of distinctive expertise. Furthermore, clinicians in each discipline are expected to be equally competent in their use of the *DSM-III-R.* In settings where white coats are worn, these uniforms are the great levelers, particularly today when gender differences are not as apparent as between physicians and non-physicians. Only a few recognizable differences may be left in the way services are provided, except in the administering of medication, which of course remains the responsibility of the (physician) psychiatrist.

Because of widespread interest (particularly by psychologists and clinical social workers) in further integrating the separate disciplines into a unitary "mental health professional" role, mental health skills have been promoted as being the same—no matter the type of problem evidenced by the patient, nor the discipline of the service provider. It is believed by many that the provision of services, even where they might be substantively different, can be brought into a singular mental health focus through the convergence of skills, perhaps because of the presumption that mental health services and psychotherapy are the same. Equating psychotherapists with mental health providers also eliminates the hierarchical issues generated by the power and influence of psychiatry.

The dictionary defines *skill* as: "Knowledge of the means or method of accomplishing a task." This definition would be helpful if all were to agree on what is meant by "means," "method," and "task." And there is the rub; in the hands of each discipline in the mental health field, these components of skill must be different or there would be no need for these different professions to exist. Skills, when separated from means, method, and task, are meaningless, and when separated from professional purpose they are even more empty of meaning.

Further, it is not useful to talk about generic skills when domain and social sanction are not taken into account. Finally, in view of the fact that skills are expressions of knowledge, they have to be evaluated in light of the particular profession's knowledge base.

In one sense, on the lowest level of abstraction, all mental health professionals, and in fact all people, use certain skills in similar ways, dependent more on personal style than on professional frameworks. For example, interviewing skills are fairly generic across all disciplines as well as human encounters. The interviewing skills needed to ask a client how he feels, to offer a supportive interviewing environment, to clarify inconsistencies in the client's story, to confront the client with reality, and to respond empathically probably would not distinguish one clinician from another, nor clinicians from supportive friends. These are examples of decontextualized skills (Rein & White, 1981) where means, method, and task are missing from the formulation. The skills in interviewing mean something when we know who the interview is with and what the interview is about. Once we add such questions to the picture, we can begin to distinguish among clinicians as far as the "who" and the "what" are concerned, because each mental health professional is trained to define the client and the interview content in a particular way.

Professional Purpose

Each mental health discipline has its own defined purposes, although in light of the blurring of interdisciplinary boundaries in the modern mental health field, the definitions seem to be almost quaint. Psychiatry is a branch of medicine where the purpose is to diagnose and treat mental, emotional, and behavioral disorders. This purpose brings a necessary medical emphasis to the definition of patient problems. Psychology has been traditionally defined as being concerned with empirical study and testing of mental processes. Social work's purpose is uniquely psychosocial. This means that the client is counselled in the context of his or her physical, social, political, organizational, and intimate environments.

A common example of the differences in the provision of services can be seen in the assessment process. The psychiatrist's focus is singularly on the patient; the psychologist's focus is on the empirical data derived from testing the patient's mental functioning; and the social worker's focus is on the patient and his or her environment. The consequent tasks are different, so the skills that are needed are different. Viewed on this level of abstraction, the tasks do not appear to be transferable across disciplines.

Domain and Social Sanction

When one gets closer to specific professionally defined services and tasks such as those related to patient discharge, it becomes more apparent that significant differences exist among the disciplines. Prescribing the appropriate psychotropic medication is confined to psychiatrists because they are physicians, and in our culture, only physicians can prescribe medication. In other cultures the prescription skill is allocated to shamans and witch doctors who use magic to cure illness. Psychologists might treat the affective/cognitive/behavioral manifestations of the patient's functioning, but nonmedically and not necessarily with a psychosocial focus. Social workers, in their clinical roles, might seek to do what psychologists do, but their professional and socially sanctioned domain is psychosocial.

Given the fact that only psychiatrists can claim a clear (medical) domain, they alone among mental health professionals can carry their mission into every setting, provide medical services to every patient, and remain unchallenged as psychiatrists. Psychologists and social workers who seek to blur the boundaries of their domains must define themselves again and again to demonstrate or to explain their roles and functions. Yet, this blurring may be a source of discomfort for those who do not seek their self-definition as therapist. Theoretically, the core purposes of psychiatry, clinical psychology, and clinical social work should never change. That is, neither the setting nor the patient problem should modify the core purpose or domain of these disciplines. Their sanction and training should determine the services they provide. Thus, a clinical psychologist or clinical social worker practicing in a labor union would not become shop stewards; in a court they would not become lawyers; in a mental health clinic they would not become psychiatrists. The question then is, is mental health a field of practice in which several disciplines carry out their distinctive tasks to provide mental health services, or is it a generic process that transcends consideration of legal and social sanction, domain, purpose, and training?

Unresolved Issues

Given that there is no debate about the distinctions among the mental health professions, it is curious that so many clinicians persist in assuming similarity in their practice and in the services they provide. Perhaps it is because all clinicians work with the same people and might agree at times as to their perception of problems or, occasionally, the cause of these problems. Yet, if it is all the same, why does it make a difference which clinician a person seeks out for help? Is the difference based on cost? Is the status differential among disciplines at the bottom of it all?

A spirited exchange between Wakefield and Specht (1992) may shed light on this oddity. Their debate about the place of psychotherapy in social work suggests that the drift toward homogenization of clinical skills in mental health may have to do with the prevailing interest in the practice of psychotherapy. This may be, after all, the source of confusion. Were there a Fifth Profession of Psychotherapy, it would have its own sanction, domain, purpose, training, knowledge base, and so forth, and commonly held skills then would be appropriate. The catch is that despite years of effort, the Fifth Profession has not won acceptance either within or outside of the mental health professions, so we are left with the distinctions. Psychiatrists, psychologists, and social workers treat the same patients, but they experience different professional training and practice within different frameworks of sanction and purpose. They do not provide the same services to their clients, because the professional distinctions determine the shape of their practices.

Endnote

1. There are, of course, others with primary responsibility in fields like nursing and education . . . clinical nurses and guidance counsellors . . . who also carry mental health roles. In addition, there are those clinicians who are activities therapists and many specialists in freestanding settings who address mental health problems.

References

Rein, M., & White, S. (1981). Knowledge for practice. *Social Service Review, 55*(1), 1–41.

Wakefield, J., & Specht, H. (1992). Debate with author. *Social Service Review, 66*(1), 141–159.

Rejoinder to Professor Meyer

Shirley Cooper

Carol Meyer, a respected colleague and my opponent here, recognizes that "there may be only a few recognizable differences left in the way services are provided." She notes further that with "the blurring of interdisciplinary boundaries in the modern mental health field, the definitions seem to be almost quaint." Agreed! The differences Meyer describes are indeed traditional, with far less relevance in actual practice today than once obtained. We are, of course, not discussing *all* of social work; our focus here is on the provision of mental health services.

Meyer further asserts that "*Theoretically* [my emphasis] the core purposes [of the different mental health professions] should never change," irrespective of setting or patient problem. In reality, these factors play a vital role in determining how mental health professionals do and *should* intervene. Patient problems do not alter, no matter to whom patients address and describe their suffering. And anyone who has had a brief encounter with managed care is hardly oblivious to the huge impact of setting (used in the widest sense) on providing or limiting services.

It is because all mental health providers require a common core of knowledge that clinical social workers plead for better clinical training, in largely deaf social work schools, and find it necessary to create their own professional organization and clinical training beyond the master's level.

Meyer further remarks that "there is no debate about the distinctions among the mental health professions." That is pure fiction. The debate rages, and more so today when scarce resources and recession worry all mental health professionals as they compete for definition and power in legislative halls, licensing laws, professional organizations, and elsewhere. Cost, status, and incomes are significant elements and factors in these turf struggles.

Meyer once again makes an astute observation when she remarks that "the drift toward homogenization of clinical skills" should reasonably evolve in creating a Fifth Profession. Life, however, is not essentially fueled by logic. My comments rest on ten years of personal experience with other mental health colleagues in designing a program, a five-year course of rigorous study, and teaching in what led to a Doctorate in Mental Health.[1] It was conceived at a time when mental health services were expanding and offering greater access in another time. It ceased to exist—no, it was destroyed—by retrenchment and recessions that vastly heightened the fears and competition for status, prestige, power, and earnings among traditional mental health disciplines.

And, finally, I remember vividly my student days when I heard Gordon Hamilton's repeated comment that what most distinguishes social work from other helping professions is our values. Social work, at its best, has and will seek to ameliorate suffering, identify vulnerabilities, restore function, and call for social justice. Sometimes compassionately, all too often too grudgingly and ambivalently, society sanctions these in the social work profession. The *clinical practice* provided by mental health social workers is part of society's sanctioned services.

Endnote

1. For a detailed description, see Wallerstein, R. (Ed.). (1991). *The Doctorate in mental health: An experiment in mental health education.* New York: University Press of America.

DEBATE 15

Has Deinstitutionalization Failed?

Arguing an emphatic YES is Ann Braden Johnson, who is a clinical social worker with nearly twenty years of experience working with the chronically mentally ill in a variety of settings from state hospitals to community-based clinics. She currently directs a mental health program in a large urban jail and writes about the mental health system in her spare time. The author of *Out of Bedlam: The Truth about Deinstitutionalization,* Dr. Johnson is now working on a book about the failure of scientific psychiatry to address the needs of human beings.

Arguing NO is Richard C. Surles, Ph.D., who has been New York's Commissioner of Mental Health since 1987. In that capacity, he is responsible for administering a state-operated system of thirty-one hospitals, two research centers, and a network of outpatient services. He has served as the Administrator of Mental Health/Mental Retardation for the City and County of Philadelphia (1982–1987), the Commissioner of Vermont's Department of Mental Health (1971–1982), and held a variety of roles within the North Carolina Division of Mental Health (1974–1977) and at the University of North Carolina (1970–1977). His publications range from studies of use of emergency services to policy analysis in areas of finance and organizing and evaluating mental health services.

YES

ANN BRADEN JOHNSON

Deinstitutionalization is a remarkably complicated concept. It has its roots in political ideology, economic reality, shifting social values, and clinical practice; and what's more, it has been applied to all kinds of institutions, including those housing juvenile offenders and the developmentally disabled as well as the mentally ill. Most simply, the idea behind deinstitutionalization is that optimal treatment of longstanding and chronic behavioral conditions will take place not in an institutional setting but in situations and under conditions most closely approximating the social and cultural norms that apply everywhere else. The term *deinstitutionalization* has come to connote both that underlying idea and, in a kind of clumsy corollary, its practical realization. This dual meaning can be confusing but is itself a clue to the very messy nature of the social problems deinstitutionalization seeks to address.

I believe that deinstitutionalization, particularly the deinstitutionalization of the mentally ill, never actually happened. While it is certainly true that at some point it became popular among social theorists and the more adventurous clinicians to believe that even the chronically mentally ill could benefit from community-based treatment rather than traditional custodial care, the chronically mentally ill were never removed from custodial care in any real way. For the most part, the chronically mentally ill who had been in state mental hospitals during the years of aggressive discharge—the state hospital census hit about 550,000 in 1955 and has been dropping ever since—were simply shifted to other custodial settings not run by the government. This paradoxical result, which might more appropriately be called *re*institutionalization, came about in large part because the drive to discharge was rooted in fiscal anxiety, not in concern for patients or their care. In 1949, representatives of the forty-eight state governments got together, agreed that for them to continue to foot the bill for lifetime care of the chronically mentally ill was to risk bankruptcy, and decided to work together to seek alternatives to hospitalization.

At first, enthusiasm for emptying state mental hospitals ran high, and early reports brimmed over with success stories. Public and professional assumptions about mental illness had indeed changed, the public was generally receptive to new ideas about mental illness, and the first patients to be discharged mostly did just fine. Unfortunately, those first patients were the ones who had families to whom they could return or were those who had been hospitalized most recently—in short, those who were the easiest to place and had the most promising futures. Still worse, this same group of misleadingly successful discharges became the pool of subjects for research studies published in the early 1960s and used ever after to justify further depopulation of the state mental hospitals.

The patients discharged afterward were not so easy to place—their families didn't want them or had died off long before—and so another custodial setting, the nursing home, was hastily adapted to fit the population. When the nursing homes were filled, the adult home, or board-and-care facility, was created to take up the slack. Census data tells the story:

Per 100,000 population:

	1950	*1960*	*1970*	*1980*
Mental hospital	407.2	351.3	213.4	108.2
Home for aged	196.9	261.9	456.2	629.6

Admittedly, the country had seen an overall increase in its elderly during these years, but that alone cannot account for the huge expansion of the nursing home population. In fact, a significant portion of today's nursing home residents are people who used to live out their days in mental hospitals, most notably the senile elderly and patients with Alzheimer's disease, while younger, more manageable mental patients are housed in privately owned and operated adult homes.

The whole idea that the mentally ill might better acquire the skills needed to lead a normal life by living among normal people rather than among other mental patients depended for its realization on the development of a wide range of community-based treatment programs. In fact, our enormous mental health system never actually produced these programs, certainly not on the scale required. What the system did manage to come up with were sedating drugs that promised far more than they could deliver, suppressed the more obvious symptoms while leaving the underlying disorder alone, and produced grotesque side effects that have turned out to be irreversible in at least 40 percent of long-term users.

Public policy is more a matter of goals and objectives than it is of implementation and practice, and so it was almost inevitable that the designers of the community mental health center would dream up a therapeutic ideal with no regard for its likely future in the marketplace. Because no one anticipated how unpopular the chronic caseload would be with mental health professionals—community-based clinics neither wanted nor knew how to deal with severely mentally ill patients, the early community mental health centers were too committed to competing with private practitioners to take on such an undesirable group, and private practitioners had less than no desire to fill their waiting rooms with chronic mental patients—the former hospital patients went untreated in the community.

In many states, community mental health center planners intended to shift state hospital workers to the new community clinics, thus ensuring that the workers kept their jobs while making good on their promise to reallocate resources to the community along with the patients. It turned out, however, that no one on the policy-making level had reckoned with the enormous difficulty of eliminating entrenched institutions. Most hospital employees were represented by strong unions that vehemently opposed hospital closings. In many cases, the state hospitals provided just about the only source of employment in the small rural towns where they had been built under an older treatment paradigm. New clinics tended to be placed in larger towns and cities, often far away, and few hospital employees were interested in relocating. Last but not least, the new community clinics gained a reputation as exciting, cutting-edge places to work in, so they attracted flocks of ambitious, with-it mental-health workers in no mood to share the limelight with the old state-hospital chronics—patients or staff.

All of these factors hobbled the community mental health movement, but what really did it in was that its true purpose was to save the states money. Once the bureaucrats in charge of state budgets found how little it cost to maintain a chronic patient on monthly visits to an outpatient clinic to renew his prescription for psychotropic medications, especially by contrast with what it cost to maintain him in an inpatient bed or even a day hospital, they were hooked. It did not take long for the states to figure out that in many instances Medicaid would pay for the outpatient care, that Medicare was available to pay for nursing home care for the senile elderly, and that SSI could be used to pay for ex-patients' room and board. Best of all, these funding mechanisms were federally sponsored, involving at the most a small contribution from the state.

The net result of this quite dramatic shift of fiscal responsibility from the states to the federal government was that the states were able to shed a political liability that had been theirs exclusively for over a century: chronic patients were able to leave the hospitals in droves, moving into single-room-occupancy hotels or rooming houses or adult homes at federal expense, free to live on their own. After years of institutional care they were totally unprepared to survive on their own, but that was certainly not SSI's problem—it never pretended to be more than a substitute for welfare. The states had made drugs and outpatient care available, so it wasn't *their* fault if the discharged patients were "too resistant" to follow up. Having finally gotten out from under the crushing burden of having to provide lifetime custodial care to a huge, ever-growing caseload, the states were not about to pick up the tab for their failure to make it in the community.

The trouble was, neither was anyone else. SSI specifically refuses to pay for the kind of therapeutic residence chronic mental patients actually need, because SSI is a living allotment, not a medical benefit. Medicaid will pay for the least restrictive care available, which means outpatient visits, even though the best evidence suggests that day hospital treatment is usually more effective for the chronic population. What housing there is exists to turn a profit for its owners and only incidentally to care for its residents. Treatment increasingly means medication only, for maximum ease of patient management.

And so we have come full circle, having invented a new form of custodial care that is famously free of locked doors and barred windows but otherwise recreates the very back wards it was supposed to replace. Liberated like the rest of us, the chronic mental patient can now choose his own lifestyle: he can spend the rest of his days in narcotized inactivity in a board-and-care facility indifferently run for maximum profit, with staffing to match; he can shuffle aimlessly around a homeless shelter that may or may not boast what is called a ''mental health component'' dedicated to dispensing his medication with maximum efficiency; or he can strike out on his own and go crazy in the streets.

In other words, we are back where we started, except that the chronic mentally ill are harder to locate now than they were when the state hospitals had them. For all the talk about community-based care, fully 70 percent of all mental health funds go to pay for inpatient care, while only about one-seventh of the millions of Americans thought to be in need of some kind of psychological assistance actually get it, according to the 1978 President's Commission on Mental Health. The architects of deinstitutionalization failed to think through the fiscal implications of many of their proposed reforms, and they were naive about the political opposition they were likely to encounter. Meanwhile, no one stopped to consider what the chronically mentally ill would look like outside a hospital, even as they were being dumped wholesale into marginal settings in marginal neighborhoods. The unfortunate result is that our society's initial willingness to rethink its attitude toward the mentally ill was squandered, wasted by opportunistic policies conceived in the name of fiscal prudence. In the end, deinstitutionalization was a slogan masquerading as a reform, the status quo disguised as change, a goal without a program. The sad thing is that it might work, if only we had the courage to try it.

Annotated Bibliography

Estroff, S. E. (1981). *Making it crazy: An ethnography of psychiatric clients in an American community.* Berkeley and Los Angeles: University of California Press.

An anthropologist lived among a group of ex-patients in Wisconsin for a couple of years.

Johnson, A. B. (1990). *Out of Bedlam: The truth about deinstitutionalization.* New York: Basic Books.

This is the most comprehensive study of the policy of deinstitutionalization both in theory and in practice. It is also written to be entertaining—at least insofar as the topic permits.

Sheehan, S. (1982). *Is there no place on Earth for me?* Boston: Houghton Mifflin.

This book tells the story of a real chronic mental patient, "Sylvia Frumkin," and documents her problems and setbacks as she moves around within the post-deinstitutionalization mental health system. It is not a happy story, but the author tells it exceptionally well.

Except for Sheehan's book, which is journalism, these are scholarly studies of mental health care in the United States at the end of the twentieth century. However, if one is to understand deinstitutionalization completely, it is essential to consider what it replaced by reading an honest account of life in a custodial state hospital. There are several examples, among them:

Farmer, F. (1982). *Will there really be a morning?* New York: Dell.

A movie star's autobiography, useful for its harrowing descriptions of life in a state hospital during the Depression.

Kesey, K. (1962). *One flew over the cuckoo's nest.* New York: Signet.

An amazingly good novel.

Ward, M. J. (1946). *The snake pit.* New York: Random House.

A novel, written by a nurse.

All three have been turned into effective and surprisingly truthful movies.

Rejoinder to Dr. Johnson

RICHARD C. SURLES

Deinstitutionalization, as Dr. Johnson affirms, was indeed applied to "all kinds of institutions"—even, until Willie Horton, persons in state prisons. She also implies that some master conspiracy existed to promote deinstitutionalization which involved the states and leaders of the national mental health movement. There is some evidence that she may be correct that at a federal level, a conscious decision was made to ignore the comprehensive needs of persons in state psychiatric hospitals in the 1960s in favor of political support for a new federal program of community mental health centers.

The best evidence of this policy decision can be found in Gerald Grob's (1991) book, *From Asylum to Community.* He notes that federal planners were aware that persons residing in state hospitals during the 1960s were largely older, unmarried, and without financial supports. Dr. Johnson is also, I believe, correct in asserting that the federal support for community mental health centers was largely based on untested assumptions and, in retrospect, failed to recognize the complexity of the needs of persons with a severe mental illness in community settings. But she also seems to assume that we have had a national public policy in mental health and that mental health professionals and leaders actually designed the current system. The references to the states also seem to imply that a state is a single entity—speaking in a single voice.

My view is that we in the community of mental health are having the wrong debate and that our distraction with the legacy of mental health promotes argument only among those who have some understanding of our culture. We, however, tend to lose sight of the fact that major policy changes in the past three decades have generally ignored the mental health debate but profoundly affected it.

If one examines the history of large declines in the census of the old state hospitals, a case can be made that mental health planners and leaders had little influence on the policies that affected those declines. Probably the most significant changes came through welfare reform and federal programs of the ''Great Society'' of the Johnson Administration of the 1960s. For example, the creation of a social security program for disabled people provided income for a class of indigent people, in which persons diagnosed with a mental illness were included. The federal Medicaid program mandated that nursing home facility care be included in the basic package of services if states chose to participate. Coverage of nursing care fostered the diversion of older, indigent Americans from state care to private nursing facilities, but there is little evidence that this diversion away from state hospitals was a goal of the reform. In addition, federal courts in the 1970s ruled that if patients or inmates were used as part of a hospital workforce, then they had to be compensated. Finally, the U.S. Supreme Court found that involuntary confinement to state hospitals was a judicial, not a medical, decision.

In the 1990s, we are again exploring major social reform. Welfare is being reconceptualized as work-fare. Reform of the health care system is under way in many states, but no coherent national agenda in health—let alone mental health—is yet present. As in the past, the issue of the impact that emerging reform will have on persons with severe mental illness does not appear to be a priority of the leaders of these new reform efforts. Keeping to the tradition among mental health professionals and leaders, we continue to debate our past while others are designing both our future and the national policy framework for treatment of persons with mental illness and disability.

Reference

Grob, G. N. (1991). *From asylum to community: Mental health policy in modern America.* Princeton, NJ: Princeton University Press.

NO

RICHARD C. SURLES

To debate the issue of deinstitutionalization, it is essential to begin with the term and acknowledge its wide variation in usage. In its most simplistic form, deinstitutionalization is cited as a national mental health policy that resulted in the population of state-owned and -operated institutions being reduced from over 550,000 beds in 1955 to approximately 100,000 in 1992. New York State alone housed over 93,000 persons in state mental institutions as late as 1955. For the most part, until the early 1960s, state institutions were the primary provider for persons with serious mental illness, and most patients admitted to state care tended to stay for long periods of time. For example, only 3 percent of the patients admitted to a New York State hospital in 1959 left within one year of their admission.

During the 1960s, the overall number of inpatient beds operated by states began to decline. However, admissions and discharges to state hospitals continued to increase as new philosophies of "aftercare" and outpatient treatment fostered shorter lengths of stay. By the late 1960s, New York State was housing approximately 70,000 patients, but admissions between 1955 and 1969 had more than doubled.

A more complex definition of deinstitutionalization involves a description of the shifting of responsibility for persons believed to be mentally ill and disabled from a fixed location, a state hospital, to a variety of settings which might be operated by state government, local government, or nonprofit corporations. In addition, the shift was also supported by the growth of a significant core of private practitioners who gave professional credibility to the concept of community treatment.

The concept of deinstitutionalization was operationalized during a period of national social reform that occurred largely outside the planning and policy development within the field of mental health. For example, the emergence of the federal Medicaid program in the late 1960s provided a means of funding for skilled nursing care for indigent persons who previously could be provided care only in state mental health facilities. Social Security also provided a fixed income stream which enabled people to leave state hospitals. Many found low-cost housing through privately operated homes for adults or, in larger urban areas, single-room-occupancy hotels.

During the 1970s and 1980s, community general hospitals began to increase their capacity to provide emergency and acute psychiatric inpatient care. Nationally, states supported the development of outpatient services, and programs of community support and rehabilitation grew. In the late 1970s, the National Institute of Mental Health began promoting a program concept called the "Community Support System" (CSS). CSS advocates cited the failure of traditional clinical outpatient programs to offer more than limited outpatient office visits or day programs. These advocates sought a more comprehensive response to the complex social supports needed for people who previously would have probably been long-term state hospital patients. By the late 1980s, most states had acknowledged the important role that community support programs can play in assisting a person with a disabling mental illness.

At its best, a single state hospital can be viewed as not only a fixed location, but also as an organized institution with a ''bundle'' of supports and services. A hospital is a comprehensive provider that, for one fee, offers housing, nutrition, social support, and medical, dental, and psychiatric treatment. Many hospitals, especially during the 1960s, also provided aggressive vocational rehabilitation services. But at its very best, the state hospital system was responding to only a very limited number of persons in need. Moreover, the state hospital system, until the 1960s, represented a virtual monopoly on mental health resources. For example, as late as 1945, almost 80 percent of all psychiatrists in the United States worked in governmental institutions as compared to 1992, when it is estimated that only 11 percent continue to work for such facilities.

Until recently, there has been a very low expectation for persons who were institutionalized to recover from their mental illness. Instead, chronicity referred to not only the status of the person's illness, but also to life expectation for the individual.

The simplistic definition of deinstitutionalization as previously described is one in which depopulating institutions is the major theme. And, even today, a public discussion continues as to the fate of the patients discharged from hospitals during the 1960s and 1970s. New York, which discharged the greatest number of patients, provides a case example. Persons in New York hospitals as late as 1979 were more likely to be elderly and to have been in the hospital for many years. One of the primary reasons for the annual decline of census of the state hospitals was the death of aging patients which, in New York alone, averaged 8,000 per year from 1965 to 1976. Even today, a significant portion of the decline in use of state hospitals results from death by natural causes or the placement of frail elderly persons into skilled nursing care. Discharge practices in New York and other states also changed dramatically, especially during the 1970s, with length of stay shortening to weeks and months rather than years.

There are many explanations of this shift in practice, including litigation, improved treatment, national standards, and access for the individual to new social programs. As previously indicated, changes in the national Social Security policy in the late 1960s provided for a limited guaranteed monthly income for those who were disabled as a result of a prolonged mental illness. By being declared disabled, a person also became categorically eligible for medical assistance under the federal/state Medicaid program.

The changes that provided income maintenance and medical assistance also stimulated the development of an alternate care system outside the control of the state hospital and, for the most part, the control and influence of the state mental health authorities. Much has been written of the development of federally selected and funded community mental health centers, but there has been only limited examination of the discharge policies of state hospitals or the practices of veterans hospitals, county hospitals, or psychiatric units in general hospitals.

The more complex definition of deinstitutionalization requires an understanding of the interactive effect of the shift in national policy that attached benefits to a disabled individual and the resulting entrepreneurial response, which produced options for persons with mental illness that were largely not anticipated in planning associated with the development of state mental health policy. New businesses were rapidly created in response to the new purchasing capacity represented by entitlement created for disabled people. Cottage industries known as "adult homes," "rest homes," and "single-room-occupancy hotels" (SROs) developed as places of residence for those who had no access to family. In states that developed a diverse mental health benefit under the Medicaid program, general hospitals and specialty outpatient clinics developed, but usually provided only limited coordination or interaction with the traditional state mental health system.

By the 1980s, an elaborate maze of mental health treatment and support systems had emerged. Private psychiatric hospitals became one of the "hot stocks" of the decade. The nursing home industry also assumed much of the role previously held by the older state hospitals, and acute psychiatric units in county or community general hospitals deflected admissions to state institutions.

During the 1970s and 1980s, however, other forces were at work that ultimately would have an unanticipated impact on many former mental patients. Two of the most adverse events were associated with access to benefits and affordable housing. First, starting in the late 1970s, the Social Security Administration began to systematically review the eligibility of those previously judged to be entitled to Supplemental Security Income benefits and, therefore, categorically eligible for Medicaid assistance. There is evidence that persons with mental disabilities were more adversely affected than any other disability group. Second, low-cost housing, to which many former patients had been and were being discharged, became less available. The recently published Federal Task Force on Homelessness and Severe Mental Illness Report (Interagency Council, 1992) states:

> Between 1970 and 1982, the nation lost more than one million SRO units as urban renewal and gentrification efforts encouraged their conversion into condominiums and other upgrade uses. . . . In New York alone, SRO units declined from 127,000 to 14,000 during that 12-year period.

Clearly, the social safety net has become more fragile for all low-income Americans. Decentralization and the dramatic variation between the states in organizing and providing benefits make even describing the consequences of deinstitutionalization difficult. The shift from highly centralized state-operated campuses to individually targeted entitlement programs has also created an environment that simultaneously provides some level of freedom of choice for persons with a psychiatric disability, while also placing these same people at greater risk during a period of changing national policies and shifting interpretation of their rights and entitlements.

The question of the success or failure of deinstitutionalization is largely irrelevant. It continues the mythology that public mental health policy is controlled by mental health professionals and that a national plan was launched for deinstitutionalization by a misguided few. It also seems to assume that ''things were better before the mental health system lost control and began the dramatic downsizing of state facilities.''

To return to past policies would require an investment of public resources that few discuss. For example, if New York State were to rehospitalize 93,000 people on any given day, and to do so in life-safe space, the state would require $8 to $9 billion annually—not including the billions more that would be required in capital cost—to bring aging facilities up to modern code. Those costs could be substantially reduced if policies of the 1960s and 1970s were reintroduced.

Those policies that permitted lower cost would require, among others:

1. That patients be utilized as workers on state farms, in laundries, food service, and maintenance but not compensated for the labor;
2. That the Supreme Court reverse its decision that involuntary confinement in a hospital represented a deprivation of liberty and was, therefore, a decision for judges and not physicians; and
3. That State hospitals would be made exempt from state and local fire and life safety codes.

The odds of returning to the older policies seem even lower than winning a state lottery.

We in mental health work within a large policy context that frequently creates significant barriers to clinical treatment and to the creation of a supportive plan of care of people with severe mental illness and disability. There are few indications that our policy environment will be made any less complex, and many examples of reform and change in state and federal policies abound. We may see major change in health care in this decade. Welfare policy is undergoing dramatic change. Mental health leaders should give priority to policy reform in which their concerns for people with severe mental illness support inclusion of an agenda of health care, social, and rehabilitative reform.

Reference

Interagency Council on the Homeless (1992). Report of the Federal Task Force on Homelessness and Severe Mental Illness. Wash., D.C.: U.S. Department of Health and Human Services.

Rejoinder to Dr. Surles

ANN BRADEN JOHNSON

It is ironic but fitting that Dr. Surles should begin his essay with a review of the many conflicting ways in which the term *deinstitutionalization* has been used over the years, because it is just this kind of circular thinking that the mental health field is so good at getting caught up in. Deinstitutionalization happened, however we define it, because it cost too much to hospitalize chronic incurable mental patients for life at state expense. Now the same patients who used to be in hospitals are out, causing problems, and we can't imagine what else to do except rehospitalize them, which we can't do because it costs too much, except that we don't know what else to do. Around and around it goes. The best minds in the business are so obsessed with counting things like the mentally ill homeless on the one hand, or defining and redefining our terminology on the other, that they never quite seem to notice that they are in charge of a thoroughly dysfunctional system.

This kind of thinking, represented in miniature by Dr. Surles' essay, suggests the very problem the mental health system faces yet can't quite accept, much less take responsibility for: we mental health professionals *are* in charge, and we *are* to blame. This is *our* mess, not someone else's: we eagerly depopulated our state hospitals in the name of community mental health when that was a hot idea; but we chose to implement community programs that merely duplicated the ones already in operation at the time—outpatient clinics, for instance—instead of creating new ones specifically tailored to the real-life needs of new caseloads, including the deinstitutionalized and the never-institutionalized. When the old models failed, we looked around for someone else to blame and found plenty of convincing candidates, including such perennial favorites as the judicial system, for deciding the mentally ill have rights just like every one else; politicians, for trying to save money by robbing state hospital budgets only to spend the money on something else; real estate developers, for gobbling up SRO housing units; or patient advocates, for insisting on pursuing individual rights and entitlements, often at the expense of the class.

So what? So what if nameless others forced deinstitutionalization on us in the form of patients' rights and legislative initiatives and cost-cutting devices and holes in the safety net? Chronic incurable mental illness is ours to deal with, and we owe it to ourselves and to our patients to do something about it. One thing we should have done long ago, and certainly could start to do now, is to face some facts once and for all: people don't need to be in a hospital to get all their custodial and treatment requirements met under one roof; small, community-based residences and small, chronic care facilities are tried-and-true models that can and should be implemented all over the country; and medication alone is no substitute for genuine care. All we've done so far is to let the patients out; now we need to do something for them.

DEBATE 16

Does NAMI Represent the Needs of All Families with Psychiatric Patients?

Arguing YES is Dr. Dale L. Johnson, who is President of the National Alliance for the Mentally Ill and has served on the National Alliance for the Mentally Ill (NAMI) board for six years. He is a Professor of Psychology at the University of Houston, where he teaches and does research in clinical and developmental psychology. He has published extensively on family support programs and has a special interest in cross-cultural research issues. His academic training was at the University of North Dakota (B.A.) and Kansas University (Ph.D.).

Rae E. Unzicker says NO. Ms. Unzicker is the Coordinator of the National Association of Psychiatric Survivors. She also serves on the Board of Directors of the National Association for Rights Protection and Advocacy, the Governor's Mental Health Planning Council (South Dakota), and on the Advisory Council to the South Dakota Protection and Advocacy Program. She speaks throughout the world on the topic of psychiatric oppression, has appeared on all the major television talk shows, and is a writer and film producer.

YES

DALE L. JOHNSON

The title question, "Does NAMI represent the needs of all families with psychiatric patients?" can be answered with an enthusiastic "yes," but only if certain qualifications are stated. Any argument without this clarification would lead only to misunderstanding.

First, it is important to understand what the National Alliance for the Mentally Ill (NAMI) is. It was founded in 1979 by people who had personal experience in living with serious mental illness and who had formed groups in their home communities in Wisconsin, Maryland, Missouri, California, and a few other states to advocate for people with serious mental illnesses. Most of the founders were parents of mentally ill people, but siblings, spouses, and other relatives were also present. The founding group also included former patients, now typically referred to as "consumers," and a few mental health professionals. In forming a national organization they stated the goal of NAMI in the preamble to the bylaws: "Members of NAMI are dedicated to the eradication of mental illness and to the improvement of the quality of life of those whose lives are affected by these diseases."

"Mental illness" at this first meeting was understood to mean severe and persistent mental illnesses such as, for example, schizophrenia, schizo-affective disorder, bipolar disorder, and major depression. The founders formed a national organization because there was no existing organization to provide the necessary advocacy focus and because the need for such an organization was great.

The goals statement indicates that the central focus of NAMI is on the well-being of the person with mental illness, and the well-being of families is secondary, although important in itself. On this question of focus there has been an interesting development within NAMI. In the early days of the organization, there was a greater emphasis on families. Families felt burdened in having to care, virtually alone, for a mentally ill person (Johnson, 1990) and wanted help from service providers. However, as NAMI developed from a few people in scattered groups to an organization with 140,000 members in 1500 affiliates in all fifty states, the focus shifted more sharply to the person with mental illness. Apparently, many of the needs of the family members for support and information have been provided by NAMI groups. This is not to say that the burden has been lifted—far from it. Most families, within NAMI or not, experience a heavy burden in providing care for the mentally ill person.

It has been understood from the beginning that NAMI would not advocate for all psychiatric patients, if "psychiatric patients" means anyone who has a *Diagnostic and Statistical Manual III-Revised (DSM-III-R)* (American Psychiatric Association, 1987) diagnosis. There has been tacit agreement that the illnesses included have as an essential cause brain dysfunction and that the presence of psychotic features is common. Beyond this, there are no sharp distinctions. For example, the anxiety disorders, including panic disorder and obsessive-compulsive disorder, quite likely involve brain dysfunction and may be severe and persistent. They may involve psychotic features, but typically psychosis appears only when the condition coexists with schizophrenia or affective disorders. Compared with the latter illnesses, anxiety disorders are generally less disabling. For example, football great Glen Campbell suffered from panic disorder but was still able to star in the National Football League. By contrast, when Lionel Aldrich, also an NFL player, developed schizophrenia, he became so disabled that he was soon on the streets as a homeless person.

In a recent survey of NAMI families, which yielded 7386 responses, diagnoses given for the mentally ill person in the family were schizophrenia, 63 percent; major affective disorder, 17 percent; bipolar disorder, 14 percent; personality disorder, 2 percent; and other, 2 percent. Thus, it is clear that the emphasis for NAMI is on the serious mental illnesses, and therefore it neither advocates for nor represents all families of psychiatric patients, nor has it ever intended to.

A key part of the orienting question has to do with the idea of representation. How can any group, even one as large as NAMI, claim to represent the needs of the vast number of people with serious mental illnesses and their families? Given that 1 percent of the population has schizophrenia and another 1 percent has bipolar disorder and yet another part of the population suffers from major depression, a conservative estimate of the number of people with serious mental illness is 3.5 percent of the population (Ron Manderscheid, NIMH, personal communication June, 1991). Thus, there are 8.4 million people with serious mental illnesses in the United States. Add to that number two family members per mentally ill person and the total is 25.2 million people. NAMI is small in this context.

Members of the NAMI Ethnic Minorities network also point out that NAMI does not have many minority members; its minority membership is certainly not proportionately represented. NAMI is also not representative by social class. There is evidence that serious mental illness is more common in lower socioeconomic strata, and NAMI members tend to be of the middle class. NAMI invites all interested people to join and has initiated an active outreach program into minority and low-income neighborhoods.

Given these considerations for perspective, it is important to note that proportional representation is not a necessity for legitimate advocacy. The United States Senate is an example with its largely Anglo, male membership, elected by women and men with the understanding that they would represent all of their constituents, whatever their gender, ethnicity, or creed. In much the same way, when I, as a NAMI member, advocate for research and services for people with schizophrenia, I advocate for all people with this illness, including my own son, and for the relatives of NAMI members who have schizophrenia, but not limited to my son or to the NAMI relatives. When we advocate before the United States Congress to have the National Institute for Mental Illness (NIMH) budget for research increased, we advocate for the well-being of all people who might benefit from this increase. If we successfully encourage pharmaceutical manufacturers to develop new and better medications, our relatives might benefit, but so might thousands of other people who have never had contact with NAMI. What is important is that NAMI members recognized the need for focused advocacy for a very large group of people who were not receiving adequate services and for whom relevant research was lacking.

There is a second issue related to representation. It has to do with how one group of people can claim to declare what another group of people needs. Can, for example, parents advocate for their children? Of course they can and always have, but what if the children are adults? Why shouldn't these adults state their own needs? These questions of representation bring us to the heart of mental illness advocacy: the question of competence to represent oneself. On this issue, if the adult child is not competent to represent himself or herself, then society has agreed that another adult may represent the person. Traditionally, that person is a near relative such as a parent, but courts also may appoint guardians to be representatives. If the adult has very low intelligence and has a diagnosis of mental retardation, and if the condition is expected to be continuous, a guardian is expected. One of the first strong advocacy groups was the Association of Retarded Citizens (ARC), an organization that comprises largely parents of children and adults with mental retardation. The legitimacy of ARC to advocate for mentally retarded people has been questioned rarely because it seems to most people right and just that this advocacy for vulnerable individuals should be undertaken by others who are competent.

The situation is different for adults with serious mental illnesses, and it is on this difference that conflict with regard to the right to advocate has arisen. People suffering from serious mental illnesses often have poor judgment, little insight into the nature of their illness (Sartorius, Shapiro, & Jablensky, 1974), and beliefs that other people do not confirm (delusions). To make a diagnosis, these symptoms must be present to such an extent that the person's ability to function independently is impaired. What makes the matter difficult is that unlike the person with mental retardation whose limitations are typically life-long and relatively unchanging, the person with mental illness often develops the symptoms after a course of normal development and typically experiences continuing symptoms in an episodic manner. Thus, some people are unable to advocate for themselves during symptomatic periods, but can advocate when symptoms have remitted. Moreover, symptom remission is often a relative matter. Many people with serious mental illnesses who undergo treatment find the major symptoms have eased, but they are left with a feeling of low motivation or little energy. These feelings, combined with the social skills deficits resulting from years of being out of touch with society's ordinary events while the individual is in a psychotic condition, make advocacy unlikely.

It is sometimes said that the best advocates for people with mental illness are those who have been mentally ill, and we in NAMI support this advocacy. However, there is still a danger that the interests of the people with mental illness who are unable to advocate for themselves will be neglected, and it is for this group that NAMI stands virtually alone in providing representation.

Claims are also made that NAMI, viewed as an organization composed of relatives of people with mental illness and ignoring the consumer members in the organization, has interests that are at odds with those of consumers. Much is made of this apparent conflict, but when consumers and relatives compare lists of what they want from service providers or what they want for the quality of life for people with mental illnesses, the differences are minor. In general, they focus on the question of enforced treatment. Even on this, most consumers acknowledge when they have become free of symptoms that they needed treatment. It is a part of serious mental illness, a product of a dysfunctional brain (Amador, Strauss, Yale, & Gorman, 1991), that one does not know that one is ill. If I am infected with a flu virus, I tell myself, these aches and this lassitude are signs of flu: I say, "I am ill." However, the person afflicted with bipolar disorder experiences a feeling of extraordinary well-being, and later a feeling of hopeless despair, but does not experience these personal changes as illness—not until through training or experience the person becomes aware of the significance of the changes in self.

A final issue relevant to representation has to do with whether the organization purporting to advocate for certain objectives has had any impact on society. NAMI certainly has. The rise in the NIMH research budget from about $80 million a year to over $700 million provides the most compelling evidence of impact, but NAMI also has had a key role in the reorganization of the Alcohol, Drug Abuse and Mental Health Administration (ADAMHA) to place greater emphasis on mental health research and services. At the local and state levels NAMI members now sit on decision-making boards and have a direct influence on the way services are provided. State legislatures have placed more emphasis on mental illness issues.

In summary, NAMI does represent and advocate for people with severe and persistent mental illnesses that have a high likelihood of being caused by brain dysfunction and involve psychosis. Secondarily, it represents and advocates for their families. The legitimacy of its advocacy is in the need to present the interests of a large group of people with major psychiatric disability who too often are unable to advocate for themselves. Recovering mentally ill people are also a part of NAMI and add their voices in advocating for all people with serious mental illnesses.

References

Amador, X. F., Strauss, D. H., Yale, S. A., & Gorman, J. M. (1991). Awareness of illness in schizophrenia. *Schizophrenia Bulletin, 17,* 113–132.

American Psychiatric Association (1987). *Diagnostic and Statistical Manual, III-Revised.* Washington, DC: American Psychiatric Press.

Johnson, D. L. (1990). The family's experience of living with mental illness. In H. P. Lefley & D. L. Johnson (Eds.), *Families as allies in treatment of the mentally ill.* (pp. 31–64). Washington, DC: American Psychiatric Press.

Manderscheid, R. (June, 1991). Personal Communication.

Sartorius, N., Shapiro, R., & Jablensky, A. (1974). The international pilot study of schizophrenia. *Schizophrenia Bulletin 1,* 21–34.

Annotated Bibliography

Hatfield, A. B. (1991). The National Alliance for the Mentally Ill: A decade later. *Community Mental Health Journal, 27,* 95–97.

Hatfield provides a useful, brief history of NAMI and provides a context for its current activities.

Johnson, D. L. (Ed.). (1990). *Training psychologists to work with the seriously mentally ill.* Washington, DC: American Psychological Association Press.

This collection of papers describes the kind of training professionals, not just psychologists, need to work effectively with people who have a severe and persistent mental illness.

Marsh, D. (1992). *Families and mental illness: New directions for professional practice.* New York: Praeger.

The author is a clinical psychologist and a mother of a person with serious mental illness. She has written this guide for professionals to outline what they need to know to work with families.

Mondimore, F. M. (1990). *Depression: The mood disease.* Baltimore: The Johns Hopkins University Press.

Evidence that major depression is a biochemical disorder. Advice for patients, families, and professionals on coping strategies and treatment.

Torrey, E. F. (1988). *Surviving schizophrenia: A family manual* (revised). New York: Harper & Row.

This book is regarded as basic reading for all families struggling with schizophrenia. Torrey, a psychiatrist, was motivated to write the book by his own attempts to cope with his sister's illness.

Rejoinder to Professor Johnson

Rae E. Unzicker

It is irresistible. Professor Johnson writes, "These questions bring us to the heart of mental illness advocacy. . . ."

It is clear. NAMI simply does not understand the concept, meaning, or purpose of advocacy. To advocate does not mean to decide what is best for another, to make choices on behalf of another, or to speak *for* another. To advocate means, simply, to represent that person/client's "expressed interest."

While NAMI purports to do this, it most decidedly does not. NAMI represents its own best interests, and what it considers to be the best interests of not only the members of their own families, but also of every "seriously and persistently mentally ill" person in America!

It is obvious. NAMI's idea of advocacy is heartless. People—their own children—are not multifaceted individuals with histories and pain and differences and suffering. They are statistics with "poor judgment, little insight into the nature of their illnesses, and beliefs that other people do not confirm [delusions]."

Without arguing the entire conceptual framework of the medical model, it is enough to say any thinking person knows both instinctively and by experience that all people are more complicated than genetics and chemistry.

Since Professor Johnson has chosen a medical metaphor (having the flu), I think it is important to state once again that there are no laws against having the flu, or cancer, or AIDS, while there are statutes in every state that punish the behavior of people labeled "mentally ill." This is the crux of the issue. Having experienced cancer in my own life, and having had the opportunity and responsibility to make true life-and-death decisions relating to my own health—in the midst of an extremely stressful time—has validated for me the exact opposite of Johnson's contention that ". . . the legitimacy of its [NAMI's] advocacy is in the need to present the interests of a large group of people with major psychiatric disability who *too often are unable to advocate for themselves*" (emphasis added).

Professor Johnson, in concert with the NAMI party line, simply refuses to acknowledge that people subjected to brutalizing psychiatric treatments are not only able to advocate for themselves, but also have beliefs and real-life experiences that other people—their parents, primarily—simply refuse to confirm or acknowledge (delusions). These experiences and beliefs form the energizing force behind the mental patients' rights movement and are at the heart of what we believe is true advocacy—in personal empowerment, freedom of choice, and the abolishment of involuntary treatment.

NO

RAE E. UNZICKER

When I began working within the mental patients' rights movement, and eventually became the Coordinator of the National Association of Psychiatric Survivors, it did not occur to me that many of the calls and letters I would receive would come from family members of people who have been psychiatrically labeled. However, approximately 20 percent of the requests for help, information, and referral we now receive come from family members. They are shocked at the ''treatment'' their sons, daughters, spouses, and others are receiving in the mental health system (Unzicker, 1989). They are frustrated by a system that promises help and then betrays both the family *and* the identified patient.

They are extremely upset by the involuntary commitment process. While many of them may have reluctantly initiated a commitment petition—or were coerced into doing so by a mental health professional—they are never told the wide-ranging ramifications: the loss of basic freedoms, the routine use of powerful and dangerous drugs, and the long-term institutionalization–transition–aftercare–follow-up–outpatient commitment cycle that may never end.

A letter received recently expresses this common outrage:

> To whom it may concern:
>
> I am a mother of a so-called 37-year-old male 'paranoid schizophrenic.' The stories I could tell you! I have had my fill of the mental health experts.
>
> I belonged to NAMI but am not satisfied. Because of reading *NAPS/News,* Kate Millett's book, and Judi Chamberlin's book, I am encouraging my son to take more responsibility. I'd like to be an advocate and encourage other clients to speak up to the professionals, not follow like whipped dogs. . . . I think my son is doing great in spite of the professionals. I believe in him. Thank you again.

NAMI is, however, one of the most powerful forces influencing public policy regarding mental health in America. It is important to note that NAMI was originally financed in part by the National Institute of Mental Health (NIMH), which provided funds and technical assistance for NAMI's founding conference. Since that time, most state mental health authorities, often through grants from NIMH, have funded start-up activities for local and statewide AMI chapters and, in some cases, are providing ongoing organizational funding.

NAMI makes clear that it is not an organization *of* ''the mentally ill,'' but *for* them. Its very name, however, is stigmatizing; we do not call people with cancer, for example, the cancerous. NAMI also makes it clear that it represents only those families whose *adult* children are labeled with the new catch-phrase for what used to be called ''chronic''; now they are called ''severely and persistently mentally ill.'' This is a useful gambit that allows NAMI to discount the opinions and experiences of anyone who has recovered or anyone who simply rejects the label. Apparently, it is NAMI's belief that it is impossible to recover and that, if one does, one was ''misdiagnosed'' in the first place. This attitude of hopelessness pervades NAMI, which places its hope in drugs and other ''treatments'' to ''control the symptoms.'' But it is, I believe, truly reflective of NAMI's official, narrow view of biological psychiatry.

For a variety of complicated reasons, NAMI has rejected any other possible view of human problems in favor of what they call ''brain disease.'' They believe, based on virtually no solid scientific evidence, that their children (most NAMI members are parents of adult children) are biologically defective. NAMI is tenacious in this belief; along with the American Psychiatric Association and drug manufacturers, NAMI has even convinced the National Institute of Mental Health to declare the 1990s "The Decade of the Brain," thus reducing their psychiatrically labeled relatives to biological organisms and denying the reality of the humanistic and authentic social, environmental, spiritual, economic, psychological, and, yes, familial, issues that have significant impacts on all human beings.

NAMI's not-so-hidden agenda is clear: to absolve themselves of guilt, blame, and responsibility for the troubles of their children. This desire to rewrite history is understandable, given the long tradition of "blame Mother" which was an outgrowth of the popularization and 1950s Americanization of Freud's ideas. However, it flies in the face of new research, most significantly that of Rose, et al. (1990), which confirms what most psychiatric survivors know—that, for many of us, our families of origin were and are toxic. In looking at Rose's research—conducted with people labeled as "severely and persistently mentally ill"—the figures are astonishing. As many as 75 percent of the clients in long-term care programs were identified as survivors of childhood sexual and/or physical abuse. To label this phenomenon as "biologically based mental illness" is both absurd and insulting. To revictimize these people in the traditional mental health system is cruel, at best. To validate their parents' denial over their own experiences is horrifying.

NAMI is staunchly anti-choice. Its official position not only favors involuntary commitment, but also actively supports the expansion of commitment criteria. Nowhere is this more evident than in the commitment process. Instead of providing safe alternatives, family members are frequently the ones who not only initiate petitions, but also testify against their own adult sons and daughters in hearings. Further, they often expect their adult children to be grateful for this unwanted intervention. Like all abusive parents, their attitude is, "Someday you'll thank me for this."

Some local and state chapters are now promoting a commitment standard known as "likely to deteriorate," which means in practical terms that people who stop taking psychiatric drugs—or who even threaten to stop taking them—can be committed with little or no due process rights. NAMI has been at the forefront of promoting loosening the criteria for the use of forced medication, not only for patients in hospitals, but also for those released through a legal mechanism called "outpatient commitment." In its most oppressive form, outpatient commitment involves having a nurse come to the patient's home and injecting him or her with Prolixin, a drug that stays in the body for up to three weeks and that creates some of the most severe side effects attributed to psychiatric drugs.

It should not be surprising, then, to reveal that NAMI proudly accepts funding for its organization from drug manufacturing companies and that drug companies regularly court NAMI for its powerful political muscle. NAMI was at the forefront, for example, of promoting the new and dangerous drug Clozaril but then, paradoxically, sued Clozaril's manufacturer for selling it at inflated prices and in package deals that would ensure a high degree of monitoring, which is crucial to this particular drug. One of its ''side effects'' is death. It seems clear that the agenda of some parents is not to ''help'' their psychiatrically labeled adult children, but to flex their powerful and controlling muscles, with the complicity of a plethora of state mental health codes that they themselves have helped to create (Blanch, 1990).

Nonetheless, people involved with the mental patients' rights movement are not unsympathetic to the very real pain experienced by family members. After all, many of those closest to us—our friends—experience difficult times when they become disturbed and disturbing. It is not easy to provide the kind of intensive, supportive caring that many people in crisis need and want; it is even more difficult for parents when already complicated family dynamics exist. This does not justify, however, the punishing, abusive, and hostile treatment parents accord to their distressed adult children whom they call, ironically, their ''loved ones.''

As I meet with local AMI members throughout the country, I have discovered that many of them came to the organization looking for personal support and that a good many of them do not support the national organization's rigid political and philosophical ideology. But due to their own grief and suffering and sense of powerlessness, they believe they cannot impact policy decisions made at the highest levels of NAMI's leadership. They are right; there is trouble within the NAMI family itself.

By its own survey, NAMI members do not represent the vast majority of parents of psychiatrically labeled people. The typical NAMI member is over fifty years old, upper middle class, lives in the suburbs, and earns more than $50,000 a year. Of course NAMI members have political clout; they have time, money, and energy, and they have formed alliances with other pro-psychiatry groups, primarily the American Psychiatric Association and drug companies. A drug company recently sponsored an all-expense-paid ''conference,'' primarily for NAMI members, to learn the newest information about the company's psychotropic drug products.

Contrast the typical NAMI member with the typical parent of a typical long-term recipient of mental health services, who is poor, a minority, alone, and living in an inner city. There are very few black or Hispanic faces at NAMI conferences.

Finally, it is apparent that while NAMI speaks of destigmatizing ''mental illness,'' in actuality it creates an ''us'' and ''them'' dichotomy. In its own organizational structure, NAMI has created a ''Client Council,'' made up of ''consumers'' (psychiatrically labeled people) who generally support NAMI's philosophy. The council is clearly a stepchild of this paternalistic and patronizing organization. ''Consumers'' who disagree with the parent organization's views are told to go elsewhere, or their disagreement is labeled a symptom of their illness. And NAMI was recently the subject of a complaint filed with the Department of Labor for firing a staff member who was a recipient of mental health services, allegedly because they refused to accommodate her stress-related disability. The ''consumer'' won.

Pat Risser (1990), an ex-patient advocate, wrote poignantly of his attempts to ''cooperate'' and build coalitions with AMI members. He writes, ''For three years, I sat on a state AMI board. For three years, I was generally not accepted as anything more than a second-class citizen. I quit, not because I am a poor teacher or ran out of patience. I quit because I was tired of being a token to satisfy some members' need to feel fair.'' Risser also points out ''. . . 'consumers' are also family members. We may be the psychiatrically labeled family member, but we are still family. Aren't we?''

References

Blanch, A. (1991) *Report of meeting on use of involuntary interventions: Perspectives of family members and psychiatrists.* Available through CSP Office, Center for Mental Health Services, 5600 Fishers Lane, Rockville, MD 20857.

Rose, S. M., Ph.D., Peabody, C., & Strategias, B. (1990). Another unveiling: Abuse background of psychiatric survivors and their neglect by mental health systems. Unpublished manuscript. Excerpted in *NAPS/News,* Summer, 1990.

Risser, P. (1991). Writer criticizes organized family movement. *NAPS/News,* Fall.

Unzicker, R. (1989). On my own: A personal journey through madness and reemergence. *Psychosocial Rehabilitation Journal, 13,* 1, pp. 71–77.

Rejoinder to Ms. Unzicker

Dale L. Johnson

Ms. Unzicker apparently does not like the National Alliance for the Mentally Ill (NAMI), and she gives us a reason in her first paragraph. Her use of the phrase ''psychiatrically labeled'' suggests a fundamental disagreement with the idea that one might actually have a real illness that is mental or psychiatric. She plays on this theme later in her criticism of medication. In the latter criticism, she ignores the research evidence supporting the usefulness of medication in reducing psychiatric and depressive symptoms.

Her statement is wrong on several issues:

1. NAMI counts on the dues and contributions of members for its operational support; it is not supported by the NIMH or any other governmental agency. She is right that some state AMIs do receive support from state mental health departments. Actually, why should they not? They can still advocate for increased funding for mental illness services and be critical of the use of these funds as warranted.
2. No NAMI conferences have been supported with pharmaceutical manufacturer support.
3. The NAMI platform does not "favor involuntary commitment." It does support the right to treatment and the right to full protection when involuntary commitment is required by the courts.

Her contention that NAMI members have reduced their relatives to "biological organisms" is to me, and NAMI members, deeply offensive. I am in this movement to get help for my son, a friendly, bright, and caring person, who was struck down by the biologically caused illness schizophrenia when he was 19. He is still friendly, bright, and caring, but he struggles with hallucinations and impaired attention. Although he is grateful for the help he has received from the antipsychotic medication clozapine, symptoms persist and result in an impaired quality of life. He needs rehabilitative assistance to return to college or to work, but this assistance has not been available. His situation is typical of that of many people who have mental illnesses, and it is a primary goal of NAMI to help all in this situation enjoy a better quality of life. The recognition that people with serious mental illnesses have brain dysfunction does not diminish them in the eyes of those who love them; on the contrary, it does help to understand their struggle.

Ms. Unzicker is right in implying that NAMI parents do not like to be blamed for causing the mental illness of their children (Johnson, 1989). Freud died in 1939 and cannot be held directly responsible for the surge of parent-blaming that took place in the 1950s and continues today, but his followers did carry his banner against families. She refers to the research of Rose et al. (1991) to support her position that families are abusive and thus responsible for subsequent illness of their children. The Rose research is too flawed to provide the support she seeks. The report did not mention diagnoses of the interview respondents and may have included a group who did not have schizophrenia or bipolar disorder. The data collected were all retrospective. Clients were interviewed about early experiences, and many reported abusive families. There was no external verification of the reports. When distressed people are more negative about early experiences than when not distressed (Lewinsohn & Rosenbaum, 1987). A common delusion among people who have psychotic disorders is that one has been mistreated severely. Some people are highly susceptible to interviewer suggestion that they have been abused (Wakefield, 1992). There is no reason why some people with severe and persistent mental illnesses might not have been abused as children, but that abuse did not cause the schizophrenia or bipolar disorder. The weight of evidence is that the essential cause is brain dysfunction.

As a resident of South Dakota, it is perhaps not surprising that Ms. Unzicker finds few ''black or Hispanic faces at NAMI conferences.'' Living in Houston, I am impressed with the ethnic diversity present in our meetings, and anyone attending the recent NAMI national convention in Washington would have been similarly impressed. NAMI is open to all people who have an interest in improving the well-being of people who have serious mental illnesses.

Ms. Unzicker's dismissal of the reality of the severely mentally ill is basic. If there were no severe mental illnesses, there would be no need for NAMI, but those of us who have seen how destructive serious mental illness is know it is real, and we have joined together in an organization called the National Alliance for the Mentally Ill.

References

Johnson, D. L. (1989). Schizophrenia as a brain disease: Implications for psychologists and families. *American Psychologist, 44,* 553–555.

Lewinsohn, P. M., & Rosenbaum, M. (1987). Recall of parental behavior by acute depressives, remitted depressives, and nondepressives. *Journal of Personality and Social Psychology, 52,* 611–619.

Rose, S. M., Peabody, C. G., & Stratogeas, B. (1991). Undetected abuse among intensive case management clients. *Hospital and Community Psychiatry, 42,* 499–503.

Wakefield, H. (1992). *Remembering 'repressed' abuse: Initial research, theoretical analysis and evaluation of claims.* Paper presented at the convention of the American Psychological Society, San Diego.

DEBATE 17

Is Managed Care Good for Mental Health Clients?

Kevin Corcoran, who is a Professor in the Graduate School of Social Work at Portland State University, argues YES. He received his M.S.W. and Ph.D. from the University of Pittsburgh and is currently completing a J.D. from the University of Houston. Dr. Corcoran's areas of interest include clinical practice, practice evaluation, measurement, and mediation. He maintains a private practice in clinical social work and dispute resolution. He is the editor of *Structuring Change: Effective Practice for Common Client Problems* (Lyceum, 1992).

Arguing NO is Carol A. Bernstein, M.D., Director of Residency Training in the Department of Psychiatry at New York University Medical Center and Associate Professor of Clinical Psychiatry. Assistant Clinical Professor of Psychiatry at the Columbia University College of Physicians and Surgeons and Associate Director for Postgraduate Education in Psychiatry at Columbia University and the New York State Psychiatric Institute. In addition, she is Chairperson of the American Psychiatric Association's Committee on Medical Student Education and a member of the APA's Joint Commission on Public Affairs. Dr. Bernstein maintains a small private practice for psychiatry in New York City.

YES

KEVIN CORCORAN

Managed Care and the Marketplace

The question of whether managed care is good for clients addresses one of society's most critical challenges—the equitable distribution of quality care in light of ever-increasing costs and limited availability. The need for cost containment and quality assurance is fueled by the fact that such essential services of health and mental health care are bought and sold in the marketplace, as opposed to being distributed as an entitlement to all citizens. Additionally, there is waste and abuse in the mental health care system. For example, it seems that every practitioner knows of programs where the clinician is expected to be a marketing agent, where the routine recommendation is to admit the patient to a hospital; that is, of course, provided the prospective patient has some form of insurance coverage. As a consequence of a marketplace approach, health care service, of which mental health represents 12 to 14 percent, was approximately 12 percent of the 1990 gross national product (Dorwart, 1990); and yet, over 37 million Americans have no health insurance and are effectively excluded from many of the services exchanged in the marketplace.

The attitude of consumers and practitioners is as if care was an entitlement. As in health care, all too often the parameter of clinical services is limited by the insurance coverage. Many consumers assume that whatever clinical services are desired is the one of choice regardless of cost; after all, "My insurance will cover it."

In many respects, this is a relatively unchecked marketplace where the buyer and seller rely on someone else to be the payer. Consequently, the current reliance on third-party reimbursement has brought with it the burdens and benefits of managed care.

What Is Managed Care and How Does It Work?

Such important goals of containing costs and assuring quality have resulted in a variety of program labeled "managed care." Managed care may be defined as "any method that regulates the price, utilization, or site of services" (Austad & Hoyt, 1992). The four general approaches to managed care are: authorization prior to initiating treatment; mandated second opinions prior to authorization of treatment; review of ongoing treatment before reimbursement and continuation; and high cost managed care review of completed treatment (Tischler, 1990). The first two approaches attempt to determine whether the services are the best available ones for the specific problem, delivered by the most cost-effective professional. The latter two methods attempt to ensure that the standard of care of services was sufficient to warrant payment.

The determination cf quality is based on various mechanisms from a simple telephone call by a case manager to extensive records review. Frequently, case managers make their decisions to authorize treatment or payment based on a form completed by the clinician. The written form documents the need for services, diagnoses, and treatment plan including short- and long-term goals that are attainable within the time limits of the insurance coverage (Osman & Shueman, 1988). Clearly, then, denial of authorization or refusal to reimburse has implications for the client in need of mental health services and clinicians who expect payment for their work.

Burdens and Benefits of Managed Care

Any program that influences from whom a client may receive services, what those services ought to be, and at what cost is understandably controversial. For example, cost containment, which authorizes short-term treatment and less expensive outpatient intervention, instead of inpatient therapy may be considered cost effective and in the best interest of the client. In reality, though, opponents of managed care may view this as an interference with the professional's clinical judgment. Given the potential for premature termination of services, the end result may be lower quality services and a continuing client need that will eventually cost even more money to resolve.

In general, opponents consider managed care to be a burden to the client and service provider by requiring even more paperwork, while concomitantly being intrusive, inconvenient, and often inconsistently administered by different insurance carriers and managed care programs. While these criticisms have some merit, much of the objection to managed care is based on clinicians' practice reliance on long-term, continuous treatment, which overemphasizes exploration and insight with clinicians taking a rather nondirective and passive role. In contrast, for managed care programs the goals of cost containment and quality assurance may be more effectively met through short-term interventions that are goal-directed, time-limited, and facilitated by an active problem-solving clinician.

This discussion illustrates that managed care creates additional problems while it ideally solves others. As Dorwart (1990) and others point out, the problems of managed care are formidable. The benefits, however, far outweigh the burdens.

Earlier we discussed how managed care attempts to control cost and assure quality by pretreatment authorization or prepayment evaluation. In essence, the pretreatment approval is designed to see that a particular clinical problem receives the most effective and the preferred practice approach (Giles, 1991). When successfully implemented by a managed care program, a client is more likely to avoid using limited resources on inappropriate, time-consuming, and costly services. The direct effect is that the clients may receive better services, and access to the more effective services is not delayed by the needless initiating and terminating of inappropriate services by clinicians who simply have an opening on their caseload.

Pre-approach methods of managed care also prevent waste of limited resources, such as taxpayer dollars, corporate employee benefits, or a client's valuable time and productivity. By approving services in advance a client is less likely to unknowingly select a professional and a procedure that are unnecessary or inappropriate for the particular problem. In many respects, then, the managed care program serves as a referral source that prevents the needless waste of money and time.

Managed care also benefits clients by creating a wider variety of choice of service providers. This is seen when a managed care program assigns a client to an equally effective, but less expensive professional. This might include referring a client to a social worker or other master-level practitioner instead of a more costly psychiatrist (Patterson, 1990). Admittedly, this is contrary to the idea of freely selecting services in the marketplace where a client might initially want "a real doctor."

In understanding managed care it is important to remember that cutting costs is not the only issue. Managed care is also concerned with quality of care. Managed care programs that evaluate ongoing or completed services are also helpful to mental health clients. The assessment of quality is much like test-driving a car after a mechanic has repaired the brakes; the major difference is that the test-drive is completed by an independent evaluator working through a managed care program. In every sense, the evaluation by a case manager is a mechanism of consumer protection. The client is prevented from paying for services that are not considered effective by someone other than the person who actually provided the service. Much like mechanics who do good brake repairs, clinicians know they do a good job and should be paid. Managed care helps clients by evaluating the standard of care before paying for it.

Clients are also helped by managed care in that these programs often require that clinicians set meaningful, obtainable, and observable goals that are reached with well-defined, planned, and deliberate interventions. This approach requires hard work by clinicians between sessions, which might not be billable hours, and is much more demanding than relying on the therapeutic relationship, nondirective techniques, reflection, group process, or other methods that, in part, are flying by the seat of the pants. Since failure to provide such structured services may result in a denial of reimbursement, clinicians have a strong incentive to keep abreast of new developments in the field. Thus, by assuring that only quality services are paid for, managed care improves consumer satisfaction by seeing that the best and more contemporary services are provided at the most effective cost.

Conclusions

The role of managed care in mental health has increased dramatically over the past few years (Edinburgh & Cottler, 1990). While its goals are cost containment and quality assurance, managed care has failed to solve some problems while also creating new ones. For example, from a 1991 survey of mental health professionals, 44 percent of a sample of social workers reported that more clients are disallowed services due to managed care; 37 percent of this sample reported that they changed their treatment approach because of managed care; and 52 percent reported that managed care shortened the length of the treatment (NASW News, 1992).

Indeed, there are problems for such programs and serious improvements are needed. When managed care is effective, though, it helps clients by serving as a referral source that matches their particular problem with a cost-effective clinician who uses specific procedures to obtain meaningful and measurable goals. Such a program prevents the waste of limited resources. Managed care also prevents clients from wasting their time with less effective and more costly services. Finally, managed care helps clients because it not only enhances the likelihood that a client will use the most effective interventions available, but also provides a strong incentive for practitioners to learn new and more effective techniques. In essence, all of these benefits are helpful to clients by containing costs while promoting the use of more effective interventions that lead to positive client change.

References

Austad, M. F., & Hoyt, C. S. (1992). The managed care movement and the future of psychotherapy. *Psychotherapy, 29,* 109–113.

Dorwart, R. A. (1990). Managed mental health care: Myths and realities in the 1990s. *Hospital and Community Psychiatry, 41,* 1087–1091.

Edinburgh, G., & Cottler, J. (1990). Implications of managed care for social work in psychiatric hospitals. *Hospital and Community Psychiatry, 41,* 1063–1064.

Giles, T. R. (1991). Managed mental health care and effective psychotherapy: A step in the right direction? *Journal of Behavior Therapy and Experimental Psychiatry, 22,* 83–86.

NASW News. (1992, April). *Survey eyes therapy fees,* 3–4.

Osman, S., & Shueman, S. A. (1988). A guide to the peer review process for clinicians. *Social Work, 33,* 345–348.

Patterson, D. Y. (1990). Managed care: An approach to rational psychiatric treatment. *Hospital and Community Psychiatry, 41,* 1092–1094.

Tischler, G. L. (1990). Utilization management and the quality of care. *Hospital and Community Psychiatry, 41,* 1099–1102.

Annotated Bibliography

Giles, T. R. (1991). Managed mental health care and effective psychotherapy: A step in the right direction? *Journal of Behavior Therapy and Experimental Psychiatry, 22,* 83–86.

This article considers the benefits of managed care as related to facilitating the use of effective interventions. The author argues that specialized treatments, usually behavioral techniques, will be used more frequently because of the demands of managed care.

Patterson, D. Y. (1990). Managed care: An approach to rational psychiatric treatment. *Hospital and Community Psychiatry, 41,* 1092–1094. Borenstein, D. B. (1990). Managed care: A means of rationing psychiatric treatment. *Hospital and Community Psychiatry, 41,* 1095–1098.

These articles are paired together to form a debate. Patterson argues that managed care provides for rational care delivery by assigning client with clinician; that managed care enhances fiscal and clinical responsibility and essentially monitors practice effectiveness. Borenstein, in contrast, argues that reviewers overseeing managed care are not objective, not qualified to review clinical judgment and particular procedures, and threaten client confidentiality. Both authors, of course, are correct.

Tischler, G. L. (1990). Utilization management and the quality of care. *Hospital and Community Psychiatry, 41,* 1099–1102.

This article reviews the history of managed care, delineates the process of utilization review, and considers the effects of managed care on the quality of care. The author astutely concludes that for more effective treatments to be used, more rigorous patient guidelines, including clinical protocols, are needed.

Rejoinder to Dr. Corcoran

CAROL A. BERNSTEIN

The fundamental premise in Dr. Corcoran's commentary on managed care services for mental health clients is that "essential services of health and mental health care are bought and sold in the marketplace, as opposed to being distributed as an entitlement to all citizens." However, many health care professionals would argue that health care is a right, not a privilege, and that marketplace economics alone do not do justice to the debate about health care delivery.

A second assumption in Dr. Corcoran's statement is that both the quality and appropriateness of treatment are adequately addressed by the insertion of a "reviewer" or "case manager" into the delivery system. Such reviewers often lack medical training and are not qualified to determine the nature and need for treatment of psychiatric patients, particularly when they rely solely on telephone consultations or medical record reviews.

Dr. Corcoran reveals the inherent bias of mental health professionals who do not treat patients with a full range of psychiatric disorders when he asserts that managed care programs with their goals of cost containment and quality assurance will redirect "practice reliance on long-term continuous treatment, which overemphasizes exploration and insight with clinicians taking a rather nondirective and passive role." This statement reflects the erroneous belief that the major form of psychiatric treatment that will be affected by managed care is long-term intensive psychotherapy. A large proportion of patients suffering from mental illness have serious *chronic* disabilities and require *prolonged* treatment and management, which is already characterized by a ''goal-directed, active problem-solving approach.'' This significant population is completely overlooked in Dr. Corcoran's argument.

Dr. Corcoran goes on to say that by approving services in advance ''a client is less likely to unknowingly select a professional or procedure that is unnecessary or inappropriate for a particular problem.'' When treatment options are driven by financial necessity, it is hard to believe that the best interests of the patient can be taken into full consideration, especially if cost escalates as a result.

Under the rubric of ''wider provider choice,'' managed care companies propose to assign clients to ''equally effective but less expensive'' professionals. This philosophy implies that the services provided by different mental health professionals are equivalent. It also eliminates professional distinctions, obscures areas of expertise, and short-changes patients.

Drs. Steven Scharfstein and Allan Beigel in their book *New Economics and Psychiatric Care* (1990) comment accurately on a fundamental difficulty with managed care programs. ''The 'less is more' approach is inappropriate for a significant percentage of [psychiatric] patients. The reality is that for many mentally ill persons their illness is catastrophic. Ten percent of the mentally ill account in most studies for 60% of inpatient days or outpatient visits. Despite all of our best efforts, unless there is developed an equitable approach to catastrophic illness within the context of the procompetition market, the burden of care of the severely mentally ill is likely to be shifted to an already underfinanced public sector even more than in recent past'' (p. 237). Furthermore, ''there are ethical and economic rules for medicine that have historically distinguished this and other professions from business. . . . In justifying the public's trust, professionals have set higher standards of conduct for themselves than the minimal rules governing the marketplace, and maintain that they can be judged under those standards only by each other, not by laymen. The ideal of the market presumes the 'sovereignty' of consumer choices; the ideal of a profession calls for the sovereignty of its members' independent authoritative judgments'' (p. 238).

In summary, the marketplace mentality of managed care programs undermines professional responsibility, violates confidentiality, blurs professional identities, and drastically curtails treatment options for the mentally ill. Managed care in its current form is no remedy for the health care crisis.

Reference

Scharfstein, Steven S., & Beigel, Allan (Eds.). (1985). *The new economics and psychiatric care.* (pp. 237–238) Washington D.C.: American Psychiatric Press.

NO

Carol A. Bernstein

The issue of exploding national health care expenditures is one of the major economic problems of our time. Between 20 and 30 percent of the population remains uninsured, creating an additional crisis for many Americans. One of the most widespread attempts at cost containment has been the development of managed care programs:

> Managed health care generally refers to the organizational management of health care in two principal ways. First, managed care can be a system of utilization review, utilization management, and benefit control. . . . The rationale for managed care is that if providers are paid a fixed amount, in advance, for patients or illness episodes, a remarkable shift in provider behavior would occur. Instead of doing more to be paid more, the health industry could actually earn more by doing less (and therefore limit what were considered fearfully escalating costs). The market place mentality of the 1980s roundly endorsed this strategy and managed care became the reigning shibboleth of corporate America. (Sederer & St. Clair, 1990, pp. 90–91)

One example of managed care delivery is the service provided by a health maintenance organization or HMO. ''An HMO is a health care system that contracts to provide a predetermined set of services to its voluntary subscribers for a fixed cost or premium. If the HMO meets its budget by careful utilization of its services it breaks even. If the HMO exceeds its budget, it then has lost money and is at risk to go out of business'' (Sederer & St. Clair, 1990, p. 91). These managed care programs are structured to place a financial limit on the delivery of service. In mental health, this will result in curtailing health care to those most in need and drastically short-changing a patient population that is already underserved. Masquerading as a panacea for skyrocketing health care expenses, managed care is merely a euphemism for managed cost.

Another basic principle of managed care is utilization review. By forcing physicians to struggle with excessive numbers of reviewers (most are nonphysicians), managed care companies have encroached on medical decision making and seriously compromised physician and patient autonomy over clinical practice. Physicians must generally report to third-party payers to meet insurance, Medicare, and Medicaid requirements. Under managed care, they are forced to report to a reviewer or case manager to justify what more than twenty years of education and training has taught them is necessary to provide indicated and appropriate treatment for their patients. Such ''partnerships'' erode the basis of state-of-the-art medical care, jeopardize the doctor-patient relationship, and make financial considerations rather than patient welfare the basis for clinical practice.

Managed care companies frequently segregate patients into groups based on medical history. For managed care organizations to remain fiscally sound, they seek to enroll a pool of subscribers who are at low risk for illness. This aspect of managed care may have the most dramatic impact on patients with serious mental illness. One would predict that patients suffering from chronic psychiatric conditions such as schizophrenia, manic depressive disorder, generalized anxiety disorder, and substance abuse disorders will be disqualified from a medical care system designed to reduce patient utilization. These are the patient groups who are most desperately in need of treatment and who, even now, do not have insurance parity with patients suffering from more "acceptable" illnesses such as chronic cardiac disease, diabetes, or cancer.

A system of health care that is designed to place a quantitative limit on the delivery of service can initially save money. Furthermore, unscientific statistical analyses of such programs may demonstrate no increase in the incidence of morbidity and mortality for a given population. Nevertheless, because those at greatest risk will be excluded from participation, it will be difficult to realistically assess the impact or benefit to patients of such cost-containment measures. Large numbers of patients could be in such a system for years, perhaps decades, before morbidity and mortality would be demonstrably increased, and the results would be catastrophic for significant numbers of them.

Historically, medical professionals may have neglected financial considerations when developing treatment strategies, but they have not placed a monetary value on human life. The very concept of a health care delivery system that rewards clinicians financially for reductions in the delivery of care is antithetical to a medical tradition that exhorts the physician through the Hippocratic Oath to "exercise [my] art solely for the cure of [my] patients."

In mental health, managed care will virtually eliminate insurance coverage for patients who need treatments such as psychotherapy, where increased rather than decreased frequency of visits may be indicated. Even patients for whom the primary treatment is pharmacologic but who require regular monitoring (such as patients taking clozaril) may ultimately lose insurance benefits or would be excluded from participation in the first place.

One of the most egregious problems with managed care systems is that these companies employ "reviewers" to determine not only who is entitled to receive treatment but by whom and for what. Most reviewers make their determinations by telephone and are not physicians. American Psych Management, a managed care company that recently contracted with New York State to provide mental health services to all New York State employees, uses such a system. If an employee wishes to receive coverage for a mental health service provided by a nonparticipant, he or she must first contact an American Psych Management reviewer whose credentials and training are unknown. These reviewers subsequently approve or deny requests for coverage based solely on telephone conversations. Most managed care companies do not provide written criteria to professionals, even those considering participation, regarding fee schedules, review timetables, and "acceptable'' procedures. As a result, while the care giver enters ''blindly'' into the contractual arrangement, the patient is left even more in the dark without any way to assess the reviewer's background, much less the provider's.

Managed care contracts frequently limit the choice of practitioners and hospital. Often these limits and choices are dictated by cost concerns at the sacrifice of clinical excellence. Practitioners are also required to submit written justification for continued treatment, generally after five or ten visits. This ''paper chase'' forces the provider to spend excessive hours dealing with bureaucratic requirements rather than taking care of patients.

Patient mental health may be jeopardized further by stressful concerns that insurance benefits are evaporating. For example, if a patient is hospitalized for depression and the managed care contract stipulates that thirty days is the limit for inpatient treatment, the practitioner must consider the possibility that the patient will deteriorate when faced with the prospect of premature discharge versus the substantial financial burden incurred for continued hospitalization. A number of hospitals have acknowledged the seriousness of this issue by including managed care and utilization review as part of the patient problem list.

Finally, one of the most appalling casualties of managed care is the confidential nature of the doctor-patient relationship. Confidentiality has always been a hallmark of the medical profession. A patient's right to privacy and the sanctity of the patient-doctor relationship are established legal precedents. Furthermore, the Hippocratic Oath states ''that whatsoever I shall see or hear of the lives of my patients which is not fitting to be spoken, I will keep inviolably secret.'' Managed care companies, by their very existence, violate the trusting relationship established between physician and patient by requiring physicians to justify to an outside party both the nature and the rationale for treatment. As these ''reviewers'' have increasing authorization to determine the frequency, duration, and type of treatment including hospitalization, the essence of the bond between physician and patient will be destroyed and the right to appropriate treatment will be forfeited.

In summary, the proliferation of managed care companies is a disaster for the mental health care system and particularly for patients suffering from severe psychiatric disorders. We must find some way to make fiscally sound decisions about the cost and practice of health care, but the managed care alternative is not a sound one if we are seriously concerned about appropriate and effective treatment for mental illness. The historical legacy of disenfranchisement of the mentally ill from our insurance system is well documented. Managed care will only make this worse.

Reference

Sederer, L. I. and St. Clair, R. L. (1990, March 19). Quality assurance and managed mental health care. *Psychiatric Clinics of North America, 13*(1), 90–91.

Suggested Readings

Edinburg, G., & Cottler, J. (1990, October). Implications of managed care for social work in psychiatric hospitals. *Hospital and Community Psychiatry, 41*(10).

Melnick, S. D., & Lyter, L. L. (1987, March). The negative impacts of increased concurrent review of psychiatric inpatient care. *Hospital and Community Psychiatry, 38*(3).

Riba, M., Greenfield, D., & Glazer, W. M. (1992, July). Utilization management and psychiatric education: Problems and opportunities. *Psychiatric Annals, 22*(7).

Scharfstein, S. S., & Beigel, A. (Eds.). (1985). *The new economics and psychiatric care.* Washington, D.C.: American Psychiatric Press.

Sederer, L. I., & St. Clair, R. (1990, March 19). Quality assurance and managed mental health care. *Psychiatric Clinics of North America, 13*(1).

Rejoinder to Dr. Bernstein

Kevin Corcoran

The primary focus of Dr. Bernstein's opposition to managed care is predicated on the restricted view that it is simply cost containment. To this end, Dr. Bernstein persuasively illustrates the argument with HMOs. After all, distributing services below a specified dollar amount while still turning a profit is health care rationing in a market economy. She further contends that this will result in disqualifying those most in need of services. There are three oversights in Dr. Bernstein's argument: (1) managed care is more than cost containment; (2) the disqualification of less preferred consumers is the current structure of the insurance industry (simply compare Aetna with Blue Cross); and (3) those most in need of services are most likely not covered by a private carrier and are excluded from much of the marketplace of mental health services.

Managed care is more than just cost containment. It also assures that quality services are delivered. In fact, the cost-containment function itself promotes quality care by the simple fact that services purchased are inspected to determine if they are the best services, delivered by the most appropriate professional who is up-to-date on the treatment techniques for that particular client problem. In contrast, Dr. Bernstein sees this as intrusion by the reviewers into physicians' unbridled autonomy in the marketplace and even sounds aghast that the reviewer might be a non-physician. This is one of the reasons managed care is needed in the first place; twenty years of schooling—and its accompanying high cost for services—may not be necessary for many client problems, such as social problems, interpersonal problems, skill deficits, or health promotion; and, of course, the list goes on.

Finally, Dr. Bernstein asserts that managed care will threaten the confidential relationship between patient and physician. All sorts of heinous things will happen then, since confidentiality is the "hallmark" of the medical profession and the "sanctity" of the patient-doctor relationship. This is a curious argument, indeed. First of all, confidential information is different from legally privileged communication, and under federal law physician-patient communication is not protected (interestingly, though, communication with a paraprofessional drug or alcohol counselor might be). Second, managed care is less concerned with what is said in treatment (i.e., intrusion) and more concerned with what treatment intends to accomplish (i.e., the goals relevant to a client problem). To allow physicians—or any other mental health professional for that matter—to stroll through the mental health services marketplace without concern for who will pay how much for what type and quality of services is no way to assure that a consumer gets what is paid for or that the needed services are received and delivered at an acceptable standard of care.

DEBATE 18

Should It Be Easier to Commit People Involuntarily to Treatment?

YES say Doctors Swartz and Sibert. Marvin S. Swartz, M.D., is Associate Professor and Head of the Division of Social and Community Psychiatry at Duke University Medical Center. He has had a long-standing interest in law and psychiatry, particularly as it applies to acute psychiatric settings. He currently is principal investigator for an NIMH-funded project on the effectiveness of involuntary civil commitment.

Thomas E. Sibert, M.D., is Clinical Associate and Associate Head of the Division of Social and Community Psychiatry at Duke University Medical Center. Dr. Sibert's main interests include training of psychiatrists and other mental health professionals in public sector psychiatry as well as educating primary care physicians about psychiatric conditions. He is currently Project Coordinator for an NIMH-funded project to train primary care physicians in the recognition and treatment of depression.

Loren R. Mosher has a different perspective as he argues NO. Dr. Mosher was educated at Stanford (A.B.) and Harvard (M.D.) and received his psychiatry training at the Massachusetts Mental Health Center in Boston and the NIMH intramural research program in Bethesda, Maryland. He served as Chief of the NIMH's Center for Studies of Schizophrenia for twelve years and directed the Soteria research project, a home-like residential nondrug treatment setting for newly diagnosed schizophrenics deemed in need of hospitalization. He was Professor of Psychiatry at the Uniformed Services University of the Health Sciences in Bethesda for eight years and continues there as a clinical professor. His most recent book, *Community Mental Health* (Norton, 1989), coauthored with Lorenzo Burti, M.D., has been translated into three languages. Currently, Dr. Mosher is Associate Director of Montgomery County Maryland's Department of Addiction, Victim and Mental Health Services.

YES

Marvin S. Swartz and Thomas E. Sibert

Over the past three decades, public policy toward involuntary civil commitment of the mentally ill in the United States has swung between two poles: medical paternalism and a due process legalistic model. Until the late 1960s, medical discretion prevailed as a standard for confinement and treatment. Physicians' authority was to confine and treat patients based on the patients' presumed "need for treatment." Medical discretion was subject to little review and oversight, leading to open-ended confinements and, in some cases, to the warehousing of patients who had no realistic chance of receiving treatment or rehabilitation.

Beginning in the late 1960s, civil libertarians pressed to narrow involuntary civil commitment criteria and introduce procedural safeguards similar to those used in the criminal justice system. For civil libertarians the only compelling justification for involuntary treatment was a patient's overt and imminent dangerousness to self or others. In response to their activism, numerous states altered their involuntary civil commitment statutes to include due process procedures, such as the right to counsel, and narrowed their standards for involuntary commitment from the broader "need for treatment." Involuntary civil commitment was no longer regarded as an issue of pure medical necessity, nor was forced treatment seen as the sole prerogative of the medical profession.

The narrowing of criteria for involuntary civil commitment was joined by further litigation that attempted to press for the right of patients confined to hospitals to be free of forced medication. While the constitutional issues surrounding the espoused right to refuse treatment continue to be murky, many states have found that patients have a qualified right to refuse treatment, and many subsequently enacted cumbersome procedural safeguards to protect against "unwarranted," forcible administration of medications.

Limiting commitment criteria to "dangerousness" and affording committed and "dangerous" patients the right to refuse treatment combined to create cumbersome and antitherapeutic treatment environments. Public sector hospitals found themselves with growing ranks of untreatable, dangerous patients while "nondangerous" but very sick patients were barred entry to the hospital due to restrictive dangerousness-based commitment criteria.

A heated debate has ensued since the late 1960s about the direction, extent, and result of these purported mental health law reforms. Psychiatrists protest the imposition of narrow commitment laws as impossible intrusions on their traditional roles as medical care providers. They also decry commitment roles as medical care providers. They also oppose commitment criteria based on dangerousness, which restrict their discretion and place them in the position of social control agents. Furthermore, critics of dangerousness-based commitment criteria argue that these criteria place undue emphasis on the *rights* of patients to be free *from* treatment and neglect the medical *needs for* treatment of the seriously mentally ill, particularly for patients whose capacity to understand the need for treatment may be impaired by the very illness needing treatment. Hence, psychiatrists argue that the mentally ill, with new legal protections, are "rotting with their rights on" (Appelbaum & Gutheil, 1978). Unfortunately, we have witnessed the continued protection of the liberty interests of psychotic individuals to ruin their lives, alienate their families and other supports, and continue on a road of chronicity and often homelessness.

A parallel process to the narrowing of involuntary commitment criteria has been the public policy of deinstitutionalization of the mentally ill. Beginning in 1955, at the dawn of deinstitutionalization, the total United States census of public psychiatric hospitals was roughly 550,000 and now has dipped well below 120,000. The promise of deinstitutionalization was that community-based care, housing, rehabilitation, and other needed medical and psychiatric services would be integrated into a community-based system of institutions. However, community-based care has never been adequately funded or coordinated and suffered further setbacks with retrenchments of funding for all social welfare programs in the 1980s.

A confluence of factors, including narrowed civil commitment criteria, the unfilled promise of comprehensive community mental health care, and lack of low-cost, adequate housing has led to a dramatic rise in homelessness. Of the roughly 3,000,000 homeless individuals in the United States, roughly a third are mentally ill. Thus, the rising tide of homelessness and the visible presence of mentally ill persons sleeping on grates, panhandling, and traveling aimlessly around the country is the most visible failure of deinstitutionalization—a process abetted by the narrowing of involuntary civil commitment criteria that bar access to the doors of the hospital. As a result, many individuals are now willing to rethink the means by which mentally ill patients are committed.

Should it be easier to involuntarily commit individuals to treatment? Our response is a qualified "yes," qualified because civil commitment statutes in themselves do not improve services. Narrow criteria provide a protection against unwarranted treatment, not a right *to* treatment or guarantees of treatment. A civil commitment statute is not a plan for developing services. Absent the will to fund and develop comprehensive mental health services, broadening civil commitment statutes will counterproductively refill the hospitals and further tax limited treatment resources. While psychiatrists would welcome a shift to greater medical discretion in initiating treatment, few would welcome greater discretion to confine in the absence of improved treatment resources. Thus, we must improve mental health systems while creating workable laws.

We strongly advocate the inclusion of "need for treatment" criteria as a basis for involuntary treatment. However, we also support the notion that deprivation of liberties in the name of treatment creates a reciprocal responsibility to provide treatment.

The American Psychiatric Association (APA) (Stromberg & Stone, 1983) has suggested a model state statute on civil commitment of the mentally ill that advocates inclusion of "need for treatment" criteria in commitment statutes. They also recognize that a need for treatment or so-called *parens patriae* confinement can be justified only when the promised benefits of treatment are realistically available. Thus, the APA stipulates in its model state statute that confinement is justified only if there is a reasonable probability that the disorder is treatable at or through the facility (Stone, 1985). Thus, we do not, nor does the APA, seek psychiatric discretion to warehouse individuals with little hope of treatment.

While laws, by and large, cannot create systems of care, flexible commitment laws may facilitate the development of a continuum of services. A majority of states now permit, and roughly half explicitly provide for, involuntary commitment to outpatient treatment. Court-ordered outpatient treatment may then be utilized as a less restrictive alternative to hospitalization, avoiding the need for hospitalization, or as a mechanism for ensuring or assisting in compliance with treatment (Mulvey, Geller, & Roth, 1987). In North Carolina, where an outpatient commitment statute has been codified since 1984, experience has shown that commitment to outpatient treatment may reduce rehospitalizations by 82 percent and lengths of stay by 33 percent (Fernandez & Nygard, 1990). In an even more flexible variant of the North Carolina law, Ohio permits mentally ill individuals to be committed to the care of the local mental health authority who may then assure compliance with treatment across a continuum of inpatient, outpatient, and rehabilitative services.

Serious mental illness is not a myth, nor is the tragedy of suffering of individuals and families of the mentally ill. Persons with severe and persistent mental illness have serious illnesses that rob them of their capacity to make informed decisions, follow through with decisions about treatment, or voluntarily participate in treatment. It is the responsibility of mental health professionals, aided by workable mental health laws, to help meet the care needs of these individuals, even if against their espoused wishes.

In summary, we support broadening of involuntary civil commitment criteria to "need for treatment" criteria for the treatment of persons with severe and persistent mental illness only insofar as legislatures and community leaders also bear the responsibility for creating and funding a reasonable continuum of care. With appropriate due process safeguards, broadened discretion to commit an individual to treatment should be used to place and hold the individual anywhere in that continuum. Involuntary commitment should include inpatient, partial, and outpatient treatment.

As a final note, we add additional caveats. We do not support treatment that does not work. Coerced treatment is a blunt instrument that should be used judiciously for patients for whom other means and choices have failed. Many patients, given choice in treatment, will comply, participate, and improve without coercion. We also believe that we are obligated to empirically evaluate coercive treatments. For instance, we need to know which treatment models that include coercion, are effective and if outcomes are improved by these methods. We also need to know more about for whom, and how, involuntary treatments work. Unfortunately, the answers to these questions are not yet known. In the meantime, judicious use of flexible involuntary civil commitment criteria are our best, albeit imperfect, remedies to the morass of noncompliance, recidivism, and chronicity.

References

Appelbaum, P. S., & Gutheil, T. G. (1979). Rotting with their rights on: Constitutional theory and clinical reality in drug refusal by psychiatric patients. *Bulletin of the American Academy of Psychiatry and Law, 7,* 306–315.

Fernandez, G. A., & Nygard, S. (1990). Impact of involuntary outpatient commitment on the revolving door syndrome in North Carolina. *Hospital & Community Psychiatry, 41,* 1001–1004.

Mulvey, E. P., Geller, J. L., & Roth, L. H. (1987). The promise and peril of involuntary outpatient commitment. *American Psychologist, 42,* 571–584.

Stone, A. A. (1985). A response to comments on APA's model commitment law. *Hospital & Community Psychiatry, 36,* 984–989.

Stromberg, C. D., & Stone, A. A. (1983). A model state law on civil commitment of the mentally ill. *Harvard Journal on Legislation, 20,* 275–296.

Annotated Bibliography

Appelbaum, P. S., (1985). Special section on the APA's model commitment law: An introduction. *Hospital & Community Psychiatry, 36,* 966–992.

This special section in *Hospital & Community Psychiatry* discusses the APA's model state statute on civil commitment from a number of different perspectives. Comments from psychiatrists, advocates, and attorneys are included.

Hoge, S. K., Appelbaum, P. S., & Geller, J. L. (1989). Involuntary treatment. In A. Tasman, R. E. Hales, & A. J. Frances (Eds.), *Review of Psychiatry, 8,* 432–450. Washington, DC: American Psychiatric Press.

This chapter provides a current and comprehensive review of involuntary treatments from legal and clinical perspectives.

Mulvey, E. P., Geller, J. L., & Roth, L. H. (1987). The promise and peril of involuntary outpatient commitment. *American Psychologist, 42,* 571–584.

This article provides a comprehensive discussion of involuntary outpatient commitment from ethical, clinical, and legal perspectives.

Rejoinder to Dr. Swartz and Dr. Sibert

LOREN R. MOSHER

Expanding Forced Treatment: Where Will It All End?

Dr. Swartz and Dr. Sibert provide readers with an admirable, seemingly well-reasoned, mainstream, properly qualified set of reasons to expand the scope of involuntary treatment to include "need for treatment."

Unfortunately, their arguments are "holeyer" than swiss cheese and unholy in their ethical implications. Let me highlight a few of their assertions (paraphrased to save space) that, in my opinion, just don't wash:

1. "Dangerous patients and the right to refuse treatment *created* antitherapeutic environments in public sector hospitals."

   Since Dorothea Dix's reform was subverted to carry out the tenets of Social Darwinism in the late 1880s, these institutions have never (with rare exception) provided therapeutic environments. Their adverse effects on patients have been documented repeatedly—long before today's more restrictive commitment laws.
2. "Narrow laws *intrude* on psychiatrists' traditional roles as medical care providers."

   The traditional relationship between medical care providers and their patients is a voluntary one. In fact, in concert with society's wishes, psychiatrists are the only class of physicians who can routinely *intrude their treatments* on unwilling patients without formal legal proceedings.
3. "Dangerousness criteria make psychiatrists agents of social control."

   All forced treatment, whatever its rationalization, is social control.
4. "Need for treatment is an acceptable criteria for commitment if treatment is available."

What constitutes "need" and "treatment" in psychiatry are basically personal opinions. If I am clever enough to invent a new "treatment" I will certainly be motivated to define as large a group as possible as "needing" it—whether they want it or not. Not surprisingly, this is also an excellent economic strategy for me.

5. "Outpatient commitment is effective and a useful addition."

   In a very thorough review of all the studies of outpatient commitment, Maloy (1992) concluded:

> A careful examination of these [outpatient commitment] empirical studies 1) establishes that the existing research literature provides no empirical evidence that involuntary outpatient commitment provides an effective means to address treatment compliance problems associated with severe and persistent mental illness and 2) suggests that expanding and improving the community mental health and social services systems could be an important, perhaps critical, factor in addressing the community needs of people with serious and persistent mental illness, thereby ameliorating the crisis of the "revolving door" patient. (p. 24)

There does seem to be some common ground held by Drs. Swartz and Siber and myself. As they note, "forced treatment will not produce a system of needed services." Where my colleagues and I differ is over the unethical use of force tied to a pie-in-the-sky hope that somehow, contrary to all previous experience and their own assertion, the resources to meet real needs will be made available. My position, congruent with Ms. Maloy's second conclusion, is that given sufficient options (i.e., resources) almost every disturbed and disturbing person will find one that she or he can accept voluntarily.

Forced treatment is always liable to abuse. Widening its scope would increase its abuse. The more power psychiatrists have, the less they will need to establish and maintain collaborative relationships with their patients. They will become less and less physicians and more and more police.

Where will it all end? It should never begin.

Reference

Maloy, K. A. (1992). *Critiquing the available evidence: Does involuntary outpatient commitment work?* Washington, DC: Mental Health Policy Resource Center.

NO

Loren R. Mosher

Giving psychiatry the power to deprive people of their freedom under the guise of treatment has allowed the flagrant abuse of human beings. Our "civilized" society condones these abuses—colectomy, arsenic injections, malaria-induced fever, lobotomy, electroshock, and most recently neuroleptic drugs—because it chooses to believe the mystification that this is ''humane medical treatment.'' Too many spirits have been annihilated in the name of psychiatric treatment:

> Mr. G was found semiconscious under a tree in his backyard by his wife and 14-year-old daughter at 9 p.m. on a cool spring night. It appeared that he had fallen or jumped from a ladder in an attempt to hang himself. A rope was dangling from a branch of a nearby tree. He was rushed by ambulance to a nearby emergency room (ER). There were no obvious rope burns, and neck x-rays were negative. Blood alcohol was .24.
>
> His family waited patiently until he slept off the effects of the alcohol. A psychiatrist was asked to evaluate. When Mr. G awoke, he and his wife discussed the situation and decided that he might benefit from mental health treatment for his depression. Although they would have preferred outpatient intervention, they agreed to the psychiatrist's recommendation of hospitalization. The couple, in their late 40s, had never before encountered the mental health system. They asked where Mr. G might be admitted voluntarily. The evaluating psychiatrist told them that only a nearby for-profit psychiatric hospital would take cases like Mr. G's because he needed to be admitted involuntarily. Without further ado, the psychiatrist, because of conflict of interest (he was part owner), asked the ER physicians to commit Mr. G to this hospital.
>
> By this act, the committing physicians violated the law governing involuntary hospitalization. They decided, without even the nominal process of adjudication, that a man *and his wife* were not capable of responsible decision making. They subjugated the couple to their arbitrary exercise of power. Within twenty-four hours Mr. G was converted to voluntary status, but when he later wanted to leave against medical advice he was threatened with recommitment—a form of rights violation commonly practiced in this institution. Mr. G stayed thirty days, the exact number of inpatient days covered by his health insurance.

Had Mr. G not had health coverage, he would almost certainly have been committed to a local state hospital—commitment there *guarantees* admission and paid transportation from the ER to the state facility. It is rather remarkable that health insurers regularly pay for this very expensive form of treatment—even when their policy holders do not want it.

It is often argued that involuntary psychiatric hospital commitment is used more frequently with marginalized and surplus persons (e.g., the poor, minorities, and optionless customers of public mental health systems) because their powerlessness makes them easy marks for deprivation of freedom. What the above case illustrates is that even the ostensibly powerful can be arbitrarily deprived of their freedom. Mr. G is well educated, an upper-level manager in a high-technology firm, married to an MBA, with a family income of $150,000 a year. He and his wife live in an elegant suburb and are seen as pillars of their church and community.

The hospitalization left what will probably be lifelong marks on this family; fearing disclosure and stigmatization, they withdrew from community activities. They mistrust psychiatrists in particular and physicians in general; hence, they avoid even routine medical care. Mr. G has suffered continually from the signs and symptoms of post-traumatic stress disorder (P.T.S.D.) as a result of his treatment in the ER and then in the hospital. Most devastating is that Mr. G will lose his security clearance and his job. A degradation process, lasting long after the event, grinds inexorably on and on.

Readers of this volume probably believe you will never be subjected to involuntary hospitalization. Because you know how the system works and the alternatives available, you have a certain degree of counterpower. However, your friends and relatives may not be so knowledgeable, and they may be subjected to forced hospitalization. Like almost everyone, they would rather not think about it. It is more comfortable to believe it will never happen. The nearly universal public disinterest and denial of the unfairness of this practice helps perpetuate it. It certainly had never occurred to Mr. G and his family that such a think could happen to them in a free society. I recommend to all this volume's readers a visit to the locked admissions unit at your local state hospital; you'll quickly be looking to get out. You'll have to be patient and nice to Nurse Rachet to do so. This is the type of setting in which Rosenhan's (1973) classic study, "On Being Sane in Insane Places," was conducted. Rosenhan showed that such places can't distinguish normal volunteers posing as patients from mad persons. He also found that once admitted, it was very hard for even asymptomatic actors to get out.

Our society gives coercive power to the legal system. Except for psychiatrists, it does not give such power to the medical system. It presumes that physicians, because of their training, knowledge, skill, authority, status, and good relationships with their patients, will be able to persuade them to accept even very painful treatments. For example, cancer chemotherapy, despite its nausea, vomiting, and hair loss is acquiesced to daily. It is also refused. Less effective alternatives, if available, may then be offered.

It is rather ironic that the branch of medicine that is presumed to be most expert in the development and use of the doctor-patient relationship to effect change is the only one that has the right to be coercive. Many would defend the profession as well intentioned in so doing, but then again we know what the road to hell is paved with.

There is not space here to detail it, but since the beginning of industrialization in the West, mad persons have been subject to deprivation of freedom, incarceration and isolation in institutions. Had this not been so, there would have been no one for Pinel to unchain, thereby insuring his place in psychiatric history. A myth has developed that disturbed and disturbing persons have been unchained so they can receive humane medical treatment—even if it is against their will. Herein lies the most basic and widely accepted mystification around this issue: "We are forcing you into an institution so we can administer medical treatment for your own good." Neither force nor incarceration are compatible with treatment. This coercive act actually makes "treatment," as usually defined by the medical profession, impossible. It violates basic tenets of medical practice by negating the need to establish a relationship and to obtain the patient's agreement to treatment. Unchained, yes; free to make their own treatment decisions, no.

Psychiatry's current biologic zeitgeist supports the position that it is not possible to have a therapeutic relationship with a person with a "diseased brain"; hence, coercion is justified. This rationalization flies in the face of decades of clinical experience and research indicating that while often more difficult, it is usually possible to establish a collaborative relationship with even the most disturbed and disturbing persons. When this is not possible, it is usually the result of multiple experiences of betrayed trust, which are then reinforced by involuntary hospitalization. It is very difficult to trust doctors who can not only behave like cops, but also deny to themselves that is what they are doing!

Why does psychiatry, with the misguided approval of society, take on this role as an agent of social control? Unlike the case described above, it's not usually motivated by greed. My view is that it is mostly the result of a serious case of we-themism. *We* do not want to expend the time, energy, and willingness to be open to understanding *them* on their own terms. As products of Western pragmatism, *we* believe that we must do something about the un-understandable *them.* When *they* don't play the game by the rules of consensual validation, *we* whistle foul and send *them* to the penalty box—to be "treated" of course, not incarcerated. For me, no matter what the rhetoric or rationalization, locking someone up against her or his wishes is imprisonment. In fact, when carefully examined, institutions that accept committed persons look more like prisons than hospitals.

Luckily *we* in society isolate ourselves from *them* by letting a willing psychiatry incarcerate and exclude *them.* The widespread not-in-my-backyard (NIMBY) syndrome attests to the degree to which society does not want to face those it has had psychiatry exclude. Society's investment in "out of mind, out of sight" is large, and it is not willing to reduce this portion of its portfolio.

Some will defend this practice of involuntary hospitalization on the grounds that legal procedural safeguards on its use will prevent its being abused. This line of reasoning is a bit like saying that slavery could be legal if only proper legal procedural safeguards were established. Once the practice is legalized, abuse is inevitable in both instances. I invite anyone who would believe otherwise to talk with a few patients who have been involuntarily committed. The least powerful (uneducated, poor, minorities, women) are usually the most abused. However, despite his ostensible power, these "safeguards" were violated with ease by the doctors of Mr. G, a high-status individual.

This is the era of consumerism in mental health. Inherent in the definition of the word "consumer" is volunteerism, choice, and options. Is this not further evidence that forced treatment is an anachronism? Would "consumers" of involuntary commitment (pardon the contradiction) support its continued use? If my own sample is in any way representative, they would answer a resounding *no!*

My position is that commitment for the purpose of forced treatment is inherently a flawed notion and hence unfixable. Both it, and its chief partner in crime, the state hospital system that takes in most committed persons, should be abolished.

NIMBYism, isolation and exclusion, abusive treatment and human degradation processes will continue so long as psychiatry has the arbitrary power to deprive individuals of their freedom in the name of "treatment." Although it has gone on for a very long time, psychiatry shall no longer be allowed to have it both ways. If coercion and deprivation of freedom are deemed necessary to control deviance, leave it to the legal system. Society should renegotiate its social contract with psychiatrists, permitting them to do only what they are, or should be, trained for—relationship-based healing, not policing of minds.

Acknowledgment

Judith Schreiber, L.C.S.W. and Ron Thompson, J.D., provided helpful comments on this essay.

Reference

Rosenhan, D. L. (1973). On being sane in insane places. *Science, 179,* 250–258.

Suggested Readings

Alexander, G. J. (1982). Freedom and insanity. *Metamedicine, 3,* 343–350.

Miller, K. S. (1976). *Managing madness: The case against civil commitment.* New York: Free Press.

Stover, E., & Nightingale, E. O. (Eds.). (1985). *The breaking of bodies and minds: Torture, psychiatric abuse, and the health professions.* New York: W. H. Freeman.

Szasz, T. S. (1978). Should psychiatric patients even be hospitalized involuntarily? Under any circumstances—no. In J. P. Brady & H. K. Brodie (Eds.). *Controversy in psychiatry.* Philadelphia: W. B. Saunders.

Rejoinder to Dr. Mosher

Marvin S. Swartz and Thomas E. Sibert

The rationale for any restriction of civil liberties, such as that involved in involuntary civil commitment, is based on an assumption that the greater good of the individual or society is served by such a restriction. Statutory procedural safeguards, such as hearings to protect due process, are employed to ensure that any abrogations of liberty are considered carefully. It is clear that what constitutes the greater good for society and adequate safeguards of liberties shifts according to prevailing values. For instance, three decades ago, halting the institutionalization of the mentally ill was a preeminent concern; today we can barely recall that debate as the homeless mentally ill live without adequate care. Today, ensuring treatment and protection for this population commands greater urgency and concern. What we value in terms of treatment, however, must still be restrained by statutory checks and balance. Dr. Mosher points out that, inevitably, in some circumstances, due process safeguards are inadequate or that what we judge to be the greater good for society proves to be misguided.

There are few arenas in which the dynamic tension inherent in this process is felt as acutely as in involuntary commitment. Dr. Mosher's response illustrates this tension well. As we have outlined, the history of professional discretion afforded psychiatrists to involuntarily commit individuals to treatment reflects a pendulum swing toward narrowed professional discretion and greater judicial authority that just now shows signs of swinging in the opposite direction. We believe this return toward greater professional latitude is inspired by the failure of many existing community-based treatment programs to provide meaningful alternatives to institutional care. In addition, there is a growing consensus that clear and sensible instances exist where the exercise of patient autonomy in the form of treatment refusal has led to ruination of health, deterioration of quality of life, and even death. Nevertheless, our endorsement of shifting commitment criteria towards "need for treatment" commitment standards from present "dangerousness standards" acknowledges that confinement for the purpose of treatment assumes that a patient will not only be confined, but will also be treated.

The public and individual weal is only served if such treatment is reasonably effective. In the past several decades, we have developed a host of effective somatic and psychological therapies and reasonable methodologies, including measures of symptomatic improvement and quality of life, with which to gauge the efficacy of treatment. We believe it only alarms already frightened patients to equate "colectomy, arsenic injections, malaria-induced fever, lobotomy, electroshock and . . . neuroleptic drugs." Though imperfect, somatic treatments have made considerable inroads in the quality of most patients' lives.

The availability and effectiveness of treatment is a pivotal issue in the involuntary commitment controversy because a major argument against commitment holds that the ostensible "benefit" of confinement, good treatment, is not available or does not result. We maintain that such treatment exists and is beneficial and stipulate that involuntary treatment should, in fact, be tied to available and effective therapy.

We disagree that coercive treatment or commitment leads to post-traumatic stress disorders (PTSD) or makes a cooperative, therapeutic relationship impossible. We also disagree that a therapeutic perspective that addresses possible biological pathology automatically excludes the prospect of or desire for a "therapeutic relationship."

We are cognizant of the fact that many mentally ill individuals retain the capacity to choose to refuse or forgo treatment. However, unlike treatment decisions regarding cancer chemotherapy in fully competent adults, at certain times, mentally ill individuals do lack capacity to judge what is in their best interest. At those times, involuntary commitment serves the individual who, according to the American Psychiatric Association's model commitment statute definition:

> . . . lacks capacity to make an informed decision concerning treatment [in that] the person by reason of his mental disorder or condition, is unable, despite conscientious efforts at explanation, to basically understand the nature and effects of hospitalization or treatment or is unable to engage in a rational, decision-making process regarding such hospitalization or treatment, as evidenced by inability to weigh the possible risks and benefits. (Stromberg & Stone, 1983, p. 301)

We think this threshold determination of diminished competency is a crucial part of an involuntary commitment standard that helps render treatment to those in need without unnecessary abrogation of freedom.

We will not address the dangerousness standards, which have as their basis societal benefit, or the notion that "nurse Ratchets" are inevitable, prevalent and sadistic, or coercive agents on psychiatric wards. We believe the latter to be untrue.

In summary, we believe that, in large part, adequate safeguards currently exist to prevent cases of capricious misuse of involuntary commitment. Psychological and somatic treatments are available to serve the interests of the mentally ill when involuntarily committed and that the incapacity to make an informed decision regarding treatment should be a crucial criterion for involuntary commitment combined with a corresponding obligation by clinicians to provide effective treatment.

Reference

Stromberg, C. D., & Stone, A. A. (1983, Summer). Statue: A model state law on civil commitment of the mentally ill. *Harvard Journal on Legislation, 20*(2), 301.

Debate 19

Have Mental Health Professionals Abandoned the Chronically Mentally Ill?

YES says Mary H. Castañuela who is currently completing doctoral studies at Columbia University School of Social Work. Recently she was a Research Assistant with an NIMH study of housing psychiatrically disabled homeless men. Other current work involves benefit-cost analysis of housing the homeless mentally ill. After receiving a M.S.W. degree at the University of Illinois at Chicago, she worked in the areas of foster care, juvenile probation, and crisis intervention and as a Program Director of the county hospital in Houston, Texas.

NO says Vikki L. Vandiver who is an Assistant Professor in the Graduate School of Social Work at Portland State University. She completed her doctoral studies at the University of Texas—Health Science Center, School of Public Health. Her areas of interest include cross-national/cross-cultural studies of services for the chronic mentally ill, case management, and health care for persons with schizophrenia. She is also a research consultant to a community mental health center.

YES

Mary H. Castañuela

Although one of the major problems in state institutions for the mentally ill was the lack of professional staff, this issue was generally ignored so long as the public could believe that they were receiving proper care. Now that the chronically mentally ill have been discharged to the community for almost thirty years, it can no longer be ignored that mental health professionals have abandoned the chronically mentally ill. The fact is, the core mental health professions (psychiatry, psychiatric social work, clinical psychology, and psychiatric nursing) lack interest in and exhibit a reluctance to work with this population. In academia, as well as among practitioners, it is evident that, "Most mental health disciplines do not place a high value on serving persons with long term psychiatric problems" (Farkas, 1990, p. 102).

The mental health professions developed in response to the problem of providing care and treatment for persons with chronic mental illness. Psychiatry emerged within the state mental hospitals, through the role of physicians as superintendents of asylums. Nurses were trained in state hospitals, many of which had schools of nursing. Social workers began working with the families of patients and were later employed in mental hospitals. Unlike these professions, clinical psychology does not have its origins in the treatment of the chronically mentally ill. Despite the much larger number of mental health professionals today than in the past, few are involved in providing direct, long-term services to the severely and persistently mentally ill.

Available data on psychiatrists show that the majority are in private practice. Having little involvement in public sector mental health care, psychiatrists generally practice in settings that do not service the most severely ill. Mechanic (1989) reports that in 1987, there were approximately 36,000 psychiatrists in active practice, with only a small proportion in institutional settings. Twelve percent were in medical schools and universities; 6 percent in community mental health centers; 4 percent in private psychiatric hospitals; and 3 percent in other hospitals. Based on these figures, 75 percent of psychiatrists were in private practice. Such specific data on psychiatric social workers, psychiatric nurses, and clinical psychologists are not readily available, since for these professions estimates are usually made for broad, general practice categories and do not specify the service population. However, in a recent NIMH study, Gottlieb (1989) reported that among the various mental health service providers, solo or group private practice continues to be the mainstream of mental health care. Persons with severe and persistent mental illness are not typically private practice clients. The choice for private practice by mental health professionals is a choice not to work with the chronically mentally ill.

Private practice is neither accessible nor appropriate for those with a severe and persistent psychiatric disorder. Service users tend to be those with less severe mental health problems who can accommodate the higher service fees, directly or through third-party payments. They are also clients who easily fit into the preferred client category. The nature of the disorders that affect the chronically mentally ill often precludes their membership in the YAVIS group—Youthful, Attractive, Verbal, Intelligent, and Successful. Private practitioners usually provide some type of psychotherapy and few, if any, of the support services most needed by those who are psychiatrically disabled. Provision of these support services requires more than weekly fifty-minute sessions of talk therapy. Research shows that the psychiatrically disabled can live and function in the community with interventions of skill and support development (Anthony, Cohen, & Farkas, 1988). They need comprehensive services that include supervised or supportive living and working arrangements; ongoing medical and mental health care; crisis intervention; and psychosocial rehabilitation.

A closer look at the services that are available and more appropriate for persons with severe and chronic psychiatric disorders is further indication that they have been abandoned by mental health professionals. When patients were cared for primarily in state institutions, there was a lack of professional staff and a reliance on untrained workers. The situation has not changed much for them since their return to community care. The boarding homes, nursing care facilities, and the more recently developed single-room-occupancy (SRO) facilities where many of them are living today are usually staffed by nonprofessionals who have little training or experience working with this population. Community residences in many cities also have a shortage of well-trained professionals. Farkas (1990) concluded that the most consistent interventions that have been offered to persons with severe psychiatric disorders are ''medication maintenance from the medical profession and caring and support from paraprofessionals'' (p. 102).

The shortage of well-trained professionals servicing the chronically mentally ill reflects the reluctance of practitioners to work with this population, as well as the resistance of mental health academics. Faculty, in general, show little interest in the chronically mentally ill. In one survey of core discipline graduate education programs in four northwestern states, faculty self-ratings on interest and competence were lowest for the severely mentally disabled than for any other population or mental health problem (Mallam, 1987). Similarly, Rubin and Johnson (1984) reported that social work students rated the chronically mentally disabled as the least appealing group with whom to work.

Throughout the country, few graduate and professional schools offer programs or relevant courses for the training of students to work with psychiatrically disabled persons (Anthony, Cohen, & Farkas, 1988). Psychiatric residency programs tend to concentrate on inpatient care of acutely ill persons who have functioned well in the past (Talbot, 1992). In social work and psychology, a strong feeling exists that course work should not focus on any particular problem or population. Rather, it should provide a general knowledge base and practice skills that are broadly applicable, whereas specialty training, such as practice with the chronically mentally ill, should be provided at the students' field practicum. Undergraduate nursing programs also lack training for work with the chronically mentally ill. In course work, psychiatric and mental health concepts are used to enrich a broad curriculum. Students' field placements in psychiatric settings are brief and not always with the chronically mentally ill (Francell, 1990). Although the mental health disciplines have programatic differences, such as those discussed above, it is clear that in psychiatry, clinical psychology, social work, and nursing alike, there is continued resistance to integrate relevant courses and field components for the training of students to work with the chronically mentally ill (NIMH, 1990).

The attitudes held by most mental health professionals and students toward the chronically mentally ill prevent any consideration of work with them. Minkoff (1987) states that these professionals share the public's negative and exclusionary attitudes toward the mentally ill. Also, this group of professionals shares the negative attitudes of the medical profession toward chronicity. Work with chronic mental patients is regarded as hopeless and unrewarding, since they demonstrate little progress. Another negative attitude that contributes to abandoning the chronically mentally ill is the distaste of mental health professionals for dependency and the lower classes. The lack of adequate training in schools and universities contributes to the endurance of these negative attitudes and the affective barriers to servicing the severely and persistently mentally ill (Minkoff, 1987).

The commitment of mental health professionals in the past to the care and treatment of the chronically mentally ill has given way to a preference for private practice and treatment of the ''worried well.'' Instead of interest and concern, negative attitudes toward the most seriously ill exist because of their chronicity and dependency. Schools and universities continue to neglect the need for appropriate training to prepare practitioners to work with them. The most severely and chronically ill are serviced primarily by inexperienced nonprofessionals. This, in effect, is the abandonment of the chronically mentally ill by mental health professionals.

References

Anthony, W. A., Cohen, M. R., & Farkas, M. (1988). Professional pre-service training for working with the long-term mentally ill. *Community Mental Health Journal, 24,* 259–269.

Farkas, M. (1990). Clinical training with a rehabilitation focus. In National Institute of Mental Health, H. P. Lefley (Ed.), *Clinical training in serious mental illness.* (pp. 102–126). (DHHS Publication No. ADM 90-1679). Washington, DC: U.S. Government Printing Office.

Francell, C. G. (1990). Comments to: Preparing nurses to work with the seriously mentally ill. In National Institute of Mental Health, H. P. Lefley (Ed.), *Clinical training in serious mental illness.* (pp. 96–101). (DHHS Publication No. ADM 90-1679). Washington, DC: U.S. Government Printing Office.

Gottlieb, G. L. (1989). Diversity, uncertainty, and variations in practice: The behaviors and clinical decisionmaking of mental health care providers. In National Institute of Mental Health, C. A. Taube, D. Mechanic, & A. A.

Hohmann (Eds.), The future of mental health services research. (pp. 225–251). (DHHS Publication No. 89-1600). Washington, DC: U.S. Government Printing Office.

Mallam, K. E. (1987, January). *Training professionals for work with persons with long-term mental disabilities.* Paper presented at the meeting of the Community Support Systems Project Directors, Richmond, VA.

Mechanic, D. (1989). *Mental health and social policy* (3rd ed.). Englewood Cliffs, NJ: Prentice Hall.

Minkoff, K. (1987). Resistance of mental health professionals to working with the chronic mentally ill. In A. T. Meyerson (Ed.), *Barriers to treating the chronic mentally ill.* (pp. 3–20). San Francisco: Jossey-Bass.

National Institute of Mental Health, Harriet P. Lefley, (Ed.). (1990). *Clinical training in serious mental illness.* (DHHS Publication No. 90-1679). Washington, DC: U.S. Government Printing Office.

Rubin, A., & Johnson, P. J. (1984). Direct practice interests of entering MSW students. *Journal of Education for Social Work, 20,* 5–16.

Talbott, J. A. (1992). Training mental health professionals to treat the chronically mentally ill. In R. H. Lamb, L. L. Bachrach, & F. I. Kass (Eds.), *Treating the homeless mentally ill* (pp. 109–123). Washington, DC: American Psychiatric Association.

Annotated Bibliography

Grob, G. (1973). *Mental institutions in America: Social policy to 1875.* New York: The Free Press.

Grob analyzes the social welfare history as well as the medical history of mental illness through an examination of the evolution of social policy. He discusses the political, social, economic, and ideological contexts under which the United States mental health care system developed into a state system.

Hargreaves, W. A., & Shumway, M. (1989). Effectiveness of mental health services for the severely mentally ill. In National Institute of Mental Health, C. A. Taube, D. Mechanic, & A. A. Hohmann (Eds.), *The future of mental health services research* (pp. 253–283). (DHHS Publication No. ADM 89-1600). Washington, DC: U.S. Government Printing Office.

A review and discussion is presented on the effectiveness of treatment and services for the severely and disabled mentally ill. Several empirical studies are included on the effectiveness of psychotherapy with this population and on the effectiveness of community support services, such as those discussed in this debate.

Bowker, J. P. (Ed.). (1985). *Education for practice with the chronically mentally ill: What works?* Washington, DC: Council on Social Work Education.

These articles discuss the development of a social work curriculum to educate students for practice with the chronically mentally ill. Rubin reviews six effective forms of service delivery to emphasize the need for an empirically based curriculum. Dincin puts forward psychiatric rehabilitation as an important new area for social work education. Rapp specifies proposals for a curriculum. Gerhart details how one school has integrated into its curriculum a direct-practice course and relevant field components.

Rejoinder to Ms. Castañuela

VIKKI L. VANDIVER

The conclusion that mental health professionals have abandoned the chronically mentally ill has been proposed a number of times, and Ms. Castañuela's position gives voice to many of these concerns. She argues three main points: (1) private practice is the preferred model at the exclusion of serving the chronically mentally ill; (2) university and academic settings neglect to provide training programs; and (3) the chronically mentally ill are served by inexperienced nonprofessionals. While these concerns are, indeed, limitations for mental health professionals, they do not uphold the conclusion that abandonment has occurred.

Issues of Private Practice

While Ms. Castañuela is correct in her assertion that there is an increase in private practice, this has not been at the exclusion of the chronically mentally ill. Private practitioners (psychiatrists, in particular) have, indeed, broadened their patient caseload, which includes treating the chronically mentally ill. Moreover, opportunities for chronically mentally ill clients to be seen in private practice reduces the stigma that they are only worthy of public mental health care, which tends to be fragmented, brief, and overwhelming. To assert that private practice settings are neither appropriate nor accessible for people with chronic mental illness is to perpetuate the notion that the chronically mentally ill belong in a two-tier system that is, by construct, exclusive.

Issues of Educational Neglect

It is questionable that academic settings are actually resistant to including formalized training programs on working with the chronically mentally ill, as Ms. Castañuela asserts. To the contrary, academic programs are better suited for generalist training on which specialization is subsequently built. While specialization is necessary to keep up with the developing knowledge, many of the skills of helping continue to require a generalist's base. Additionally, most programs (e.g., nursing, psychiatry, and social work) have courses in mental health proportional to other clinical courses.

Issues with Nonprofessionals

Ms. Castañuela refers to examples where inexperienced and nonprofessional staff are frequently responsible for the care of chronically mentally ill people. It is incorrect and perhaps paternalistic to suggest that only those who are "professional" (i.e., with advanced degrees) are able to provide quality care for the chronic mentally ill. This claim precludes an appreciation for the numerous self-help groups, peer and family groups, and volunteers who extend their knowledge and experience to provide effective services beyond the formal mental health care system. Clients live in a world blended with more nonprofessionals than professionals; thus, the knowledge gained from both groups can provide critical life skills and support necessary for community survival.

Conclusion

Despite Ms. Castañuela's well-presented argument, it is not an easy task to polarize such a complex issue. To ask if we have abandoned the chronically mentally ill is to further bifurcate a concept that has little relevance in describing a level of professional involvement that is continuous and not dichotomous.

What Ms. Castañuela describes as limitations or deficiencies in the role of mental health professionals can also be seen as its strengths. Private practitioners who see the chronically mentally ill not only help those with chronic mental illness, but also provide relief to overburdened public mental health settings by offering shorter waiting lists, quieter settings, and longer visits. As for education's neglect, Ms. Castañuela indirectly illustrates that the lack of a specialized mental health program contributes to the benefit of curricula by maintaining a focus on common human needs (e.g., health, social supports, resources, and caring people). Last, nonprofessionals can offer normalization that is needed to deal with day-to-day challenges of living with chronic mental illness.

To conclude, a more accurate view of mental health professionals is not to see them as abandoning the chronically mentally ill, but simply as players in a continuum of services, ranging from professional and the public to the paraprofessional and consumer participant. While Ms. Castañuela and I depart on the issue of abandonment, we would ultimately arrive at the conclusion that mental health professionals play a pivotal role in the care of people with chronic mental illness. To what degree and success that is accomplished remains a topic for continuous discussion.

NO

VIKKI L. VANDIVER

In spite of the increasing national and international attention given to the needs of persons with chronic mental illness, some suggest that this vulnerable population has been abandoned. Frequently cited arguments revolve around three primary points: legislation, services, and personnel working with persons with mental illness. In terms of legislation, deinstitutionalization is considered by some to reflect abandonment through public and professional indifference (Morganthau, Agrest, Greenberg, Doherty, & Raine, 1986; Atwood, 1982). As for services, the increasing rate of psychiatric illness—including more than one million people with schizophrenia who, in 1986 were unaccounted for by the service delivery system (Armat & Peele, 1992)—results in additional demands on an overburdened and underfunded service delivery system. And, finally, proponents of the abandonment position cite practitioners' orientation to psychotherapy that devalues psychosocial services and views persons with chronic mental illness as undesirable clients (Gerhart, 1985).

The assertion of an abandoned population would have us believe that nothing exists and no one cares for the chronic mentally ill. However, this argument challenges this notion and asserts that mental health professionals have not abandoned their commitment to the chronically mentally ill. The continued commitment to this population is illustrated through examples drawn from legislation, shifting services, and a change in personnel, which now incorporates and emphasizes the active role of the consumer and his or her family.

Abandonment: Mistake or Misunderstanding

By definition, abandonment means "to give up completely" (Guralnik, 1984). Abandonment of the chronically mentally ill would mean that society and its professionals have given up. To assert that the mental health profession has abandoned the chronically mentally ill is not only incorrect, it is also a misunderstanding of the very concept of abandonment as well as a discount of the dedication and obligation of various politicians, professional leaders, and service delivery personnel who have worked diligently to help the mentally ill.

Legislation of Non-Abandonment

It is well established that mental health policy of the last two decades contributed to the decline and restructuring of many mental health service systems. Deinstitutionalization emptied many state psychiatric hospitals with insufficient financial and practical alternatives given to the communities that suddenly found themselves unprepared to treat the mentally ill. Moreover, deinstitutionalization occurred at a time when fiscal conservatism was the norm, federal dollars for mental health programs were slashed, and Social Security rolls were purged of people with mental disabilities. However, some things were positive with deinstitutionalization.

Recognizing the changing face of mental health policy, many politicians, practitioners, and concerned community leaders argued for the need to develop adequate and available community-based resources. Critics often cite deinstitutionalization as the culprit and source of abandonment. Quite simply, however, the problem was not deinstitutionalization so much as the failure to have funding follow the chronically mentally ill into the community.

In spite of the original misappropriation of funding for community-based services, many notable accomplishments occurred that illustrated continued professional commitment. For example, care for persons with severe mental illness became the highest priority for public mental health services (Koyanagi & Goldman, 1991), as seen in the State Comprehensive Mental Health Services Plan Act 1986 (P.L. 99-660). This significant legislation called for state and local agencies to coordinate their efforts in serving people with mental illness through consumer, family, and advocate input. This legislation provided funding for services such as case management, psychosocial rehabilitation, and various work programs.

Other legislation further illustrates the continued commitment to the chronic mentally ill. For example, the Disability Benefits Reform Act of 1984 broadened the criteria for people with disabilities to preclude termination of benefits (Koyanagi & Goldman, 1991). Additionally, the NIMH Community Support Program, which survived as a demonstration program throughout the budget- and program-slashing years of the Reagan administration, later served as the main model for service delivery systems.

In essence, these legislative and policy initiatives emerged at a time when the political and fiscal climate was not favorable to people with mental health disorders. It was through the concerted efforts of mental health professionals, families, consumers, and advocates working together to respond to the deinstitutionalized person's needs that these policies were developed and programs implemented. These efforts, albeit only a start and not enough, were the result of an involved and proactive mental health professional community and not one that had given up.

Responsive Service Delivery Systems

Those asserting abandonment suggest that mental health professionals are no longer interested in working with people with mental illness. This argument is due, in part, to a lack of appreciation by many professionals for the environmental conditions affecting the mentally ill, as well as a preference for private practice. In other words, it has been claimed that mental health professionals care less about the mentally ill and favor the comforts of the private practice setting. While this may be true for many, and some would argue far too many, it is not the case for all professionals or for certain disciplines, such as nursing, public health, community psychiatry, and social work. The evidence of non-abandonment is seen in services that are responsive and consumer-driven. Probably the two most persuasive examples are the increasing number of consumer empowerment groups and peer-professional case management services, both of which strive to mobilize resources and advocate for more responsive services.

Moreover, the legislative initiatives have encouraged and mandated the development of responsive service systems. Consequently, many dedicated professionals have created community-based programs to serve the mentally ill while simultaneously encouraging consumers and their families to rely on their own needs and preferences for services. The most visible of these consumer-driven organizations is the National Alliance for the Mentally Ill.

Further, in many communities efforts by mental health professionals of various disciplines (i.e., case managers) have helped supplement state and local services (Swayze, 1992). Among the most effective service systems are those that enlist outreach to provide linkage to a vast network of formal and informal service components. Efforts to involve the natural support systems (e.g., clergy, boarding homes, schools and colleges, community and business leaders) have all been within the auspices of case management and illustrate caring and commitment in spite of limited financial resources.

This network approach has resulted in an increase in services that address the needs of the mentally ill, even though such services are often not within the formalized mental health system. The result is a more responsive social service system that creates a partnership between providers and recipients of services that attracts individuals who have avoided more traditional services, such as the homeless mentally ill dual diagnosed (Bachrach, 1992).

Such concerted efforts by mental health professionals and consumers reflect responsive services and do not indicate that the profession has abandoned the mentally ill. Those arguing abandonment may not give sufficient credit to these efforts, because the resources mobilized are frequently outside the auspices of the formal mental health service system. This is also seen in the services that have been developed to confront the health concerns of people with mental illness. For example, in 1981 not a single Medicaid case management program existed, but by 1986 nineteen states had such programs, serving 651,000 individuals (Robinson, 1991). Here, again, the evidence illustrates an absence of abandonment.

Shifting Personnel

While legislation has encouraged and mandated community-based services, these changing services have, in turn, resulted in changes in personnel who are committed to helping the mentally ill. In spite of recent increases in the number of mental health professionals working in private practice settings, which is due in part to reimbursement opportunities, mental health professionals of multiple disciplines continue to serve people with severe mental illness. A report by Knesper, Pagnucco, and Wheeler (1985) confirms that psychiatrists, more so than social workers and psychologists, cared for the more seriously mentally ill, whereas professionals with less than a bachelor's degree made up 23 percent of the work force in mental health organizations.

Moreover, the number of disciplines serving the chronic mentally ill has expanded beyond psychiatry to include clinical and community psychology, nursing, social work, public health, rehabilitation, and consumers themselves. Consequently, abandonment may seem to appear because no single profession is responsible for solving the problems faced by people who have a chronic mental illness. There has also been an increase in certain disciplines that work with the mentally ill. Specifically, there has been an increase in the work force of nurses (29 percent), social workers (18 percent), and physicians other than psychiatrists (11 percent) (NIMH, 1991; Dial, 1991). This lack of professional parochialism also means that no single discipline is to blame for what appears to be abandonment.

At the same time, it can be questioned whether professionals have ever abandoned the chronic mentally ill. For example, in a survey completed over a decade ago, psychiatrists reported that 15.5 percent of their patients had a diagnosis of schizophrenia; psychologists reported that 5.0 percent of their patients had a diagnosis of schizophrenia; social workers reported 7.2 percent, and primary care physicians had 5.8 percent. While these figures may seem low relative to entire caseloads, they do not reflect abandonment; the prevalence of schizophrenia is approximately 1 percent of the general population (Kaplan & Sadock, 1991). Moreover, schizophrenia is much less common than "neurotic" or "relationship" problems, which formed the majority of the practitioners' caseloads.

Additionally, professional organizations are uniting their efforts to better serve psychiatric populations. One example is the rapid growth of the American Association of Community Psychiatrists, which represents a coalition of researchers, frontline clinicians, and advocates who are dedicated to serving their communities and patients in spite of inadequate funding, shrinking programs, and changing role expectations (Bachrach, 1991). These staff trends do not indicate a professional community that is turning its back on this special population.

Conclusions

Persons with mental illness possess a variety of needs that were not present when institutional incarceration was the treatment norm. The last two decades saw increasing growth in the subgroups of chronically mentally ill people who are homeless, abuse drugs and alcohol, and are the new "never institutionalized" mentally ill. While the laudable intent of deinstitutionalization may be criticized for failing to ensure that funds followed the mentally ill into the community, legislation, consumer-driven services, and dedicated personnel have responded. It is short-sighted to conclude that the profession has abandoned this population. However, the magnitude of the problems that remain make even the substantial improvements seem minimal. Thus, even though the mental health profession has not abandoned the mentally ill, the number of people with chronic mental illness is increasing; services have been restricted, thus exacerbating the psychotic condition; and some political leaders have shown themselves to be neither kinder nor gentler.

While it has been argued that the mental health profession has continued its commitment and been actively involved in caring for the mentally ill, this by no means implies that legislation, services, and personnel are either adequate or readily available. What this does mean is that legislation, services, and personnel are working simultaneously to create new changes and that we have not relinquished the enthusiasm for the cause.

References

Armat, V., & Peele, R. (1992). The need-for-treatment standard in involuntary civil commitment. In H. R. Lamb, L. L. Bachrach, and F. I. Kass (Eds.), *Treating the homeless mentally ill.* (pp. 183–202). Washington, DC: American Psychiatric Association.

Atwood, N. (1982, March). Professional prejudice and the psychotic client. *Social Work, 27,* 172–177.

Bachrach, L. (1991). Community psychiatry's changing role. *Hospital and Community Psychiatry, 42,* 573–574.

Bachrach, L. (1992). What we know about homelessness among mentally ill persons: An analytical review and commentary. In H. R. Lamb, L. L. Bachrach, and F. I. Kass (Eds.), *Treating the homeless mentally ill.* (pp. 13–40). Washington, DC: American Psychiatric Association.

Dial, T. (1991). Surveys by APA find sharp decline in private practice as primary work site for psychiatrists. *Hospital and Community Psychiatry, 42,* 1183–1184.

Gerhart, U. (1985). Teaching social workers to work with the chronically mentally ill. In J. Dincin, U. Gerhart, C. Rapp, A. Rubin, and J. Bowker (Eds.), *Education for practice with the chronically mentally ill: What works?* (pp. 50–67). Washington, DC: Council on Social Work Education.

Guralnik, D. (1984). *Webster's New World Dictionary.* New York: Warner Communications.

Kaplan, H., & Sadock, B. (1991). *Synopsis of clinical psychiatry.* Baltimore: Williams and Wilkins.

Knesper, D., Pagnucco, D., & Wheeler, J. (1985). Similarities and differences across mental health service providers and practice settings in the United States. *American Psychologist, 40,* 1352–1364.

Koyanagi, C., & Goldman, H. (1991). The quiet success of the national plan for the chronically mentally ill. *Hospital and Community Psychiatry, 42,* 899–905.

Morganthau, T., Agrest, S., Greenburg, N., Doherty, S., & Raine, G. (1986, January). Abandoned. *Newsweek,* pp. 14–19.

National Institute of Mental Health. (1991). NIMH survey ties staffing increases in mid-80s to growth in number of mental health agencies. *Hospital and Community Psychiatry, 42,* 1179–1183.

Robinson, G. (1991, March). Choices in case management. *Community Support Network News, 7,* 1, 12–13.

Swayze, F. (1992). Clinical case management with homeless mentally ill. In H. R. Lamb, L. L. Bachrach, & F. I. Kass (Eds.), *Treating the homeless mentally ill.* (pp. 203–220). Washington, DC: American Psychiatric Association.

Annotated Bibliography

Knesper, D., Pagnucco, D., & Wheeler, J. (1985). Similarities and differences across mental health services providers and practice settings in the United States. *American Psychologist, 40,* 1352–1369.

This article examines national survey data of professional behaviors from four main disciplines: psychiatry, social work, psychology, and primary care medicine. The authors test eight central hypotheses and conclude, in part, that psychiatrists reported the highest percentage of case mix of people with severe mental illness and that providers who worked in either private practice or public settings saw people with chronic mental illness.

Koyanagi, C., & Goldman, H. (1991). The quiet success of the national plan for the chronic mentally ill. *Hospital and Community Psychiatry, 42,* 899–905.

This article examines the recommendations of the national plan of the 1980s and how the major public health financing programs (i.e., Medicare, Medicaid, SSI, and SSDI) were influenced by mental health care advocates. The authors stress the need for interdisciplinary teamwork to ensure that policy implementation and funding for these programs remain an agenda for the future, especially in light of continuing health care financing debates.

Bachrach, L. (1992). What we know about homelessness among mentally ill persons: An analytical review and commentary. In H. R. Lamb, L. L. Bachrach, & F. I. Kass (Eds.), *Treating the homeless mentally ill.* (pp. 13–40). Washington, DC: American Psychiatric Association.

This article provides a critical review of the political, clinical, and social issues confronting the homeless chronic mentally ill person. The author challenges conventional policy that places care for the chronic mentally ill person on the states and recommends strategies for improved service planning.

Rejoinder to Dr. Vandiver

MARY H. CASTAÑUELA

The argument presented by Dr. Vandiver is based on a lack of clarification and specification of the issue. The question of abandonment of the chronically mentally ill by mental health professionals is distinct from the general question, "Have the chronically mentally ill been abandoned?" This question lends itself to an obvious "no" response, easily justified by pointing out anything that anyone is currently doing for this population. Vandiver sets up a straw man by stating that to assert abandonment is to say, "Nothing exists and no one cares for the chronically mentally ill," and defining abandonment as "to give up completely."

As evidence for continued professional commitment, Dr. Vandiver cites the general mandates, provisions, and goals of mental health legislation. She draws the conclusion that these policies emerged as a result of the efforts by mental health professionals, families, consumers, and advocates, but does not specify who the professionals were or what their role was in those efforts. More importantly, any legislation must be implemented and evaluated before it is lauded. Dr. Vandiver offers no information on effects of the policy on those with chronic mental illness or on the practice choices of psychiatrists, clinical psychologists, psychiatric social workers, and psychiatric nurses.

Although the needs of the chronically mentally ill have not changed much, their move from institutions into the community has necessitated different and innovative service interventions that are provided by varied mental health personnel. Vandiver states accurately that a responsive delivery system and shifting personnel are evidence of non-abandonment of the chronically mentally ill. However, these factors are not evidence that psychiatrists, clinical psychologists, psychiatric social workers, and psychiatric nurses have not abandoned this population. She makes broad, general statements about "a more responsive social service system," "a vast network of formal and informal service components," and "an increase in services," without providing data to support such statements.

Finally, "mental health professionals" do not include everyone who works with or is involved with the chronically mentally ill (i.e., physicians, mental health aides, families, consumers, legislators). The professions that have a common interest in the study and treatment of psychiatric illnesses are psychiatry, clinical psychology, psychiatric social work, and psychiatric nursing. Evidence from the practice and academic areas of these professions makes it clear that they have abandoned the chronically mentally ill. Acknowledgment of their abandonment does not in any way discredit the concerted efforts of dedicated individuals. However, these efforts and their results cannot be viewed as substitutes for the past involvement of the core mental health professionals.